# the women's guide to the wired world

# the women's guide to the wired world

A User-Friendly
Handbook and Resource Directory

## BY SHANA PENN

The Feminist Press
at The City University of New York
New York

Published by The Feminist Press at The City University of New York
The City College, CUNY, Wingate Building
Convent Avenue at 138th Street, New York, NY 10031
First edition, 1997

Library of Congress Cataloging-in-Publication Data

Penn, Shana.
    The women's guide to the wired world : a user-friendly handbook and resource directory
/ by Shana Penn.—1st ed.
    p. cm.
Includes bibliographical references and index.
ISBN 1-55861-167-3 (alk. paper)
1. Internet (Computer network)—Directories.  2. Women's computer network resources—
Directories.  I. Title.
ZA4201.P46 1997
025.04—dc21                                                                                    97-10031
                                                                                                        CIP

This publication is made possible, in part, by a major grant from the The AT&T Foundation.
The Feminist Press would also like to thank The Sister Fund, Joanne Markell, Caroline Urvater, and Genevieve Vaughan for their generosity in supporting this publication.

Text design by Ascienzo Design, New York
Typesetting by CompuDesign, Jackson Heights, New York
Printed on acid-free paper by WebCom Limited.
Printed in Canada.

03 02 01 00 99 98 97     7 6 5 4 3 2 1

For the Network of East-West Women

# Contents

# Acknowledgments

I want to thank all the people who helped make this book possible. Several women contributed chapters on a variety of subjects: Debra K. Floyd, Amy Goodloe, Liza Weiman Hanks, Nina Beth Huntemann, Cheryl Lehman, Sonia Jaffe Robbins, Melissa Leigh Stone, and Victoria Vrana. Several others provided ongoing consultations and/or text for sections of the books, including Donna Axel, a human rights lawyer; Barbara Ann O'Leary, a co-founder of Virtual Sisterhood; Galina Venediktova, Russian program coordinator at the Network of East-West Women; Michael Weil, production manager at Young and Rubicam; and Karen Wickre, a co-founder of Digital Queers. I also want to thank those women who granted me on-line interviews, answering a host of questions regarding their Internet activity, including Joan Korenman, creator of a variety of on-line gender resources and Olga Lipovskaya, director of the Petersburg Center for Gender Issues.

I especially want to thank Jean Casella, senior editor at The Feminist Press, whose keen editorial insight and direction carried the book through its various stages of development and strengthened the final product. Sara Clough, assistant editor at the Press, maintained a steady hand in the editorial process and was, along with Jean, a pleasure to work with.

Finally, I want to thank everyone at the Sandra Dijkstra Literary Agency for their support and representation of my work.

Shana Penn

Washington, D.C.

July 1997

The Feminist Press extends a special thank you to the AT&T Foundation for its generous support of the publication of this book and for its continued support of The Feminist Press's publishing program.

# Introduction

# WOMEN ON-LINE

## A Virtual Reality!

> *Universal access [to the Internet] isn't enough—*
> *there's also the crucial question: "Access to what?"*
>
> —JOAN KORENMAN
> creator of Gender Related Electronic Forums and WMST-L

*The Women's Guide to the Wired World* is an informative, user-friendly how-to book for those of you who are just becoming acquainted with the Internet, and for those of you who are already "converted" and want to make the most of your time, money, and energy while using on-line tools and searching for quality on-line resources. It is tailor-made to introduce you both to the technology and to the wealth of resources that can help women make informed decisions about our lives.

The Internet is rich in electronic resources that can point you to, for example, academic and employment opportunities specifically for women, reproductive and sexual health care, and support systems for lesbians and women of color. The sheer volume and variety of resources is absolutely breathtaking, and this book is one of the first that will equip you to take greater advantage of them. Here you will find resources that address the specific needs of women from diverse social, political, ethnic, age, occupational, and economic backgrounds. You'll also learn helpful tips for clear communication and information management to ease your entry into this sometimes chaotic terrain. And you'll be introduced to some of the women telecommunications experts from around the world whose collective vision of the future forecasts ways in which electronic communication will strengthen women's lives globally.

In the tangible present as well as in the far-off future, the Internet can serve you generously—offering you time- and cost-saving benefits, whether you're a graduate student who is carving out a professional career, a working woman who is already juggling a job and a family, an activist, an independent scholar, or a retiree. Through the Internet, you can commune with old friends and make new friends anywhere in the world without hiking up your monthly telephone bill. Best of all, you won't have to leave your home or office to gain access to library databases, museums and galleries, magazine digests, and discussion groups and bulletin boards on subjects as wide-ranging as health care, parenting, educational and business opportunities, legal services, international networking, travel and entertainment, and media. The growth in numbers of Internet users in the 1990s and the mushrooming of on-line services point to the power of Net access. This book facilitates your ability to enter into what has until now been the mostly male preserve of electronic communications—and to enter on your own terms.

By the time you read *The Women's Guide to the Wired World,* there will probably be many new Web sites, bulletin boards, and other on-line resources available to you. And that's good news, because first and foremost, this book shows you how to explore the Net and make your own discoveries. By the time you read this book, there will also be new approaches to the Net, new forecasts about its potential, and new theories about technology and society, and about technology, society, and gender. This book will help you become familiar with the prevailing debates about the Internet so that you'll feel *au courant* with the public discourse as it evolves. In addition, the newest ideas and most up-to-date resources are being collected and posted to the book's Web page on The Feminist Press's Web site at `http:\\www.ccny.cuny.edu\fempress\wiredworld` to supplement the materials you'll find in *The Women's Guide to the Wired World.*

I have been privileged to witness firsthand the expanding knowledge and power women achieve when they learn to effectively utilize electronic communications. Between 1994 and 1996 I designed and oversaw the building of the first women's electronic network for the former Soviet Union and Central and Eastern Europe. From Washington, D.C., I directed the Network of East-West Women (NEWW), an international communications network linking hundreds of women's nongovernmental organizations in thirty countries across the former Communist region. The electronic network that our organization created, called NEWW On-Line, serves an international community of academics, journalists, human rights activists, artists, parliamentarians, lawyers, businesspeople, technology and medical professionals, environmentalists, private and government foundation officers, and United Nations program officers—all of whom are interested in women's swiftly changing position in societies that are making the transition to democracy. Currently, NEWW operates six electronic conferences and two World Wide Web sites, in English and in Russian. It is also developing an information management system and on-line resources for women who work in the fields of international development and women's human rights.

The Internet training programs that my staff and I designed when building the electronic network have been tried and proven successful among women of all ages, classes, and cultures, and in countries with varying technical capabilities—from the United States to Russia to Albania, Ghana, and India. We produced an e-mail user's manual, which was distributed at Internet demonstrations during the 1995 United Nations' Fourth World Conference on Women in Beijing, China.

Along with the cadre of women trainers at NEWW, I have learned how to translate technical skills into laypersons' language, whereas many male trainers and computer guides adopt an overly technical language that is off-putting to many trainees, regardless of sex. While both men and women could benefit from quality technical guidance, women's access lags behind and deserves special attention.

I was motivated to write this book because the demand was simply impossible to ignore. In my work, I learned that most North American women don't know where to go for hands-on training or quality electronic resources. It has been very exciting to assist women from diverse backgrounds who were eager to take greater advantage of the technology and its offerings, and to learn how electronic communications can satisfy their information needs. I wanted to share that excitement—

and the benefits of my experience—with as many women as possible.

The value of an Internet user's guide and resource directory for women is evident in the benefits and opportunities that electronic communications offer us. As women, we have specific personal and social concerns, all of which are addressed in abundance on the Internet. But how to find the resources that best reflect our wide-ranging interests? How to know where the most useful offerings are located—and which ones to avoid?

Joan Korenman, based at the University of Maryland, collects and regularly updates invaluable lists of electronic gender-related forums. In an e-mail interview in July 1996 I asked her how women should be thinking about electronic communications as its popularity increases. She responded:

> As you note, electronic communications is becoming the channel through which all of us—women and men alike—will receive much of our information. People without access to this technology will be like those at an earlier time who lacked access to books and literacy. Given present-day socioeconomic arrangements, this issue may impact more on women than on men. Those of us in relatively privileged circumstances must work to ensure that access to information technology is readily available to everyone, both in the United States and around the world.
>
> But even universal access isn't enough—there's also the crucial question: "Access to *what*?" What information will be readily available? Whose novels and poems will we read? Whose theories will we study? Whose history will we learn? Women's studies has struggled to bring to light women's experiences and accomplishments. (Indeed, The Feminist Press has been at the forefront of that effort.) But now we must be just as dedicated to making sure that women's experiences and accomplishments are fully represented in the electronic world. And we can't do so unless we participate in that world. If we do not, there is a real danger that much of what we have all worked so hard to accomplish in women's studies will be lost, and women's experience will once again be rendered invisible.

There are Internet resource books for making money on Wall Street; for finding love; for legal and government resources. Recently, separate books have discussed why women should use electronic communications, described how they can use it, and listed specific sites of interest to women. But no book has done all three things; and none has explored in-depth—and seriously evaluated—the wealth of informational resources that would enrich the lives of women in all our diversity.

Where women's resources are listed in general guides and reference books, the selections are arbitrarily chosen and insufficient in number. Topics such as "automotive: cars" occupy more pages of the industry standard, *The Internet Yellow Pages,* than does the subject "women." Yet on-line resources for women are plentiful, and can be found on Listservs, Usenet newsgroups, Gophers, and World Wide Web sites. And more are being developed every month on all of the public and private networks. The volume of on-line information, support groups, services, products, and networks that this book makes available exemplifies the potential and promising market that women represent. It's time to serve the needs of this growing audience of women Internet users.

*The Women's Guide to the Wired World* draws upon the expertise of the women who are helping to construct the information superhighway and who are breaking ground in their own right. These women experts include Debra Floyd, who creates electronic forums for people of African descent at the Institute for Global Communications; Nina Beth Huntemann, a telecommunications analyst who studies women's political use of computer technology; Cheryl Lehman, a feminist professor of accounting and financial management and on-line maven; Sonia Jaffe Robbins, who moderates on-line meetings; Melissa Stone, who for many years developed the computer and on-line capacities of environmental science institutions in Europe and the former Soviet Union; Victoria Vrana, who leads e-mail training workshops with the Network of East-West Women for women in the United States, Europe, and Russia; Liza Weiman Hanks, a lawyer and contributor to *MacWorld On-Line*; and Amy Goodloe, proprieter of Women Online, who is a computer trainer, Web site designer, and publisher of on-line resources targeting lesbian users. Because their work reflects how women relate to the technology, they've been invited to contribute to various technical and resource chapters in this book.

*The Women's Guide to the Wired World* is divided into two parts:

PART 1: THE BASICS AND BEYOND. The opening part of the book covers the information you will need to enter the world of the Internet and use it to its maximum potential—and yours. It includes a basic explanation of electronic communications; the equipment and information you need to go on-line; the ABCs of Internet tools—general guidance in using tools and facilities such as e-mail, discussion forums, Internet research tools, and the World Wide Web; some innovative uses of the Internet, including how to conduct on-line meetings; user-friendly tips and answers to frequently asked questions; and a review of the current debates and controversies surrounding the Internet.

PART 2: THE RESOURCES. This part of the book includes guidelines for conducting Internet research plus thirteen extensive, annotated resource lists on personal, educational, professional, commercial, political, media, local/national/international, technical, women-oriented and general topic areas. More than one thousand addresses and sites were carefully selected for inclusion. These are described in the chapters, with commentary and easy-to-follow instructions for accessing each resource.

At the end of the book you will find a glossary defining every term that appears in the book enclosed in asterisks—*like this.* Glossary words are highlighted the first time they appear in running text (as opposed to boxes or lists) in each chapter. You'll also find information on the women who contributed to the book, a bibliography of recommended readings, and a subject index for easy access to all the information covered.

Welcome to the wired world! Good luck and enjoy! And don't forget to visit the on-line *Women's Guide to the Wired World* on The Feminist Press's Web site at http:\\www.ccny.cuny.edu\ fempress\wiredworld.

# Part 1

# THE BASICS AND BEYOND

This section will introduce you to electronic communications tools and their applications: electronic mail, Listservs, Usenet newsgroups, Gopher sites, FTPs, and the World Wide Web. In addition, it will walk you through the new and exciting process of moderating on-line meetings. You can flip through the pages and select what you need to learn depending on how familiar you are with the Internet.

The explanations and instructions for each tool are presented in discussions of the following:

- How each tool operates
- The services and providers that support them
- The software and hardware needed to use them
- Tips on how to maximize their use
- "Real world" examples of how women use each tool

Each chapter also includes words of advice, where appropriate, from women who are well-versed in the particular tool. They can help you know what to expect when you go on-line.

Halfway through this part of the book you'll find a chapter on "Netiquette," or on-line etiquette. At the end you'll find answers to some questions that are sure to come up as you enter the world of cyberspace, and a discussion of some issues, especially relevant to women, which have arisen as a result of the electronic revolution.

# 1

# ELECTRONIC COMMUNICATIONS
## What Our Mothers Couldn't Teach Us

### WHAT IS ELECTRONIC COMMUNICATIONS?

*Electronic communications* is a technology that transmits information from computer to computer via telephone lines and/or cables. There are three basic forms of electronic communications:

- E-mail
- Discussion forums and bulletin boards: Usenet newsgroups, mailing lists/Listservs, conferences, Internet Relay Chat
- Internet research: FTP sites, Gopher, World Wide Web

**E-mail** is a simple way to send and receive messages with family, friends, and colleagues who live in the same town or who are thousands of miles and several time zones away. E-mail fosters conversation—the casual, consensual kind you might have on the telephone.

The various **discussion forums,** such as *Usenet newsgroups,* *mailing lists,* and *Listservs,* and *Internet Relay Chat* allow you to engage in discussions or *chat sessions* and *post* announcements onto *bulletin boards* on topics of special interest—from employment discrimination to safe sex to pregnancy and birth. On-line discussions can be moderated or unmoderated, friendly or *flaming,* informative or supportive.

**Internet research** is carried out through the "network of networks," which is actually a set of technical standards and policy agreements that permit interconnections among most computer *networks* worldwide. On the Internet you can gain access to a vast array of free data, libraries, and other on-line resources around the world on almost any subject imaginable. You don't simply go "on the Net," although you may frequently hear that expression used (or misused). Rather, you log-in to someplace in particular—for example, an electronic magazine, library, or store.

This guide will introduce you to the necessary first steps for connecting on-line, sending and receiving e-mail, exploring discussion groups and bulletin boards, and conducting research (or *surfing*) on the Internet, using such standard tools as *Gopher,* *Archie,* *Veronica,* *FTP,* *Telnet,* *World Wide Web,* and so on.

### WHAT KIND OF EQUIPMENT DO I NEED TO USE ELECTRONIC COMMUNICATIONS?

To get started in electronic communications, you need only four pieces of equipment:

- A computer
- A modem

- A telephone line
- Communications software to link together the modem, computer, and telephone line

A *modem* is hardware that allows you to communicate with another computer over telephone lines. The word *modem* is an acronym for modulator-demodulator. A modem converts and modulates computer information into sound information that is carried across telephone lines. A modem at the other end demodulates the audible information back into computer information.

*Communications software* manages the connection between your computer and the on-line communications system to which you are connected. Communications software enables you to do the following things:

- Make use of the modem
- Manage information exchange between your computer and the on-line system (host or server)
- Send information *to* the host
- Capture and store information *from* the host

This process is discussed in detail in part 1, chapter 2.

> In a world of decreasing public spaces, but increasing bureaucracy and profit-driven private-sector interests, electronic communications technology provides arenas to talk freely to one another about our experiences, and to even plan actions for change. The discussion groups I choose to hang out in directly affect my daily life, just as my geographically close friends and family do. That's the power of communication in any form. I just happen to take part via a computer, modem, and telephone line.
>
> —NINA BETH HUNTEMANN
> University of Massachusetts, Amherst

### HOW MUCH COMPUTER EXPERIENCE DO I NEED TO USE ELECTRONIC COMMUNICATIONS?

You don't need to know any kind of programming at all. Your computer already has a word-processing program. Your modem comes with communications software. All you need is training—and practice, practice, practice.

You should know the basics of how to use your computer—how to turn it on; create, open, save, and close files; use the word-processing program; and print and delete files. But you don't have to be a computer genius to use the technology.

### THE TOP FIVE ADVANTAGES TO USING ELECTRONIC COMMUNICATIONS

1. **It's really fast.** When you send information electronically, it travels at much faster rates than by post or even by fax. A one-page fax might take several minutes because the information must be converted from paper to an electronic form, while the same text sent electronically may take well under a minute to send.

2. **It's inexpensive.** Although your initial start-up costs may be less expensive with a fax (since you have to have a modem and computer to communicate electronically), in the long run, electronic communications will save you money. You'll never need to buy paper and toner. If you use electronic communications properly, you won't accumulate phone bills comparable to the bills for fax usage. Because the electronic text travels very quickly, you spend less time on the phone line than you would sending a fax of the same text, and accrue a smaller bill. In addition, you can usually link into national and even international networks with a local call rather than a long-distance one.

3. **It's intimate.** Electronic exchanges tend to be informal, more like a postcard or Post-it note than a letter. You can respond immediately to a message or query, in the same day or hour that you receive it. This helps the sender and receiver feel as though they are in close proximity to one another.

4. **It's efficient, effective, and productive.** Electronic communications allows you to send one message to any number of e-mail users simultaneously. It also allows you to correct or edit other people's work with a minimum of effort because the text is already in electronic form. Therefore, a message can be e-mailed over long distances, and the receiver can easily make comments or corrections directly into her computer and then send it back to the originator or on to a third party. For example, you can send a draft agenda to participants in an on-line meeting, notify them of a deadline for returning their revisions to the agenda, and then send out the final agenda that will begin an electronic discussion.

5. **It's collaborative.** With electronic communications you can collaborate with others on-line to carry out an endless variety of projects. For example, you can write or edit articles or set an agenda collaboratively, as described above; discuss ideas and experiences; organize meetings or events locally, nationally, or internationally; and exchange research materials.

## WHAT ARE SOME OF THE USES OF ELECTRONIC COMMUNICATIONS?

Electronic communications is efficient for professional use and effective for keeping in touch with friends and relatives. And yet, the critics of *telecommunications* shake their heads and warn that electronic communications is to the 1990s what television was to the 1950s. They say it is a media conspiracy and, like television, it isolates people in their homes, where they sit alone, lonely and glassy-eyed, pressing buttons before a spellbinding screen.

But electronic communications at its core is *interactive,* and much more educational than television. Moreover, language, research, and literary skills are vital to maximizing use of the technology—just as important as computer skills.

In fact, electronic communications is the most serviceable tool I have ever used for communicating, networking, and retrieving information—all of which I do every day. For five years I directed an international communications and resource network for women's grassroots organizations in Eastern Europe and the former Soviet Union. I regularly communicated with our advisory board and supervised staff and projects in more than twenty countries. One of our main projects was the building of an electronic communications network for women's advocacy groups in the former Soviet bloc. Of course, it makes sense that I rely on electronic communications to carry out my work. But the ways I use the technology are no different from the ways you might use it in your work or private life. As you scan the lists that follow, you'll see that the verbs point to the very common and universal nature of electronic communications applications.

In the workplace you can use electronic communications to do the following:

- Send internal office communiqués
- Develop and direct projects and staff
- Argue, debate, discuss, and strategize on policy and management issues with staff and outside consultants
- Co-author or co-edit articles, reports, and proposals
- Advertise products or services
- Take orders for products or services
- Update your membership or customers on current events or new products
- Disseminate membership applications or brochures on request
- Announce general meetings and special events
- Collaborate on projects locally or globally
- Conduct research and arrange and coordinate field research
- Network and exchange informational resources with other organizations or businesses
- Notify your board of directors or head office about urgent matters
- Nurture relationships with funders or clients
- Post calls for papers and job applications

In your personal life you can use electronic communications to do the following:

- Maintain long-distance relationships with family and friends
- Talk to your partner when either of you is traveling
- Invite friends to parties
- Gather information on subjects of interest
- Communicate with others on special interest topics
- Purchase consumer products and request catalogs
- Subscribe to magazines and mailing lists
- Explore the world at a leisurely pace

Using electronic communications, I have also learned how to buy a house, give myself a breast exam, and choose a qualified chiropractor. (Sitting in front of a computer is a merciless predicament for my lower back!) I have read Radio Free Europe reports and congressional daily records. (Okay, not everyone's idea of fun.)

Electronic communications alters the pattern, shape, and texture of communication and informational exchange. It changes your expectations. Like a winged messenger, you are able to send messages in a matter of minutes. The speed at which electronic communications functions increases your productivity and improves your communication skills. It also creates a lateral exchange of information: suddenly, communication begins fanning out in many directions at once, which has a democratizing effect on the senders and receivers of information, as well as on the social value of the tool itself. Electronic communications is, after all, a very social tool, encouraging interaction that is both intimate and worldly, and inspiring a sense of connectedness across geographic and cultural borders. Often, people who might never meet in person come together in *cyberspace.*

Though electronic communications does not replace traveling to visit one another, it does make possible a new mode of regular exchange that, like every other medium, becomes part of the whole. Its unique contributions are the simultaneity of conversations and the increased access to resources, both of which spread authority, and thereby the power of decision-making, among a larger number of participants—what some call a "lateral power structure."

## BUT WHAT IS CYBERSPACE—AND AM I SURE I WANT TO GO THERE?

The comedian Lily Tomlin once described the vast, networked, electronic community as "BacoBits scattered across the salad bar of cyberspace." Most of us know what BacoBits are—but what is cyberspace? Is it magic? Is it a highway leading to a romanticized, sci-fi future? Is it a place, or a state of mind?

I most like Esther Dyson's working definition. Dyson is a pioneering force in the computer and telecommunications industries, both here in the United States and internationally, and has a far-reaching, down-to-earth vision of cyberspace and electronic interconnectivity. Think of real estate, she persuasively argued in *The New York Times Magazine*. Real estate is "an intellectual, legal, artificial environment constructed *on top of* land. Real estate recognizes the difference between parkland and shopping mall, between red-light zone and school district, between church, state and drugstore. In the same way, you could think of cyberspace as a giant and unbounded world of virtual real estate. Some property is privately owned and rented out; other property is common land; some places are suitable for children, and others are best avoided by all but the kinkiest citizens." ("If You Don't Love It, Leave It," July 16, 1995).

In cyberspace, there are thousands of places to visit. You can go to places like cafés and restaurants; you can go to bookstores, newsstands, shopping malls, and movie theaters; you can check out bulletin boards and enter large, small, and medium-sized communities made up of like-minded people. In cyberspace, notes Dyson, "communities are chosen by the users, not forced on them by accidents of geography. This freedom gives the rules that preside in cyberspace a moral authority . . . [and] if you don't like the rules, you can just sign off."

The fact that you engage in electronic communications in the privacy of your home or office potentially provides you with enough space to contemplate how to use this tool purposefully. I have worked with a Polish e-mail trainer named Roma Ciesla who says that, especially after years of living under Communist censorship, electronic communications' unregimented info-flow makes her feel like she has the world in her home and a home in the world; it has helped her shape a social identity that feeds her self-esteem—plus, she enjoys feeling up-to-date.

Having worked in countries with limited technical capacities, I am even more aware how easy it is to use Internet tools in the technologically advanced United States. I know many women in other parts of the world who live without functioning telephones, telephone lines, overnight delivery services, or reliable postal systems—or who have never had the open-ended access to the array of resources that inform and support North American women's lives. For them, electronic communications is a lifeline. For you, it may be less essential—but it can still open up a whole new world of choices in communication and information-gathering.

There's no denying it: electronic communications is a worthwhile investment. The pay-off is edifying, enriching, fun, creative, and inspiring. For some people, it's a spiritual experience. For others, it's purely utilitarian. But for most users, myself included, it's virtually impossible to recall life before electronic communications entered my day-to-day reality.

## HOW DID THE INTERNET GET STARTED?

Sonia Jaffe Robbins, who authored "A Brief History of the Internet" in the *NEWW On-Line User's Guide* (Washington, D.C.: Network of East-West Women, 1995) provides the short version: In the late 1960s the Rand Corporation, the United States' foremost cold war think tank, was given the following problem to solve: How would U.S. government and military authorities communicate in the event of a nuclear attack? The answer that these cold warriors proposed was to create a network with no central authority, one that would be designed to operate in and endure even a worst-case scenario.

In 1969 the U.S. Department of Defense funded this proposal, called ARPANET (Advanced Research Projects Agency Network). However, the federally funded researchers and military strategists quickly began using ARPANET as a high-speed electronic post office, sending messages back and forth among universities. Soon after, ARPANET users created a way to send a single message to many people simultaneously. In this way, mailing lists for special interest groups were born. (One of the most popular mailing lists back then was for sci-fi-philes.)

In more recent times, Internet usage has skyrocketed. In the West, this increase has coincided with the ever-growing sales of personal computers, as well as with the proliferation of commercial networks. In the former Eastern bloc and in some developing countries, computer communications spreads as telecommunication infrastructures are improved.

## HOW ARE WOMEN AND WOMEN'S GROUPS USING ELECTRONIC COMMUNICATIONS?

I have found that inventing new ways to utilize electronic communications can be fun and exciting (and even an integral part of the electronic package). But I first gained inspiration and new techniques from the many women and women's organizations who were on-line long before me. Women-oriented and feminist activity abounds on the Internet, and has been percolating since the mid-1970s. Many individuals and organizations have been creating their own services or have claimed their own territory on many of the commercial, educational, and not-for-profit organizational networks. Here are a few examples:

1. **The Boston Women's Health Book Collective** (BWHBC), which authored the self-help classic *Our Bodies, Our Selves,* and Arrow, a women's health group in Southeast Asia, have been communicating via e-mail for several years. In 1994, the electronic exchange of regional data enabled the BWHBC to quickly alert Arrow to the alarming fact that a drug Asian women were being given for birth control was actually sterilizing them.

2. **WomensNet** is a network that services the telecommunications needs of not-for-profit women's organizations who seek to interlink their networks locally, nationally, and internationally (including Arrow and BWHBC). Committed to increasing women's access to telecommunications technology, WomensNet acted as the primary provider of computer communications for the thirty thousand non-governmental organizations (NGOs) represented at the United Nations Fourth World Conference on Women in 1995. The Beijing conference marked the first time women from around the world realized that global communications could enable them to collaborate with each other—and to sustain that connection well into the future. WomensNet was created by Susan Mooney, a visionary woman in her mid-twenties who proudly claims that she has no formal computer training. WomensNet is one of several networks—others include PeaceNet, EcoNet, and LaborNet—that form the **Institute for Global Communications** (IGC). IGC is the U.S. member of a global activist network called the Association for Progressive Communications (APC). (See part 2, chapter 1, for more information about WomensNet and many of the other U.S.-based forums mentioned here.)

3. Another interactive on-line service for women is the commercial provider, **Women's Wire.** Headquartered in San Francisco (as is WomensNet), Women's Wire offers a range of resources and services comparable to its not-for-profit counterpart, such as information about women's studies programs, women's colleges, and the education of girls; archives on the women's movement; women's health issues; and resources for women in technology. Women's Wire was originally developed on America Online, then broke away to become autonomous; since late 1995, it has been housed under CompuServe. Along with new commercial resources, Women's Wire continues to provide innovative services and resources such as an the Older Women's Network, career and finance information, a spirituality forum, and women's magazines. In 1995, CompuServe also became the first large commercial network to support a women's forum. Amy Bernstein, an associate editor at *U.S. News & World Report,* successfully persuaded the magazine to sponsor **Women's Forum,** coordinated by Women's Wire.

4. Many individuals spend their leisure time developing on-line resources. For example, Sarah Stapleton-Gray of Alexandria, Virginia, created **Feminist Activist Resources on the Net,** a vast store of information, ideas, and networking opportunities which can be found on the Web. The

offerings include Current Feminist Issues, Feminist Activist Calendar, and Feminism Fun and Games.

5. **Women's rights advocates in Russia** network electronically to retrieve Internet news on global women's issues and to broadcast the information through local mainstream media. During the political changeover in the former Soviet bloc, as new laws and constitutions are being made, Russian women's rights advocates are also using electronic communication to distribute abstracts and critiques of draft legislation that concerns women. Under the Soviet government, draft legislation used to be announced in newspapers, but in the transition to a democracy and a free market economy, newspaper publishers opt to sell print space to advertisers rather than publish draft laws. So women are taking it upon themselves to disseminate pertinent legislative information. For example, in 1994 the Russian parliament drafted a proposal to eliminate abortion from health insurance policies after decades of government coverage. Women needed to act quickly to inform their constituencies, appeal to parliamentarians, organize public debates, and produce alternative policy proposals. Electronic communications became a vital element in their successful fast-response effort.

6. **NEWW On-Line** is the name of the electronic network built by the organization I directed to facilitate dialogue and activism among women's rights advocates East and West. NEWW On-Line is a means to the end of reinforcing the advocate's need for the local, national, and international exchange of ideas and experiences. One of the services NEWW On-Line provides is sending and delivering e-mail messages for colleagues who lack the technology; we call this service the electronic post office. Similarly, in Berlin, Germany, **ZIF,** the Women's Information Center, acts as an electronic librarian, conducting Internet research for Eastern European women's groups that lack full Internet access. (See part 2, chapter 2, for information on these and other international forums.)

## WHAT ARE SOME OF THE STANDARD TOOLS FOR EXPLORING THE INTERNET?

The various tools for electronic communications are fully discussed in part 1, chapters 3 through 8. But because these terms will come up as you begin to enter the world of electronic communications—as you go about choosing a network and getting yourself on-line—some brief definitions are provided here.

*Text-based* electronic tools include:

1. **E-mail,** as described earlier in this chapter, enables you to send and retrieve messages from one computer to another over telephone lines. (See part 1, chapters 2 and 3.)

2. **Usenet newsgroups, Listservs and mailing lists, and Internet Relay Chat** are used for ongoing moderated discussions, unmoderated chat sessions, posted announcements, and news updates on specific topics. Telecommunications whiz Esther Dyson calls these "real communities," where groups of people converse among themselves. Some individuals actively

participate in conversations with each other, usually through posted messages; others listen and observe. (See part 1, chapter 5.)

3. **Gopher** sites are for gaining control over your Internet browsing and research work. You wade through a series of hierarchical menus, placing *bookmarks* at the sites where you will want to return. Bookmarks help you keep on-track as you delve through layers of files. Once you find what you want, you download it. (See part 1, chapter 7.)

4. **FTP (File Transfer Protocol)** sites are for browsing through and retrieving full text files and programs from *remote computer* data archives. Technology writer Mitzi Waltz calls FTP the "workhorse of the Internet." (See part 1, chapter 7.)

5. **Archie** and **Veronica** are used for searching FTP and Gopher menus more effectively. Archie is an index to FTP sites, a *command-driven* *search program* that is available via Gopher and the World Wide Web. Veronica is an index to Gophers that allows you to search either single or compound terms. (See part 1, chapter 7.)

6. **Telnet** is for accessing a remote *host* computer inexpensively. When you Telnet into a computer system, you are *logging on* as if you were working at a computer on the network you are calling. Because you are not being charged for the long-distance telephone call, you will happily save yourself money. You can Telnet into library card catalogs, or you can access an interlibrary loan system to order books and periodicals from your local library. Most *Internet service providers* offer Telnet as one of their Internet options. (See part 1, chapter 7.)

In addition, you will learn about *graphics-based* tools. Many people think that the graphically based World Wide Web is easier to use than the text-based tools, because with the help of a *Web browser,* you can use a mouse to click onto different informational sources, to move around from one host computer to the next, and to view graphics. *Web sites* certainly are more visually pleasing, because you can view formatted text that uses boldface and italics and a variety of fonts and colors, as well as graphics. Although you cannot engage in chat sessions, you can access graphic information such as maps, photographs, and cartoons, as well as video and audio offerings which are not otherwise available. (See part 1, chapter 6.)

These tools won't make too much sense until you open an account and start using them. The first step, then, is to choose a network, communications software, and an e-mail program—all of which are explained in the next chapter.

# 2

# HOOKING UP
## Choosing a Network and Other First Steps

Now that you understand the theory and structure behind electronic communications, you need to know some general information about *networks* and *communications software,* and how to get yourself on-line.

In this chapter, you will learn about the following:

- The different types of networks
  - On-line vs. off-line
  - Text-based vs. Graphic-based
  - Educational
  - Organizational
  - Commercial
  - Free-nets
  - Local
  - Bulletin board systems
- Communications software
  - Network-specific software
  - Generic software
  - Parameters and settings
- Dialing-up and Logging-in
  - Local dial-ups
  - Manual dial-ups
  - Logging in and passwords
  - Scripts and macros

### CHOOSING THE NETWORK THAT WORKS FOR YOU ON THE NET

Choosing a network—that is, an ***Internet service provider,**\* or ISP—is the single most important factor in your *cyberspace* experience. There are hundreds of different pathways onto the Internet. Networks are companies that have dedicated phone lines at their central offices and computers which are wired together and configured to send and receive messages. These are what can be called *host* computers. Networks are connected to the Internet, and the Internet transmits messages from one network to another. Networks rent the use of their dedicated lines to customers, either by the hour, the month, or the year.

The network you choose determines the price of communication and research, the ease or difficulty of use, and the amount of information and services available to you, as well as the kinds of information offered. Every network has its own character, just as communities take on a certain character because of the people who create them. You are probably familiar with the names of many U.S. commercial providers. But you might be surprised to learn that they are quite distinct from one another. CompuServe is professionally and technically oriented; America Online emphasizes entertainment services for the young, upwardly mobile, and predominantly singles set; Prodigy is family-oriented; and Women's Wire bridges the Internet's gender gap with its "fe-mail" orientation.

Many networks also offer special "product lines" that are created exclusively for a network's user base. Because these network-created resources are available only to network subscribers, they should influence your choice of a network. Different networks also arrange access to resources differently. For example, PeaceNet prioritizes its resources under social change categories such as conflict resolution, human rights, and environment. In contrast, a commercial network such as America Online classifies resources under weather, shopping, travel, entertainment, and chat sessions. On both networks, you will find information sources on almost any topic that interests you, from weddings to women's environmental organizations. But it will take more or less time to locate a particular resource, depending on the network you choose.

With thousands of Internet service providers from which to choose, the selection process can be dizzying. Many formerly local ISPs like Erols or the Well are now going regional or national, and competing with the well-known commercial on-line services like America Online and CompuServe. The dedicated ISPs connect you directly to the Internet and provide you with an e-mail address and mailbox, as well as access to the World Wide Web, Usenet newsgroups, FTP, Gopher, and Telnet. They generally offer unlimited connect time for a flat monthly fee. The commercial on-line services do not always have access to a full range of Internet services, but do offer subscribers many network-created resources and easy-to-use software packages. They sometimes charge additional hourly fees for Internet access.

To select an ISP that suits your needs, first seek advice from friends who are Internet mavens. What services did they choose, and why? Are they satisfied customers? In addition, consider the following criteria:

1. What are the monthly charges? Are there additional hourly charges for high-volume use, and are you likely to accrue them?
2. Is a full range of Internet services (e-mail, Web, Gopher, FTP Usenet newsgroups, Telnet) offered?
3. What kinds of special, network-specific services are offered?
4. Are women- and feminist-oriented resources offered and easily accessible?
5. Are technical support services available by e-mail and telephone?
6. How long has the ISP been in existence, and is it likely to be around a year or more down the road?
7. Is it difficult to get on-line during peak hours?
8. Does the ISP update its equipment?
9. Are SLIP and PPP connections available?
10. Does the ISP allow you to build your own Web site? What are the costs?
11. Can the ISP accommodate your telecommunications needs when you travel? Does it offer national access (through local dial-ups across the country) and an 800 number?

On the World Wide Web, you can survey the thousands of ISPs available. Borrow a friend's account and visit the following Web sites:

- "The List," at http://www.thelist.com, which claims to have the largest list of ISPs (5,023), searchable by country, state/province, area code, or name.
- Listings for Canada at http://www.herbison.com/herbison/iap_canada_meta_list. This site also offers a "meta-list" of international ISPs.

---

**Q:** Why is women's Internet use increasing?

**A:** Since the hardware (PCs, modems, communications software) and know-how has moved beyond traditionally male circles—computer science departments, military institutions, and transnational corporations—electronic communications technology has been integrated into wider spheres—the workplace, commercial space, leisure services, and so on.

I'm not at all surprised that women are finding ways to make the Internet a part of their everyday activities. But it is crucial to remember, if women want to shape the future of Internet technology, that the creators and financial supporters of all the computer technology industries are still overwhelmingly represented by men.

—NINA BETH HUNTEMANN
University of Massachusetts, Amherst

---

### On-line Networks vs. Off-line Networks

Technically, there are two general categories for electronic communications networks: on-line and *off-line.*

An **on-line** system allows you to work directly with the host computer or through the host to reach the Internet. It uses only one communications program. It allows you to connect to and interact directly with the host computer, which means it allows you to write and save messages on that computer, not your own.

With an on-line network you can choose which e-mail messages you would like to delete, *download,* or forward. The connection to the host computer enables Internet research. On-line networks usually charge a monthly fee plus an hourly rate. Even if you use an on-line network, you can—and should—choose to do some of your work off-line. For example, you should compose your e-mail messages before you connect to the network to *upload* the messages, reducing your on-line time—and your hourly charges.

An **off-line** system, sometimes also called UUCP or "store and forward," can use two communications programs. One program is for writing and reading messages. You write all of your e-mail messages ahead of time and address each one, as if you were folding them into stamped and addressed envelopes. After you have prepared your messages, you may start a second program. This program automatically *dials-up,* *logs-in,* downloads all your new mail, uploads all your prepared mail, and *logs-off*. (You'll learn what all these terms mean later in this chapter.) It is quick and simple and minimizes the use of the phone line (which is very important for users in countries with poorly constructed and unpredictable phone systems). Off-line networks usually charge per *kilobyte* sent and received. Off-line networks are very easy to use, but limited. You cannot choose which messages you would like to download. Since you are being charged per kilobyte, if someone sends you a large file, you must download and pay for all of it. Moreover, you cannot access the Internet with an off-line network. To use the Internet, you must be connected to a host computer or to the computer from which you want to retrieve files.

---

**INTERFACE CHOICE: TEXT vs. GRAPHICS**

Different networks (and different communications software programs) offer you different types of interface. The interface affects how information appears on your screen and how you interact with it. Text-based networks and software use file menus, typed commands, and function keys. You never need to touch a mouse to use them. Graphics-based networks and programs have pictures and icons which you activate by clicking the mouse.

---

## INTRODUCING THE NETWORKS

The networks can be broken down into different "types." These types of networks are described in the following section, with a brief analysis of their cost, user *interface,* Internet access, type of information provided, and level of technical (and sometimes emotional) support. See the Feminist Press Web site for an annotated list of many of the U.S. networks and service providers and information on how to contact them.

### EDU: Educational

Educational networks are those directly related to universities and institutions. They developed from the original ARPANET (described in part 1, chapter 1) and NSFNET (National Science Foundation Network). If you can obtain an account on an educational network, do so. EDU networks provide a high degree of Internet access at a low cost.

COST:  For many years, EDU networks were free for students and faculty. However, this is rapidly changing as the National Science Foundation withdraws its funding from the Internet. Still, at the moment, universities continue to charge rock-bottom prices, averaging $10 to $20 a semester for unlimited use.

USER INTERFACE:  The way your mailbox and the Internet appear on your screen can range from clunky and *text-based* (all words, no pictures) to fully *graphics-based.* Software varies from one university to another.

INTERNET ACCESS:  Most educational networks provide full Internet access. These networks were some of the first architects and mainstays of the Internet. However, some universities do not yet have access to the *World Wide Web.*

TYPE OF INFORMATION:  Educational networks are naturally one of the best places for academic resources and scholarly pursuits. Of particular interest to women are women's studies syllabi, curricula, periodicals, discussions, and academic job listings.

SUPPORT:  It is usually very simple to set up an account on a university network (provided you are part of the university). Call your campus computer center and they will give you a password and *login.* If you use a computer which is part of the campus computer network (a computer in a university office, computer center, or library), it is likely that you will not need to install a *modem* or software. Using your home computer to access the network will require extra set-up. Often the support centers are staffed with students, paid and unpaid, who tend to be over-worked, so you will need to be patient. The level of support services varies among different educational institutions.

## ORG: Not-for-Profit Networks

Not-for-profit networks are nationwide, topic-specific networks run by not-for-profit organizations. These began in the mid- to late 1980s and are still proliferating. Examples include PeaceNet, EcoNet, LaborNet, ConflictNet (for conflict resolution issues), WomensNet, HandsNet (for social service professionals), Earthlink, and HomeoNet (for homeopathic medicine and research). Not-for-profit organizations that have their own private networks, like the United Nations, are also classified as ORG networks. Occasionally, access to not-for-profit networks is restricted to professionals and not-for-profit organizations working in the field of focus. ORG networks are particularly useful for not-for-profits, especially those that use the Internet for more than research. These networks provide suggestions, technical support and low-cost host computer space for creating *conferences,* *mailing lists,* *Gophers,* and *Web sites.* Organizational networks serve every region of the world.

COST:  Not-for-profit networks do cost money, although they try to provide the best service for the lowest cost possible. Monthly fees range from $10 to $20, with hourly rates from $1.50 to $6 after six to ten free hours per month. Their costs for Gopher, *newsgroup,* *mailing list,* and Web space are considerably lower than those of commercial networks. Some even provide free space to not-for-profit groups.

USER INTERFACE:  Many of the larger ORG networks have fully graphics-based, easy-to-use software. Some still use generic software and have text-based menus. One of the disadvantages of not-for-profit networks is that they sometimes lack *local dial-ups* for smaller towns, so users must use designated 800 numbers, which are more expensive because services charge higher on-line rates for use of these numbers.

INTERNET ACCESS:  The larger not-for-profit networks have full Internet access and usually help other organizations create their own informational resources on the Internet. Smaller ORG networks are still catching up.

TYPE OF INFORMATION:   This is where ORG networks differ the most from commercial networks. Not-for-profit networks provide information about their topics of focus—women, peace, labor issues, social services, homeopathic medicine, and so on. Not only are their Internet menus organized to provide quick and easy access to these outside-the-mainstream resources, but they often carry conferences, *chat sessions,* and databases on political topics that are not accessible from other networks.

SUPPORT:  Support at ORG networks is usually very responsive and thorough. The one drawback reflects the problem of all not-for-profits: understaffing. Often you'll find yourself holding the line for voice support or waiting for them to return your call. On-line support is more efficient than voice support, and on-line technical support conferences and manuals are extremely useful.

### COM: Commercial Networks

Large commercial networks such as CompuServe, Delphi, America Online (AOL), Prodigy, and Microsoft Network (MSN) receive the most media attention and are the best known in the United States. There are also many smaller commercial networks which provide different levels of Internet access and services for local areas.

COST:  Larger commercial networks charge from approximately $20 a month for unlimited use; or from $12 to $15 a month for about ten free hours, with additional charges accruing for additional hourly use. Smaller networks usually provide different levels of access at varying costs; for example, an "e-mail only" account would cost less than one with full Internet access. The costs are high for opening and maintaining Web, Gopher, FTP, and conference sites. However, competition continues to drive prices down.

USER INTERFACE:  The large commercial networks differ from one another in look and feel; in fact, this is the way in which they differ the most. AOL's sophisticated graphical interface has become the desirable standard interface, and its Web *browser* is rated one of the best. To use most commercial networks, you'll need to download the necessary software upon opening an account. Ease of installation varies. Some smaller commercial networks still run text-based menus.

INTERNET ACCESS:   By the end of 1996 all of the major networks had begun providing full Internet access. Some do not yet provide Internet space for individuals, businesses, or organizations. Smaller COM networks provide such services, but the fees are high.

TYPE OF INFORMATION:  Again, this is where commercial networks differ greatly from one another and from other types of networks. In general, commercial networks provide commercial material (including advertising and shopping services); information on finances, travel, and hobbies; interactive chat sessions on an infinite number of topics; and news services. Each of the larger COM networks has forums and discussions that can be found on that network only. These networks frequently hold special, scheduled on-line interviews and events with media, entertainment, and political celebrities. Many product vendors, especially the computer and multimedia companies, place their information exclusively on one network. If you have special interests or regularly interact with specific businesses or vendors, it is worthwhile to investigate the options before selecting a commercial network.

SUPPORT:  As with many other networks, there are usually two kinds of technical support, on-line and telephone support, and response time varies.

### Free-nets

Free-nets usually provide electronic communications services to local or regional areas. Free-nets usually have limited Internet access, sometimes only providing users with *e-mail* and a limited number of local conferences. They often have time restrictions under which on-line time may be limited—for example, two to four hours per day. These networks are limited in size and in number of users. Most rely on volunteer energy—a good way to meet your local Internet community in the flesh and learn more about networks.

COST:  Free-nets really are free! To keep their costs down, some users have an account on a free-net solely for e-mail usage, and an account on another network for Internet activity.

USER INTERFACE:  To keep costs low, many free-nets have clunky, text-based interfaces. It is usually difficult or expensive to dial-in to these networks from other cities.

INTERNET ACCESS:  Most free-nets do not have Internet access. Some provide limited Internet services such as Telnet and FTP.

TYPE OF INFORMATION:  Free-nets provide information you will not be able to find on other networks. They usually have discussions and postings about local governments, events, businesses, schools, and so forth. The blend of *virtual* and "real" communities is said to revitalize businesses.

SUPPORT:  These small networks can be understaffed and overextended, resulting in slow or limited support. However, if you need someone to pay a house call and examine how you have hooked your modem to your computer, they'll help you. It might be the only chance you'll have to get this kind of in-person service. Also, many community networks provide free training and orientation, or they'll barter for volunteer service.

### Local ISP: Local Internet Service Providers

Local Internet service providers are quickly becoming one of the best ways to get on-line. Small companies are opening up at an astounding rate all over the country,  and many established providers are expanding regionally or nationally. They offer every level of Internet access for some of the lowest prices around. Newspapers and magazines abound with offers of "Unlimited Internet Access for $9.99 per month." The trick with local ISPs is finding the legitimate, reliable companies. Some of the better known providers include Pipeline, Digex, Panix, Portal, TIAC, and the Well.

COST: Local ISPs offer low and sometimes almost bulk rates for Internet access. For example, Erols offers unlimited Internet access and use for $160 a year, or about $14 a month. Prices can drop as low as $10 a month. Research carefully any ISP advertising rates like $2.99 a month; there is probably some fine print which adds at least another $20 to your bill. Flat-fee rates are more economical than hourly or per kilobyte charges and allow you to surf at your leisure.

USER INTERFACE: Most local ISPs provide their own software packages, which usually include popular, common, and easy-to-use programs like *Eudora* and *Netscape.* Ask about the software program before you commit. Anything "homegrown" and text-based is probably not worth using with these networks.

INTERNET ACCESS: Almost all local commercial networks provide full Internet access as well as e-mail-only accounts. They may also be capable of putting your whole business or organization on-line with a direct T-1 connection if you so choose. (T-1 lines are cables that provide direct Internet connections, without the use of telephones or modems, and are most commonly used by ISPs, universities, and corporations.)

TYPE OF INFORMATION: Local ISPs often do not provide their own content, meaning you will not find network-specific information like AOL's chat rooms or PeaceNet's alternative news services. Local ISPs are a doorway to the Internet and nothing more. You may want to use an account on these networks for Internet research only and save yourself some money in the process.

SUPPORT: Support on these networks varies. Often the sales departments are staffed with temporary phone people who don't seem to know the first thing about the Internet. Like other small businesses, some local ISPs seem to be understaffed and can be unresponsive. Others are much better. Ask friends or other users about their experiences to determine the quality level.

## BBS: Bulletin Board Systems

Bulletin board systems are similar to free-nets in that they are extremely small and will only service a local area. (People from outside the area can use the BBS if they are willing to make a long-distance call.) Some BBSs are free; others charge a low fee. BBSs are almost always run by individuals or small groups. If you have your own computer and can install a separate phone line, then it is easy to put up your own BBS.

COST: BBSs are inexpensive or free as long as you can access them with a local telephone call.

USER INTERFACE: BBSs are almost always text-based, sometimes using difficult commands.

INTERNET ACCESS: Usually BBSs only provide e-mail, with some file transfer capabilities. Some give you Telnet capability as well.

TYPE OF INFORMATION: BBSs are known for unusual or specific information. For example, your town may have a local BBS for dentists in the area. Often the information is technology-related.

SUPPORT: Again, a BBS may provide you with the rare opportunity to see a support person in the flesh. Since BBSs are usually run by one or two people, voice support is limited.

### Interoffice Networks

Many businesses and organizations now have their own internal networks. These networks are free, but are limited to e-mail and occasionally office conferences. They are usually limited to office employees; you cannot send or receive mail to or from anyone outside the in-house network. These systems provide information you cannot find elsewhere, such as directions to the company picnic or the minutes from a staff meeting. The software is generally simple to use.

### COMMUNICATIONS SOFTWARE

There are as many different kinds of software as there are networks. Your choice of software depends on the type of computer you have, the network you choose, and the functionality you desire. Your software, like your network, can make electronic communications easy or frustrating to use.

---

**A NOTE ON PROTOCOLS**

When you are downloading and uploading on an on-line system, at some point your computer may ask you which protocol you want to use. (This doesn't happen in off-line systems, because these systems transfer files automatically and choose the appropriate protocol for you). Protocols are the different languages computers speak—the various ways they send information back and forth across the phone lines. Some protocols are faster than others. Some have built-in error correction. Error correction allows the computer to check each little piece of information that comes over the phone line to make sure it did not get scrambled or deleted on its journey. Some common protocols are ASCII, xmodem, ymodem, zmodem, kermit, and FOP. ASCII is used for text files only; it cannot send binary files, which includes all graphical files. It is important to make sure you tell your host computer and your own computer to use the same protocol. (Some communications software programs, such as ProComm Plus, automatically detect which protocol you are using and set themselves appropriately.)

---

Communications software enables you to "talk" to your modem, which interacts with your telephone line. It enables you to dial the number you need to connect to your network and to hang up. Your software also talks to your computer and tells it to prepare to receive a file, place files in specific folders or directories, and send specific files through the phone line (via the modem) to the host computer and finally into the wide world of the Internet.

Your software also tells your modem and computer which *protocol* (such as *ASCII* or *binary*) you want to use to send and receive messages. You can set this as a default, indicating you will always use a certain protocol, or you can choose the protocol each time you transfer files.

Because all software programs are unique, it isn't possible to instruct you to press this key or click on that icon to initiate an action. Instead, the following section will explain the types of software and e-mail programs you might encounter so that you can select a program that best suits your needs, or identify the type and capabilities of the software you may already have.

### Network-Specific Software

Many Internet service providers, especially the large commercial networks, have developed their own software programs. The network will either send this to you by snail mail in the form of floppy disks (which you must then install on your own computer) or tell you to download the software when you open an account. This software is usually graphical, easy to use, and well supported by the network's technical staff via voice or e-mail. Network-specific software usually contains special features, such as a button for reaching support at the network or a customized address book function. This software can only be used on the network which provides it. In general, you cannot use other communications software to reach these networks.

### Generic Software

A generic software program is a program that can be used with different networks. However, it cannot be used with *all* networks. These programs differ for IBM/PCs and Macintosh computers. Some of the well-known programs for Macs include Microphone II, Red Ryder, and White Knight, while ProComm Plus and MTEZ are widely used on PCs.

Eudora is a popular, graphics-based, generic e-mail program that is available for both Macintosh and IBM/PC computers. It acts like a housekeeper and automatically takes care of many of the small tasks that you would otherwise do manually. For example, it downloads and deletes messages for you, and can thus save you lots of money, because if you do not delete messages you will be charged for them. Some other mail programs also do this kind of housekeeping for you.

Another important distinction in communications software lies with the software's interface—text-based or graphics-based. Some people prefer one kind of interface over the other, depending on the network with which they interact, their previous computer experience (whether they use Windows, a Macintosh, or a DOS shell), and their personality. Some people simply prefer words and key commands to pictures and the mouse, or vice versa. If you already use a computer, you probably know your preference. Regular e-mail users or people with accounts on different networks usually have more than one type of communications software on their computers.

Generic software can often be obtained as *freeware* or *shareware.* It can also be purchased in computer stores. There are now many new commercial packages like "Internet in a Box," which are also generic communication software programs. These packages are generally conglomerations of many small programs which can be obtained as freeware or shareware.

Modems usually come with a simple, generic communications software as well, although they tend to be limited in their capabilities.

### Shareware and Freeware

Shareware and freeware are software programs ranging from e-mail editors to screensavers. These programs can be downloaded directly from the Internet.

**Freeware** is just what it sounds like—software that is free of cost. Often, these programs are created by individuals who sincerely enjoy giving away their nifty gadgets to fellow users. All they may ask for in return is an e-mail message from you, giving feedback and helping to identify "bugs," or problems with the program.

**Shareware** programs are applications, usually developed by individuals, which require a small fee. These are also found on the Internet. Sometimes creators of shareware distribute their programs on faith, asking users to send a $5 to $25 check for use of the program. The days of faith-based payment, however, are rapidly ending. Most shareware programs now require you to register. This entails sending a check to the creator, who then sends you a password or a registration number. Only after you have that number can you use the shareware.

### Parameters and Settings

Among other things, you will use your communications software to set your *parameters,* which you should find under the "parameters and settings" menu. These tell your computer and modem exactly how to transfer information.

The first part of your basic **communications setting** usually designates the number of *bits* (units of computer information) your computer sends in one package. The number is almost always eight or seven. The second and third parts specify the **parity** and **stop bit**—added bits which help the computer check itself to ensure the complete and correct transfer of a package of information. One of the most common communications settings is "8 bits, no parity and 1 stop bit"—written as "8-n-1." (It is likely that your network will tell you which settings it requires, so you will not need to worry about these technical details.)

**Modem settings** are also important. You can tell your communications software how fast your modem runs, or how fast you want it to run. This is called the **baud rate** (pronounced "bawd" or "bod"), and it refers to the number of *bps* (bits per second) your modem can transfer. Most American modems today are 14,400 baud rate modems, commonly referred to as 14.4, or 28,800 baud rate modems known as 28.8. Older modems run at speeds of 9,600, 2,400, or even 1,200 bps. Since the amount of time it takes to transfer determines how long you stay connected to your network—which, in turn, increases or decreases your costs—you can understand why the baud rate is crucial. Under modem settings you will also need to indicate a **COM port**. This tells your computer *where*—at which *port,* or connection point—it will find your modem. This setting is most often COM port 1.

Other settings include **protocol settings,** which can indicate a default protocol to use, and **file settings,** which designate default directories or folders to receive and send mail. Your communications software's manual should include detailed descriptions of all of these settings.

### DIAL-UP AND LOG-IN

Once you have selected the network and software appropriate for your needs, you will need to learn how to connect to your network—what's known as dialing-up and logging-in.

**Dialing-up** refers to the process of dialing your host computer through a telephone line and connecting to it. **Logging-in** means telling the host computer exactly who you are so that you may gain access to the part of the computer that allows you to use e-mail and receive your e-mail messages. Again, because all software and networks require unique commands in order to operate, what's outlined here are the general premises behind making those connections, as well as some of the basic steps.

It's important to remember that unless you have a direct connection to the Internet (which you might have with an EDU account) you will be telling your modem, through your communications software, to contact your host computer through an actual telephone line.

If you are using a telephone line that you usually use for voice (telephone) communication, you will not be able to call anyone while you are on-line. If anyone calls you, they will receive a busy signal. Keep this in mind when you are trying to call a friend whose phone is busy for three hours—she may be on-line.

If you have call-waiting on your phone, you must turn it off before you begin. You can often tell your computer to do this automatically. Otherwise, an incoming call can interrupt your on-line session and disrupt data transfer. Your local phone company can tell you how to deactivate call-waiting.

Because you are using regular telephone lines, your e-mail connection is subject to the same kinds of problems as a phone call. Your network is equipped to handle massive numbers of telephone calls because it has special lines. Even so, you may sometimes receive a busy signal, especially if you use a small commercial network, a freenet, or a BBS. Bad weather and natural disasters also affect phone lines. In addition, the basic telecommunications infrastructure in a country affects that country's capacity to handle electronic communications. Many users in developing countries and in Eastern Europe, for example, have an extremely difficult time using e-mail due to their countries' weak infrastructures.

## Local Dial-Ups

Just as you are using "real" telephones lines, networks are "actual" places with tangible computers that are situated in offices with suite numbers that are housed in real office buildings. These network headquarters are usually located in large cities, which may or may not be close to your home or office.

If you are "calling" the host computer over the telephone line, how is it possible to avoid massive long distance charges? The larger networks have made arrangements with small companies all over the country who are often Internet service providers themselves. These agreements allow you, the user, to call the small company in your city or area by dialing a local telephone number. The company will then connect you to the host computer at your network. You pay the local company through your network. For example, if you pay your network $2 an hour for connect-time charges, the network may pay the company $.50 of that hourly fee. *Local dial-ups* allow you to maintain the same account on the same network if you move, or to access your account as you travel. Your network will provide you with a list of local dial-ups when you open your account.

## Manual Dialing

Your communications software usually allows you to dial-up in two ways. The first way is by dialing manually. Manual dialing means that you type in all the commands necessary to tell your modem to dial the number for your host computer. Luckily, these commands are simple and you only need to know three.

First, tell your software you want to dial-up. Then, type in your first modem command, `at` or `atz`, and press ENTER or RETURN. These commands are abbreviations for "attention," and inform your modem that you are speaking to it. The commands ensure that your computer and modem are connected and that everything is working properly. If it is, the term `ok` will appear on your computer screen.

The second modem command to type is `atdt`. This tells your modem "attention dial tone." Follow this command with a space, then the number of your host computer. Type in the telephone number exactly as you would if you were making a voice call, using a 1 if it is a long-distance number, or a 9 if you need to connect to an outside line. Complete the command by pressing RETURN or ENTER. Here's what first appears on the computer screen when I try to reach my network's host computer:

```
atz
ok
atdt 986-6066
```

If you are communicating internationally, you should be aware that telephone lines use two types of signals, tone and pulse. Most telephones have a switch that changes them from one to the other. Telephone lines in the United States use tone. From Eastern Europe and other parts of the world, you might need to type `atdp` for "attention dial pulse."

The only other modem command you really need to know if you are manually dialing is `ath` for "attention hang up," which tells the modem to disconnect the phone.

After you tell your modem to dial a number, you will hear a series of clicking and beeping noises; these are the sounds of a number being dialed on a touch-tone phone, but at a much faster pace. And when you have successfully connected, you can't miss hearing a long, piercing sound. This crashing sound is good: it means you are linking to your host computer.

## Logging-In

After you connect to the host computer at your network or to the computer at your local dial-up, you will be asked to identify yourself.

Usually, after connection, the words `Welcome to such-and-such network` or `Connected at 9600` will appear on your screen. (The number is the baud rate.)

Next you will see a log-in prompt. The word `login:` will appear on your screen with a blinking cursor to the right of it.

Your *login* is your e-mail "name." When you open your account, you will designate your login. Some people use their first and/or last name. Some people use the name of their business or organization. It is a good idea to keep your login simple so that people can easily remember it. Your login becomes the first half of your e-mail address; you will use it every time you use e-mail.

This is what I see on my computer screen as I log-in:

```
Welcome to WomensNet
login: shanapenn
password: ******
```

After you type in your login, your network will give you a password prompt. Like your login, your password is chosen by you when you open your account. (Sometimes your network will give you a temporary password which you use the first time you connect. Afterwards, you can change your password.) When you type your password, you will not see it on the screen. You may see asterisks, dots, or nothing at all. The actual password remains invisible on the screen to help protect your account's security.

Because your password is your security, you will want to choose one that is not obvious. You might try mixing up lower- and uppercase letters, or using numbers and punctuation marks, if your network will allow it. It is a good idea to change your password regularly.

### Scripts and Macros

Your network may also allow you to dial-up and log-in using a *script* or *macro.* In fact, with some of the fully graphical network programs you may not even have the option of dialing manually. Scripts and macros are small software programs built into your communications software that act like mini tape recorders. A script may execute a series of commands written ahead of time by the creators of the software. Or it may record commands that you type in and replay later. Either way, the commands run whenever you click on an icon or choose the name of the script from a menu. For example, many commercial communication software packages have service providers such as America Online, Prodigy, and Delphi listed in a menu or displayed as a series of icons. If you choose one of these networks, your modem will check itself and dial a number—usually an 800 number—for the network. This saves you the trouble of manual dialing.

The ability to record your own script can make dialing-up and logging-in very simple. Find the command in your menu that turns the "recorder" on. (Microphone II, for example, calls this command "Watch Me." But the command name may be more generic, like "record macro.") Your communications software will ask you to name your macro. You can give it any name you want (but make sure you remember it!)

Next type in all the commands described in the sections on manual dialing-up and logging-in. After you send your password and choose your terminal type, turn the recorder off. The next time you want to connect, all you will have to do is click on your new icon or choose the script name in a menu.

Congratulations! You have waded through a lot of technical material. Now the fun part begins: it's time to send an e-mail message.

# 3

# A MAILBOX OF ONE'S OWN
## Getting Started with E-mail

Electronic mail, or *e-mail,* offers you a simple way to send and receive messages from computer to computer over telephone lines. Like telephone communication, e-mail offers instant gratification. Like the postal service, it allows you to exchange written documents—only you don't need stamps or envelopes, and you don't need to leave home to visit the post office.

E-mail will probably be the first Internet tool you'll learn, and the one you'll use the most. Of the 20 million people on the Internet, more than two-thirds primarily use e-mail. Because e-mail is so popular, many kinds of mail programs offering a variety of options have been developed for different computers. Because there is so much diversity in systems, this chapter will teach you how to use e-mail regardless of the specific mail system you have.

In this chapter, you will learn the basics that all e-mail users need to know:

- How e-mail works, and what people use e-mail for
- E-mail addresses: how to create one, how to decode them
- The components of an e-mail message: the header, body, and end-of-message marker
- Uploading and downloading: sending and retrieving mail
- Locating e-mail addresses and address directories

## HOW DOES E-MAIL WORK?

When you open an e-mail account, you are renting space on a *host computer.* A host computer is a big, powerful computer owned by a *network.* It is located in the office of your network, most likely in a major city. This host computer sends and receives your e-mail and connects directly to the Internet.

Because they are using telephone lines, calls through your *modem* are telephone calls—and long-distance calls, of course, can cost a lot of money. To help you save money, most networks around the world have made arrangements with access providers, or *local dial-ups.* These are companies with computers in towns other than the city where the network's host computers are located. They let people call their computers, which in turn call the host computer. This way, you don't have to pay long-distance charges.

E-mail does not necessarily require Internet access (i.e., you can use e-mail for internal office communication). However, if you have Internet access, you can use the Internet to e-mail all other Internet users. You can also send e-mail messages among different kinds of computers—IBM/PCs, Macs, and Amigas, mainframes and terminals.

## WHAT ARE SOME USES OF E-MAIL?

With e-mail, you can do any—or all—of the following things:

- Send messages to one person
- Send a message to many people simultaneously
- Send a message to a predefined list of users
- Send text files
- Send binary files such as graphics, formatted text, spreadsheets, programs, and audio and video attachments
- Edit and/or forward a message to which you are responding
- Distribute electronic newsletters
- Send out announcements to mailing lists
- Receive messages from network management systems or other computer programs and services
- Store messages in files just as you would hard copies
- Save one message in several files at once for cross-referencing

**Q:** What is important about e-mail for Russian women?

**A:** It enables us to network, to learn about the activities of groups in other countries, to discuss the possibility of organizing mutual actions, to find new friends and projects. To express love.

—OLGA LIPOVSKAYA
Petersburg Center for Gender Issues, St. Petersburg, Russia

## WHO USES E-MAIL?

Many universities, federal institutions, and private companies communicate using e-mail, from the University of California, to the United States Holocaust Memorial Museum, to Apple, Lotus, and Microsoft. Many women's organizations also rely on e-mail, including the Native American Women's Health Resource Center in South Dakota, the Georgetown Law School Sex Discrimination Clinic in Washington, D.C., and the National Organization for Women.

It is estimated that 30 million people in two hundred countries on seven continents make up the total world e-mail community. According to a 1995 survey conducted by the Georgia Tech Institute, only 10 percent of users have been women. We should be aiming for a 50/50 gender ratio before the year 2000. And in fact, we may be well on our way to achieving an on-line gender balance, especially if the widespread use of e-mail at the 1995 United Nations Fourth World Conference on Women in Beijing is any indication of the growing numbers of women being trained in the technology.

---

**ADVENTURES IN E-MAIL**

In preparation for the Fourth World Conference on Women, the UN arranged travel for Eastern European participants journeying by train from Poland to China, via Siberia and Mongolia. Two hundred women joined the nineteen-boxcar adventure. During their two weeks of travel, they received on-board e-mail training via satellite. Victoria Vrana, the chief staff techie in the Washington office of the Network of East-West Women, was one of the fifteen e-mail trainers on the train and also the satellite runner. Every time the train pulled into a station, Victoria would carry a one-hundred-pound satellite dish out of the train, turn on the computer, send and receive messages, then race to retrieve the satellite dish before the train huffed and heaved toward Beijing. In this way, women from around the world were able to send 250 welcome messages to the trainfarers as they headed toward the largest world conference on women ever held.

---

## GETTING INTO E-MAIL

Using e-mail may represent your first experience in electronic communications. As you enter this new world, you may feel a bit overwhelmed. Sometimes *cyberspace* seems like a huge labyrinthine skyscraper, with so many doors and enticing signs that it's hard to know where to go first, where each door will lead, or how to return to the original hallway. While it is important to maintain a sense of control over your use of the Internet (and while it is this book's job to make sense of these tools for you), you should also remember that a part of every learning process is occasionally feeling lost and groping for your way. If you feel lost and hopeless, turn off the modem and go for a walk outdoors. Review these instructions and try again later.

Mail metaphors may help you to conceptualize the e-mail process. You sign up for a mailbox at a post office. To send mail, you first write the message, making sure you know the address where you'll be sending it. Then you address your message, drop it in the slot, and send it off. If you like you can store a copy in a file folder. To receive mail, you open your mailbox and pick up any new messages that have come in. You place the mail you've received in a file. Next, you close your mailbox and open up the file where you stored the message to read it. The steps really are that simple.

So let's get started! You've selected a network and communications software. You've *dialed-up* and *logged-in.* What's next? Find your mailbox. Your network probably has several options other than mail. The e-mail part of your network will probably be called "mail" or "inbox." You might see an icon with an envelope or another related symbol.

Here's a sample opening menu from WomensNet:

```
WomensNet Commands:
    c    Conferences
    m    Electronic mail
    i    Internet services
```

```
d     On-line databases
u     User directory
n     News finder
s     Setup: change your password, language, terminal type
e     Extras
bye   Logout
```

Your selection (3 or 'h' for help):

On this network, you would simply type m at the prompt to get into e-mail.

Remember, from this point on you will be "talking" to two computers. Almost all commands you type will be commands that talk to the host computer.

## THE COMPONENTS OF AN E-MAIL ADDRESS

E-mail addresses may look formidable, but they do follow a certain logic. Just as your street address tells the postal service exactly where you live, your e-mail address tells where you live in cyberspace. Each e-mail address consists of two parts connected by the @ sign. For example:

shanapenn@igc.apc.org

It is important to remember that e-mail addresses do not contain spaces between any of the elements. If a space must be shown, it may be replaced by an underscore (_), a dot (.) or hyphen (-), or a dash (—). Also remember never to type a period at the end of an e-mail address; this is not needed, and will only confuse the computers. It's also useful to know that by convention, e-mail addresses appearing in text are often bracketed by the the < and > symbols, like this: <shanapenn@igc.apc.org>. These symbols are there only to clarify for the reader where an address begins and ends; you *do not* type these symbols when you address an e-mail message.

The part of the address to the left of the @ sign is your **\*userid,\*** which stands for user identity, or user name. It may be unique to you, like your name, or it may be shared, like the name of an organization. You can usually choose your userid. Many people create userids by joining the first letter of their first name with their surname. (Women, especially, often prefer gender-neutral userids for all the expected reasons.) The userid part of the above e-mail address is shanapenn.

The other elements of the address, which follow the @ sign, cannot be chosen. The @ sign is always part of an e-mail address, and it means exactly what it symbolizes: the word *at*. To the right of the @ sign are the **\*domains,\*** which tell the computer where to find the place at which you receive mail. The domains are hierarchical, separated by dots, and read from right to left.

The part of the address that occupies the farthest right position is called the top-level domain. In international e-mail addresses the top-level domain often indicates the country, such as us for the United States or jp for Japan.

Within the United States, the top-level domain most often indicates a type of network. Some common network domain abbreviations are as follows:

| com | commercial | gov | government |
|-----|------------|-----|------------|
| edu | educational | mil | military |
| org | organization | net | network |

Reading from right to left, the next level domains can indicate where the user's computer is located, the name of her organization, and the name of her host computer. An address will not necessarily include every one of these components. Here are two examples of e-mail addresses:

sophia@nws.aubg.bg

sophia = userid
nws = the name of the computer
aubg = where the machine is located (at the American University at Blagoevgrad)
bg = country (Bulgaria)

sisters@sovam.com

sisters = userid (for an organization called the St. Petersburg Center for Gender Issues)
sovam = the name of the computer
com = commercial network

## THE COMPONENTS OF AN E-MAIL MESSAGE

Every message consists of a header, a body, and an end-of-message marker.

The **message header** is the "stamped-and-addressed envelope." It includes the destination, return address, and "cancellation" postmark. The message header includes several pieces of information—some created by the person (or program) sending you the message, and the rest created by the various e-mail programs on the computers that forwarded the message from the sender to you and received the message on your behalf.

If you display a stored e-mail message, you will see the message as your mail program sees it. (Unless you purposely saved the messages *without* the headers.) Some of the information you will see in the header relates to the message itself and may be of interest to you.

The **"To:"** field indicates to whom the message is being sent. A message can be addressed to one or more people; next to the "To:" you should see one or more names, separated by spaces—for example:

shanapenn@igc.apc.org  day@cais.com  mcat@aol.com

E-mail can be addressed to individuals; to programs that accept e-mail; to previously created abbreviations ("aliases"); to the name of a mailing list (in which case all of the list's subscribers will receive the message); to abbreviations for mailing list names; and even to files in which certain names appear, if your e-mail system supports this feature.

The **"Subject:"** field indicates the message's content, as determined by the sender. Subject text should summarize the message and motivate the receiver to read it as quickly as you might wish.

The **"From:"** field indicates who sent the message, usually including their "real" name as well as their e-mail address. E-mail systems automatically input this information for senders, so they do not have to type out their name and address on every message.

The **"Date:"** field indicates the date and time when the message was created, as recorded by the sender's computer. (Remember that it reflects the sender's time zone, not yours.)

The **"cc:"** field indicates any others to whom the message has been sent. Some programs also provide a "bcc:" field, which indicates that a blind copy has been sent.

The **"Reply to:"** field indicates where to send responses. This may at times differ from the sender's address.

Other message header fields include **"Received:," "Return-path:,"** and **"Message-ID:."** They tell you more information about how the message was routed to you. The "Return-path:" field, like "Reply to:," tells you where to send a message if you want to respond. The "Received:" field indicates what computers the message was routed through. "Message-ID:" is a unique number given to every e-mail message.

The **body** of an e-mail message is like the body of a snail mail message, beginning with "Dear So-and-so" and ending with "Yours Truly." It's where the sender says whatever she has to say. It can be brief and businesslike or long and heartfelt. It can contain lists, agendas, or responses to questions asked in someone else's e-mail.

The **end of message marker** is the final part of an e-mail, which commonly says something like "Transfer complete," to indicate that the message was sent. This marker is automatically inserted by the computer at the end of a message.

Here is a sample e-mail message from my account at IGC, the Institute for Global Communications:

[HEADER]

```
From DMcGrory@sct-po.biz.uiowa.edu Fri May 3 15:10:32 1996
Return-Path: DMcGrory@sct-po.biz.uiowa.edu
Received: from ns-mx.uiowa.edu (ns-mx.uiowa.edu [128.255. 1.3]) by
igc7.igc.apc.)
Message-Id: <199605032210.RAA29829@ns-mx.uiowa.edu>
Received: by pink-floyd.uiowa.edu (cc:Mail translation to SMTP) on Fri
May 03 17:05:40 1996
To: neww@igc.apc.org
Date: Fri, 3 May 96 16:07 CST
Subject: For Shana Penn - CEELI/NEWW COLLABORATION
Status: R
```

[BODY]

```
Dear Ms. Penn,

As you may recall, we met earlier this spring in Moscow at the book
launching held at the USIS Center.  At that time, we discussed the
possibility of collaborating on a gender issues law oriented semi-
nar and I later e-mailed our proposed program for a workshop on
violence against women in Russia.

We have set dates for holding these workshops in St. Petersburg and
Moscow on June 12 & 13 for the latter and June 17—19 for the for-
mer. It would be most helpful if you could provide us with names and
telephone numbers of Russian lawyers, prosecutors, and judges who may
be interested in attending these events. Health care workers and cri-
sis center counselors are also welcome. If you can help us out on this,
we'd greatly appreciate it.


All the best,


D. McGrory,
ABA-CEELI Legal Specialist
```

[END OF MESSAGE MARKER]

```
—Transfer complete, hit <RETURN> or <ENTER> to continue—
```

## UPLOADING AND DOWNLOADING: SENDING AND RETRIEVING E-MAIL

Sending and retrieving e-mail is the act of transferring files from your computer to your host computer, and vice versa. This requires you to be connected to your network. But when you work in e-mail, it's important to remember that while some things must be done on-line, many others can be done *off-line.*

**On-line** means that you are connected to the network. You must work on-line when you transfer messages you have received to a computer file and when you send messages from a computer file via e-mail.

**Off-line** means that you are working only on your computer. You are not connected to the network. You are not using your modem, you are not hooked into any one else's computer, and you are not spending any money. You should be working off-line when you read your mail, print out messages, and write your responses or compose new messages. Working off-line saves you money—and believe it or not, most of your e-mail work will be done off-line.

## Downloading: Retrieving E-mail

E-mail messages do not come directly to your computer. Your mail is stored in your mailbox on the host computer, much as it would be in a postal mailbox. You must always check your mailbox to see if you have mail.

When you open your mailbox (often called "inbox" on e-mail programs), expect a message similar to this one:

```
You have new mail messages.
Reading folder: incoming . . . 35 messages 5 new 7 unread
Type 'u' for next unread message, '?' for command summary, 'h' for help."
```

If you have new or unread e-mail messages, you will want to retrieve them: you must bring the e-mail files from the host computer to your own. This is called *downloading.* There is more than one way to download. Some networks, especially off-line networks, download your mail for you in a big group, or batch. The problem here is that you cannot choose which messages you want. You may wind up with a lot of junk mail. If so, simply delete it.

Other networks and software allow you to simply save individual messages onto your hard drive. You can look over an index of messages in your mailbox, indicating the senders and subjects of each, and then download only those you want. An index of messages received might look something like the following sample, which comes from the electronic mailbox of the Network of East-West Women:

```
Mail: (i)ndex (u)nread (w)rite (c)apture (d)elete (s)ave (h)elp
(q)uit: i

Date    #  Subject                                Lines  From

----    -  -------                                -----  ----

Dec 3   1  Report for November                     188   neww
Dec 7   2* local service providers                 578   PMCDONALD
Dec 7   3* Re:local service providers              204   spierce
Dec 7   4* news from Murmansk Women Congress       172   IRINA
Dec 8   5* Re: Internet providers                   46   ginsburg
Dec 10  6  Schedule for 1997                       113   naeemf
Dec 10  7  Fwd: DC Bosnia Calendar 10               50   AndrewEiva
Jan 10  9  WWW stats: NEWW Home Page                37   root
Jan 10  10 Re: 1997 THE YEAR OF WOMEN              179   wlo

— Hit    <RETURN>         for more —
```

When you select the message you want to save, your software automatically chooses the correct *protocol* for transferring the file. Depending on your *Internet service provider* and mail program, you will either set up a download protocol or remind your computer every time you download. In the latter case, you must first tell your host computer that you want to download a message or messages, usually by typing a command. The host computer will usually ask you which protocol you would like to use.

You must also tell your own software that you are going to download. Your computer usually asks you what you would like to name the new file and where (in which folder or directory) you would like to store it. Then it will ask which protocol you are using.

Once a message is safely stored on your computer, you should delete that message from the host computer (along with any messages you aren't interested in reading); otherwise, you might be charged a storage fee.

Remember that every minute you spend on-line may cost money. It is best *not* to read your messages on-line, but rather to download them and read them from a file saved on your own computer.

### Reading and Responding to E-Mail Messages Off-Line

To read the e-mail you have downloaded, open the computer file that contains your new e-mail message. You can do this from within your word processing program. Now your message will appear on the screen. You can read it, edit it, add to it, print it, or delete it.

You will want to answer at least some of your messages. Always answer messages off-line. When you finish writing your mail in a word processing application, save your document. Most of the time, you have to save e-mail in a text-only format, rather than in your own word processing program. Your program may call this text-only format "text only," "text only with breaks," "ASCII," or "DOS text file." Use your program's HELP key to find out how to save in a text-only format.

You should also make sure you will remember what your file is named and where it is saved, so that you will be able to find it when you get on-line. Some people keep a notepad by their computer and write down the names of their e-mail files as they save them.

### Uploading: Sending E-Mail

*Uploading* is the other side of downloading. It means sending a message from your computer to your host computer through the phone lines, and instructing the host computer to send your message to its recipient.

As you prepare to send your messages, think back to make sure each has been saved in a mailable format. Then check to make sure you know the e-mail address of each person to whom you want to send a message. When you're ready to go, dial-up and log-in, and go on-line.

Whenever you send an e-mail message, you will be asked to fill in the user-generated parts of the header outlined earlier in this chapter. Your computer will provide the field names. One of these fields will be "Subject:"; the information you type in here will become part of the header of your recipient's message, and will appear in her list of messages received, so remember to be as specific as possible. If you are sending a message to a specific person at a shared account (an organization, for example), you should put that person's name in the subject line.

Your mail program will probably offer you a final opportunity to check or change your message before you send it; for example, you might see these options:

```
(f)ormat (c)hange (r)eview (e)dit (a)dd (s)end (q)uit
```

While you don't want to spend a lot of time working on-line, don't take these options lightly. Remember that in most systems, once a message has been sent, you can't stop it.

In addition to sending your own messages, you can forward to a third-party a message you have received from someone else. You can also attach a filed message—your own or someone else's—or document to a new message you are sending. The file will be sent along with your message. (Make sure your attachments are properly formatted, too.) You should find the "Forward" option and the "Attachment" or "Enclosure" option in your e-mail program.

## ELECTRONIC ADDRESS DIRECTORIES

When you need an e-mail address, you can let your fingers do the walking—but don't be discouraged if you hit a dead end. A number of **electronic address directories** of Internet users exist on-line, but none is comprehensive. The problem is that no one is paid to create and maintain directories. Those that exist are published voluntarily by people who develop directories in their spare time. Most networks have created address directories which you can use to locate users on your network.

One way to access address directories is to e-mail the WHOIS service/directory maintained at the Internet Registry. WHOIS can be reached via e-mail, *Telnet,* or a local service provider. Its address lists are limited to people who are broadly involved with creating or maintaining the Internet. Send an e-mail message to mailserv@ds.internic.net. In the "Subject:" and "Message:" fields type HELP, and you will receive a message back on the same day.

You can also access directories that keep track of e-mail addresses via a mail transfer standard called X.500. You can find these directories via a local service provider or via *Gopher* (see part 1, chapter 7) by looking for an item like /Phonebook on any and all Gopher menus.

KIS (Knowbot Information Service) is an automated e-mail address information system that searches archives of addresses at WHOIS, X.500, and other predetermined sites via Telnet or e-mail.

Universities track changing e-mail addresses for students, faculty, and employees with CWIS (Campus Wide Information System). It is accessible via CWIS and Gopher servers.

## KEEPING YOUR E-MAIL ORGANIZED

Be prepared: messages will pile up in your mailbox more quickly than you ever expected. Many of these will be messages you don't want to delete. But you do want to remove them from your mailbox, or it will grow much too cluttered (and also possibly incur storage fees).

All undeleted incoming mail should be downloaded and saved on your own computer. It's wise to set up a system of directories or folders on your computer in which you can keep your e-mail messages organized—and thus easy to locate next time you want to refer to them.

You can set up any system for organizing messages that suits your needs. For example, you can make one general "incoming" folder for messages received, and one "outgoing" folder for messages you plan to upload. Within each folder, you can make sub-folders according to month, subject, or person/organization. I organize e-mail into month-by-month folders (1/97, 2/97, 3/97, and so on). Inside each monthly folder I categorize mail according to projects, organizations, or people. Obviously, every person will order her mail differently. The important thing is to plan ahead.

## GETTING GOOD AT E-MAIL

Practice makes perfect—or, as they say in Poland, *Ucz sie a dojdziesz do wprawy*. The best way to master e-mail is to use it as often as possible, and in as many different ways as possible. Practice with your on-line friends and start taking advantage of opportunities to use e-mail in your work. As you practice, try to do each of the following things, and they will soon become part of your normal e-mail routine:

1.  Check to see if you have mail.
2.  Scan your list of incoming messages by sender and subject line.
3.  Download and read your new messages.
4.  Save, file, print, and/or delete messages you have received.
5.  Write and upload messages—lots of them!
6.  Forward a message you have received.
7.  Attach an existing message or document to one you are sending.
8.  Save and file the day's index.
9.  Organize your computer files for incoming and outgoing messages.
10. Send a query to your on-line technical support asking for some kind of technical assistance that you might need.
11. Send me a message at shanapenn@igc.apc.org.

Welcome to the world of e-mail. And if you're nervous about "Netiquette," read on for some important tips.

# 4

# GERTRUDE STEIN ON-LINE
## User Tips for Clear, Safe Communication

*"Netiquette is Netiquette is Netiquette"*

Now that you have some of the tools you will need to engage in on-line communications, you may be wondering how computers alter the nature and quality of an interaction, and how you can cultivate lively, meaningful exchanges—whether they be with friends or strangers, or between two people or more.

Remember, in an electronic exchange you are conversing without audible and visual cues: neither tone of voice nor body language enhance an on-line conversation. All the subtleties, nuances, and pleasures that speaking, listening, and gesturing provide cannot be re-created on your computer screen—at least not without great ingenuity or state-of-the-art technology. The impersonal nature of an exchange via computers tends to breed both respectful sensitivity and sometimes, unfortunately, intractable adversity.

Depending on the user, the absence of conventional signals for human interaction and the complete anonymity among strangers can stir intrigue, confusion, recklessness, caution, or a desire to create new, appropriate communication norms. It can feel a little bit like entering a foreign country: you may speak the language, more or less, but you don't know all the idioms or the customs, and the street signs don't always make sense to you.

This chapter is a kind of visitors' guide for travelers to the wired world. It introduces you to on-line customs, conventions, and idioms, and recommends ways for you to control the quality of your electronic communications. The information in this chapter should be useful to you even if you are an on-line novice using only e-mail. It will become even more useful as you move on to things like discussion groups and on-line meetings, described in subsequent chapters.

To foster a sense of community and citizenship on-line, users of electronic communications have created guidelines for civil, humane interactions known as *Netiquette,* a word which obviously derives from *Net* and *etiquette*—and means just that. Netiquette encourages healthy on-line communications norms, so that users may accurately represent themselves and avoid offensive provocations. Netiquette guidelines do not yet specifically or directly address on-line sexism per se. The protocols tend to be very general—for example, be brief and be polite, and do not underscore gender or race awareness. Nonetheless, it is within the scope of Netiquette to add antisexist and antiracist directives to the prevailing game rules, especially as women users grow in numbers and begin to strategically influence Net usage.

At the time of this writing, in 1997, women users have not yet begun to advocate on-line against sexism in an organized fashion, though lists of preventatives and protocols are being passed around in *cyberspace* and in some of the new writings on women in the electronic communications world. The later part of this chapter will look at some examples of what happens when communication breaks down and becomes sexist and abusive—for instance, when, where, and how women experience sexual harassment on the Net, and how you can protect yourself. But the best place to start is with a list of Netiquette norms—Net conventions, symbols, and lingo that are known the world over.

## THE BASICS OF NETIQUETTE

Certain conventions have developed among users concerning the text of *e-mail* and other on-line communications. It's important to keep these in mind whenever you compose a message, especially when you are first starting out.

1. Tackle one subject per message. This allows you to make the subject line of the message specific—which in turn makes it easy for the recipient of your message to file the message for future reference.

2. Read your message before you send it. Be sure that it says what you want it to say, that it has been carefully proofread, and, perhaps most importantly, that you wouldn't mind if it is disseminated to the public. (Remember that messages received by one person can be forwarded to others with one click of the mouse.)

3. Respect people's privacy. E-mail is not a good forum for gossip because, unlike the telephone, it creates a record of your message. Be especially careful when mailing to a shared account, where your message may be read by more than its designated recipient. It's wise to observe this simple rule: Never write something that you wouldn't be able to say to another person face-to-face. Likewise, respect people's privacy if you are part of a shared account, and do not read messages that obviously belong to others.

4. Try to be brief. Respect for the preciousness of people's time, computer storage capacity, and paper supplies will be greatly appreciated by your readers.

5. Be ethical and legal. Do not assume that communication standards break down just because electronic communications has a quality of anonymity. Things like libel and copyright laws may still apply. (See part 1, chapter 9, for a discussion of Internet copyright guidelines.)

6. Respect the conventions of your on-line community. Before you actively participate in a discussion group, observe the messages being exchanged to gain a sense of the discussion's tone and direction. You will quickly notice that social conventions vary from one on-line site to another.

7. Be careful not to provoke arguments. It is easy to misinterpret tone and offend people,

unintentionally as well as intentionally. Be careful not to send angry messages because they can easily instigate a messy, drawn-out argument, especially on *mailing lists* and *Usenet news-groups*—which can, in turn, undermine a group process, sometimes irreparably.

8. Be a teacher. Be patient and forgiving of other people's mistakes, especially with newcomers. Help people by sharing your knowledge.

---

**Q:** What do you like about e-mail? What don't you like?

**A:** I like the promptness of communication, quick access to what I need, no need to bother with envelopes/stamps/fax buttons, the possibility of learning new communications programs.

I don't like the overload of information, time wasted sorting out what is not needed, excess of useless information, dependency on technology when Russian phone lines may break at any time, a certain lack of privacy because twelve people share one account and can only afford one account.

—OLGA LIPOVSKAYA
Petersburg Center for Gender Issues, St. Petersburg, Russia

---

### Special Tips for International Electronic Communications

When your electronic messages cross international borders, it's important to keep in mind some additional rules of Netiquette.

1. Cultural differences: Remember that some *Listservs* and newsgroups have participants from many countries, some of whom will not understand American slang or references to pop culture or geographical locations. Make sure you explain a reference that others might not understand.

2. Language differences: If you are writing in English to someone whose native language is not English, please be sensitive to her need for simple language use. Avoid long sentences, complex sentence structures, and difficult vocabulary.

3. Cost differences: In some regions of the world, *UUCP* is the only service provider that e-mail users can afford. This kind of service provider charges users per *kilobyte* of materials sent or received, which means that large documents, especially if sent without permission from the recipient, can wipe out someone's monthly income.

### USING INDICATORS

To ensure effective, efficient, and personalized e-mail communication, it's important to include certain **indicators** in your electronic messages.

1. When you send a message, indicate whether or not you need a response, and how quickly. For example:

```
Please let me know immediately whether you received this message.

Please respond to this message by Tuesday, March 10.

No response is necessary.

Comments are due at the end of the month.
Please confirm your participation as soon as possible.
```

2. Because all communication takes place in front of a computer screen and not in person, electronic communications can feel cold and impersonal. To humanize the communication, locate yourself in time and space. For example:

```
Good morning. It is sunny and warm, and I am sitting at the kitchen
table with a cup of tea and a copy of your letter, dated June 3rd.

A thunderstorm cut off the electricity tonight, and I am writing to
you by candlelight on a battery-run computer! If this message sud-
denly stops short, please understand why.
```

3. When responding specifically to questions or comments you have read in a message, repeat the comments you are addressing as a memory aid for the recipient. It is also possible to cut and paste the specific questions from the message you received into the one you will send. For example:

```
In response to your question, "What time will you arrive in New
York?": I will arrive at 10 in the morning.
```

## USING EMOTICONS

Once you enter the wired world, you'll quickly discover strange symbols in the messages you receive. These may look like typos, but they are actually emotional icons, or *emoticons.* Emoticons are typographical symbols used on-line to contribute tone and feeling to electronic messages. They are useful in providing otherwise cold text with more accurate expression. For the most part, emoticons range from cute to corny, and though you may never use them yourself, you'll at least need to recognize them. The following is a list of some well-known emoticons.

| | | | |
|---|---|---|---|
| :-) | smiling | :* | kissing |
| :-D | laughing | $-) | greedy |
| :-( | frowning | X-) | I see nothing |
| :'-( | crying | :-X | I'll say nothing |
| :-o | shock | :-L | drooling |
| ;-) | winking | :-P | sticking out tongue |
| {} | hugging | @--'--,-- | a rose |

In addition, users have developed ways of highlighting text in the absence of boldface or italics, which cannot be used in text-only files. Capital letters or asterisks are used to emphasize words. Asterisks are preferable, because caps too often convey shouting and make for highly unpleasant reading.

## LEARNING THE LINGO OF THE INTERNET

Once you become a Net user, you'll discover that the speed and brevity of electronic communications has fostered all kinds of shorthand acronyms. Use the following list as a reference so that you won't be surprised or confused when these acronyms appear in messages. And try using some yourself!

| | | | |
|---|---|---|---|
| AFAIK | as far as I know | IYSWIM | if you see what I mean |
| AFK | away from keyboard | IAE | in any event |
| BAK | back at keyboard | IOW | in other words |
| BBL | be back later | LOL | laughing out loud |
| BFN | bye for now | NRN | no reply necessary |
| BRB | be right back | OIC | Oh, I see |
| BTW | by the way | OTOH | on the other hand |
| FYI | for your information | ROTFL | rolling on the floor |
| GTRM | going to read mail | | laughing |
| HTH | hope this helps | SOL | sooner or later |
| IMO | in my opinion | SYL | see you later |
| IMHO | in my humble opinion | TTYL | talk to you later |

BTW, even though Netiquette evolved to encourage civilized on-line behavior, you are bound to bump into shorthand rudeness, such as these kinds of acronyms:

| | | | |
|---|---|---|---|
| FRO | fuck right off | RTFM | read the fucking manual |
| GAL | get a life | WGAS | who gives a shit? |

IMO, SOL we need to create a shorthand response to nasty acronyms—and to sexist and racist messages as well. I imagine they might include:

| | | | |
|---|---|---|---|
| SOY | shame on you | TBTN | take back the Net |
| STOP | sexist terminology outta place | WRY | who raised you? |

IOW, don't be surprised by offensive behavior and don't stand for it. Ally yourself with those women and men who are challenging and changing it.

**RESOURCES ON NETIQUETTE**

Resources on Netiquette and related topics can be found at these Web sites:

• *The Net: User Guidelines and Netiquette* is Arlene Rinaldi's popular guide to healthy communication via e-mail, discussion groups, Telnet, FTP, or the Web. You can find this at the Web site <http://www.fnu.edu/rinaldi/netiquette.html>.

• *The Core Rules of Netiquette* by Virginia Shea includes the author's ten golden rules of responsible Net behavior. Visit the Web site <http://www.bookport.com/publishers/1887164/nqhome.html>.

• *Life on the Internet: Netiquette* provides advice on polite usage: <http://www.screen.com/understand/netiquette.html>.

• *Business Netiquette International*, at <http://www.wp.com/fredfish/Netiquette.html>, offers communication tips for professional and business discussions, with an emphasis on international business.

• *Don't Spread That Hoax!* by Charles Hymes tells you how to detect and avoid Internet hoaxes, and also relays several famous hoaxes. The Web site address is <http://www.crew.umich.edu/~chymes/newusers/think.html>.

• *The Smiley Dictionary,* a guide to emoticons, can be found at <http://olympic.polytechnique.fr/~violet/smileys/>. You'll also find a plain text list of emoticons, *The Unofficial Smilie Dictionary* at Gopher site <gopher://vega.lib.ncsu.edu:70/00/library/reference/dictionaries/smilies>.

• The Web site <http://www.ucs.umd.edu/staff/amato/AC/main.html> provides a listing of acronyms and abbreviations found in e-mail messages and newsgroup postings, with their definitions.

## MUGGING WITH A MODEM: ON-LINE SEXUAL HARASSMENT AND ABUSE

Let me begin by saying that I do not personally know anyone who has been sexually harassed on the Internet—nor have I myself ever been harassed or abused. Moreover, the feminist Listservs that I've opened and monitored for several years have not been plagued with sexist intruders. The most offensive *posting* my organization ever received on a Listserv addressing women's rights in post-Communist countries was an announcement that encouraged Russian women to be mail-order brides and take advantage of the opportunity to marry rich American businessmen.

Those who write about on-line harassment agree that relatively small numbers of harassment incidents have occurred or been reported—although rudeness, obscenities, and sexual come-ons are flung far and wide through cyberspace by reckless riders of this reinless terrain, regardless of Netiquette rules.

While the reported incidents may be few in number, on-line sexual harassment is real, and has seriously frightened women who have experienced such abuse—several of whom have published their stories. The list of resources at the end of this section will point you to some relevant print and on-line resources.

The most important thing you can do, as women communicating electronically, is be alert to the patterns that precipitate abuse and the precautions you can take, both individually and collectively, in order to be safe on-line.

## WHAT ARE ON-LINE HARASSMENT AND ABUSE?

Varying opinions exist among women Net users as to what comprises on-line harassment. For some women, e-mail requests for a date or for sex signify harassment. Other women believe that if you visit a *chat room* or a Usenet newsgroup for singles where you receive a lewd proposition or sexual comments, you are not necessarily being harassed. An unexpected advance, made via a discussion group for singles, which is rejected by one person may be acceptable to another. On the other hand, an uninvited sexual advance made on alt.feminism, a Usenet newsgroup on feminist issues, might be regarded as offensive, though it may also be treated as a distracting, naughty comment by a fraternity initiate. However, sometimes an uninvited intruder persists in sending sexual solicitations, and a woman user justifiably feels trapped. In such cases, you can take steps to stop the unwanted invitations—and these steps are described below.

### A NOTE ON THE USE OF TERMS

In this chapter, the word *abuse* is used in its most general, dictionary-defined sense, without reference to any usage of the term by the legal or psychiatric professions. Abuse, for the purpose of this discussion, is intentional mistreatment—in this case, through language designed to hurt or offend others. The use of the term *harassment*, too, does not refer to any legal definition of sexual harassment, but to a pattern of repeated, hostile, and often threatening verbal—or, in the case of the Internet, written—attacks. What makes it *sexual* harassment is not simply the fact that it's directed toward a woman, but the fact that it's directed toward her *because* she is a woman.

But first it is important to understand that on-line abuse frequently occurs in discussion groups which have nothing to do with dating, sex, or feminism. It can explode in the most unexpected places—for example, in a discussion group on cats or movies or copyediting. The first time I witnessed on-line abuse was when I visited a newsgroup on Asian Americans. To my horror, I read a string of postings debating why Asian American women should be regarded as America's most desirable whores. Disgusting diatribes ensued describing slanty eyes, smelly cunts, and so forth. While none of the newsgroup users was being singled out and directly attacked, the discussion topic was racist, sexist, and thoroughly offensive. To my surprise, no one challenged the inappropriateness of the remarks. Instead, other topics were picked up and developed; occasionally someone revisited the vulgarity, as if to exercise the muscles of abuse.

## HOW AND WHERE DO ON-LINE HARASSMENT AND ABUSE OCCUR?

To begin with, it is unlikely that you will receive unwanted, offensive messages in your mailbox if you are not engaging in a Listserv or Usenet newsgroup. These are the locations where abusive dynamics are usually sparked. Rarely is a woman targeted out of the blue. She has to be regarded by her abuser as having in some way instigated the assault. In the eyes of the harasser, it is her fault that she is being stalked and harangued with abusive, threatening e-mail messages. She must have "asked for it."

Communication on Listservs and Usenet newsgroups is somewhat akin to the telephone party lines of yesteryear. You join in a pool of ongoing conversations where you can remain anonymous as long as you like, since you are not interacting face-to-face with your fellow discussant(s). Newsgroups are more anarchic than Listservs, because they are rarely moderated and community guidelines are seldom observed. If the discussions on either forum are not moderated, they tend to get out of hand and become breeding grounds for dissension, backstabbing, and sometimes civil war. When this happens, peer pressure is the only means for galvanizing the collective support required to reestablish peace and civility.

The pattern I am going to describe as sexual harassment also spurs on-line racism and other forms of abuse. (Debra Floyd discusses a racist incident in part 2, chapter 6.) Here's what can happen: You participate in a Usenet newsgroup where someone uses perverse or sexist language. You reply to the sender with a friendly reminder to stay within the bounds of civil behavior, which it is your right and responsibility to do according to the rules of Netiquette, and often according to the rules of the on-line service or Listserv facilitator servicing the discussion group. Your message infuriates the person, who quickly responds with a verbal assault. If you have reprimanded someone for sexism or if it is obvious that you are a woman, you can expect a sexist assault. You might open your e-mail and find "SHUT UP, BITCH" or "FUCK YOUR DADDY" splashed across your computer screen. You might be more angry than frightened and respond in kind, or forward the message to the discussion group. Another user might rise to your defense and attempt to quash the offender. Others plunge into the fray, either to protect or chastise you. The argument escalates. Statements fly back and forth. Suddenly you are caught up in the middle of a *flame war.* Quality control has disintegrated and chaos has subsumed communication.

This is not necessarily on-line harassment (*yet*), although it is certainly a mess. As if in a downward spiral pulled by the force of gravity, the insults continue. Next, you receive another abusive message, this time from an anonymous poster—that is, someone whose real name is not identifiable and who is using a fake e-mail address. More crude messages follow, perhaps including violent pornography, from numerous fake e-mail addresses. You cannot tell if the messages are coming from one or several senders. They keep coming, swarming down upon your mailbox like a hive of killer bees. They include threats—such as warnings that the poster of the messages is going to pay you a real-time visit in your home.

This *is* on-line harassment. What should you do?

## HOW CAN I STOP ON-LINE HARASSMENT?

There are a variety of actions you can take to stop harassment. To put an end to a situation like the one described above, you should do the following:

1. Document your harassment. Keep a paper trail of all messages you receive and send. Do not ignore the messages; the offender will not disappear.

2. Notify the *Internet service provider* used by the sender who is perpetrating the harassment. Contact the systems operator (*sysop*) or the postmaster at the site where the abusive message originated. You may be told that the sysop can only catch the offender in the act of posting a message. If that is the case, or if the postmaster does not respond, contact whoever supplies the site, climbing the ladder of management until you find someone who will be responsive.

3. Post a message to the Listserv or newsgroup where the flame war erupted. In your message, threaten to call the police. Often this is effective and the messages will stop.

4. Apply peer pressure. Notify the other users of the Listserv or Usenet newsgroup that the discussion has led to you being harassed. Share the harassing messages with the group. According to most accounts of abuse, the victim receives helpful support from the on-line community, which will usually rise in her defense. Friends of mine in Russia, where there are no laws against in-person sexual harassment, tell me that when they have been sexually harassed by a member of their community, they galvanize the support of family and friends to fend off their attacker. I suggest something similar for an on-line situation. You may be surprised at the support you will receive, but you shouldn't be. Remember, most people want to adhere to the rules of the game and maintain Netiquette.

5. Post messages to other Listservs informing Net users of the harassment. Solicit advice from other users on how to track down an anonymous message, and how to create a safer space for discussions. If you are able to track down the sender, which requires learning more about the inner workings of the Internet than you may have been prepared to learn, you can forward the abusive messages to the person's real e-mail address. This is usually the most effective way to stop the harassment.

6. Unsubscribe to the Listserv or newsgroup where the flame war began. You might oppose this solution because it means you are censoring yourself, but on the other hand, you may be eager to remove yourself from the scene where the trouble began.

## ARE ON-LINE HARASSMENT AND ABUSE AGAINST THE LAW?

Can on-line harassment be prosecuted? Sexual harassment is usually defined as occurring in the workplace or on campus, not in an electronic discussion. On-line harassment, for the most part, stands outside prevailing legal definitions of sexual harassment. There are criminal and civil laws that address certain kinds of on-line abuse. For example, it is against the law to use another person's name to send mail, or to make threats through a means of interstate commerce. In addition, defamation or libel break the law, as does intentional infliction of emotional distress.

Keep in mind, however, that federal law does not regard insulting behavior as harassment.

The incidents must be objectively regarded as abusive and threatening to one's physical and/or emotional well-being. It is not easy to prosecute on-line harassment. In general, cyberlaw is still being formulated. As of the present moment, many feminist Net spokespersons, especially those who are anticensorship, recommend combating on-line harassment with nonlegal remedies. These tend to be more immediate; they're effective; and they will not fuel the controversies over whether more regulation is needed on the Net.

## WHAT CAN I DO TO PREVENT HARASSMENT AND ABUSE IN THE FIRST PLACE?

Until and unless society's attitudes toward women undergo considerable change, it is inevitable that some sexual harassment and abuse will take place—on the Internet, just as in the world at large. And it is important to remember that, in spite of what your abuser might think, women do not "provoke" or "deserve" harassment or abuse.

Nevertheless, knowing the ways of the world, it is wise to take certain steps to reduce your chances of being the victim of on-line harassment or abuse.

1. Preserve your anonymity. Some women use gender-neutral *userids* so that they are not singled out for their gender. Some women even prefer not to use their real last names in their userids, since these can be looked up in a telephone directory.

2. Preserve your privacy. Do not include your real life address and phone number in your e-mail messages, especially messages to shared accounts, Listservs, or newsgroups.

3. Respond quickly and firmly. If you receive unwanted advances or abusive messages, make sure you inform the sender—immediately, and in no uncertain terms—that you do not want to receive them. Carefully compose a response, ask a friend or two for feedback, then send the reply as soon as possible.

4. Choose your on-line forums carefully. Exercise caution when you select Listservs and newsgroups to participate in. Subscribe to moderated discussion groups, or to ones with very clear Netiquette rules to which users faithfully adhere, or to private Listservs where you have to apply for admission. If you're not happy with the way discussions are going, don't hesitate to unsubscribe.

5. Choose your Internet service provider wisely. Some on-line services monitor their discussion groups, and may take steps to deflect or respond to abuse situations; others do not.

6. Install *filters* in your e-mail program. Filters are available which will remove unwanted messages from a specific sender. Consult other users or your on-line service to find filters compatible with your e-mail program.

## THE LONG VIEW: ON-LINE HARASSMENT AND CENSORSHIP

There's been a good deal of debate recently on whether—and to what extent—communication on the Internet should be censored, regulated, or monitored by the government. Laws have been proposed, passed, repealed, and modified. But most of these laws have to do with on-line pornography, not with the kind of harassment and abuse discussed in this chapter. (For more on on-line censorship debates, see part 1, chapter 10.) And in any case, these laws are being made, for the most part, by old white men—who are, as experience shows, not the best people to decide what's good for women.

On the other hand, on-line sexual harassment *is* a form of censorship if women are being silenced as a consequence. The free speech of women is threatened when women are verbally abused or threatened; or when their participation in discussion groups is curtailed by male users; or in any other comparable scenario that discourages or prohibits women's free and safe use of electronic communications.

The best solution seems to be to take measures to ensure our safety, comfort, and freedom to communicate into our own hands, within our own on-line communities. There are steps we can all take to see that, over the long run, women will be able speak freely, with a minimum of harassment or abuse, in the on-line world.

The first and possibly the most effective step you can take is to educate your Internet service provider, and demand that efforts be made to protect users from harassment and abuse. Encourage others—women and men—to do the same. This way, you will be helping to create safe, harassment-free communities for yourself and other women without legal censorship. If people who enjoy harassing women want to "express themselves," they can simply go elsewhere to do it. (And if everyone takes these steps, the abusers may some day end up with no one but each other to talk to!)

### A FEMINIST ETHICS OF THE INTERNET

Netiquette is largely concerned with cultivating a civilized exchange of information and copyright protection, writes Cheris Kramarae of Women, Information Technology, and Scholarship (WITS), an ad hoc group of academics dedicated to safeguarding women's Internet presence and nondiscriminatory on-line practices. If Netiquette guidelines were influenced by feminist ethics, which WITS recommends, then we'd be considering "the importance and distinctiveness of nonviolent connections and of showing respect for life and life-giving in women's and men's experiences in many geographical areas," notes Kramarae. "Our concerns would then not be as much about freedom of speech and the right to publish electronic pornography as about providing valuable communication tools to help children learn to be interdependent and caring of others. There is another, even more encompassing approach we might consider. Ecofeminist theory and practice ask us to extend the ethical relationship not just to all humans but to living nature in its entirety. We could consider a quantum ethics which comes from seeing new universal connections and a holism that comes from understanding the system as a system. "Paying attention to the ideological themes in our talk about electronic communication, and considering principles of feminist ethics, should help us to critique the ethics of electronic communication/information patterns, develop a new gender sensitivity, and offer fresh ideas about what more universal communication might become."

For example, America Online (AOL), which offers a wide assortment of chat rooms, also adheres to a code of behavior that prohibits obscenity and harassment. AOL monitors its on-line sites, which is very attractive to some of its clientele. (However, even AOL is not always successful in censoring offensive behavior until you issue a complaint. Thus, signing up with AOL is not a fool-proof defense against harassment.)

Getting the commercial Internet service providers to incorporate any kind of anti-sexist (or antiracist) policies will probably be an uphill battle, since these services hardly acknowledge that their women users may have special concerns, interests, or needs. For example, if you call Prodigy or America Online and ask a sales representative what their network offers women, you'll be told—as I have been from one year to the next—that their services appeal to everyone, regardless of gender. In other words: What's gender got to do with it?

Another step you can take to fight on-line harassment, abuse, and sexism in general is to organize, organize, organize! Generate new interest in and discussions about how to create conditions that encourage free speech for women in cyberspace. Create new Netiquette guidelines that discourage on-line sexism and disseminate them everywhere.

---

### RESOURCES ON ON-LINE HARASSMENT

Resources on on-line harassment and abuse, censorship, and related topics include the following:

- Stephanie Brail's "The Price of Admission," in the book *Wired Women,* edited by Lynn Cherny and Elizabeth Reba Weise (Seattle: Seal Press, 1996), is a thoughtful personal essay on Brail's own experience of on-line harassment.
- *The Internet for Women* by Rye Senjen and Jane Guthrey (North Melbourne, Australia: Spinifex, 1996) has a good chapter on "Gender Issues on the Internet," which includes discussions of sexual harassment and censorship.
- The Internet Advocate Web site at `http://silver.ucs.indiana.edu/ ˜lchample/netadv.htm` provides up-to-date information about Net censorship issues, including links to other civil liberties sites and to companies that manufacture net-blocking software.

---

Now that you've learned something about Netiquette and about Internet self-defense, it's time to move on to the next step in electronic communications: the wide and varied world of virtual conversations.

# 5

# VIRTUAL CONVERSATIONS

## Usenet Newsgroups, Conferences, Mailing Lists, Internet Relay Chat

*Victoria Vrana*

Now that you have mastered sending \*e-mail\* messages, how do you participate in the multi-person discussions that are taking place all over the Internet? These are conversations on every subject imaginable—topics as broad as "feminism" or as narrowly focused as "symbolism in the literature of Virginia Woolf." Discussions on the Internet can be unstructured free-for-alls, with everyone talking at the same time, or structured and moderated forums, where participants are reminded to stay focused on a topic and communicate thoughtfully and succinctly.

Virtual conversations take place in three basic forms, each of which will be discussed in detail in this chapter:

- Usenet newsgroups and conferences
- Mailing lists/Listservs
- Internet Relay Chat and chat rooms

\*Usenet newsgroups\* and \*conferences\* are non–\*real-time\* discussions that are housed on specific computers all over the Internet. You, the user, "go" to a newsgroup and see an index of messages, or \*postings,\* to the list. You can then read, \*download,\* and post messages from within the newsgroup.

\*Mailing lists\*, also known as \*Listservs,\* also reside on \*servers\* around the Internet, and are accessed through e-mail. You subscribe to a list, and then messages are sent directly to your mailbox. To post to the mailing list, you send an e-mail message to the list address. The message is then automatically sent to all subscribers.

\*Internet Relay Chat\* (IRC) and \*chat rooms\* are the much-hyped, real-time forms of communication in \*cyberspace.\* IRC can be used by anyone with full Internet access, whereas chat rooms, forums, and so forth take place within specific networks.

## USENET NEWSGROUPS AND CONFERENCES

Newsgroups and conferences can be compared to both interactive bulletin boards and slow-motion conversations. They are on-line places where people from all over the world exchange information, news, and opinions on specific subjects. You "visit" a newsgroup or conference and read messages at your leisure. You can post a new topic or respond, or "follow up," to a posting already created, thus adding to the *thread* of a conversation. Others respond to your postings, either to the newsgroup itself or to your personal e-mail box. You can also download and forward messages you read. (Note that an e-mail message sent to a newsgroup or conference can be referred to as a "posting," "topic," or "article.")

Usenet newsgroups can be accessed through various *Internet service providers.* In contrast, conferences, while a similar form of communication, take place within specific *networks* and can only be accessed by people with accounts on that network.

Each newsgroup or conference has its own personality. Some are purely informational, with postings designed to be read, but not responded to. For example, a network may have its own conference where it posts messages about changes in fees, technical issues, or new software. Others are very social, like `alt.singles`, where people chat and flirt as their means of getting acquainted. Some discussions are quite heated, like `alt.feminism`, with fast-flying debates and commentaries. All of these "conversations" are an integral part of the living, breathing, and typing community which make up the Net. They are places worth exploring in order to get a sense of the organism behind the cables and software.

---

**Q:** What are some examples of how women best use the Internet?

**A:** For the most part, when I think of how women best use the Internet, I think of things like discussion forums that can provide both more nuanced information than most Web documents and a broadened community among people with similar interests. For women in academia, discussion forums in their field can help them become better known and better connected without having to be part of the old boys' network. I think, too, of ways in which activist women use discussion forums and other e-mail technologies for getting the word out, marshalling support for (or opposition to) legislation and legislators, etc. The Internet is also valuable for finding information about, say, women's health issues and for getting in touch with others who have experience and understanding about these issues.

—JOAN KORENMAN
University of Maryland, creator of Gender Related Electronic Forums and WMST-L

---

### Welcome to Usenet

Usenet began in 1980 as a network of *UNIX* computers, mostly based at universities. It arose out of the need for users to exchange information about the UNIX operating system, but like the Internet itself, was quickly taken over by discussions on other topics. Its technical aspects and community guidelines were created by the people who were using it the most; these guidelines are still being developed and refined today.

Usenet is not a network, software program, or *protocol.* It is an informal, loosely structured society made up of the people who use Usenet newsgroups. Newsgroups (or "groups," for short) exist on servers all over the Internet. Each group is managed by the administrator of the actual site (computer) on which the group resides. The administrator does not necessarily moderate or facilitate a discussion, but instead controls the information flow and the technical demands. Administrators do have the ability to close down groups or provide access to new ones. Internet service providers choose the newsgroups to which their users will have access.

There are approximately twenty thousand newsgroups "out there" now, with the number increasing daily. Most networks do not carry all newsgroups. Sometimes you can request access to a specific group if it is not already available via your network. If newsgroups become a large part of your Internet life, you may want to shop around for an ISP which carries most groups or allows you to request new ones. If you use a service provider without full Internet access, you may not be able to tap into newsgroups at all. You may want to choose a new or additional provider in order to experience newsgroups.

## How to Access Usenet Newsgroups

Find the section of your network's main menu that sends you to newsgroups. Usually you can "go" to a newsgroup simply by typing in its name. An index of postings will appear on your screen.

Here's a sample excerpt from an index of postings on the `soc.feminism` newsgroup:

```
soc.feminism


11/05/96      1*soc.feminism References (part 3 of)      2

                                           tittle@netcom.com

11/25/96      2*Why do some feminists fear religion      7

                                   gq342@cleveland.Freenet

12/09/96      3*Men and Feminism (Bly's Problems)      4

                                               jym@igc.org

              4 Men who supported equality      5

                                   Unknown@its.brooklyn.com

12/10/96      5 various: rants, pickiness, 2nd lang      3

                                   morphis@physics.niu.edu

Conf: (i)ndex (u)nread (w)rite (c)apture (v)isit (g)o (e)xit (q)uit ?
```

Here's a key to reading the information you'll find in the index of postings:

| [DATE OF POSTING] | [SUBJECT OF POSTING (asterisk indicates a posting unread by you)] | [NUMBER OF RESPONSES] |
|---|---|---|

```
11/05/96      1*soc.feminism References (part 3 of)      2

                                           tittle@netcom.com
```
[SENDER'S ADDRESS]

To read a posting, you can double click on it or type in its number and press ENTER or RETURN.

Your software program will allow you to reply to the message or post a new topic. The command may be as simple as typing w for "write" or clicking on an icon of a pen.

For instructions more specific to your communications software and Internet service provider, refer to your manual or contact your technical support person.

## Exploring the Newsgroups

Newsgroup names reflect their content. These names are organized according to a structured hierarchy of terms which indicate general themes. New newsgroups are usually named using previously created terms. This means that most addresses begin with a familiar abbreviation, which helps users find the groups that will interest them or the appropriate place to post a certain topic. As with all Internet addresses, the parts of a newsgroup names are separated by dots, and there are never any spaces within a name.

The following are some of the terms used to indicate broad content categories for newsgroups. You will find these terms in the farthest left position in a newsgroup name:

alt  alternative—Unusual topics or non-mainstream or "alternative" views

biz  business—Different aspects of business, including starting your own business

comp  computers—Technical specifications and problems, hardware and software, computer development, programming, and computer science

misc  miscellaneous—Anything and everything else that does not fit into other categories

news  newsgroups—News about Usenet newsgroups, including Netiquette, technical aspects, and how-tos, with lots of good information for new users

rec  recreation—Everything from travel to tennis to tobogganing

sci  science—Subjects related to the scientific disciplines (excluding computer science)

soc  social—Two possiblilities: newsgroups that are social in nature (e.g., places to meet others) *or* newsgroups dealing with general social issues

talk  talk—Impassioned debate on a diverse range of topics

## Usenet Netiquette

The best way to get a sense of the "dos and don'ts" of Usenet Netiquette is to observe it. Spend time following the articles and threads of various groups before posting something. Think of a newsgroup as a conversation or a meeting that is taking place in a room. If you walked into the room, you would join the group, listen for a while, and see if you were interested. If you weren't interested, you would leave and maybe try another room. If you were interested, you'd begin contributing to the discussion. But you probably wouldn't want to suddenly interrupt or change the discussion topic.

Unfortunately, some people abuse the openness of newsgroups and undermine the group spirit by *flaming* or *spamming.* **Flaming** is a vitriolic attack on someone for their opinion, their grammar or writing style, their e-mail address—or just for the heck of it. Counter-flaming is a response to this attack, and it usually does little more than provoke the flamer. Many *newsreader* software programs now have something called a *KILL file* which can help deal with, but not erad-icate the pains and annoyances of flaming. KILL files function like mail *filters.* Unpleasant as the name is, KILL files will automatically remove all postings with a specific subject line or from a spe-cific user or site, including cross-postings and follow-ups to the unwanted postings.

**Spamming** is the posting of the same message to many newsgroups or e-mail addresses. Usually the message is an advertisement for real (or unreal) services or products. Some spam-mers actually get paid by companies doing the advertising and are trying to make a business out of it. This is one of the absolute evils of Usenet, and the community combats it in various ways. First, spammers are chastised and shut out by other users. Second, programs called *spam detec-tors* run on many Usenet sites. These detectors monitor newsgroups and look for articles which are posted again and again to different newsgroups. People who watch the spam detectors will erase a message like this when it is found. (By the way, the term *spamming* has its origins in a Monty Python skit!)

*Lurking* means you read but don't post, listen but do not speak. You can and should always begin by lurking in a newsgroup, conference, mailing list, or chat room. This is a good way to get the feel of the new community you may or may not decide to join. However, be forewarned: news-groups, conferences, and mailing lists allow you to lurk invisibly, but IRC and chat rooms usu-ally announce your presence (by flashing your log-in on the screen when you "step in"); subsequently, other users may address you directly and encourage your participation.

Much of the Netiquette for Usenet resembles the established guidelines for e-mail exchanges. On newsgroups, as in e-mail, it's important to be clear and be brief, to respect the feelings of others, to be careful about copyrights and source citations, and so on.

Other guidelines, including the following, are especially relevant to group discussions:

1. Think about your audience, and be careful what you say about others.
2. Don't blame system administrators for their users' behavior.
3. Don't assume that a person is speaking for her organization.
4. Don't post the same message more than once.
5. Don't post to multiple newsgroups.
6. Read all follow-ups and don't repeat what has already been said.
7. When you follow up on a posting, summarize what you are responding to.
8. When appropriate, respond to another user's e-mail box rather than posting a follow-up to the newsgroup.

9. Don't use newsgroups as a resource for homework assignments.

10. Don't use newsgroups as an advertising medium.

These guidelines and others are published on-line in the article "A Primer on How to Work With the Usenet Community," by Chuq Von Rospach. The entire text can be found in the newsgroups usenet.news.announce.newusers and usenet.news.answers.

## CONFERENCES

Conferences look and function very much like newsgroups. However, they usually can only be accessed by users of the network on which the conference resides. For example, the Association for Progressive Communication (APC) has hundreds of conferences about different aspects and issues of global activism, such as wilpf.hotline, sponsored by the Women's International League for Peace and Freedom, which has "regular updates on legislation on such issues as disarmament, racial justice and an end to U.S. global intervention." It works the same way a newsgroup does, but only users with accounts on an APC network can view the conference.

Conferences also have their own informal Netiquette rules, but do not necessarily have the same atmosphere as the Usenet community. Conferences, like newsgroups, can be moderated or unmoderated. Many conferences have *FAQs* which describe the discussion and whether or not it is being moderated. These are usually the first topics in the index.

Moderated conferences are run by individuals (or organizations, institutions, or businesses). The moderator managing the conference receives each posting in his or her mailbox before it reaches the actual conference. The moderator can then decide whether or not the article is appropriate to forward to the conference. This can be a time-consuming process (some conferences receive as many as a hundred articles per day), but worthwhile if the postings address a specific topic being discussed. It's important to respect the volume of the moderator's responsibilities and be patient when you post something that does not immediately show up on the conference.

## MAILING LISTS

Mailing lists resemble newsgroups in that they are locations for discussion about specific issues that do not take place in real-time. They differ from newsgroups and conferences in that they take place through e-mail. Anyone who has an e-mail account can access the thousands of mailing lists that exist. Even with only the most basic e-mail skills you can take part in correspondence on an almost infinite number of topics. You can send mail to as many as a thousand people with just one message.

Mailing lists also reside on specific computers around the Internet, many at universities. But instead of "visiting" that computer, you send or receive postings from mailing lists directly from or to your e-mail box. First you must subscribe to a specific mailing list. Once you have subscribed, all postings to the list get delivered to your address directly through e-mail. To post to everyone on the list you only have to send a message to one e-mail address. It is that easy!

Mailing lists are run by software programs like Listserv, *Majordomo,* or *Listproc,* three names with which you will get acquainted. Listserv is probably the most widely used program, and often people refer to mailing lists simply as Listservs. These programs subscribe new users, send new postings to all subscribers, and end people's subscriptions upon request. They can also sometimes tell you who is on a list and provide descriptions of any lists previously created by the person who started the list you are interested in. These tasks are all functions of the software program. But there are also sometimes real people who moderate a list just as they would a newsgroup, receiving all postings first and deciding whether they will continue on to the subscribers.

### How to Subscribe to a Mailing List

If you want to participate in a mailing list, there are three things you must know: the list name, the subscription address, and the list address.

To subscribe to a mailing list, first send an e-mail message to the **subscription address.** Leave the "subject:" field blank. In the body of the message, write either subscribe listname your firstname your lastname your e-mailaddress or simply subscribe listname. Include your name for lists running on Listserv-type software. Don't include your name for lists using Majordomo software. You can determine the type of software by the subscription address itself. If "Majordomo" is in the address, it's Majordomo software. If not, it's in the Listserv family and will possibly have "Listserv," "Listproc," or "Request" in the address.

For example, here's a subscription message sent to the mailing list GLAS.SISTERS, a Russian-language forum on women's rights issues in the former Soviet Union:

```
To: neww@glas.apc.org
Subject:


Subscribe Glas-Sisters Shana Penn shanapenn@igc.apc.org
```

Remember that these are commands, being sent to a computer and not to a human being. Anything extraneous will not be understood by the computer, so it will reject your subscription. Sometimes the computer will respond to incorrect commands, explaining to you (not always in clear friendly terms) what you did wrong or what you need to do. Some lists will ask you to send a second message to the subscription address as confirmation, possibly with a specific numeric "password." This reduces the possibility of users being subscribed without their consent. (This happens infrequently and probably will never happen to you. But if it does, contact the list administrator and your network's systems operator.)

Once you subscribe to a mailing list you will usually receive some kind of welcome message describing the list, its rules, and how to unsubscribe. Be sure to keep this message so that you can find it again.

### How to Post a Message to a Mailing List

When you want to post a message to a mailing list, you e-mail to the **list address,** which is different from the subscription address. This address sends your message to another part of the computer that serves the mailing list, which in turn sends your message as e-mail to all the list's subscribers. If you send your posting to the subscription address, the computer will not understand it, nor will anyone read it. Conversely, if you send your subscription message to the list address, as many as thousands of people will receive it in their e-mail box.

You can post to a list without being subscribed, which is a great way to spread news or announcements. Again, this should not be used for advertising or spamming. Your posting should always be appropriate to the topic and community at hand.

### How to Unsubscribe from a Mailing List

There's no way to browse or sample a mailing list. The only way to find out if you will really be interested in a specific list is to subscribe. You may discover it was not what you wanted, because you don't care for the quality of conversation or because you are suddenly receiving a hundred messages a day—more than you and your mailbox can handle. In such cases you will want to know how to unsubscribe immediately.

To unsubscribe from a list, you can send an e-mail message to the subscription address with unsubscribe or sign-off in the body of the message. Here's the message you would send to unsubscribe to the GLAS.SISTERS mailing list:

```
To: neww@glas.apc.org
Subject:


Unsubscribe Glas-Sisters
```

Remember, your welcome message should tell you the specific commands you can use to unsubscribe.

### Managing Mailing List Overload

The challenge of mailing lists is learning to manage the information you receive. If you are subscribed to more than one list or to heavily trafficked lists, you might receive a shocking flood of e-mail in your mailbox. Some e-mail programs, such as Eudora, can be configured to sort the mail into various predesignated folders. For example, you could create a folder called "URGENT" for messages from your boss, "LOVE" for e-mail from your partner, and "LISTS" for mail from your mailing lists. New mail would be sorted into the different folders by words in the subject line or the e-mail address of the sender.

In my office, we have a separate e-mail account for all of our mailing list subscriptions. These messages are skimmed and sorted by staff and interns and comprise a significant part of our e-mail research. We also use mailing lists to carry on discussions and meetings among our members and staff (see part 1, chapter 8). Mailing lists comprise an essential part of our communication with users who have e-mail-only accounts.

Mailing lists are free of charge, but can have hidden costs. If you pay for your e-mail account by kilobytes received and sent, you must pay for every message automatically sent to you, whether or not you are interested in the message. Usually such accounts are only used with UUCP or off-line networks in second and third world countries. U.S. users should not have to worry about the costs of receiving mail, but should be sensitive to the international participants in any given discussion. For instance, instead of posting your entire thirty-page article to a mailing list, post a summary with your e-mail address and let other users contact you directly to request the entire text.

## INTERNET RELAY CHAT (IRC)

IRC is one of several forms of real-time conversations on the Internet. It was created in Finland in 1988 by Jarkko Oikarin. IRC does not belong to a specific commercial network, and anyone whose network provides access to IRC can use it. It is similar to Usenet in that the IRC world has its own language, commands, and characters, which have developed over time as thousands of people in sixty different countries have used it to talk about every subject under the sun.

Real-time conversations are perhaps the most exhilarating, confusing, and potentially intimidating places on the Net. But once you have a little bit of practice and a grasp of the basic commands and maneuvers, IRC can allow you to talk to people anywhere, cheaply and "in-person."

### How to Use IRC

Start by obtaining an IRC *client* or software program (or use your ISP's program if it provides access for you) to communicate with a server in an IRC network. These networked servers are connected to one another to exchange information instantaneously. The largest IRC network is Eris Free net (EFNET), but others, like Undernet and Dalnet, can also be used. Some popular clients are WSIRC, mIRC, and InteRfaCe. They can be obtained by anonymous *FTP* (see part 1, chapter 7) or through the *World Wide Web* (see part 1, chapter 6). Once you have your client set up or have found a doorway in through your Internet service provider, you are ready to enter this new world of bedlam and delight.

When setting up your client, you will choose a nickname. You can use anything you like, up to nine characters (without any spaces). You are also asked for your actual name when setting up IRC software. This name will appear when anyone using IRC enacts the /WHOIS command. Some people feel uncomfortable with giving complete strangers their first and last names. You can put in a fake name at this point, or choose a gender-neutral name. However, keep in mind that with most Internet activities the server, network, or computer you are using can be traced if someone really wants to do so. Take some precautions but keep a healthy dose of reality at hand. And never discuss anything over the Internet that you wouldn't discuss on the telephone unless you utilize *encryption* (see part 1, chapter 9).

### Moving Around IRC

The IRC world is composed of *channels,* more like CB radio channels than television channels. IRC channels are virtual rooms or spaces where people discuss certain topics. The subjects are much more fluid here than in the Usenet realm. Anyone can open up a new channel with a few commands, and whoever begins a channel becomes the channel operator. The official topic of conversation can be changed by the operator with a few keystrokes, and it is not uncommon for people to change the topic frequently. Just as channels suddenly appear, they abruptly disappear, closing when the last person on the channel leaves. Channels can be very hectic and crowded; then it is almost impossible to determine who is talking and when. They can also be private, invitation-only places between two or three people.

All IRC commands begin with a forward slash. When you first connect with an IRC server you can use the /LIST command to see a list of all the open channels (except those that are secret), the number of users participating in each one, and the topics.

To join a channel, simply type /JOIN and the channel name. Names start with a # or an &. Channels with # names are global: anyone around the world can join. Channels with & names are only for your specific IRC server and are not always considered a part of the IRC proper. Once you've joined, lines of text will scroll across your screen next to the "speakers'" nicknames.

To join in a conversation, simply type what you want to say and press ENTER or RETURN. You'll soon see your own nickname and words on the screen. Usually the rule is to make short statements. This is not the best place for a long monologue.

A nickname with @ in front of it belongs to the channel operator (known as ChanOp or Op). The channel operator has the capacity to kick people off a channel, share channel operator privileges with someone else, or formally change the topic. People are usually kicked off only because of bad behavior—harassing or dumping of large amounts of unwelcome material into the channel.

To leave a channel, simply type /PART channelname.

## Private IRC Channels

Creating a private channel can be an inexpensive way have a conference call–style talk with friends and family all over the world. Set up a time to meet, agree on a channel name, sit down in front of your computers in your respective time zones, and chat away, live and private, all at significantly less cost than multiple long-distance phone calls. To create a channel, simply type the /join command followed by a channel name you create. You are then the channel operator and can set the parameters of your conversation. You can make it secret, private, or invitation-only. These are somewhat advanced IRC commands and should be attempted after you feel familiar with the system. Check out an IRC FAQ or computer information newsgroup for further details.

## IRC Commands

More than one hundred commands make up the IRC language. You don't need to know many to get started in IRC, but the more you know, the better you will be at maneuvering through the world of IRC. Commands always begin with a slash, and are case-sensitive. The following is a list of some common IRC commands:

| | |
|---|---|
| /AWAY yourmessage | Leaves a message that you are not available |
| /BYE | Exits you from your IRC session |

| `/HELP` | Gives you a list of commands |
|---|---|
| `/JOIN channelname` | Enters you into the identified channel |
| `/KICK nickname` | Boots the identified nickname off the channel |
| `/LEAVE channelname` | Exits you from the identified channel |
| `/QUERY nickname` | Starts a private conversation with the identified nickname |
| `/TOPIC newtopic` | Changes the topic of conversation on the channel |
| `/WHO*` | Provides a list of users in the channel |
| `/WHOIS nickname` | Gives the identity of the identified nickname |
| `/WHOWAS nickname` | Gives the identity of a nickname who has exited |

For a full list of commands, you can FTP "The IRC Primer FAQ" at `cs.bu.edu` in the directory `/irc/support`.

## Some IRC Tips—and Pitfalls

IRC users rely on shorthand language to facilitate the rapid response associated with real-time talk. Messages need to be brief; otherwise they are hard to follow. *Emoticons* and familiar computer acronyms like `BRB` (be right back) and `BBL` (be back later) are favored among IRC users. (See part 1, chapter 4, for a list of emoticons.) In addition, `HI` is a greeting you should use when you first enter a channel, and `RE` is a repeat `HI`, used when you come back into a channel after you've left for a while.

One of the hazards of the IRC frontier is **Nick Collision Kill.** This violent name refers to the phenomenon that happens when you enter a part of IRC where someone with the same nickname is hanging out. You are both "killed"—kicked off your IRC servers—as soon as the duplicate nicknames are detected. You will lose your connection to IRC and must re-enter with a different nickname.

Sometimes stalkers intentionally use common or specific nicknames to thwart others. These people are usually detected and barred from IRC. Use a creative nickname to avoid this catastrophe.

For more information about IRC, visit the Web site `http://www.singnet.com.sg:80/public/IRC/index.html`.

To put a face to a name of an IRC user, try the IRC Picture Gallery at the Web site `http://www.powertech.no/IRCGallery`.

To find out about IRC games, which are common on many channels, go to the Usenet newsgroup `alt.irc.games` or visit the Web site `http://www.cris.co./trieger/irc/games.html`.

## CHAT ROOMS, FORUMS, AND OTHER REAL-TIME CONVERSATIONS

Many Internet service providers, especially the larger commercial networks, have their own forms of real-time conversing. These are much simpler to use then IRC, but may cost you more (in higher network per-hour charges) and lack a little of the frontier atmosphere. The advantage is that you don't need to know any specific or complicated commands. Instead you can simply click on handy icons to change rooms, send your own text, or send a personal message to someone.

Networks like America Online and CompuServe have separate parts of their systems and software programs dedicated to chat rooms. Each looks and feels a bit different from any another. The public forums are often moderated or "guided," and language can be restricted. Most of the big networks are beginning to provide special entertainment—specific times and days when you can catch an on-line "program" or visit with a celebrity or expert. Often, the text you can type is limited to a line or two per entry.

Chat rooms are where much of the sexual activity is taking place on the Internet. Rooms of the "flirt" variety are filled with offers of cybersex. The personal tastes expressed are infinitely varied, and you can go off to a private room and play with your gender and sexuality as much as your log-in and fingers will allow. (For more on cybersex sites, see part 2, chapter 9.)

You can also use chat rooms to talk to people you know on-line. As with IRC (but much more simply and, again, probably more expensively) you can plan a time for both (or all) of you to be on-line and open a private room. This can be a wonderful way to keep in touch with friends and family when you are overseas or traveling.

Now that you have some of the important electronic communications tools under control, you may be ready to pay a visit to the place everyone is talking about: the World Wide Web.

# 6

# THE WOMAN NAVIGATOR
## Welcome to the World Wide Web
### *Victoria Vrana*

*"Web sites are important because they make information freely available to all people, at all times, and can be accessed anonymously."*
—Amy Goodloe, Lesbian.org, Oakland, California

The *World Wide Web* (WWW or Web) is the newest, most exciting, and fastest growing medium in the world today. Its widespread popularity is understandable, because with its *graphics-based* browsing tools, you only need to point and click to navigate your way through the Internet. Unlike *text-based* tools for using the Internet, or a reorganization of file structures like *Gopher* or *FTP,* the Web takes the Internet to a new level, surpassing all previous programs with its capabilities. The Web enables you to do all of the following, and more:

- experience color, graphics, sound, three-dimensional interaction, and video
- access Web, Gopher, FTP sites, e-mail, and Usenet newsgroups through one interface, called a browser
- take advantage of hypertext, a sophisticated and flexible way of linking Internet sites together
- interact with information providers through forums, live chat areas, and other aspects of Web sites
- utilize a new medium for publishing, entertainment, information, and business

The World Wide Web is the Internet of the future, providing access to a wealth of resources in a simple-to-use, multimedia format.

In this chapter you will learn about the following:

- The World Wide Web's beginnings
- The Web's infrastructure: hypertext, hypermedia, hyperlinks
- How the Web is organized: Web sites, home pages, navigational tools, and internal search tools
- The Web's programming language and protocol: HTML and HTTP
- Addresses on the Web: Uniform Resource Locators (URLs)
- Web browsers: tools for navigating the Web
- Getting connected to the Web and moving around in Web space
- Hotlists for saving and filing sites
- Transferring Web materials
- Search engines for finding what you need on the Web

## THE GENESIS OF THE WEB

The World Wide Web was developed in 1989 at CERN, a particle physics laboratory in Geneva, Switzerland. By 1990 the first practical Web application was created and demonstrated. Between January and December of 1993 traffic on the World Wide Web increased 187 times, and in June of 1993 the first Web *search tool* was introduced.

The CERN Web site is the definitive source for information on the Web's development. You can find it at the following address: `http://www.cern.ch`.

## THE WEB'S INFRASTRUCTURE: HYPERTEXT, HYPERMEDIA, HYPERLINKS

*Hypertext* is a way of linking related information together through key words. Instead of files being organized into some kind of hierarchical structure like a directory or a menu, documents are connected to one another at different points, interlinking information into a weblike form.

Hypertext is a non-linear way of presenting information and documents; it allows an author of a document to provide connections to any number of other documents relevant to a subject. Such connections are called links, or *hyperlinks.* On the World Wide Web, words that serve as links are highlighted in a text; sometimes they appear in a different color, and sometimes they are boldfaced or underlined. By clicking on a link with the mouse, you call up a new file and it appears on your screen.

For example, imagine that you saw this sentence on your computer screen:

> Hypertext and hypermedia, the infrastructure of the World Wide Web, were first conceptualized fifty years ago, long before the Internet existed.

If the underlined words were hypertext links, you would be able to select them, one at a time, by clicking on each word with your mouse. When you clicked, a new document would appear on your screen that related in some way to the word chosen. The link hypertext might present you with a history of hypertext; hypermedia might link to the Webster's dictionary definition of hypermedia; World Wide Web might bring up on your screen a guide to using the Web; and Internet might take you to a description of tools and their applications.

*Hypermedia* provides the same kind of linking as hypertext, but with other forms of media, such as graphics, sound, or video. Visualize a map of Europe on your screen. You might be able to click on Lithuania and instantly "go" to a server in Vilnius which displays information on Lithuanian culture and history, in English and Lithuanian. Then perhaps you could click on a phrase in Lithuanian and receive an audio clip which pronounces the word aloud.

One of the important things to remember about hypertext and hypermedia is that the creator (also called "author") of a Web site determines what links exist. Hence, the logic behind linking is subjective, and not always what the reader expects. For example, if the author of a *Web site* wants to link the word *the* with a picture of herself, she can. You may want detailed information on a certain topic in a Web site, but if the author did not provide it, you will have to search other Web sites for sources of the information you need.

However, most Web authors want their sites to be useful and popular, so they try to develop a logical structure to their links. It is helpful to remember that even the most logical structure winds itself, weblike, through *cyberspace,* delving deeply into one subject area, spreading laterally from link to link, circling back to a starting point. A Web author's links may reveal how her mind works in ways she didn't expect—and in exploring the site, you may find your own mind working in unexpected ways as well!

> When I conceptualize a Web site, I do a lot of planning on good old paper, using a pencil and making lots of diagrams and flow charts. These are essential for a Web site of more than a few pages. Then I move the organizing over to the computer, using a text editor to arrange ideas before actually starting to put together the Web site.
> — AMY GOODLOE,
> Lesbian.org, Oakland, California

## THE ORGANIZATION OF THE WEB

The Web consists of **Web sites**. These are collections of hypertext/hypermedia files called **pages**. Almost all sites have an introductory page called the *home page.* It is often designed as a table of contents, showing the areas of information covered in the particular site. Pages are connected through links. Links can also send the user to an entirely different Web site.

The Network of East-West Women's home page looks like this:

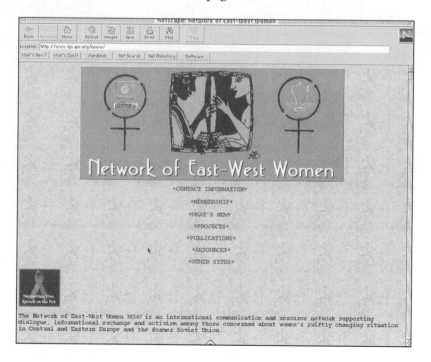

At this home page, all of the main categories are hypertext. (You'll notice that they are all starred.) If you can click on any one of them, you will be taken to another screen where you will find more information on the topic. For example, if you click on *MEMBERSHIP* you will go to a Web page describing NEWW's membership offerings, annual dues, and so on. If you return to the home page and click on *PUBLICATIONS*, you will go to a listing of past issues of the Network's biannual newsletter, e-mail instructions and resource manuals, gender studies bibliographies and course syllabi, and suggested reading lists of law-related articles and books.

By the way, the term *home page* has a second meaning. Sometimes it is used to refer to the page that appears when you start up your Web *browser,* which serves as your home base for surfing the Web. (Browsers are discussed in detail later in this chapter.) A HOME button will usually appear on every screen you explore. If you click on this button, it will return you to this opening page. (If you are using your workplace's browser, you will probably open directly to the home page of your institution's Web site, and the HOME button will take you back to this page.) The HOME button is the fastest way to interrupt a search or prepare to end a Web session.

Many Web sites have built-in **navigational tools** for moving around within a site. These are usually in the form of "buttons" at the bottom of a page which can send you backwards or forwards through a Web site. Some sites simply have a HOME button at the bottom of each page which connects you back to the home page of that site. Some sites also have **internal search tools** which let you search the entire site by key words or phrases.

Web browsers also supply navigational tools to help you move around the Web; these will be discussed later in this chapter.

## THE LANGUAGE OF THE WEB: HTML AND HTTP

The World Wide Web required the creation of a new programming language, HTML, and a new protocol, HTTP. **Hypertext Mark-up Language (HTML)** has two functions: First, it permits authors to send designed text—text using boldface, italic, different type fonts and sizes, and type specially placed and formatted—over the Internet. Second, it also allows Web site publishers to link any word or graphic to any other of their choosing.

*E-mail* and *Gopher* documents travel over the Internet only in plain, uniform *ASCII* text. HTML allows Web documents to look like the formatted documents you can create in most word-processing and desktop publishing programs. And with HTML you can create links to other pages within your own Web site, to someone else's Web site, to a piece of *freeware* you want to provide, to a sound or video clip, or to a "mailto" where the reader can send an e-mail message.

**Hypertext Transfer Protocol (HTTP)** is the language computers use to transfer Web pages over the Internet. In other words, HTTP enables you to "move" around the Web.

*A Beginner's Guide to HTML* is an excellent introduction to the programming language of the Web. It can be found at the following Web site: `http://www.ncsa.uiuc.edu/demoweb/htm-primer.html`.

## WEB ADDRESSES: UNIFORM RESOURCE LOCATORS (URLs)

An entirely new form of Internet address was also created with the advent of the Web. *Uniform Resource Locators (URLs)* (commonly pronounced "you are el," and sometimes "earl") represent Web sites, pages within a Web site, *FTP* sites, Gopher sites and *Usenet newsgroups.* (For more information on accessing FTP and Gopher files via the World Wide Web, see part 1, chapter 7.) Once you learn to dissect and decode them, URL addresses can help you understand the parts and content of a Web site or needed document.

To decipher a URL, the first thing you need to know is that a URL address is made up of three parts. Reading from left to right, the first part is called a **protocol**, the second part is the **host name**, and the third part is the **file path**.

Protocols specify the type of site, and include the following:

| | |
|---|---|
| `http` | World Wide Web sites |
| `ftp` | anonymous FTP sites |
| `gopher` | Gopher |
| `news` | Usenet newsgroups |

The protocol is usually followed by a colon and two forward slashes, for example:

`http://`

`ftp://`

`gopher://`

For Usenet newsgroups, however, the protocol is followed by a colon only, with no slashes: `news:`

The host name includes everything before the first single forward slash.

The file path includes everything from the first single forward slash onward (including the slashes themselves). The terms in the file path, separated by single slashes, can be directories, file names, or Web pages.

Here is an example of a URL address for a Web site, with a breakdown of the components:

`http://www.igc.apc.org/neww/ceewomen/efka.html`

`http://` is the protocol; it indicates that this is a hypertext file on the World Wide Web.

`www.igc.apc.org` is the name of the host computer; it tells you that this Web site resides on the Institute for Global Communications' Web server.

`/neww` is the first part of the file path; it is the address for the Web site of the Network of East-West Women.

`/ceewomen` is a second part of the file path; it indicates the Central and Eastern European Women's page, which is part of the NEWW's Web site.

/efka.html is the final destination you will reach via this file path; it is a link to the Web page of the Polish women's organization eFKa.

So—working in the other direction—the entire URL specifies the exact address of the HTML document for the Web page of eFKa, which is a link from the Central and European Women's page, which is part of the NEWW Web site, which resides on the Institute for Global Communications's Web server, which is accessed via the World Wide Web!

You will note that the very last part of a URL, on the far right, tells you about the format of the resource you can retrieve. If you wish to download the resource, you will need to pay attention to this ending so that you can choose the proper protocol for downloading. URL endings include the following:

| | |
|---|---|
| .html | hypertext file |
| .htm | hypertext file made on a PC |
| .txt | text file |
| .gif | image file |
| .jpeg | image file |
| .au | sound file |
| .mov | video file |
| ?string | URL leads you to a query |
| #anchor | URL leads you to a specific place in the directory |

## WEB BROWSERS

To access the Web you use software programs called *Web browsers.* Browsers are "windows" that let you move around cyberspace. They enable you to visit and explore (or "view") a Web site of your choice. They communicate with remote computers over great distances, putting the immense resources of the World Wide Web at your fingertips.

*Graphics-based* browsers allow you to move around by pointing and clicking, and give you full access to formatted type and graphics. Browsers can also be *text-based,* providing you with a text-only view of the Web. You navigate using the arrow keys and pressing ENTER at links. If you use a text-based browser, you cannot view or download images or other media. (Instead, images are usually replaced by the word *image*, or by a descriptive word such as *logo*, *map*, or *flower*.) Text-based browsers are faster than graphical ones, because loading graphics consumes a lot of on-line time. They are also often the only gateway to the Web for users in the Third World or post-Communist countries. If you can live without graphics, text-based browsers can do many other things that graphics-based browsers can do. However, it is difficult to take full advantage of the Web without its unique graphic and multimedia offerings.

You'll want to choose browser software that lets you make use of other tools, such as Gopher and FTP, as well as Web sites. The most popular browser today is Netscape Navigator. Other graphical browsers are Microsoft Internet Explorer and MacWeb. A well-known text-based browser is Lynx.

Some *Internet service providers* give programs like these to their users. Others (like America Online and CompuServe) have created their own software in an attempt to make their networks even more specialized and to keep all profits at home.

## GETTING CONNECTED AND GETTING AROUND

To use the World Wide Web, you must make a kind of "pretend" connection to the Internet, called an *SLIP*/*PPP* connection. Every browser and service provider makes this connection a bit differently.

Many software programs are set up to make an SLIP/PPP connection and turn on your browser simultaneously. This can often be achieved simply by clicking on an icon that says "Web," "WWW," or something similar. Other programs separate these two steps. First, you use one program to make the connection (again, by simply clicking on a button labeled something like "Connect" or "Open") and then you start your browser program. Your manual or service provider can tell you exactly what to do.

A browser usually opens by going to a Web site you have designated. To visit another Web site, you need to know its URL address. The browser provides you with a specific area in which to type in the address. In Netscape, for example, this area is called an "dialog box," and appears above the browser window. After you key in the address, and wait a few minutes or a few seconds (depending on the speed of your modem), you will have arrived at the selected site.

Once you are at a Web site, you can move around a single page by using the scroll bar if the entire page does not fit on your screen. (You can widen the window to see as much as possible on your screen.)

With navigation buttons, you can move around inside a Web site, all around the Web, or from Web site to Gopher to FTP and back. In Netscape, the navigation buttons appear above the browser window, as does the dialog box..

You can also move around by clicking directly on links, or by typing a new URL in the dialog box. Remember that, like Gophers and anonymous FTP sites, Web sites are housed in different computers all over the Internet. You may be jumping from Japan to Argentina in three clicks.

Browsers provide you with many nifty options. You can change the size and font of documents you view, and even view pages in Cyrillic or other non-Latin alphabets. You can view the source code of a page, the HTML language used to create the document, which is great for budding Web publishers. You have the usual "file" and "edit" options for saving, printing, copying, etc. You will probably find an icon that takes you to the browser creator's HELP Web page, which tells you all the choices available to you; these pages are updated frequently as browsers develop newer and better capabilities.

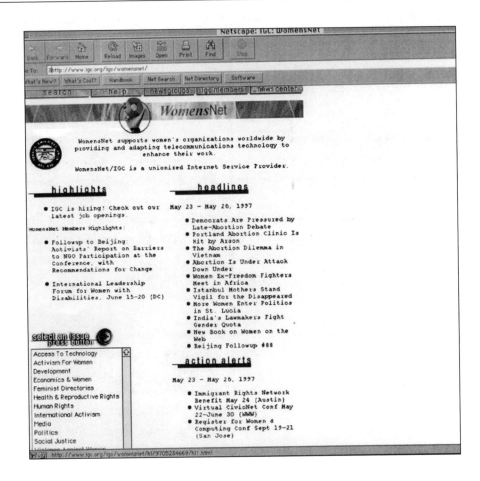

## HOTLISTS

Most browsers allow you to save sites you like or use frequently into a file called a *hotlist.* A hotlist functions much as *bookmarks* do in Gopher. When you reach a site you want to return to, you usually click on an icon to add the URL to your list. By saving the URL to your list, you make it easy to revisit the site whenever you want to. To go directly to this site later, simply open your hotlist and click on the URL. Many browsers let you organize your saved sites into different lists, under category headings you designate. For example, I have different lists for sites dealing with "Women," "International," "Non-profits," "Search Tools," and "Internet Issues."

## DEALING WITH GRAPHICS

Graphics, one of the great benefits of the Web, can also be one of its drawbacks. Because graphic files are very big, they can take a long time to transfer, or load, from the Web site to your screen. If a site is graphics-intensive, you can wait up to five minutes for it to load. This is why most people suggest using a 28.8 *modem* for viewing the Web.

Most browsers provide you with a "stop" function that will interrupt the loading of graphics. This may be in the form of an icon or a command in the menu. You can use this if you are getting impatient and want to stop and click on a new link. You can often tell your browser not to load graphics automatically through your "preference" or "option" files. This way, you will be given the option of loading the text from a site without its graphics. Your manual or ISP should have further details on such options.

## DOWNLOADING OR TRANSFERRING DOCUMENTS

One of the nicest aspects of the World Wide Web is that you no longer have to "download" documents, per se. When you connect to a Web site, a copy of the site is temporarily placed on your hard drive (in your disk cache, to be exact). To obtain a copy of the text, graphics, or source code, you need only go to your "File" menu and choose "Save."

When saving a document from the Web, take note of your "file type" option. "Source" will save the HTML code of a document, which makes the text very difficult to read, but is useful if you want to see how someone else formatted text on their Web page — for example, if you want to reproduce the look of the text on your own Web page. Choose "Text," if you can, to save only the basic text. You can also print Web pages while you are connected to them. (This usually takes a great deal of time and sometimes the edges of a page are cut off.)

### THE PERILS OF DOWNLOADING

Saving text and graphics from the Web is as easy as a few clicks. But beware! Many graphics—including things like logos—are copyrighted items, and not in the public domain. Therefore, it is illegal to copy them to your hard drive without permission. How copyright applies to text on the Web is hotly contested. Authors, publishers, and site providers all have differing views, and courts have not yet decided definitively.

It can be useful to think of saving a copy on your hard drive as making a photocopy. It may be all right to keep it for your own reference, but don't use someone else's text or graphics on your own site without citing the source and, usually, without getting permission. (See part 1, chapter 9, for more guidelines on "fair use" of copyrighted materials on-line.)

## SEARCHING THE WEB

There are hundreds of different ways to search the World Wide Web. No tool could possibly provide a complete search of all the information on the Internet, but many are trying, creating whole new structures for cataloging information in the process. Tools called *search engines* are popping up like mushrooms. Yahoo is one of the oldest, but there are also Alta Vista, Lycos, InfoSeek, Web Crawler, Inktomi and more.

Search engines almost always have a space where you can type in a key word or phrase and send it to the engine. To narrow the results of your search, choose your key words carefully, and try to be as specific as possible—and use the "plus" sign to search for word combinations. For example, if you were searching for information about me, such as my biography, my place of work, or a list of my publications, you would want to type `shana + penn` in the search box. This way, your search engine will give you a list of entries that contain *both* of these words, not one or the other. If you typed only `shana penn`, the search would give you listings of every *shana* and of every *penn* to be found on the Web—including Shana Alexander, Sean Penn, William Penn, Robert Penn Warren, and many more.

The results of the search will appear on your screen in the form of a clickable page, so that you can go directly to the site you want. Different search engines will produce varied results, so be sure to try a few if you can't find what you are looking for at first.

As the popularity the Web—and the competition among software producers—grows, search tools are providing different options to corner parts of the market. Architext Software's eXcite Netsearch claims to search by concept as well as by key words. Magellan Internet Directory lets you search for "Green Light" sites which screens out "adult" material. InfoSeek Professional charges $4.95 per month for fifty specialized searches like medical news and corporate profiles. Many search engines also provide some reviews of selected sites, giving you a more complete description and sometimes even a rating. Again, try out different tools. You will be sure to find one that fits your needs and preferences. And if your favorite search tool isn't satisfactory in all cases, try another one.

Here are the names and Web addresses for some of the top search engines:

| | |
|---|---|
| Alta Vista | `http://altavista.digital.com` |
| Excite | `http://www.excite.com` |
| InfoSeek | `http://infoseek.com` |
| Lycos | `http://www.lycos.com` |
| Magellan | `http://www.mckinley.com` |
| Web Crawler | `http://webcrawler.com` |
| Web Wombat | `http://intercom.com.au./wombat` |
| Yahoo | `http://www.yahoo.com` |

Search engines can open up new opportunities to conduct efficient, effective research on the World Wide Web. For details on other forms of research on the wide world of the Internet, read on to the next chapter.

# 7

# VIRTUAL RESEARCH
## FTP, Gopher, Archie, Veronica, Telnet
### *Victoria Vrana*

The Internet provides an almost infinite wealth of information and resources. With an Internet connection, you can access innumerable documents, sounds, pictures, software programs and now even consumer products and services anywhere in the world. A high school student in a rural area can search the Library of Congress. A women's studies scholar in Kyrgyzstan can find course syllabi at the University of Wisconsin. A businesswoman can search for potential clients at Yahoo's site on the *World Wide Web.* If you have just a little bit of know-how and a basic understanding of the concepts behind on-line research tools, computers can supply you with endless possibilities.

Computers store information in files. The files may contain text, or software code, or photographs and other visual images, or even digital music. On many university, library, and other research-based computers, a portion of these files are freely available to the public. Is it possible to gain access to them from where you sit, in front of your own computer screen? Yes, it is. In addition to the Web, there are several different ways to locate information and conduct research, using various tools. This chapter will explain how to use the following tools:

- FTP and its companion tool Archie
- Gopher and its companion tool Veronica
- Telnet

It's important to know that *FTP* and *Gopher* are tools used to search and transfer files. They cannot be used to access the graphical pages found on the World Wide Web. Advances in Web technology now enable you to access FTP and Gopher files through the Web, but the reverse is not possible. (See part 1, chapter 6 for more information.)

**FTP**, which stands for **File Transfer Protocol**, is one of the oldest forms of information transfer available on the Internet. It is a standardized, *text-based* means of retrieving copies of files and programs from *remote computer* data archives. You use your computer and Internet connection to *log-in* to remote computers, examine file directories from data archives, and transfer the files directly to your home hard drive, where they can be executed, edited, printed, and passed on. In addition to giving you access to endless amounts of research materials, FTP is one of the best ways to access the thousands of *shareware* programs, no-cost *freeware* programs, and sound and graphics files that await you on the Internet. In addition, some sites accessed through FTP contain social and cultural resources ranging from news releases to music and poetry to recipes to medical information to travel advice.

*Anonymous FTP* is a form of FTP which enables you to connect to specific sites, search, and *download* documents, files, or programs using the *login* "anonymous." You can use a program called **Archie** to search anonymous FTP files on a particular subject. You can also access FTP via e-mail and the World Wide Web.

In this chapter, you will learn how to perform the following essential components of FTP research:

- Access a server or install a client program
- Locate and transfer files
- Decode encrypted or compressed files
- Use Archie to browse and gain access to FTP files from around the world

**Gopher** is a simpler tool than FTP and anonymous FTP for accessing and transferring files. Gopher sites are hierarchically organized menus through which you navigate using your cursor or mouse. This action is described as "burrowing" or "tunneling;" thus the choice of name for this tool. A search tool called **Veronica** can be used to help you burrow your way through Gopherspace. Transferring Gopher files is as easy as downloading your *e-mail.* Gopher sites are interlinked, and you can move from one computer to another on the Internet simply by pressing ENTER.

While it is important to know how to make use of Gophers, you should also be aware that due to the advent of the Web, Gopher research will eventually become outdated and the same research will some day be done via the Web. (Web searches are discussed in part 1, chapter 6.) Until that time arrives, however, you will want to conduct much of your research in Gopherspace, and this chapter will show you how to do the following:

- Access a Gopher client
- Burrow through Gopherspace
- Save files using bookmarks
- Use Veronica to search Gopherspace

This chapter will also look at **Telnet,** a function of the Internet that connects you to a remote computer, enabling you to actually use the programs on the remote site.

## FTP AND ANONYMOUS FTP

"Concealed within this obscure acronym is one of the most powerful tools on the Internet." This is what the Net experts at the Insistute for Global Communications say about FTP, which plays the crucial role of library of the Internet. It can in fact be helpful to think of FTP as your key to a mammoth electronic library. FTP sites are places where thousands of public files are collected.

Using FTP, you can locate research materials and "check them out" of the library by downloading them and saving them on your own computer. But you never have to return them, because every item that is checked out is really only copied, so the original never leaves the library's "shelves."

As early as 1971, users of the ARPANET (which later became the Internet) were thinking of ways to expand the use of this powerful new network. FTP—a *protocol* that allows users to transfer files from one computer to another—was created. The corresponding set of commands which grew into small computer programs, or *clients,* were also called FTP, and *servers* that provided access and files were referred to as FTP sites. So the term *FTP* can refer to an Internet tool, a computer protocol, or a virtual place; it can also be a verb (as in, "I FTPed to SURnet the other day and found a lot of useful freeware").

FTP works when you use a *client* to access a remote computer called the *server.* You type in the address of the specific server you want to reach and your client connects to that computer. With FTP you must actually log-in to the new computer, just as you log-in to your e-mail account. You must have a login name and a password. Once you are admitted into the server, you can call up a list of files and directories, and delete files or move files to different directories. You can also download (or FTP) files to your hard drive.

Of course, most individuals, institutions, businesses, and networks today are not telling strangers the logins and passwords to their computers. So on the heels of FTP, a second process called anonymous FTP was created. Operators of servers put files they want the public to be able to access in a specific part of their computers. Users can FTP to these sites and log-in anonymously by typing the universal login "anonymous." The password required is usually your e-mail address.

### Accessing FTP Sites

To access a specific anonymous FTP site, you will need to know its address. Many FTP sites are listed in part 2 of this book. The best way to find addresses of other FTP sites is in other books, in magazines, and on the Internet itself. FTP indices can be found at *Web sites,* including the following:

*Archieplex: http://pubweb.nexor.co.uk/public/archie/servers.html

*Virtual Shareware: http://www.shareware.com/

*Winsite: http://www.winsite.com

Like e-mail addresses, all anonymous FTP addresses consist of *domains,* which are names of directories and subdirectories, separated by dots. There are never any spaces in an anonymous FTP address. For example, ftp.igc.apc.org is the anonymous FTP address for the Institute for Global Communications. On the Web, FTP sites have URL's beginning with the protocol ftp://.

There are several different ways to access information in FTP file libraries. You can do so via the Web, Telnet, or an FTP client software program.

If you use a Web *browser* you won't need specialized software programs or a password. Web browsers mainly enable you to access anonymous FTP sites. They can identify *ASCII* and *binary* files for you, which is a nice feature.

To retrieve files over the Web, start your browser as you normally do. Then tell the browser to to load the FTP server by typing in its *URL* in the address box. The browser will log-in to the FTP server and show its home directory. Files and directories in the home directory will appear as *hyperlinks.* You can move to the directory you want by clicking onto it. Your browser will then show its contents, and you can click onto the file you want.

The instructions for downloading a file will depend upon the browser you use. For example, if you use Netscape Navigator, you simply click the file name of the file you want. Once the file has been downloaded, you will probably be able to look at it, and then save it if you so choose. Your browser will probably not be able to show you program files; instead, you will need to save these directly. (See part 1, chapter 6 for more on using Web browsers.) This is probably the easiest way to access an FTP site, though no option proves much speedier than any other.

If you are not going through the Web, you will need specialized FTP client software. There are many different FTP clients available. You can use a *UNIX* FTP program if you have a *shell account.* Or there is an FTP package with a *SLIP*/*PPP* account for either Windows or Macintosh. The *graphics-based* Windows and Mac programs are more convenient because they automate the process of logging-in, and because you can point and click to change directories and download text files.

Sometimes, as with IRC, your *Internet service provider* will already have a client installed on its system for your use. You can see if you have access to an FTP client by typing FTP at your main menu or by asking your service provider. Many graphically based Internet software packages include a simple-to-use, clickable program like Turbogopher.

As with any Internet tool, the actual commands you type depend on your software and service provider. What will be covered in this chapter are the basic concepts of using anonymous FTP through an FTP client program.

### FTP TEXT COMMANDS

Most graphically based FTP programs will offer you point-and-click options for navigating through FTP sites. When you use FTP with a UNIX program you will need to know several simple commands. (You should be aware that FTP *is* case-sensitive, and most commands should be typed in lower-case letters).

| | |
|---|---|
| dir | Lists the files in the current directory on the remote computer |
| ls | An alternative command for listing files; can be used if dir does not work |
| cd | Changes the directory on the remote computer |
| get | Downloads a file from the remote computer to your local ISP |
| mget | Downloads multiple files |
| put | Uploads a file to the remote computer |
| bye | Logs off the remote computer |

To access a site, start up your FTP client program or go to the section of your ISP which allows you to use FTP. You may find FTP right at the main menu, as it is on the following menu from the Institute for Global Communications:

```
                    I N T E R N E T   S E R V I C E S

[1] Gopher — internet information services (GOPHER)
[2] Web — World Wide Web (WEB)
[3] Telnet — log into another system (TELNET)
[4] FTP — File Transfer Protocol (FTP)


Select a number (? for help or q to quit): 4
```

If you selected FTP from this menu, you would see a message on the bottom of your screen telling you that the computer was Retrieving Directory../. The next screen would look like this:

```
Specify the site you want to connect to, for example:
    Host: ftp.ipc.apc.org

Host:
```

At this prompt, you would type in the name of the FTP site you want to search. Once you have entered an address, your client will begin connecting you to the remote computer where the FTP site is located.

With some FTP clients, including all UNIX clients, you will be asked for your userid; type anonymous at this prompt. With all clients, you will be asked for your password; your e-mail address serves as your password. Once you send your password, you will probably be greeted with a few lines of text telling you about the server you have just accessed and maybe even the e-mail address of its administrator. You will then either see a directory of files or a command prompt. If you do not see the directory itself, you need to type in the command dir to access the directory.

Here's a sample from a directory of files at the ftp.igc.apc.org FTP site:

```
Institute for Global Communications


- - ->   [1]  .forward (.0k) [Aug 15 18:36] <Bin>
         [2]  New-stuff [Jan 28 19:41]/
         [3]  README (.0k) [Jan 2 21:57]
         [4]  bin [Sep 12 06:41]/
         [5]  dev [Sep 12 o6:44]/
         [6]  download [Feb 1 10:35]/
```

```
[7] etc [Sep 12 06:41]/
[8] pub [Sep 27 03:50]/
[9] upload [Jan 31 13:o1]/
[10] usr [Sep 12 06:44]/
```

Press ? for Help, q to Quit, u to go up a menu

## Locating and Transferring

The directory structure of FTP sites is one of the more confusing aspects of the tool. Directories list all of the files and subdirectories found at a specific FTP site. Unfortunately, these almost always have names like those listed in the sample, so it can be difficult to maneuver within an anonymous FTP site unless you know exactly what you are looking for. For this reason, FTP is less suited to browsers than its more user-friendly cousin, Gopher, and it's best to have a clear destination in mind when you use FTP. You can move from one directory to another in FTP by pointing and clicking or by using the cd command for "change directory."

When you find the file you are looking for, you can download it, which means you transfer a copy of it from the remote to your own computer. Graphically based FTP client programs often allow you to begin this process by clicking on the file that you want to download. In *text-based* programs you will need to cursor to the file you want and use the text command get to download the file. When you are finished, *log-off* by typing the quit command.

Your communications software transfers the file from your ISP's computer to your computer. It's the same software that you use to download or *upload* files from and to your mailbox. Contact your ISP support service for specific instructions. Once the copy of the file is saved on your own computer, it is yours to read, edit, print, or send.

You can upload files to a remote computer as well as retrieve them. When you prepare to upload a file to an anonymous FTP site, you usually place it in a directory called /upcoming. Connect to your ISP, select the FTP option on the menu, and follow the general instructions for logging-in to the remote computer where you want to upload your file. Open the specific directory where your file will go by typing the cd command and then incoming: cd incoming. To send the file type put filename. When the file has been transferred, log-off by typing the quit command, just as you did after you downloaded a file.

## Compression and Encryption

Often files in anonymous FTP sites, especially software programs, are compressed and/or encrypted. *Compression* makes the files smaller so they can be transferred more quickly. *Encryption,* a kind of encoding or scrambling, is used for security reasons, and for other reasons as well. Some forms of encryption make the file easier and safer to transfer and ensure that pieces will not be lost in transmission. You can tell if a file has been encrypted or compressed by looking at the *file extension,* which appears after the final dot in the file name. These extensions also tell what program has been used to compress or encrypt the files. Some common file extensions, and their corresponding program names, are as follows:

| | |
|---|---|
| .uu | uuencode |
| .Z | compresws |
| .gz | GNU compress, gzip |
| .tar | Tape Archive |

These additional file extensions may be found on Mac files only:

| | |
|---|---|
| .hqx | BinHex |
| .bin | MacBinary |
| .sit | Stuffit |
| .sea | Self-Extracting Archive |

You can find corresponding software programs to decode these files in yet another anonymous FTP site. Newer FTP programs may decode common file types automatically for you. Encoded files are considered binary files and must be treated as such. They cannot be downloaded using an ASCII *protocol.* Your software program might recognize this automatically or you may have to specify this yourself. Check with your systems operator or ISP manual to determine your program's capabilities.

For answers to FAQs about anonymous FTPs, go to the Web site maintained by Perry Rovers at http//www.iaehv.nl/users/perry/ftp-list.html. This site contains information on using FTP, automating FTP sessions, setting up an anonymous FTP server, and using Archie.

## ARCHIE

FTP may be the library of the Internet, but it can often seem like a library without a card catalog. The Internet doesn't have a main warehouse where everything is stored in an orderly fashion according to a filing system, and where new resources and new versions of resources are added in their appropriate places. Nor is there a central databank or catalog, with listings under the familiar author, title, or subject categories, of the Internet's vast resources. This can be frustrating and intimidating, especially for new users, because you must know the address of the resource you need before you can find it at an FTP site. Fortunately, however, there is a tool called Archie which enables you to search FTP sites by subject, using key words.

In the late 1980s, three students at McGill University in Montreal, Canada, created a program called Archie to help users find specific files on FTP sites. This database system catalogs files on anonymous FTP servers. These servers are responsible for updating file lists from various sites and then "talking" to each other and exchanging information so as to create a complete and up-to-date list of files. This complete list is duplicated on various public sites which users can access to search for the files they want.

Archie can be accessed in three ways: through an Archie client on your Internet service provider or by Telnetting to an Archie server; through e-mail; or through a Web *interface* called Archiplex.

If you use Archiplex to access Archie via the Web, you will be provided with a series of point-and-click commands you can follow to conduct your search. If you want to access Archie through a client or server or through e-mail, use the instructions that follow.

## Accessing Archie through a Client or Server

If your ISP has an Archie client, you can find out merely by typing `Archie` at the main menu. You can also use Telnet to access a remote Archie server directly. (Telnet is discussed later in this chapter.) Archie servers can be found at addresses around the world. The following is a list of a few of the servers in North America:

| | |
|---|---|
| `archie.uqam.ca` | Canada—Quebec |
| `archie.cs.mcgill.ca` | Canada—Quebec |
| `archie.unl.edu` | U.S.—Nebraska |
| `archie.rutgers.edu` | U.S.—New Jersey |
| `archie.ans.net` | U.S.—New York |
| `archie.sura.net` | U.S.—Maryland |

For a complete listing of Archie servers, type `servers` from within an Archie client. Remember to always use the site closest to you.

If you are using an Archie client or have Telnetted to an Archie server, you need only type `ofindoe` and the word, combination of words, or partial word for which you want to search. The resulting list of files will scroll across your screen. Each item on the list will identify the host computer, the location (a string of domains separated by dots), the name of the file, possibly its size, and the last time it was updated. Sometimes the list may include one or two lines describing each file, but don't count on it.

## Accessing Archie Through E-mail

To access Archie through e-mail you simply send an e-mail message to an Archie server. The address is `Archie@`, plus the name of an Archie server. For example, to send an e-mail to the Archie server in Maryland, the address would be: `archie@archie.sura.net`

In the body of the message, type `find` followed by the key word or words you are searching for, then `set mailto`, followed by your e-mail address, followed by `quit`. For example, here is an e-mail message that could be sent to search on the key words *Latvia* and *women*:

```
find latvia + women
set mailto shanapenn@igc.apc.org
quit
```

The results of your search should be mailed to you in a few hours. Remember that as with Listserv subscriptions, you are sending this e-mail message to a computer, not a person. Extra comments like `thanks a lot!` will only confuse the computer and make it reluctant to do any work for you.

For tips on choosing key words that will effectively limit your search results, see part 1, chapter 6. To get a complete list of Archie commands, type `help` from within an Archie client or server. To get more information than you probably ever wanted to know about Archie, type `manpage`.

## FTP Tips and Netiquette

When you use research tools like FTP and Archie, a few useful tips—and a few special rules of Netiquette—can help you avoid pitfalls and respect other users.

1. Try to access FTP files outside of normal business hours. Transferring files can use a lot of the remote site's computing power, which otherwise would be used for whatever the computer's main function is. When servers are accessed too frequently they are forced to place restrictions on public access.

2. Try as much as possible to use the Archie server closest to you.

3. When you log-in to an FTP site, look for the file labelled `readme` or `index`. These files will introduce you to the site and how to use it.

4. The best information on an FTP site is often located in a directory called `pub`.

5. Remember that most FTP files are compressed to save disk space and downloading time, so you will need to use a decompression program, which you can find on many FTP sites.

6. You'll find that software on FTP sites is often outdated. You can find out about the latest software versions, and where to locate them, on computer-related *Usenet newsgroups* and *mailing lists.*

7. Beware of *viruses* that may accompany downloaded software. Be sure to scan for viruses whenever you download software from an FTP site.

8. When you download files, do so into a temporary directory. This way, if a transfer doesn't completely work, your existing files won't be affected in any way. If you overwrite, you may find that your directory is empty.

## GOPHER

Gopher changed the face of the Internet from a rather complicated, awkward visage to a friendly, easy-going countenance. Developed at the University of Minnesota in April 1991, Gopher provided the first simple and uniform way to access and retrieve information from servers all over the world. Unlike FTP, which requires the user to know commands and wade through murky directories, Gopher's interface can be picked up by anyone in a matter of minutes.

Gopher is a menu-driven tool, meaning that files are organized into straightforward menus instead of directories. Gophers can "point" to other Gophers and link directly to them. These interconnecting sites at servers around the globe make up the world of Gopherspace.

Files are organized into menus with simple titles that are actual descriptive words instead of strange, hard-to-interpret directory or file names. The user navigates around a Gopher using a few keystrokes, arrow keys, or a mouse. Downloading is also just an ENTER key away. And like anonymous FTP sites, Gophers are created by institutions and organizations who have information to make public—for free!

### Accessing Gopher

Gopher, like FTP, follows the client-server relationship. The best way to use it is to access a Gopher client. Your Internet service provider may be running one; to find out, just type `Gopher` at your main menu. It is also easy to obtain a good Gopher client program. Graphical interface Gopher software has made a simple task even easier. It is worth investing in or finding on the Internet a program like Turbogopher, the Gopher Book, or MacGopher.

From within these client programs you can type in the name of a Gopher and watch its menu appear on your screen—no logging-in or passwording required. Gopher addresses look like FTP addresses, with no spaces or @ signs. They often begin with the word *gopher*, as in `gopher.igc.apc.org`.

### Navigating Through Gopherspace

The name "Gopher" suggests the tool's function, which is to "go for" files and retrieve them for you. In addition, it is a historical gesture to the University of Minnesota's mascot, the beloved gopher. But it also refers to the "tunneling" you do as you move in and back out of menus to look for a useful or interesting file.

To tunnel around you only need to move the arrow keys (up and down) to different menu items. The left arrow key will take you out of a current menu back to the previous one. When you find a menu item you want to burrow into, simply press ENTER or the right arrow key—or, if you have a graphical interface, just click on the item.

When you've selected your item, somewhere on your screen (often at the bottom right-hand corner for text-based Gopher clients) your program will tell you what it is doing, like "Retrieving Directory" or "Retrieving File." Be patient. Gopherspace reflects an actual physical space, too. The menu item you choose may be connecting you to a computer in Finland, so it can take some time. Sometimes servers are full or unreachable for some reason. Take a deep breath and try again.

To download a file from Gopher space, go to the directory where the file is listed, select the file you want, and download as you would from the index of a mailbox. The precise downloading process varies depending on your ISP; consult with your ISP's support service if you need help.

A great place to start exploring Gopherspace is something called "ALL THE GOPHERS IN THE WORLD," found on the menus of many Gopher clients. This is just what it sounds like—all the Gophers in the world organized by region and country. Just pick your favorite country and dig in. Gophers also often have something like "ABOUT THIS GOPHER" as the first menu item. Reading this file can save you a lot of time.

Here's a sample opening Gopher menu:

```
Internet Gopher Information Client v2.1.3

  Internet Resources

  [1]  All the Gophers in the World by Region/
  [2]  Search Gopherspace using Veronica/
  [3]  Gopher Jewels/
  [4]  Interesting Gopher Resources/
  [5]  Anonymous FTP
  [6]  FidoNet/
  [7]  Free-Nets (Community-based Nets)
  [8]  Internet Guides and Materials/
  [9]  Internet Hunt/
  [10] Libraries/
  [11] Mailing Lists/
  [12] National Information Infrastructure/
  [13] Telnet/
  [14] Usenet/
  [15] World Wide Web/
  [16] Roget's Thesaurus/
  [17] Bay Area Internet Literacy (BAIL)/
  [18] This Area for Experimentation/
```

## Bookmarks

Most Gopher clients allow the user to create *bookmarks,* another great time-saving device for navigation. When you find a Gopher or a particular menu item which you may want to explore more later, you can save its address directly onto a small file in your client. This file is called a bookmark. When you want to return to that Gopher, you open the bookmark and select the entry you want. You can usually create several bookmarks for different research topics like "Women," "Travel," "Gender Studies," and "Fish." With bookmarks, you can create your own virtual reference library right on your hard drive.

## VERONICA

Veronica gives Gopher use ten times the simplicity, power, and fun. Created at the University of Nevada, Veronica is the acronym for Very Easy Rodent-Oriented Net-wide Index to Computerized Archives. Like Archie, Veronica allows you to search with key words for any topic under the sun. But instead of searching the directories at FTP sites, Veronica searches Gopher titles and menu items. Servers in different countries have the sole purpose of searching and cataloguing Gophers all day long to make sure the most up-to-date resources are available through Veronica.

### Accessing Veronica

Veronica is accessed directly through Gopher clients, so you need no special software or commands to use it. Simply find a Gopher with a menu item like "SEARCH GOPHERSPACE WITH VERONICA." Usually such a menu will give you additional documents about Veronica and how to conduct a search.

For example, if you select menu item [2], from the Gopher menu on the previous page, you will see the following screen:

```
[1]  What is Gopher?

[2]  What is Veronica?

[3]  Searching Gopherspace using Veronica (try this first)/

[4]  Searching Gopherspace using Veronica (try this second)/
```

If you select item [3] from this menu, you will see this:

```
[1]  How to Compose Veronica Queries - June 23, 1994/

[2]  Frequently Asked Questions (FAQ) about Veronica - June 13, 1995/

[3]  More Veronica: Software, Idex-Control Protocol, HTML/

[4]  Find GOPHER DIRECTORIES by Title word(s) (via PSINet) <?>

[5]  Find GOPHER DIRECTORIES by Title word(s) (via SCSNevada) <?>

[6]  Find GOPHER DIRECTORIES by Title word(s) (via NYSERNet) <?>

[7]  Find GOPHER DIRECTORIES by Title word(s) (via UNAM) <?>

[8]  Search Gopherspace by Title word(s) (via PSINet) <?>

[9]  Search Gopherspace by Title word(s) (via SCSNevada) <?>

[10] Search Gopherspace by Title word(s) (via NYSERNet) <?>

[11] Search Gopherspace by Title word(s) (via UNAM) <?>
```

Veronica menus give you a choice of several servers through through which you can search, because servers can sometimes be full and not accept your search request. This is one drawback to Veronica, but you can often get around it by trying a server in a different country or time zone where it is the middle of the night. Always remember that there is a corresponding real, physical dimension to all this virtuality. Computers break down, lines can be overloaded, electricity can go out—anything can be happening as you move around the world from behind your desk.

After you've selected a search command from the menu, you begin the search by simply typing in one or more key words and pressing ENTER. Your search results will appear as a brand-new Gopher—a new menu of items that reflect your key words.

Here is a sample from the beginning of a search of Gopher directories using Veronica:

Find Gopher Directories by Title
Words to search for
african    american    women

[1]  Foster, Frances Smith, Written by Herself: Literary Productions
[2]  *  110A.  African  American  Women  Writers/
[3]  *  146  Spirituality  in  African  American  Women/
[4]  African  American  Women/

You can access any of the new Gopher items by selecting one. You can bookmark the search results and explore them later.

For a searchable list of worldwide Gophers, connect to gopher://main.morris.org:70//llgopher_rot%3a%5b_servers%5d.

To find more information on using Gophers, try gopher://gopher.tc.umn.edu:70 and select from the menu info about gopher folder.

## REMOTE LOG-IN: TELNET

Telnet is a function of the Internet which connects you to a remote computer—a computer other than the one you are working on. Unlike FTP, which transfers files back and forth, Telnet enables you to actually use the programs on the remote site. For example, you can Telnet to computers that have programs which perform searches or which provide information about the weather. Telnet expands the capacity of your computer and gives you access to programs you do not have or your computer is not capable of executing.

Many people use Telnet to check their e-mail from a network other than their usual service provider. For instance, if you were staying at a friend's house in Germany and you had an e-mail account at a university in Texas, you would not want to make a long-distance telephone call just to access your mailbox. But if your friend had an account with a German Internet service provider, you could work through that ISP to Telnet to the computer of your university and read your e-mail from there. You would basically be using your friend's account as a doorway to the Internet, then traveling to your own host computer and directly interacting with it.

Once you have made a Telnet connection, the commands and menus you see on the screen are not from the computer you are working on or from the Internet service provider you started out with; they come straight from the remote computer. When you type anything into your keyboard, the commands go through the Internet to affect the remote computer you are connected to, wherever in the world it is. Telnet, as you might deduce, is especially useful when traveling.

### Using Telnet

Your ISP may provide you with Telnet capabilities and a program in its software. You should be able to begin the program by typing Telnet at the main menu, selecting it from the menu, or clicking on the appropriate icon.

When you receive a prompt, type in the address of the machine to which you want to Telnet and press ENTER or RETURN. (Like Gopher and FTP addresses, Telnet addresses consist of parts separated by periods, with no spaces.) For example: Host: login.ipc.apc.org.

You should next then see a message on your screen which tells you that the computer is attempting to make its connection. If the connection is successful you will see a welcoming message which indicates that you are now connected to the remote computer. This message usually tells you what the "escape character" is. This is what you can type to quickly disconnect from the remote computer. If your Telnet session "hangs" (gets stuck, freezes), this key or combination of keys can rescue you by allowing you to escape from the session. Here's a sample welcoming message:

```
Connected to igc2.igc.apc.org
Escape character is _^]

Institute for Global Communications (ipc.apc.org)
Need Help? +1-415-561-0000
type new to open a new account
login:
password:
```

After you connect to the remote site, you may be asked for your login and password. If you are Telnetting to your own e-mail account, you should already know how to access it. Public Telnet sites either tell you how to log-in or do not require this step.

Once you are inside the remote computer, you can make use of programs stored on it. If you are accessing your mailbox, the commands and interface should be familiar to you. Public spaces often provide you with a menu and/or an extensive help file.

Using Internet research tools may seem challenging—but with Archie and Veronica to help you, the process is easier than it sounds. And whatever challenges you encounter will be more than balanced by the rewards, since even a modest mastery of virtual research tools opens up a vast world of information to you. If you're ready for a new challenge, then move on to the next chapter, where you find worldwide communication at your fingertips through on-line meetings.

# 8

# BREAKING NEW GROUND

## Moderating On-Line Meetings
### *Sonia Jaffe Robbins*

It's 11:30 on a Monday night as I sit down in front of my home computer in New York City. I log-in to my *e-mail* account so I can begin moderating an on-line, international board meeting of women representing twenty-four countries for the Network of East-West Women. (I am a co-founder of NEWW and consult as a communications coordinator.)

My day is ending, but it's 5:30 A.M. in Poland, 6:30 A.M. in Bulgaria, and 7:30 A.M. in St. Petersburg, Russia, where some of the board members live. As one of two co-moderators for the meeting, I want all the board members to have the first documents in their e-mail inboxes when they open them in the morning.

This meeting will involve no travel expenses, no hotel reservations, no photocopying of packets—in fact, the meeting will cost very little, though it will require a considerable investment of time, thought, patience, and discipline from all involved, both moderators and participants. These women activists in Central and Eastern Europe and the former Soviet Union are using cutting-edge technology—yet they have little or no experience with on-line communications.

This will be the fourth e-mail meeting NEWW's board of directors has held since the creation of NEWW On-Line, an electronic *network* of and for women advocates in the post-communist region. As the moderator or co-moderator of each of these meetings, I am exhilarated by the potential the Internet holds for such meetings—not only for international groups, but for any women's organization. E-mail is a new and efficient way to hold any kind of meeting, whether it involves a few people preparing a document together, chapters of an organization or business enterprise comparing notes, or a coalition of groups getting together to set a common agenda. E-mail meetings are a great option for people living in the same city when they can't find a mutually convenient time to meet in person or on a conference call. E-mail meetings are invaluable for starting up new organizations, coalitions, or businesses. And they are money- and time-savers for individual members or chapters of regional, national, or international groups.

In this chapter, you will learn how to conceptualize and conduct an e-mail meeting, using examples from NEWW's board meetings. It will show you how one international feminist organization has used the technology, and provide guidelines on how you can adapt your organization's structure and current meeting habits to the on-line environment.

## E-MAIL MEETINGS VS. F2F MEETINGS

Certain elements of an e-mail meeting will be familiar, because they are identical to the elements of an ordinary face-to-face meeting (or F2F meeting, in on-line shorthand).

- E-mail meetings have agendas.
- E-mail meetings have lists of participants.
- E-mail meetings have background documents which participants receive prior to the meeting.
- E-mail meetings have schedules.
- E-mail meetings have votes.
- E-mail meetings have minutes.
- E-mail meetings require prior organization and coordination.

Other elements of e-mail meetings will seem very new and different to participants accustomed to meeting F2F.

- E-mail meetings may not, at first, feel like meetings at all, because each participant remains physically alone, in her own space.
- E-mail meetings are like writing notes or leaving messages on an answering machine, since participants send and respond to e-mail at different times.
- E-mail meetings usually take place over a longer period of time—days or even weeks, rather than an hour or two.
- E-mail meetings require special efforts and frequent e-mail exchanges to keep people "in the meeting."
- E-mail meetings require agendas and deadlines that take realistic account of time differences and the fact that they are being fit into participants' other activities.
- E-mail meetings cannot utilize audio and visual aids, because exchanges must be designed to meet the requirements of *ASCII,* the basic e-mail text format.

You will probably find that e-mail meetings have certain advantages over F2F meetings.

- E-mail meetings focus on ideas and language; it's what people "say" that matters in the on-line world, not what they look like or how their voices sound. (And you can attend an e-mail meeting in your pajamas!)
- E-mail meetings give people time to carefully think about controversial issues and respond thoughtfully to disagreements or interpersonal conflicts.
- E-mail meetings don't have to happen at any particular time or place, but at the convenience of each of the participants.

You should also be prepared to adjust to some disadvantages. Many of these can be overcome, at least in part, through mutual efforts by the participants.

- E-mail meetings allow no tone of voice or body language to supplement the words. (However, there are computer approximations called *emoticons.* See part 1, chapter 4.)

- E-mail meetings—especially those including participants who have never met—may seem more formal than F2F meetings. Extra care needs to be taken to assure that e-mail meetings are personalized.

- E-mail meetings' dependence on ideas and language can place at a disadvantage those who feel less adept at expressing themselves in writing. Extra care needs to be taken during these meetings to encourage participation from those who seem reluctant to send messages.

- E-mail meetings can also place at a disadvantage participants who are less experienced with the technology or the format. Extra training before a meeting may be useful to familiarize participants with the e-mail meeting process.

- E-mail meetings cannot take advantage of the graphic and formatting capabilities of computers. (However, even using the bare bones of ASCII, you can design clear and attractive materials. See the box near the end of this chapter for some tips.)

## WHAT IS AN E-MAIL MEETING?

An e-mail meeting consists of any number of people, each with a computer, *modem,* and access to an *Internet service provider* or e-mail provider. The moderator(s) of the meeting send e-mail messages to the participants and the participants send e-mail messages to the moderator. (Meeting participants can also send e-mail to each other, just as participants in F2F meetings can meet one-on-one outside the main meeting room. However, they are encouraged to share with the rest of the group any private talks, if they pertain to the meeting.)

E-mail meetings work best if software is available on at least one of the moderators' e-mail provider's systems to set up an electronic *conference,* a *bulletin board,* or a *mailing list* (although it is possible for one of the moderators to send all the meeting messages to a previously created list of e-mail addresses). The e-mail address of each meeting participant is recorded with the automated software, and the software automatically sends all messages *posted* to the meeting or conference to all those subscribed.

E-mail meetings also work best if the automated software permits "moderated" conferences, which means that all e-mail sent to the meeting or conference e-mail address will be checked by a human moderator and posted with the appropriate subject heading, so e-mail meeting messages will be easily seen in each meeting participant's e-mail directory or index of messages. Moderated meetings also permit observers, who can read meeting messages but can't respond directly.

## THE ROLE OF THE MODERATORS

Most of the tasks described in this chapter will be handled by the **moderators**. Your first experience with e-mail meetings is likely to be as a participant rather than a moderator. However, this chapter should give you the advantage of understanding what goes on "behind the scenes" to make your meeting run smoothly—and it may also encourage you to take on the challenge of meeting moderation.

The moderators can be any members of your organization or group who have a good overview of how your group works and who know at least some of the people who will be participating in

## E-MAIL MEETINGS VS. ON-LINE MEETINGS

I've sometimes used the terms *e-mail meeting* and *on-line meeting* as if they were interchangeable. In fact, they are not. An e-mail meeting is an on-line meeting, but an on-line meeting may not be an e-mail meeting. If everyone attending your e-mail meeting has access to Netscape and the World Wide Web, you may be able to hold your meeting there.

You can even supply Netscape to those meeting participants who don't have graphic access to the Web. Documents formatted in HTML for the Web can be sent via e-mail and read in Netscape on computers not connected to the Web. Using Netscape, either on the Web or only on participants' computers, permits you to include text formatting and graphics (like charts and illustrations) in your documents.

If all participants have access to the Web, software such as Hypermail permits an e-mail list to appear on the Web and allows messages to be sorted in different ways, making it easy for participants to look for all the messages with a particular sender or subject line.

Chat sessions can also now be set up on the Web—IRC and Netscape Chat are two ways to do this. This is real-time communication, rather like a telephone conference call. Chat sessions are efficient and immediate, but they require everyone to be available to meet at the same time, and are less subject to moderation.

E-mail meetings are the simplest on-line meetings. If you are just starting out, it's wise to have your initial meetings by e-mail. Then, if your technology and budget are up to it, you can try these more ambitious methods.

---

the meeting. They could be your director or the chair of your board, but they could just as easily be staff people or even consultants. The moderators of the first e-mail meeting will probably be self-selected or appointed, but it is a good idea for moderators of subsequent meetings to be chosen by meeting participants, especially if a nonhierarchical structure is of value to your group. The moderators should have access to everyone in the organization or group with information that will move the meeting along.

A good moderator is essential to the success of any kind of meeting, but she is particularly necessary for e-mail meetings, where each participant is in her individual office or home, sitting in front of her computer or reading printouts of the e-mail meeting messages. The moderator has to make participants feel they are part of a group working together, even though they are not in the same room—or even the same time zone.

It can be very effective to have two co-moderators, to share the work and bounce ideas off of each other. If your group or organization has different constituencies, having co-moderators can help assure that power is shared among these constituencies. For example, my organization has one moderator from Eastern Europe and one from the West.

Each of the moderators should be skilled at abstracting ideas from other people's written communications and be able to summarize positions fairly, even if she doesn't agree with them herself; she must be able to separate her own opinions from those she is summarizing.

Being a moderator may feel strange at first, but you learn very quickly through experience, and even a little experience can make you appear to be an expert. IMHO (in my humble opinion), being a good moderator can feel like being a good mother. You put your ego aside and concentrate on facilitating others' communication. You encourage participation by seeing both the forest (the meeting as a whole) and the trees (the myriad individual points being made). It can be quite exhilarating to be an effective moderator of an e-mail meeting as it unfolds and develops a life of its own, and it's equally exhilarating, as a moderator, to see your suggestions embraced, or embroidered, or modified, or even rejected by meeting participants.

---

**SPECIAL CONSIDERATIONS FOR INTERNATIONAL E-MAIL MEETINGS**

Because my organization's board is made up largely of women for whom English is a second language—or even a third or fourth language—moderators face an additional challenge: making the documents easy to read for non-native speakers of English. This means that native English speakers must try to keep vocabulary and sentence structure simple, avoid long sentences and subordinate clauses at the beginnings of sentences, use figures instead of words for numbers, use only widely recognized idioms, and spell out in parentheses the meanings of abbreviations.

At the same time, non-native speakers must remain aware of homonyms (a hazard for native speakers as well) and use spelling and grammar checkers. In addition, we have found that non-native English speakers are hesitant to take on the task of moderating the meeting precisely because they feel insecure in our only common language. However, it can be extremely useful to have one moderator who is a non-native speaker, and who can proofread all documents with the specific goal of pointing out language or concepts that may not be clear to everyone.

---

## THE STRUCTURE OF AN E-MAIL MEETING

Setting up and conducting an e-mail meeting involves the following basic steps:

- Coordinating responsibilities: delegating tasks among the technical facilitator, the co-moderators, and others
- Making an agenda: deciding what to talk about
- Wielding an electronic gavel: getting the meeting started
- Facilitating communication: reading the messages of meeting participants
- Writing the moderators' summaries: moving the meeting along and bringing it to a close

### Coordinating Responsibilities

In addition to the moderators, every e-mail meeting needs someone who is designated as the **technical facilitator**. E-mail meetings work best when they are technically moderated—that is, when a person posts the messages sent by each participant, to assure that they have the proper subject headings.

This function can be filled by one of the co-moderators or by a separate person, perhaps someone who already handles the technical aspects of the computer system for your organization.

Moderators and the technical facilitator should know what one another's responsibilities are so that messages don't fall between the cracks and work isn't duplicated.

The tasks for each meeting should be listed in advance and divided among the moderators and the technical facilitator. Each moderator and facilitator should know the schedules of the other participants, especially if their work for your organization or group is volunteer or part-time. (For example, the co-moderators for two of NEWW's board meetings also teach, so we had to know when we were not available to check or respond to e-mail. We also had to know who would be able to respond immediately, if that became necessary.)

Moderating tasks should be evenly divided, so that one person is not always responsible for the "easy" parts (sending thank-you notes, for example, or tallying votes) and another responsible for the "hard" parts (summarizing the discussion to date or inviting more discussion).

Co-moderators, in consultation with each other, should also feel free to consult with or seek additional information from the organization's staff, board members, consultants, or anyone else who might be able to provide background or answer questions that arise during a meeting. Such consultations may be extremely helpful—and necessary—to moderators when they are drafting the agenda, writing background documents to be sent at the beginning of a meeting (or asking others to write them), answering questions raised by participants during a meeting, or writing the meeting summaries.

---

### WHAT THE TECHNICAL FACILITATOR DOES

The tasks of the technical facilitator include:

- Managing the mailing list for the e-mail meeting
- Ensuring that the e-mail address for each meeting participant and observer is included in the mailing list for the meeting
- Posting each response from a meeting participant to the meeting conference
- Ensuring that each posted response includes the name of the member who posted it
- Knowing the proper subject line for each posted response

The technical facilitator should be notified when meeting participants are having technical difficulties—for example, when a meeting participant is not receiving messages, when her e-mail address is not working, or when her computer is broken. The technical facilitator can mediate (or "interface") with other technical experts, if necessary, to solve the problem.

---

### Making an Agenda

Agenda-setting is simply deciding what to talk about, and it is the same whether you are meeting F2F or on-line. It's wise, however, not to have too many substantive issues in one e-mail meeting, because any issue that requires a lot of discussion will take a lot of time via e-mail. In fact, if an issue is controversial and requires immediate decision, it should be the only topic on an e-mail meeting agenda.

E-mail meetings depend on thorough preparation, just as F2F meetings do. Preparation is even more important for e-mail meetings because the opportunity for spoken negotiation is absent. Adequate consultation before the meeting can forestall feelings that anyone's position has been ignored—feelings that could intensify without the opportunity to speak F2F. (Remember: Because written e-mail documents lack the nuances and tone of voice carried by spoken words, they can tend to seem less friendly and more forceful. This is why e-mail blossoms with smiley-faces and other emoticons, which may seem silly, but are essential to convey the human being behind the words.)

You will find a sample agenda for an e-mail meeting later in this chapter.

## Wielding an Electronic Gavel

Establish a date for beginning and ending the e-mail meeting. Be sure that all your participants will be available during the meeting period; if anyone will be missing for part of the meeting period, the moderators should find out when they will be gone and when they will return. If the moderators know that people are unavailable, they won't hassle them with reminder messages.

Prepare background documents to send out before the meeting starts. At a bare minimum, these documents will consist of:

- an introductory letter
- minutes of the previous meeting
- a draft agenda
- supporting documents needed for informed participation

INTRODUCTORY LETTER:   This functions as a cover letter, and it sets the framework for the meeting. The letter states the starting and ending dates of the meeting. It also lists each document that will be sent for the meeting; each document should have a number and a title, and the title should correspond to the agenda item title to which document refers. The letter should clearly state the specific decisions or processes that are necessary to complete the meeting, and note the deadline(s) by which discussion or decision on particular agenda items are to be completed. (Every step of an e-mail meeting should have a clearly defined deadline!) The letter concludes with the meeting schedule. To overcome the formality and distance of e-mail meetings, it's nice to start this letter with some personal piece of information, like the weather or your state of mind or a particular issue you are facing. Here is a sample introductory letter from a NEWW board of directors meeting:

NEWW ISC
MEETING 3, FEBRUARY 1-MARCH 2, 1996
DOCUMENT 1: Introduction Letter

Dear ISC members:

It is winter everywhere. In New York, it is cold and icy; in Tver, there is lots of snow but also lots of sunshine.

This meeting is starting when you receive the draft agenda and this introduction letter. This letter lists the documents you will receive for Meeting 3 and the dates they will be sent by the co-moderator in the U.S.:

FEBRUARY 1
DOCUMENT 1: This letter
DOCUMENT 2: Summary of moderators' changes to minutes of Meeting 2
DOCUMENT 3: Draft Agenda for Meeting 3

FEBRUARY 2
DOCUMENT 4: Suggestions for how to organize ISC meeting materials
DOCUMENT 5: Background for Agenda Item III: Shana Penn's description of how NEWW projects have been approved up to this point
DOCUMENT 6: Background for Agenda Item III: Questions or discussion

We look forward to hearing from you in Meeting 3.

Sonia Jaffe Robbins in New York
Valentina Uspenskaya in Tver, Russia
Co-Moderators, Meeting 3

MINUTES OF THE PREVIOUS MEETING:   These are a compilation of the moderators' summaries from the previous e-mail meeting. Minutes should be sent out well before the next meeting starts, and those who participated in the previous meeting should be given two weeks to approve or to note corrections. Corrections should be reviewed by the moderators and passed on to participants in the new meeting.

DRAFT AGENDA:   The draft agenda for an e-mail meeting will look much like the agenda for a traditional meeting. It should include the document title(s) and number(s) that are relevant for each agenda item. It should also include the deadlines for discussion and decision responses. The first agenda item should always be signing in to the meeting and approval of the minutes. What follows is the agenda for the NEWW board meeting introduced above:

NEWW ISC
MEETING 3, FEBRUARY 1-MARCH 2, 1996
DOCUMENT 3: Draft Agenda

I. Sign in, changes to this draft agenda, and approval of the minutes
of Meeting 2.
DEADLINE: FEBRUARY 6


II. Old Business.
In Meeting 2, ISC participants agreed that a discussion about whether
and how consensus could work in an on-line meeting should begin on
NEWW's general conference, women-east.west. That discussion has begun.
NO DECISION NEEDED


III. New Business.
What criteria will the ISC use in selecting NEWW projects?
DEADLINE FOR RESPONSES: FEBRUARY 12
Decision will be made after trial use in applying criteria.

SUPPORTING DOCUMENTS:   These should be more or less identical to documents participants might receive in a folder at or before the beginning of an F2F meeting. They might include, in addition to the agenda, a list of expected participants, and background information about the organization or information in support of different positions on agenda topics. It is important to be sure that e-mail meeting participants have these documents before the meeting actually starts, so they will have time to read through them, think about them, and make suggestions for changes.

Once you have supplied participants with the necessary documents, you can actually begin the meeting. This can be as simple and direct as one of the moderators sending an e-mail message that states, "The meeting is starting today"—the e-mail equivalent of banging a gavel.

Because the familiar activities of walking into a meeting room and sitting down together are not available, the beginning of an on-line meeting can feel particularly amorphous. You might ask each meeting participant to send a message by a specific date, to sign-in and indicate that she is ready to take part.

Sending an immediate welcoming message in response to each sign-in message helps the person signing in feel that there is someone waiting to hear from her. Include a personal note if you have time; since e-mail meetings offer no opportunity for smiles, handshakes, or hugs, it is essential to provide a personal touch. In fact, an opening agenda item for a first e-mail meeting might be for each participant to send a brief personal self-introduction—the on-line equivalent of "going around the room" at an F2F meeting. This is particularly useful if many of the meeting participants have not met. If you have the time and the funds, a collection of photographs can also be collected and distributed by snail mail.

## Facilitating Communication

E-mail meetings that cover great distances require a lot of contact between participants and moderators. At the beginning of the meeting, it's important to answer every message, even if it's just a thank you for signing in. It is also important to respond quickly to any questions.

It is important for moderators to read all participants' messages promptly throughout the e-mail meeting. Unlike the general participants, moderators must read messages not only to formulate their personal responses, but to keep the meeting on track and running smoothly. Moderators may frequently need to send brief, private e-mail messages to various participants to refocus the discussion, clarify a point, or encourage participation. As you read through participants' messages, keep a number of goals in mind.

1. Read between the lines. A good moderator at a F2F meeting listens to what speakers say, but also always watches for nonverbal cues. Since nonverbal cues are missing on-line, a good on-line moderator needs to be sensitive to what is not written as well as what is written. Does a brief response mean the participant has no other comments, or does it mean she is hesitant to express an opinion that may be contrary to others'? Is a participant's comment clear or ambiguous? Does the ambiguity reflect a personal confusion, or does it touch on an issue that needs teasing out?

2. Keep the meeting focused. See that the meeting moves along and does not stray from the agenda. For example, if a meeting participant mentions a topic that does not apply directly to the agenda issues, the moderator might send a private e-mail message suggesting how that topic could be addressed in another way—perhaps by bringing the issue to the general membership or by writing an article in the organization newsletter. Or the moderator might conclude that an issue is too big for the e-mail meeting to settle by itself.

3. Identify communication problems. The moderators should be sure they understand what each participant has written. If you are not sure, it's best to e-mail the participant and ask for clarification. (If the meeting participants are in the same city or even country, a telephone call might be better.) If a request for clarification reveals that a participant's earlier message was misunderstood, make sure that the participant's clarification is posted to the conference and identified clearly as "CLARIFICATION." At times, you may want to suggest ways that ideas can be rephrased to ensure a clear understanding by all participants.

4. Make sure everyone is heard from. If some people seem not to be participating, send e-mail messages to those who have not been heard from and request their views. Ask why they have not been responding. Ask if any help would make participation easier. Don't forget telephone follow-up, if your budget permits.

5. Enforce deadlines. As the deadline approaches for each agenda item, the moderators should check to see that a quorum of participants has responded. If a quorum has not yet responded, the moderators should send e-mail reminders or make follow-up telephone calls, to see what problems, if any, are holding up participation.

**Writing the Moderators' Summaries**

By preparing summaries throughout the meeting, moderators can show the progress of discussion and indicate whether agreement is close. The moderators' summaries bring together in one document the highlights of all the messages to date, and offer a precis of the opinions, ideas, and suggestions. Moderators' summaries are especially important when critical discussions are taking place.

Summaries will be of either discussions or votes. Creating a summary of votes is easy: simply tally the votes and report the results. Summaries of discussions are more complex. You might think of the process as a form of textual analysis. Look for similarities and differences in the meeting participants' responses. Be attentive to whether a response is concrete or philosophical, whether it makes a suggestion or asks a conceptual question. When writing the summary, you might think of yourself as a filter for others' opinions. Use language that describes rather than judges or evaluates. If you, while acting as moderator, want to present your own ideas to further the discussion or come to a decision, describe it as a "moderator's suggestion."

Following certain general guidelines may help you use summaries to conduct efficient, effective meetings.

1. Separate areas of agreement from areas of disagreement, and outline each clearly. First identify the issues on which participants agree; this is encouraging to the meeting. Then look at whether disagreement seems superficial or fundamental. Don't avoid fundamental disagreement. You may present possible solutions not suggested by meeting participants, but don't try to force consensus where it does not exist.

2. Manage disagreement without suppressing it. If all but one person agree on a particular point, remember to include the dissenting view. Include in the summaries participants' reasoning for different viewpoints.

3. Keep the meeting's content on track, but don't ignore important side issues. Participants' contributions may reveal new issues that the agenda does not mention. Analyze these issues and include them in the summaries if they are relevant.

4. Identify participants' decisions once they have clearly been made. Describe whatever action must be taken, and who will be taking this action. If a subcommittee is to be formed, make sure there are sufficient volunteers for the subcommittee. Include deadlines for the action.

5. Know when to quit if a decision is not reached. The moderators' summary may indicate that additional discussion is needed, or that some topics should become agenda items for future meetings.

## SOME TIPS FOR MODERATORS OF E-MAIL MEETINGS

In addition to the thoughtful work of setting agendas, reading and responding to messages, and preparing summaries, moderators must perform many more "mechanical" or "clerical" tasks. These tasks, too, are essential to a productive e-mail meeting.

TRACKING MESSAGES. E-mail meeting moderators must keep track of and save all messages from participants. These are essential for preparing summaries and minutes, and should be preserved as part of the organization's permanent record. There are three ways to keep track of meeting messages: on computer disk (each message is downloaded and kept in a directory), which can be further divided into subdirectories named for each agenda item; on paper (each downloaded message is printed out and kept in a manila folder); or on a chart (each message received is recorded by date on a chart). In fact, it is best to do all three, rather than rely on just one method. This may seem like repetitive work, but redundancy is the safest course.

CREATING EFFECTIVE SUBJECT LINES AND DOCUMENT HEADERS. How can you be sure your meeting participants won't miss your e-mail meeting messages among the dozens they receive daily? For each meeting, it's a good idea for the moderators to establish naming conventions. This means selecting certain words or characters to begin the subject lines of all meeting-related messages. It's also a good idea for the subject line to include the topic of the message. (This can get tricky, because the number of characters in a subject line is limited.) The subject line of each message should also correspond to the header of the document contained in that message. For example, for the NEWW board meeting outlined in this chapter: `Subject: ISC M3 Agenda III Mod. Summ.` The moderators should communicate the naming conventions to all participants before the meeting begins, and the moderators and/or the technical facilitator should make sure that all messages have the appropriate subject headings before forwarding them to participants.

ESTABLISHING REALISTIC DEADLINES AND SCHEDULES—AND KEEPING THEM. Keep your deadlines realistic. Allow people time to read, think, and respond thoughtfully. If participants are not meeting their deadlines, the moderator will have to send reminder messages. Nagging is no fun—in fact, it can be the hardest part of the meeting for both moderators and participants. But it is also a necessary part of e-mail meetings.

E-mail meetings can be hard, time-consuming work for all participants, and especially for the moderators. But they are tremendously exciting, too. When a moderator checks her e-mail each day and sees all the responses coming in, she can feel like the hub of a magically working, invisible sisterhood. So when you come home tired to a full mailbox, remember this: pulled together by electrons, bits and bytes, our words whirring silently over the telephone wires, we are using this technology to knit together our own empowerment.

# 9

# FAQs
## Frequently Asked Questions—and Their Answers

*The important thing to remember is that this is not
a new form of life. It is just a new activity.*

—ESTHER DYSON

EDventures and Electronic Frontiers Foundation

### WHAT'S THE ABSOLUTE MINIMUM HARDWARE NEEDED TO GO ON-LINE? CAN I USE A MAC SE OR A 386 PC?

These computers are adequate if you don't mind limiting your access. If you only use a *shell account,* which is the cheapest kind of Internet access, you can run various *text-only* programs that let you send and receive *e-mail,* retrieve software or files from *remote computers,* and navigate a text-only version of the *World Wide Web.* If you want more options, then you'll need at least a 386-based machine that runs Windows, with four megabytes of RAM. You'll also need at least a 14,400 *baud* *modem.* To browse the Web with *Netscape,* you'll need even more RAM.

### WHAT HAPPENS IF I ACCIDENTALLY HANG UP OR MY MODEM IS ACCIDENTALLY UNPLUGGED?

Get back on-line, and don't worry; your modem is probably intact. If you were in the middle of *uploading* or *downloading,* start again. If you were in the middle of writing a message on-line, you probably can't retrieve it. You'll have to begin writing it over again.

### CAN I RETRIEVE A MESSAGE THAT I'VE MISTAKENLY DELETED?

Yes, most *networks* make it possible for you to "undelete" messages, usually by typing UND.

### WHAT CAN I DO IF MY MESSAGES ARE RETURNED TO ME?

Returned mail, or *bounced* mail, most frequently results from errors in the way you've typed an address. Check the address to make sure it's correct; then try sending it again. If your mail is returned again, you may need to check with the recipient to make sure her e-mail address has not changed. You can also try checking in an electronic address directory. (See part 1, chapter 3.)

### WHAT DOES "HOST UNKNOWN" MEAN?

Host unknown means that the computer that hosts the address to which you are sending mail couldn't be found. Try resending the message later; the problem is usually that the *host computer* was down when you tried to get the message through.

## IS THERE A CYBERSPACE EQUIVALENT TO POSTAL SERVICE CHANGE-OF-ADDRESS CARDS? WHAT DO I DO IF I CHANGE MY E-MAIL ADDRESS?

Unfortunately there is no equivalent thus far. If you change your address, you must send out messages to your crucial correspondents. Remember to unsubscribe from *Listservs,* and, if you want to remain in their discussions, to resubscribe when you have your new account. If you switch *Internet service providers* it is helpful to retain your old account and let it overlap for a few days with the new one so that addresses are readily available to you when you are sending out notification of your change. Mail sent to your old address after you've discontinued it will be returned to the sender.

## WHEN SUBSCRIBING TO A LISTSERV, THE DIRECTIONS SAY TO WRITE "YOUR NAME." DOES THIS MEAN MY REAL NAME OR MY E-MAIL ACCOUNT NAME?

You may write either name, or even something else, since the Listserv program automatically finds your e-mail address. Each system has a HELP command which can assist you with terms specific to that system. Find it by typing HELP in a message and send it to LISTSERV@hostaddress.

## WHAT CAN I DO TO ELIMINATE UNSOLICITED MAIL?

Write to the postmaster at the site where the mail originated. Send your message to postmaster @site.domain. Describe your problem and ask for action to be taken. Another alternative is to use a mail *filter* program.

## WHAT IS A MAIL FILTER PROGRAM?

A mail filter program allows you to choose an author, subject, or content for elimination. Any time a message arrives with information which fits into your chosen category, the filter separates it out for you and enables you to delete or file it quickly. This type of filter comes as part of a mail package; check with your service provider if you would like to use one.

## I SUBSCRIBED TO SEVERAL LISTSERVS AND AM OVERWHELMED BY ALL THE MESSAGES FILLING MY MAILBOX. WHAT CAN I DO?

You can unsubscribe to some of the Listservs or you can choose only those lists that are moderated, in which case the moderator does a lot of the editing and filtering for you. (For more options, refer to part 1, chapter 5.) New users should also be advised to choose your Listservs carefully, and avoid oversubscribing. The results can be overwhelming!

## ARE MY E-MAIL MESSAGES REALLY PRIVATE?

No, not at all. Any e-mail sent over the Internet can be intercepted, not only by a hacker but also by the postmaster or *sysop* (systems operator) at your ISP. The sysop tracks your e-mail use for accounting purposes: where and when you send mail; how long you are on-line per session; how long each message is. The postmaster can read any bounced or returned e-mail. So e-mail is not private, even though it may feel like a private activity, because you are sitting all alone at your computer when you compose and mail your messages.

Security software such as PGP (Pretty Good Privacy) can give you some protection, but it is, as the name implies, limited. Otherwise, it is recommended that you scramble messages that you feel you need to keep secret. In Internet terms, scrambling or *encryption* means encoding messages by using algorithms, thus making an e-mail message incomprehensible to anyone who does not know the secret code. Unfortunately, there are not yet laws to govern cyberspace privacy the way there are to protect mail sent through the U.S. Postal Service. (See part 1, chapter 10, for resources on this subject.)

### DOES BIGOTRY EXIST ON-LINE?

Unfortunately, yes. On-line homophobia, racism, and sexism are all too common. Hate groups are having a field day on-line. The Simon Wiesenthal Center, a Los Angeles group which studies the Nazi Holocaust and also tracks Neo-Nazi activity, posts information on the various kinds of hate files that are uploaded to the Internet in the United States. More than fifty groups distribute their vitriolic propaganda on-line. For example, the bulletin board of the far-right Minutemen uploads homophobic and racist texts from Chicago. A music label called Resistance Records, which produces white-supremacist music, is developing an Internet site where users can download the album jackets and lyrics to its music. Neo-Nazis even use electronic communications technology to promote computer hate games.

Along with the bigotry exhibited by organized hate groups, there's ample evidence of reckless, rude, politically incorrect *flaming* on Listservs and *Usenet newsgroups.* In these instances, an organization is not formally touting its prejudiced message; instead, individuals are randomly, recklessly shooting off at the mouth when you least expect it. (For more information on on-line bigotry and how to combat it, refer to part 1, chapter 4, on sexual harassment, and part 2, chapter 6, on resources for women of African descent. You can also contact the Simon Wiesenthal Center: webmaster@wiesenthal.com.)

### WHEN I QUOTE FROM INTERNET RESOURCES, IS IT NECESSARY TO CITE THE SOURCES?

Documents considered published works—including anything that has been published in print, like an article or a book—need to be fully cited, even if you have copied them from an on-line source. If you are quoting a long excerpt from a published work—or the entire work—you may be required not only to cite the source, but also to request explicit permission from its author or publisher to reproduce the work. It's a good idea to familiarize yourself with fair use guidelines, just as you would need to if you were writing something for publication in print. "Fair use" means how much of another person's work you can fairly—and legally—reproduce without permission from that person.

Materials created on computers and circulated via e-mail usually belong to the category of unpublished materials, and can be cited by describing the nature and source of the material to the best of your ability.

Citing on-line materials helps make the Internet a useful and viable resource for other scholars and surfers. Sue A. Dodd of the Institute in Social Science has written a detailed and useful document on the subject entitled "Bibliographic References for Computer Files in the Social Sciences: A Discussion Paper" (not to be reprinted unless proper attribution is made, as the text clearly states). Dodd writes: "The good news is that researchers are beginning to cite computer files in the reference sections of social science journals. The bad news is that for every person who does cite his or her data source, another twenty to thirty continue to provide no citations. This means that valuable data sources will not be indexed by bibliographical services such as *Social Science Citation Index;* and more importantly, the next researcher who would like to analyze these data may not have sufficient information to acquire them." (Sue Dodd, Institute in Social Science, University of North Carolina, Chapel Hill, N.C. 27599. To obtain a copy of this paper, contact Sue Dodd at USDODD@UNCVM1.BITNET.)

### DO I HAVE TO SEEK PERMISSION TO REPRINT GRAPHICS FOUND ON WEB SITES?

Yes. It is illegal to reproduce these materials without permission. Send a request for permission to reprint the material to the producer of the site or of the specific material you wish to use; include a description of where and how you want to reprint it.

### IF I RECEIVE A PERSONAL MESSAGE AND PASS IT ALONG TO ANOTHER PERSON, IS THIS FAIR USE?

It is probably unfair, though you might still have an "implied license" to reproduce the message. (For instance, if the message asks for help on a non-private matter, there might be an implied license to pass it along to others who might be able to help.)

### CAN I INPUT AND UPLOAD AN ARTICLE TO A LISTSERV OR NEWSGROUP FROM A NEWSPAPER OR MAGAZINE THAT DOESN'T HAVE ELECTRONIC VENUES?

The print media might be available on an on-line service; therefore, it would probably be unfair. If the issue of the newspaper or magazine is still available in bookstores and on newsstands for purchase, then this would also make it unfair. The point, in this case, is that you should not be undermining a publication's ability to sell the material it owns.

### CAN I FORWARD SOMEONE ELSE'S MESSAGE FROM ONE NEWSGROUP TO ANOTHER?

This is probably fair because the message was posted for public consumption, and because the person posting it has no commercial interest in selling the message.

### CAN I QUOTE A FEW SENTENCES FROM A NEWS ARTICLE THAT I'VE DOWNLOADED?

This is probably fair as long as you reprint only a few sentences.

The conditions and considerations that apply to copyright and fair use on the Internet are relatively new, and, like other privacy, property, and protection issues, the details are still being hashed out. Some of the issues are comparable to those dealing with fair use in other media, but many concerns are new and Net-specific.

These examples of fair use issues are adapted from Q&As created by Larry Lessig, David Post, Eugene Volokh, and others at the Cyberspace Law Institute and Counsel Connect. For many more examples, and for all kinds of helpful information on on-line legal issues, contact the Cyberspace-Law for Non-Lawyers Listserv. This is an announcement-only Listserv, not a discussion list. To subscribe, send a message to LISTPROC-REQUEST@COUNSEL.COM; include the command SUBSCRIBE CYBERSPACE-LAW Firstname Lastname in the body of your message. An open discussion about these issues is held on the archive Web site at http://www.cli.org/cyberspace.

Some of the questions raised by the development and growth of electronic communications *don't* have simple answers. For women, several of these questions are especially difficult to resolve—and, at the same time, especially important to think about. Read on for some thoughts on these cyberspace controversies.

# 10

# SUBJECT TO DEBATE

## On Space, Free Speech, and Censorship

The introduction of a new communications technology always arouses controversy. The Internet's impact upon us has been compared to that of television, radio, and even the Morse code. The most notable difference is the rapidity with which we've become aware of and captivated by the Internet. That which inspires also provokes. The Internet's emergence has fueled the fires of public and legal discourse, as reported in the more familiar forms of media such as television, newspapers, and magazines. As each day brings new Internet users, it also brings new questions. Who has access to the Internet? Who controls it, and determines its course? Will it democratize access to information, or concentrate it in the hands of a technical elite? Will it be maintained as an open communications system, or will governments and corporations ultimately control it? How will it develop—from its basic infrastructure, costs, codes, languages, and networks to the legal framework, formats, and on-line cultures?

Two of the issues surrounding the rise of electronic communications are discussed in this chapter. The first concerns the implications of women's marginal presence on the Internet, as compared with that of men. Should we be surprised that surveys show greater numbers of male users than female users? Is this a result, as the popular media concludes, of female fears, both of technology and on-line harassment? I think not, for reasons I will discuss in the first part of this chapter.

The second issue involves burning questions about free speech versus protection from harassment and unwelcome pornography. Legislative and public efforts to regulate the Internet have sparked a national controversy over the last few years: To censor or not to censor? With help from lawyer Donna Axel, I address this question in the second half of this chapter.

### CLAIMING SPACE

*The Internet was 84.5% male and 82.3% white. Until now.*

—Guerrilla Girls poster, found at the GG Web site

*The Internet was 84.5% male and 82.3% white. So what?*

—Response to the poster, found at the GG Web site

In the books, articles, and on-line conversations on women and *cyberspace* with which I'm familiar, three questions tend to guide the discussions:

1. How many women are using the Internet?
2. Is it safe for women on-line?
3. How are women occupying the space of cyberspace, both as individuals and collectively?

The third question, more than the first two, motivated me to write this book, because it asks us to consider the qualitative experience of women's Internet presence, both as creators and users of electronic resources. We may represent less than 50 percent of Internet users, according to the statistics, but there's nothing marginal about women's demonstrated technical mastery of Net tools and resource offerings. Moreover, the numbers are changing so rapidly that no one can pin down the ratio of women to men users for more than a month at a time. With regard to sexual harassment, the incidents are more uncommon than common, and more predictable in certain locations than in others. In addition, as described in part 1, chapter 4, there are numerous ways to face-off against harassment and abuse on the Net. Thus, when we consider women's presence on the Internet only in numbers, or only in terms of the sexual harassment being enacted on computer screens, we risk allowing the real subject—*women users*—to become obscured.

Until recently, both the statistics on women's on-line presence and the media portrayal of women in cyberspace have underscored our marginality in the world of electronic communications. However, the numbers do not indicate how women *use* the Internet. Why does a woman go on-line? What kinds of information are specifically designed to inform her life? Who are the hard-working women generating the Net's content on behalf of their gender?

As the lists of resources presented in this book reveal, women can be found everywhere on the Net; there's nothing obscure about how we claim space and use it to our benefit. Especially in academia, women have been developing and making use of Internet resources for more than a decade. Already a vast store of women-oriented resources exists on-line, and it is growing rapidly. Increasingly, women's advocates are making ingenious use of the Net as a tool for addressing women's personal and social needs.

The statistics also don't tell us, nor does the media investigate, whether the Internet's gender imbalance might be a result of unequal *access* to the technology. Who has access and who doesn't? According to a survey conducted by the Institute for Research on Women and Gender at Columbia University, professors and students point out that access is determined by class, "which is intersected by gender and ethnic differences" (*Feminist News* 13 [October 1995], 3). Debra Floyd tells us in her chapter on resources for women of African descent (part 2, chapter 6), it shouldn't surprise us that traditionally underserved populations are underrepresented on the Internet. And the most underserved populations in this country are poor people, people of color, and, of course, women.

The results of a survey in early 1995 showed that only 10 percent of U.S. Internet users were women (Georgia Tech Institute, GVU's Fourth Annual WWW User Survey, http://www.cc.gatech.edu/gvu/user_surveys/). Fortunately, as concerns the numbers of women using the Net, demand may be stimulating supply. With every new survey of women's usage, the statistics show rapid growth in some areas—as well as a daunting lack of growth in others. The fall 1995 survey by the Institute for Research on Women and Gender revealed several important trends.

• Women's Internet presence was up to 29.3 percent. Of Web users, women represented 32.5 percent. The increase, however, occurred largely in college students and in K-12 educators.

• There are more women Web users between the ages of 16 to 20 years old than men: women in this age group represent 14.2 percent of all users, while men represent 11.5 percent. In the older age groups, however, men still outnumber women.

• The percentage of female users drops significantly when university-affiliated Internet users are not counted in such surveys. According to the Institute, "There is more gender equality in 'net' use within universities than on the commercial  services and in government."

• Notwithstanding the gender imbalance on the Net, U.S. women are being integrated into the Net user population faster than are women in other countries.

These last two statistics reinforce the point about access. Where women have greater access to electronic communications—for example, in school or university settings, or in industrialized countries in general—they use it in greater numbers. The final statistic also demonstrates, once again, the power of women's solidarity. The most outstanding reason that more and more North American women are being integrated into the Internet population is that a wide range of training and mentoring programs, managed by and for women, have gained popularity across the country in the last two years. With clever names like Technomama, Webgrrls, Spiderwoman, and Webmistresses Unite!, these in-person and on-line training workshops and support groups are making the Internet accessible and tangible for increasing numbers of women. In addition, new community programs, such as the Community Technology Centers' Network, are bringing the technology into low-income districts in cities throughout the United States. While none of these programs represents an effective solution to the gender, race, and class discrimination that permeates the computer and telecommunications industries, women's dedication to bringing women and other underserved populations on-line has greatly contributed to an increase in the numbers of users and technical developers from those populations.

The integration of women's expertise into all aspects of the Internet's development is the next step for women to take. Women's experience and knowledge need to influence prevailing approaches to regulation and free speech, content, usage, technological innovations—in other words, the combined ingredients that create what Cheris Kramarae, a spokesperson for the ad hoc group Women, Information Technology, and Scholarship calls "an hospitable communication environment." That would require strategic planning and collective organizing, at the levels of both user and technician.

The issues around which women might organize have now crystallized. Statistics need not stop us; they are constantly shifting, and we have power to make them shift even faster. Harassment may censor women in the immediate sense, but not over the long term—unless we allow it to. There is work to be done by those of us who want to advocate and influence the inner workings and long-range evolution of electronic communications to serve human needs, including the need for a democratic, participatory communications culture. The Internet's potential to enrich women's social position everywhere in the world is manifest. We should not underestimate its power—our power, on-line.

> Women and girls should have integral roles in the conception, design, content, use, implementation, economics, and legal policies of electronic communications networks on a local, national, and international level. The current user mix, along with a social environment which discourages female usage of electronic networks, continues to exacerbate the gender gap and has put females at a stunning disadvantage. Women are vastly underrepresented as designers, users, and contributors on the electronic networks. Our goal is an hospitable communication environment for *all* users.
>
> —CHERIS KRAMARAE
> Women, Information Technology, and Scholarship (WITS)

## CENSORSHIP IN CYBERSPACE

In the world of cyberspace, few issues are as thorny or divisive as the issue of government regulation and censorship of the Internet. Individual Internet communities—various networks or discussion groups, for example—have long wielded guidelines which exclude certain types of content. But the question of general government restrictions on the free-flowing communication that takes place over the Internet is another question altogether. Donna K. Axel, an attorney working in the area of human rights, contributed the following discussion of Internet censorship issues.

The issue of whether the Internet should be regulated—and if so, how—has stirred up the legislators, incensed free speech advocates, and divided women.

Many legislators are using the issue of pornography on the Internet to justify far-reaching regulation of the Net. Consequently, the courts have been asked to weigh the need to restrict certain obscene materials on the Internet against First Amendment guarantees of free expression, as well as against the privacy concerns of both individual users and business enterprises.

In 1995 the U.S. Congress passed the Communications Decency Act, increasing government regulatory power over the Internet. In June of 1996, a panel of federal judges granted a preliminary injunction against the law, ruling it an unconstitutional restriction on free speech. The judges likened communication over the Internet to conversations, which are well-protected by the First Amendment, rather than to broadcasting, which is subject to considerable government restrictions. (It's legal to say just about anything on the telephone, but many types of words and images are banned from television and radio.) As long as communication over the Internet is principally characterized as conversation, the highest level of legal protection will be afforded users, including those who upload pornography (with the exception of child pornography, which is banned under distinct laws).

While the Justice Department has plans to appeal the judges' decision to the U.S. Supreme Court, it seems likely that the Court would find the law unconstitutional, since it is not likely to revise its earlier view that pornography is speech, protected under the First Amendment.

In any case, legislative efforts to monitor Internet communications are, in practical terms, a bit outlandish, since any attempt at regulation would require a censorship board to evaluate the content of each and every document before it is uploaded. This would require massive government intervention. The Internet is a vast collection of mainly private computer networks, connecting millions of users in an estimated 150 countries. There are more than seventy thousand private computer bulletin board systems in the United States, and even more private business networks. Material uploaded at any of these millions of sites would need to be subject to review by government regulators. Thus, any attempt to regulate communication on the Internet would threaten not only the First Amendment rights of users, but also their essential privacy rights.

Government regulation would, in effect, take the Internet out of the hands of the everyday users and undermine the existing communities which are the backbone of the Net. And since the proposed regulatory legislation was first introduced, these communities have been mobilizing to oppose the legislation.

Donna Axel is on the mark. The government is already waging new battles that undermine free speech. One example is the campaign to ban *encryption,* which is the means of encoding messages by using algorithms, thus making the messages incomprehensible to anyone who does not know the secret code. (For more on encryption, see part 1, chapter 9.) Since all *e-mail* can be intercepted, software programs have been designed that can encrypt your e-mail and protect your privacy, though none of these programs is yet foolproof.

There are two specific items here—encryption and freedom of speech. Last year [1995], Congress passed the Communications Decency Act, after very little debate. It was censorship, pure and simple. Fortunately, last month [June 1996] a Federal appeals court ruled the law unconstitutional. God bless those judges. They came in knowing little about the Net, but they opened their minds and said that the Internet was more like a soapbox than television and much more democratic.

As for encryption, the Government keeps trying to do what governments naturally do: control people. They would like to ban encryption to make it easier for law enforcement to listen in on people. In principle, all they want to do is stop crime. But the fact is encryption is defensive technology against big government, big business, big crime. I'd rather have defensive technology than leave the power to snoop in the hands of people I might not trust. Basically, the intelligence community wants this.

—ESTHER DYSON
EDventures and Electronic Frontiers Foundation
(from "The Cyber-Maxims of Esther Dyson," interview with Claudia Dreifus,
*The New York Times Magazine,* 7 July 1996, 16–17)

The attempts to ban encryption are certainly relevant to women users, especially those of us who use the Internet for professional and advocacy purposes. Imagine that your rape counseling and prevention center is collecting personal information from domestic violence victims on-line. Or that you are organizing abortion clinics nationwide via the Net to combat violent assaults on clinics. If your on-line communications was denied the protection afforded by encryption and could be easily intercepted, you might think twice before choosing to conduct your research or lobbying activities on-line. The same work might be carried out by some combination of telephoning and postal mail—but not necessarily as quickly, affordably, or effectively. The potential prohibition of encryption threatens women's freedom to communicate on-line privately and safely. We need to add our voices to those in opposition.

Likewise, freedom of speech in cyberspace is a women's issue. While there is misogynistic pornography available on the Internet, and while many women are understandably appalled by its existence, the solution does not lie in allowing government to censor the Internet on our behalf.

A government that manipulates the pornography debate to argue for regulation, and thereby the protection of women and children, might also exploit other issues that make women vulnerable, such as on-line harassment. And regulation, as a means to counter sexual harassment, would only replace one form of censorship with another. Neither is sympathetic to women's on-line experience and needs.

Free speech, free expression, and free association inspire the widespread use of the Internet everywhere in the world. These freedoms are more, not less, essential to traditionally disempowered citizens like people of color and women, and it is in our interest to take an active role in preserving them.

A more conscious approach to ensuring freedom of speech, and the rights and responsibilities associated with it, is the next task at hand. Rather than continually react to government interference, we might act more expediently to resolve the problems and challenges that participation in virtual reality produces. How we approach the problems that are of particular relevance to women will help legitimize and expand our on-line presence. At the same time, in the way that the particular sheds light on the general, our articulated concerns will also help untangle the complicated issues that all free speech advocates are struggling with. Women's on-line experience, from the satisfying to the problematic, has the potential to validate and strengthen the general campaign for free speech on-line. Our contributions might make us indispensable.

Voters Telecommunications Watch posts regular updates on Internet-related legislation in the U.S. Congress. To receive postings, send the e-mail message `subscribe vtw-announce Firstname Lastname` to `listproc@vtw.org`.

# Part 2

# THE RESOURCES

The Internet's decentralized nature can make searching for information a tedious task. Conventional key locations such as libraries, which catalog old documents and new ones, simply don't exist. Search engines help you locate materials but no one engine contains files of everything to be found on-line. In addition, new sites are created every day, and there is no easy method for keeping track of them. Joan Korenman, who has been tracking gender resources on the Net since 1991, emphasizes:

> I think both women and men need better resources for finding and evaluating information. Though I value the Internet for its potential to empower, I'm finding that as more and more people develop Web sites and other on-line resources, it becomes harder to sort through them all to find sites offering truly useful, up-to-date, and reliable information. I think it's especially important that information targeted to women be accurate. Many women have been brought up to be fearful of technology. If they try to send messages to an e-mail list or access a Web site and fail because the information is no longer correct, they may decide that they've done something wrong and that they simply aren't cut out for this sort of thing.

The purpose of this resource directory is, in part, to help women gain the confidence to explore the wired world by providing a large annotated list of high-quality "entry points," with clear information on how to access each one and helpful comments and tips. The directory contains useful information for women with a diversity of backgrounds, racial and ethnic heritages, physical abilities, sexual orientations, political orientations, occupations, lifestyles, and geographical locations.

To prepare this section, I polled hundreds of women from diverse backgrounds to learn what subjects they would want to access on the Internet, and gave each subject its own chapter within this section, so the user can maximize her use of information and services available on each of thirteen subjects.

Each chapter has subcategories on the featured subject and lists the best resources for each category. By "best," I mean those resources that are excellent starting points for exploring each category, with easy-to-follow links to other facilities. Some are lively support groups, which will give the user a healthy sampling of how discussions proceed on-line. Others are bibliographies, articles, and periodicals on a given subject. Still others are Web sites or mailing lists created by key organizations, which can offer expert information and advice. All of the resources were selected with the aim of helping the user make the most of her time and energy while at the same time encouraging her to confidently explore additional sites.

Each listing includes the tool and address needed to access the resource, along with additional comments and description. In some chapters, sidebars illustrate the kinds of information found at a particular site. Quoted commentary comes directly from the creators of the sites.

The information in part 2 is drawn from the recommendations of a group of co-researchers—women who create the resources, use them regularly, and professionally analyze their value. We used eleven criteria for deciding which resources would be listed in each category:

1. Will women from diverse class, race, and ethnic backgrounds find resources that take into account their specific high- or low-income and multicultural needs and preferences?

2. Are the resources drawn from local, national, and international sources?

3. Does each chapter enable the user to use a variety of tools and protocols for accessing an array of topics and subtopics?

4. Is the menu easy to understand?

5. Are there links to other sites? Did the creator of the resource take the time to develop other links?

6. Does a World Wide Web site make effective use of graphics or is it primarily text-based?

7. Is the Gopher easy to maneuver? Are the directions clear?

8. Is the newsgroup excessively flaming? Does it stay focused on the topic? Is it sexist, racist, or otherwise offensive? (Newsgroups are not moderated.)

9. Is a mailing list/Listserv well moderated?

10. Do the tools and facilities provide quality information?

11. Are the resources true to their subject titles?

Each chapter provides both women-oriented and general information on a particular subject. For example, the chapter on health resources covers reproductive health care and breast self-exams, as well as physical disabilities and arthritis.

Many resources could have fit into more than one chapter, and sometimes it was difficult to decide where a resource should be placed. For example, lesbian parenting is in chapter 5, family resources, but it could just as easily been in chapter 8, lesbian resources. So if you don't find what you're looking for right away, check the subject index for other possible locations.

Please remember that Web sites and other locations change addresses or close down yearly if not more frequently. New sites are opened every day. In order to keep updated on changes and additions, or to let us know about a favorite site missing from this book, please refer to The Feminist Press's brand new Web site, at http:\\www.ccny.cuny.edu\fempress\wiredworld. Meet you there!

# 1

# PUTTING GENDER ON THE AGENDA
Women's Resources and Organizations in the United States

*An eddy of estrogen in the vast sea of testosterone that is the Internet.*
—from Leslie's World Of Chicks http://www.gslis.utexas.edu/~ldevlin/woc.html

As I explored the Internet for this chapter's resources, I began to notice the many ways in which women operate in *cyberspace.* From computer to computer to computer, women use *telecommunications* to assert their autonomy, claim territory, exchange information, hone a marketable skill, and express their visions of global harmony. The Net, it seems, is both a safe and fertile space for women—to experiment with voice, to create community, to advocate for a cause, to come out, to hang out. Some, especially younger women, are staking their own space and proudly (sometimes literally) calling it their own. You'll probably discover, as I did, women's *Web sites* with names such as Amy's Obsession, Beth Lapides' Un-Cabaret, Chelle's Cozy Corner, Gopher Donna, Lichto's Land, Linda Brookover's Queens Site, and Nikki Craft's Homepage. In addition, some women seem to be experimenting with the medium to reinvent themselves, such as those who have created Web sites called Cyber-Sappho, Geekgirl, Net Chick, Nrrd Grrl, Ratgrrl's Hideout, and Sassyfem.

The creators of sites like Ratgrrl and Sassyfem know their technology and how to market themselves in a commercial, not quite literary world. These young women who are spending their free time developing Web sites are not using their modems to cruise for guys and score a date. They are trying (and, granted, sometimes trying too hard) to make the Internet a hip, appealing place for women to be.

Of course, the offerings for women go far beyond satisfying individuation processes, as you'll notice in the array of resources that I've selected for this chapter. Some of the oldest feminist organizations in the United States have well-developed, highly informative Web sites, such as the Feminist Majority and NOW (although Ellie Smeal and Patricia Ireland aren't doing the uploading themselves). Some of the best support groups for women in academia and in business are on-line, such as WMST-L (Women's Studies Listserv) and MBA-Women (Women with MBA degrees Listserv). Today you can find the self-help health classic *Our Bodies, Our Selves* on the Net, as well as Women's White Pages (a directory of women-owned businesses) and Women's Web Magazine, which addresses a wide range of interests. The most prevalent kinds of on-line resources to be found cater to improving women's quality of life, such as Feminist Activist Resources on the Net, Gender Equity in Sports, Internet Resources for Women's Legal and Public

Policy Information, Women's Feature Service, Women's Health Issues, and Women's Political Hotline.

In this chapter, you'll find an assortment of resources focusing largely on social issues of relevance to women. Women's advocacy organizations have made ample and ingenious use of the Internet to campaign, build coalitions, distribute news alerts, and link to like-minded groups across the United States. Included in this chapter are listings of women's nongovernmental organizations (NGOs), hotlines, policy research institutes, grassroots groups, and government agencies, divided into the following categories:

- The arts
- Campus activism
- Directories of women's organizations and search engines
- Economic discrimination
- The environment
- Feminism

- General resources for activists
- Legal and policy issues
- Networks
- Other women's spaces
- Politics
- Reproductive freedom
- Violence against women

## A REMINDER ABOUT LISTSERVS AND MAILING LISTS

Lists with Listserv or Listproc addresses are managed with automated software. To subscribe to such a list, send this message to the address given: SUBSCRIBE Listname Firstname Lastname "Listname" is the name of the list, and "Firstname Lastname" is your real name, not your userid. Lists with a Majordomo address use a similar message, minus your name unless otherwise instructed. For other lists, follow the instructions given. If you have problems sending messages to a list, ask your system provider's support staff for help.

—JOAN KORENMAN
Creator of Gender Related Electronic Forums and WMST-L

Over the last few years, feminist and women-oriented resources have proliferated. You'll find that some are underdeveloped, which may result from the fact that some organizations do not yet devote full-time labor to their on-line activities. Many sites are repetitive, making you feel like you're circling through the same list of names and addresses over and over again. Obviously, it's still a new field and still under construction as numerous Web sites forewarn. The electronic offerings included here belong to what I think of as a "first generation" of resources and services. I've assembled those I consider the most focused and thorough, and the easiest to learn from and navigate. I suggest starting with a Web *home page* of one of the women's service providers, such as WomensNet or Women's Wire, to understand how information is categorized and the links established.

## THE ARTS

| | |
|---|---|
| *What* | **CYBER-SISTERS** |
| *How* | Mailing list |
| *Where* | Send the message SUBSCRIBE.CYBER-SISTERS to MAJORDOMO@PMEDIA.COM to subscribe. |
| *Comments* | Unmoderated list for women in the arts who use the Internet for artistic exploration and also meet here to network with other women in the arts. |

| | |
|---|---|
| *What* | **International Alliance for Women in Music** |
| *How* | Listserv |
| *Where* | Send the one-word message SUBSCRIBE to IAWM-REQUEST@ACUVAX.ACU.EDU to subscribe. |
| *Comments* | List for members of the IAWM and for musical women interested in joining. |

| | |
|---|---|
| *What* | **Women Artists Archive** |
| *How* | Web |
| *Where* | http://www.sonoma.edu/library/waa |
| *Comments* | Contains information on more than one thousand women artists from the Middle Ages to the present. Located at Sonoma State University, California. |

| | |
|---|---|
| *What* | **Women in Theater** |
| *How* | Listserv |
| *Where* | Send message to LISTSERV@UHCCVM.UHCC.HAWAII.EDU to subscribe. |
| *Comments* | Forum for artists and scholars on feminism, race, sexualities, class, and gender, as related to theater and performance. |

| | |
|---|---|
| *What* | **Women Writers and Artists** |
| *How* | Listserv |
| *Where* | Send the message SUBSCRIBE WWA-L Firstname Lastname to LISTSERV@PSUVM.PSU.EDU to subscribe. |
| *Comments* | Discussion forum for women on creativity. |

| | |
|---|---|
| *What* | **Women's Studio Workshop** |
| *How* | Web |
| *Where* | http://www.webmark.com/wsw/wswhome.html |
| *Comments* | Provides information about the Studio Workshop, a not-for-profit artists' organization that provides workspace for artists; grants, fellowships, and exhibition opportunities for visual artists; and a Summer Arts Institute. |

## CAMPUS ACTIVISM

| | |
|---|---|
| *What* | **Campus Green Vote** |
| *How* | Web |
| *Where* | http://www.agc.apc.org/cgv/ |
| *Comments* | CGV is a not-for-profit, nonpartisan project of the Center for Environmental Citizenship to train and organize a national network of young voting environmentalists. There are offerings such as Green Your Campus, Green the Government, Blueprint for a Green Campus, and an Activist Profile Network. |

**Q:** As electronic communications becomes increasingly popular in the United States, how should women be thinking about its use?

**A:** We should get out there and become a presence. We should encourage all the women we know, whether feminist or not, to get on-line and not feel intimidated, either by the technology or by any weirdos they meet on-line (whatever their definition of "weirdo" may be). We should develop links with each other, both on-line and in real life. There needs to be a sense that there are just as many kinds of women, and feminists, on-line as there are in the real world. Global connections between feminist groups should be enhanced. Maybe we could have periodic check-in's to a Web site, on different issues, and do the following:

1. Generate letter or e-mail campaigns where a women's issue is under attack
2. Keep tabs on how our government and each other's governments are keeping up with the Beijing conference's Platform for Action
3. Coordinate media campaigns on women's issues
4. Hook up women's groups that have access to electronic communications with those that don't

—SONIA JAFFE ROBBINS
NEWW On-Line, New York

| | |
|---|---|
| *What* | **CAN-YFN (Campus Activists' Network, Young Feminist Network)** |
| *How* | Mailing list |
| *Where* | Send message to CANET@PENCL.MATH.MISSOURI.EDU to subscribe. Type canet for subject header; type SUB CAN-YFN Firstname Lastname in the body of the message. |
| *Comments* | Ongoing discussion among feminist activists at U.S. universities. |
| *What* | **CCOAR (Coalition of Campus Organizations Addressing Rape)** |
| *How* | Mailing list |
| *Where* | Send message to ERIBET@ORION.OAC.UCI.EDU. Type subscription in the subject heading; in the message include your name, e-mail address, and the four- to eight-letter password you want to use. |

*Comments*    Moderated discussion list for activists, educators, and researchers working against
rape. Includes conference and event announcements, job listings, discussions of rape
education advocacy, and research. Subscribers will be approved by the listowners.

*Tidbit*    When you subscribe, specify whether you want to receive the list's daily messages
in one big post.

*What*    **Progressive Student Network**

*How*    Gopher

*Where*    `gopher://fr.cic.net:70/11/Politics/ProgStudNet`

*Comments*    Information on the Progressive Student Network, a national network of student
groups founded in 1980 at Kent State University dedicated to social and political
change. Includes information about about PSN's activities: conferences, meetings,
caucuses, publications, actions, and demonstrations.

## DIRECTORIES OF WOMEN'S ORGANIZATIONS AND SEARCH ENGINES

*What*    **Feminist Internet Gateway**

*How*    Web

*Where*    `http://www.feminist.org/gateway/master.html`

*Comments*    Lists fifty-five organizations, each with an established Internet presence, and pro-
vides their e-mail addresses. Includes American Medical Women's Association,
League of Women Voters, Ms. Foundation, NOW, Planned Parenthood, SisterLove,
Women Against a Violent Environment, Women and Rural Economic Development,
WHAM! and Women Leaders Online.

*What*    **Directory of Women's Professional Organizations**

*How*    Web

*Where*    `http://www.feminist.org/gateway/womenorg.html`

*Comments*    Approximately ninety listings of business, law, medical, philanthropical, and sports
organizations. Full addresses minus e-mail. Developed by the Feminist Majority
Foundation.

*What*    **The Electra Pages**

*How*    Web

*Where*    `http://electrapages.com/`

*Comments*    Seven thousand resources from the database of the Women's Information Exchange,
which also brought us the National Women's Mailing List. Organized in four different ways: geographic location; type of organization/business/service; geographic
location and type of organization; alphabetic listing.

*What*    **Femina**

*How*    Web

*Where*    `http://www.femina.com/`

| | |
|---|---|
| *Comments* | Aliza Sherman of Cybergrrls developed this extensive directory of organizations and resources arranged into nineteen categories, with approximately eighty to one hundred topics per category. Links include Art, Business and Finance, Computer and Science, Education, Entertainment, Family, Girls, Health, Religion, Shopping and Products, Sports and Fitness. New listings are added daily. A truly impressive search engine, well-conceived and always helpful. |
| *Tidbit* | Aliza Sherman can be contacted at `asherman@interport.net`. |
| *What* | **Feminist Activist Resources on the Internet** |
| *How* | Web |
| *Where* | `http://www.igc.apc.org/women/activist/femresou.html` |
| *Comments* | Well known as the most complete listing of activist resources and organizations. Developed by Sarah Stapleton Gray (`sarahg@netcom.com` or `http://www.clark.net/pub/s.gray/sarah.html`), who has become the Internet manager for NOW. |
| *What* | **Gender-Related Electronic Forums** |
| *How* | Web |
| *Where* | `http://www-unix.umbc.edu/~korenman/wmst/forums.html` |
| *Comments* | Probably the most developed listing of academic, professional, and activist mailing lists and Listservs for the United States and internationally. Regularly updated, thoughtful, extensive. Its creator, Joan Korenman, is heroic! |
| *Tidbits* | Korenman depends on many sources of information to maintain the Gender Related Electronic Forum. From time to time, she says, "I'll run searches on Liszt, a search engine with probably the largest database devoted to e-mail lists." She also welcomes suggestions and information from individuals and invites you to notify her of additions or changes at `korenman@umbc2.umbc.edu`. |

**Q:** What kinds of resources for women need to be better developed?

**A:** There need to be more resources for women not affiliated with an academic institution or private business, which often provide training, Internet access, and technical support for their employees and students. Women who work part-time jobs without benefits, or who work at home, will not have the taken-for-granted exposure to electronic communications that teachers, students, and full-time professionals enjoy. What is needed are more public-access terminals in local libraries, women's shelters, senior citizen centers, and the like. Hand-in-hand with the equipment and Internet accounts must be free or low-cost training and technical support, offered in the same public arenas.

—NINA BETH HUNTEMANN
University of Massachusetts, Amherst

| | |
|---|---|
| *What* | **National Women's Mailing List** |
| *How* | E-mail |
| *Where* | wie@wco.com |
| *Comments* | Created by the Women's Information Exchange, NWML has been part of the communications backbone of the women's movement for more than fifteen years. Individuals register in the areas in which they want to get mail, then grassroots feminist and progressive organizations reach them via postal mailings. |

| | |
|---|---|
| *What* | **Search Directory on Women's Resources** |
| *How* | Web |
| *Where* | http://wwwomen.com/ |
| *Comments* | The self-proclaimed "premier search directory"—and indeed, it is, with listings and links to everyone and everything associated with improving women's personal, professional, and public lives. |

## ECONOMIC DISCRIMINATION

> *"The ceiling isn't glass; it's a very dense layer of men."*
>
> —ANNE JARDIM

| | |
|---|---|
| *What* | **Dataline** |
| *How* | Web; Gopher |
| *Where* | http://www.cyberwerks.com/dataline for Web site; gopher://cyberwerks.com:70/11/dataline for Gopher site |
| *Comments* | Reports on current and seminal glass ceiling cases in the United States. Includes articles on "Mapping the Glass Ceiling," "Three Levels of the Glass Ceiling," "Women and the Law," and "Women Rising in Management." |

| | |
|---|---|
| *What* | **FEMCON-L (Feminist Economists)** |
| *How* | Mailing list |
| *Where* | Send message to LISTSERV@BUCKNELL.BUCKNELL.EDU to subscribe. |
| *Comments* | Discussion/support group for feminist economists. |

| | |
|---|---|
| *What* | **Women and Economic Issues** |
| *How* | Web |
| *Where* | http://www.igc.apc.org/women/activist/work.html |
| *Comments* | Part of WomensNet; has very useful links to the Women's Bureau at the U.S. Department of Labor, Supreme Court cases dealing with the Equal Pay Act, assistance programs for homeless women, and the Prostitutes' Education Network, among others. Definitely worth touring. |

| | |
|---|---|
| *What* | **Women's Bureau, U.S. Department of Labor** |
| *How* | Web |

| | |
|---|---|
| *Where* | http://gatekeeper.dol.gov/dol/wb |
| *Comments* | Information about the Women's Bureau, its programs and activities, fact sheets, press releases, and special reports. |

| | |
|---|---|
| *What* | **WOMENWORK** |
| *How* | Listserv |
| *Where* | Send message SUBSCRIBE WOMENWORK to MAJORDOMO@HUMANISM.ORG to subscribe. |
| *Comments* | Discussion on women and work, economic empowerment in developing countries, economic hardship/crisis. |

## THE ENVIRONMENT

| | |
|---|---|
| *What* | **ECOFEM (Women and the Environment)** |
| *How* | Mailing list |
| *Where* | Send message to LISTSERV@CSF.COLORADO.EDU to subscribe. |
| *Comments* | Discussions on women and the environment, from the local to the global. Includes grassroots activism, legislative advocacy, treaties and conventions, publications, course syllabi, and events announcements. |

| | |
|---|---|
| *What* | **Feminists for Animal Rights** |
| *How* | Web |
| *Where* | http://envirolink.org/arrs/far/home.html |
| *Comments* | Information from FAR, a national educational organization dedicated to ending abuse against women and animals, between which the groups' advocates find many interconnections. Explains where the group stands on the testing of animals to further AIDS research and many other issues. |

In April 1993, when a nuclear accident occurred in Tomsk, Russia, releasing radioactivity into the atmosphere, local officials released very little information about the event. Local activists, who happened to be meeting in Tomsk with colleagues from all over Russia at that time, quickly traveled to the affected area, gathered accurate details about what had happened and made the information widely available through the e-mail network.

—LYNN RICHARDS
Surviving Together, ISAR

| | |
|---|---|
| *What* | **SEAC+WOMYN (Student Environmental Action Coalition)** |
| *How* | Mailing list |
| *Where* | Send message to LISTPROC@ECOSYS.DRDR.VIRGINIA.EDU to subscribe; type SUBSCRIBE SEAC+WOMYN Firstname Lastname in the body of the message. |
| *Comments* | Women's environmental activist list, organized by the Student Environmental Action Coalition. |

## FEMINISM

| | |
|---|---|
| *What* | **ABIGAILS-L** |
| *How* | Mailing list |
| *Where* | Send the message `SUBSCRIBE ABIGAILS-L` to `LISTSERV@NETCOM.COM` to subscribe. |
| *Comments* | Feminist activist discussion list on gaining full and equal rights through immediate actions. Evolved from the `Beijing95-Women` list. |

| | |
|---|---|
| *What* | **Bridges** |
| *How* | Listserv |
| *Where* | Send message to `LISTSERV@ISRAEL.NYSERNET.ORG` to subscribe. |
| *Comments* | Moderated list on Jewish feminist identity and activism. |

| | |
|---|---|
| *What* | **Cybergrrl Webstation** |
| *How* | Web |
| *Where* | `http://www.cybergrrl.com` |
| *Comments* | Cybergrrl creator Aliza Sherman developed this visually entertaining and informative guide to women's political and personal resources, from SafetyNet, a compendium of domestic violence resources, to Sneakergrrls, a personal fitness and health "library," to Webgrrls, listings of local groups and classes for women techies and users. If you become a Webgrrl (or boyyy), Aliza will make a link to your Web site. Cybergrrl looks like Supergirl's younger sister. |
| *Tidbit* | Sherman's creations are produced under the rubric of Cybergrrl Internet Media, her developer of interactive content and communities on the Internet, World Wide Web, and commercial on-line services. |

| | |
|---|---|
| *What* | **FEM-ALERT** |
| *How* | Mailing list |
| *Where* | Send the message `SUBSCRIBE FEM-ALERT` to `MAJORDOMO@FEMINIST.ORG` to subscribe. |
| *Comments* | Created by the Feminist Majority to provide regular information on key feminist issues and on Feminist Majority's Web developments. |

| | |
|---|---|
| *What* | **Feminism Fun and Games** |
| *How* | Web |
| *Where* | `http://www.igc.apc.org/women/feminist.html` |
| *Comments* | Refers you to on-line feminist humor, science fiction, comics, and film reviews. Could be more fun and gamey. |

| | |
|---|---|
| *What* | **Feminist Majority and the Feminist Majority Foundation** |
| *How* | Web |

*Where*  http://www.feminist.org/welcome/1_fmf.html

*Comments*  A testament to this more than twenty-year-old institution's ability to keep abreast of technological as well as political currents, and use them to strategic advantage. The Feminist Majority has always strived to win women's equality through research and effective action, and it has now developed a strong Internet presence, with quality graphics and numerous links to other feminist organizations and pertinent topics, to help accomplish its goals. The group's sophisticated on-line offerings reflect the organization's dedication to effectively transmitting its message.

*What*  **FEMINISTS**

*How*  Mailing list

*Where*  Send the e-mail message SUBSCRIBE FEMINISTS FIRSTNAME LASTNAME to LISTPROC@ECHNYCC.COM to subscribe.

*Comments*  Ongoing discussion on feminist issues.

*What*  **Guerrilla Girls**

*How*  Web

*Where*  http://www.voyagerco.com/gg/

*Comments*  The Guerrilla Girls are a world-renowned group of women artists and art professionals who, over the last ten years, have been making posters about discrimination. "We wear gorilla masks to focus on the issues rather than on our personalities. . . . The mystery surrounding our identities has attracted attention and support. We could be anyone; we are everywhere." GG's site contains three main categories: "Expose Yourself," "Love/Hate Mail," and "Posters." The group's posters, on- or off-line, and its Web graphics are divine examples of feminist humor.

*Tidbit*  Try reading e-mail the Guerrilla Girls receive in their regularly updated mailbox: GuerrillaGirls@voyagerco.com. Then send them a message yourself!

*What*  **Jewish Feminist Resources**

*How*  Web

*Where*  http://world.std.com/~alevin/jewishfeminist.html

*Comments*  Not for nice Jewish girls only, this site provides assorted links to Jewish feminist and lesbian topics as well as to cultural and religious sites, Jewish history and organizations worldwide, education, scholarships, and publications. Heavy on text, low on graphics.

*What*  **Leslie's World Of Chicks**

*How*  Web

*Where*  http://www.gslis.utexas.edu/~ldevlin/woc.html

*Comments*  In 1996 Leslie Devlin's World Of Chicks was number three on the Whole Internet Catalog's Top fifty List, and understandably so. It is funny, informative, and graphically sophisticated—a pleasure to surf.

| | |
|---|---|
| *Tidbit* | Contact Leslie Devlin—also known as America's other favorite redhead—at `ldevlin@gslis.utexas.edu`. |
| *What* | **National Organization for Women (NOW)** |
| *How* | Web |
| *Where* | `http://now.org/now/home/html` or `http://www.now.org/` |
| *Comments* | The home page presents NOW's main links to Fight the Right, Take Action, Key Issues, News, Contacts, and Info. Contains reports and legislative updates on affirmative action, abortion, economic equity, electoral politics, racial and ethnic diversity, and violence against women. Few graphics; some links more developed than others. |

- Because of sex discrimination, women are paid less than 75 cents for every dollar men are paid for full-time employment, and most employed women are self-supporting heads of households or necessary contributors to a family income.

- Millions of older women are condemned to lives of poverty because the Social Security system perpetuates this injustice; women over sixty-five average less than 60 percent of what men average in annual social security income.

- Female-headed families in the U.S. are four times as likely to be poor as male-headed or couple-headed families. According to the National Advisory Council on Economic Opportunity, at the present rate, five years from now the poor will be made up almost entirely of women and children. NOW refers to this phenomenon as "the feminization of poverty."

—From NOW's General Information Page
`http://www.now.org/`

| | |
|---|---|
| *What* | **Feminism Resource File** |
| *How* | FTP |
| *Where* | `ftp://rtfm.mit.edu/pub/usenet/news.answers/feminism/resources` |
| *Comments* | Resource file for the newsgroup `soc.feminism`; links to organizations, publications, bibliographies, and other sources that appear in the newsgroup. |
| *What* | **Third Wave: Young Feminist Activists** |
| *How* | Web |
| *Where* | `http://www.feminism.com/thirdwave.html` |
| *Comments* | Home page of Third Wave, a member-driven national nonprofit organization devoted to young feminist activism for social change. |
| *What* | **Virtual Estrogen: Because there isn't enough of it in real time** |
| *How* | Web |
| *Where* | `http://jupiter.rowan.edu/~aldr7850/` |
| *Comments* | Entertaining, visually pleasing, informative site, with links to a wide range of orga- |

nizations and subjects (i.e., Leslie's World Of Chicks, Blue Stocking, and the Global Fund for Women). You'll find links to Women and Computers, Domestic Violence, Feminist Homepages, Gender Issues, General Resources, Gay and Lesbian Rights, and Fun Links.

| | |
|---|---|
| *What* | **Women Online** |
| *How* | Web |
| *Where* | http://www.women-online.com/ |
| *Comments* | Created by Amy Goodloe; contains links to Internet resources, mailing lists, international news, and Web design promotion for women-owned businesses. A colorful guide to building Web sites. Wonderful animated graphics. |

| | |
|---|---|
| *What* | **WRAC-L (Women's Resource and Action Centers)** |
| *How* | Listserv |
| *Where* | Send message to LISTSERV@DARTMOUTH.EDU to subscribe. |
| *Comments* | Discusses issues and resources of relevance to women's centers, both freestanding and university-based. Open to staff and affiliates of women's centers. |

## GENERAL RESOURCES FOR ACTIVISTS

| | |
|---|---|
| *What* | **Activist Oasis** |
| *How* | Web |
| *Where* | http://www.workshop.matisse.net/~kathy/activist/tools.html |
| *Comments* | Great media tools, with links to news and journalism, U.S. government, state governments, political parties, and political sites on the Net. You can jump to CNN, AP services, Today's Internet News, and What's Up at the White House, among others. |
| *Tidbit* | Send comments and questions to Kathy Watkins at dtv@well.com. |

| | |
|---|---|
| *What* | **The Electronic Activist** |
| *How* | Web |
| *Where* | http://www.berkshire.net/~ifas/activist/ |
| *Comments* | Contains e-mail addresses for U.S. congressmembers, state legislators, and media. Click on a name and send a message from your Web browser. |

| | |
|---|---|
| *What* | **Fundlist** |
| *How* | Listserv |
| *Where* | Send the message SUBSCRIBE FUNDLIST FIRSTNAME LASTNAME to LISTPROC@LISTPROC.HCF.JHU.EDU to subscribe. |
| *Comments* | Discussion forum covering a wide range of fund-raising issues. |

| | |
|---|---|
| *What* | **Human Rights** |
| *How* | Usenet newsgroup |

| | |
|---|---|
| *Where* | soc.right.human |
| *Comments* | Ongoing discussions on human rights issues. |

| | |
|---|---|
| *What* | **Impact Online** |
| *How* | Web |
| *Where* | http://www.impactonline.org/ |
| *Comments* | Site of Impact Online, a not-for-profit organization that aims to foster community activism using telecommunications as an advocacy and organizing tool. Educational and informative, with great graphics, it will inspire you to imagine all kinds of uses for e-mail and other Internet tools, from staging a charity auction to choosing a volunteer management computer program. |

| | |
|---|---|
| *What* | **Meta-Index for Not-for-profit organizations** |
| *How* | Web |
| *Where* | http://www.duke.edu/~ptavern/pete.meta-index.html |
| *Comments* | Contains information on human rights, civil liberties and politics, health and human services, and the environment. Also links to some of the foremost lists of not-for-profit organizations and resources for not-for-profit groups and activists. Awarded the 1995 Best of Web Nonprofit Sites by Impact Online as well as the Magellan Four-Star Site award. |

| | |
|---|---|
| *What* | **Philanthropy Links** |
| *How* | Web |
| *Where* | http://www.duke.edu:80/~ptavern.pete.philanthropic.html |
| *Comments* | Provides resources for research and educational programs and Listservs on issues of social change. Also links to the Internet Nonprofit Center, the Philanthropic Initiative, the Foundation Center, and other philanthropic sources. |

| | |
|---|---|
| *What* | **Progressive Activitism** |
| *How* | Usenet newsgroup |
| *Where* | Misc.activitism.progressive |
| *Comments* | Information from progressive groups in the United States. |

| | |
|---|---|
| *What* | **Progressive and Nonprofit Organizations on the Net** |
| *How* | Web |
| *Where* | http://www.garnet.berkeley.edu:3333/progorgs/progorgs.html |
| *Comments* | Offers links to youth organizations and networks, socialist and left groups, environmental groups, gay organizations, women's rights organizations, and not-for-profit groups on-line. |

| | |
|---|---|
| *What* | **Web Active** |
| *How* | Web |

| | |
|---|---|
| *Where* | http://www.webactive.com |
| *Comments* | Information and links to all that's happening in on-line activism. |

## Additional Sites for Activists

- Amnesty International On-line: http://www.abanet.org
- Artists Against Racism: http://www.vrx.net/aar/
- Committee to Protect Journalists: gopher://gopher.igc.apc.org:5000/11/int/cpj
- The Human Rights Gopher: gopher://gopher.humanrights.org:5000/1
- Human Rights Watch: http://www.uottawa.ca/~hrrec/
- LaborNet: http://www.igc.apc.org/labornet/
- National Child Rights Alliance: http://www.ai.mit.edu/people/ellens. NCRA/ncra.html
- PeaceNet: http://www.peacenet.org/peacenet/
- Turn Left: http://www.cjnetworks.com/~cubsfan/liberal.html

## LEGAL AND POLICY ISSUES

| | |
|---|---|
| *What* | **American Civil Liberties Union** |
| *How* | Gopher |
| *Where* | gopher://gopher.aclu.org:6601/11/legislative |
| *Comments* | Includes congressional voting records and information about the ACLU and its work. |

| | |
|---|---|
| *What* | **Feminist.Com** |
| *How* | Web |
| *Where* | http://www.feminist.com/up.html |
| *Comments* | Finally, Feminist FaxNet (created by the Center for Advanced Policy), a weekly report on hot policy items from our nation's capital, has now acquired an on-line presence. Offers weekly news alerts and updates on policy issues and legislation of concern to women. The on-line site also offers postings from women-owned businesses, women's health resources, articles, and interviews. Serves as a home for many women's not-for-profit organizations. |

Voters Telecommunications Watch posts updates on Internet-related legislation in the U.S. Congress. To receive postings, send the e-mail message subscribe vtw-announce Firstname Lastname to listproc @vtw.org.

| | |
|---|---|
| *What* | **FEMJUR (Feminism and the Law)** |
| *How* | Mailing list |
| *Where* | Send message to LISTSERV@LISTSERV.SYR.EDU to subscribe. |

| | |
|---|---|
| *Comments* | Ongoing, unmoderated discussions on a wide range of issues regarding feminist law, theory, legal texts, professional support, and more. Sometimes tedious, as are most lists—or, as one subscriber says, as is the law. |
| *What* | **Internet Resources for Women's Legal and Public Policy Information** |
| *How* | Web |
| *Where* | `http://asa.ugl.lib.umich.edu:80/chdocs/womenpolicy/`<br>`womenlawpolicy.html` |
| *Comments* | Links you to Internet resources on legal and public policy issues concerning women's lives, including health care and reproductive rights, lesbian rights, mothers and children, violence against women, sexual harassment, women of color, women with disabilities, and labor rights. Also includes links to general legal sources. |
| *What* | **Law Students, Women-only** |
| *How* | Listserv |
| *Where* | Send your name and e-mail address to `OWNER-XXANDLAW@LAW.WISC.EDU` to subscribe. |
| *Comments* | Discussions on woman as "outsider" in legal culture. |
| *What* | **Legal Rights of Women** |
| *How* | Web |
| *Where* | `http://www.launchsite.com/womensrts/` |
| *Comments* | Advertises and excerpts a women's legal rights book, "the only text ever published to legally define in one book federal and state law applying to over 200 subjects that most affect the lives of women. The purpose of this text is to bring to one source the legal principles most affecting the personal, business, family, and civil rights of women." |
| *What* | **National Journal of Sex Orientation Law** |
| *How* | Web |
| *Where* | `http://sunsite.unc.edu/gay/law` |
| *Comments* | Special focuses include reports and studies on lesbian and gay issues; transcriptions of proceedings, panels, and programs; briefs filed by litigators in major cases throughout the United States; and traditional law review scholarship on sex orientation. |
| *What* | **NOW Action Alert** |
| *How* | Mailing list |
| *Where* | Send message `SUBSCRIBE NOW-ACTION-LIST` to `MAJORDOMO@NOW.ORG` to subscribe. |
| *Comments* | Sponsored by the National Organization for Women; offers legislative updates and action alerts. |

| | |
|---|---|
| *What* | **PAR-L (Canadian Women's Issues)** |
| *How* | Mailing list |
| *Where* | Send message to `PAR-L-SERVER@UNB.CA`; type `SUBSCRIBE PAR-L Firstname Lastname` in the message to subscribe. |
| *Comments* | Moderated, bilingual (French and English) list on policy, action, and research on Canadian women's issues, begun by the Canadian Advisory Council on the Status of Women. |

## Additional Sites on Legal and Policy Issues

- AFL-CIO Home Page: `http://www.aflcio.org/`
- American Bar Association: `http://www.abanet.org/`
- Attorneys Without Borders: `http://www.asf.be/asf/`
- Children's Defense Fund: `http://www.tmn.com/cdf/index.html`
- Department of Justice Information Center: `http://www.ncjrs.org` or via e-mail: `askncjrs@ncjrs.org`
- Lawyers Committee for Human Rights: `gopher://gopher.igc.apc.org:5000/11/int/lchr`

# NETWORKS

| | |
|---|---|
| *What* | **WomensNet** |
| *How* | Web |
| *Where* | `http://www.igc.apc.org/womensnet/` |
| *Comments* | A nonprofit computer network for individuals and organizations working on women's rights. WomensNet provides e-mail accounts, Internet access, Web publishing, consulting and training, to help women adapt telecommunication tools for their information and access needs. There are unique information resources on WomensNet such as databases and conferences on feminist issues, plus opportunities to create your own mailing lists, conferences, and Web sites. |
| *Tidbit* | For more information you can also send an e-mail message to `womensnet@igc.apc.org`; attn: Susan Mooney. |

| | |
|---|---|
| *What* | **Women's Wire** |
| *How* | Web |
| *Where* | `http://www.women.com/guide` |
| *Comments* | Both an on-line service and a Web site, now part of CompuServe. Since its debut several years ago, the entrepreneurial San Francisco–based service has offered an excellent and diverse range of resources, appealing to feminists and women in general, including older women. Under CompuServe, the resources are the same, though the presentation is definitely more commercial, with lots of slow-to-load, obviously expensive promotional advertisements for Clinique cosmetics and Ford automobiles. Colorful graphics, but annoyingly slow; it may be possible to access the same |

or similar information faster elsewhere. On the other hand, it's practically an institution, being the first service provider to appeal to women.

## OTHER WOMEN'S SPACES

| | |
|---|---|
| *What* | **Amazon City** |
| *How* | Web |
| *Where* | http://www.amazoncity.com |
| *Comments* | Calls itself the "first city for women on the Internet"—or anywhere, for that matter! May still be under construction when this book is published, so stay tuned! |
| *Tidbit* | Contact city@planetamazon.com to put your business in the city. |

| | |
|---|---|
| *What* | **GrrrlTalk** |
| *How* | Web |
| *Where* | http://mediacity.com/cyberboarder/Features/Grrltalk/grrltalk001.html |
| *Comments* | Guide to lesbian and lesbian-friendly conversations on the Internet. |

| | |
|---|---|
| *What* | **Where the Girls Are** |
| *How* | Web |
| *Where* | http://www.eskimo.com/~susan/girls/htm |
| *Comments* | Filled with links to high-quality feminist Web sites such as WomensNet, NOW, and Feminist/Women's Studies, as well as to lesser-known but important locations such as the Older Women's League, Women's History Month Collaborative Encyclopedia, and BaseCamp Seattle. Regularly updated. |

| | |
|---|---|
| *What* | **Women's Web** |
| *How* | Web |
| *Where* | http://cyber.sfgate.com:80/examiner/womensweb.html |
| *Comments* | Contains news, Internet resources, and a forum for discussing women's issues. |

## POLITICS

| | |
|---|---|
| *What* | **Center for American Women and Politics (CAWP)** |
| *How* | Web |
| *Where* | http://www.rci.rutgers.edu/~cawp/ |
| *Comments* | Information from CAWP, a research, education, and public service center, based at Rutgers University, which promotes greater understanding and knowledge of women's relationships to politics and government. The site also works to strengthen women's influence and leadership in public life and provides current updates on women candidates, fact sheets on women officeholders, publications, and CAWP programs. Also includes links to other resources on women and politics. |

| | |
|---|---|
| *What* | **President's Interagency Council on Women** |
| *How* | Web |
| *Where* | http://www.whitehouse.gov/WH/EOP/Women/IACW/html/IACWhome.html |
| *Comments* | Established in August 1995 to carry out the Platform for Action as formulated at the UN Fourth World Conference on Women in Beijing, the PICW will also carry out additional initiatives that support the equal rights of women and girls. Site contains the National Action Agenda, a survey, and contact names and addresses. |

## REPRODUCTIVE FREEDOM

| | |
|---|---|
| *What* | **National Clinic Defense Project** |
| *How* | Web |
| *Where* | http://www.feminist.org/welcome/defense.html |
| *Comments* | Created by the Feminist Majority Foundation, the NCDP is the nation's largest clinic access project working to keep women's health clinics open in the face of antiabortionists' harassment and violent assaults on clinic workers and patients. Site includes information on the NCDP, an index of affiliated and independent clinics, and updated news about antiabortion blockades, as well as success stories. |

| | |
|---|---|
| *What* | **WOMEN-CLINICDEFENSE** |
| *How* | Mailing list |
| *Where* | Send the message SUBSCRIBE WOMEN-CLINICDEFENSE to MAJORDOMO@IGC.APC.ORG to subscribe. |
| *Comments* | Discussion and information on reproductive rights and abortion access, especially geared for abortion providers, clinic workers, clinic escorts, and legal defenders. |

## VIOLENCE AGAINST WOMEN

| | |
|---|---|
| *What* | **Domestic Violence** |
| *How* | Gopher |
| *Where* | gopher.berkeley.edu; go to Libraries and Academic Support/Research Databases and Resources by Subject/Women_Gender Studies/Womens Wire Gopher/Women's Health/Eating Disorders/Domestic Violence |
| *Comments* | Explains what constitutes domestic violence, giving statistics on abuse rates, national polls, injuries and fatalities, reports to police, and resulting deaths. Includes case studies and results. |

| | |
|---|---|
| *What* | **Family Violence Prevention Fund** |
| *How* | Web |
| *Where* | http://www.igc.apc.org/fund |

*Comments*   Offers information to service providers for battered women, statistics on incidents in the United States, and personal stories.

*What*   **FAVNET (Feminists Against Violence Network)**

*How*   Listserv

*Where*   Send message to `MDUBIN@IX.NETCOM.COM` to subscribe.

*Comments*   Discussions on domestic violence issues from professionals and survivors.

*What*   **Feminist Majority's Domestic Violence Information Center**

*How*   Web

*Where*   `http://www.feminist.org/other/dv/dvhome.html`

*Comments*   Provides fact sheets, hotline resources including telephone numbers for every state in the United States, and listings of domestic violence Internet sites.

*What*   **Intimate Violence**

*How*   Listserv

*Where*   Send message to `listserv@uriacc.uri.edu` to subscribe; type `INTVIO-L Firstname Lastname` in the body of the message.

*Comments*   Devoted to discussion about intimate violence, including partner abuse, sexual abuse, and incest.

---

### CYBER SUPPORT FOR BATTERED WOMEN

What happens when a battered woman goes to the library to look for information? With the increase in public access points to the Internet, an on-line search has become a real alternative. The information provided could offer advice about how to find a helping agency and/or leave an abusive relationship. An on-line search is an attractive possibility for several reasons. All inquiries are anonymous. The site is passive information waiting for someone to log on. No one knows who has been making inquiries. There is no self-imposed obligation, on the part of the person inquiring, to the person supplying the information. No answers to give, just material to read, consider, and possibly download. There is no commitment to act—at least not until ready to do so. There will be no long distance calls appearing in the next phone bill. From the perspective of those maintaining the site for battered women, the on-line information available can be kept up to date, and can point a woman to a helping agency when she is ready to take another step.

—JO SUTTON
*Women'space Magazine/Ezine* 1:4 (1996)

---

*What*   **PAVNET (Partners Against Violence Network)**

*How*   Listserv

*Where*   Send message to `MAJORDOMO@NAL.USDA.GOV` to subscribe; type `SUBSCRIBE PAVNET` in the body of the message.

| | |
|---|---|
| *Comments* | Sponsored by the U.S. Department of Agriculture, Partners Against Violence hosts national and international discussions on antiviolence issues, including initiatives, prevention programs, implementation, problem-solving, and networking efforts. |
| *What* | **SafetyNet: Domestic Violence Resources** |
| *How* | Web |
| *Where* | http://www/cybergrrl.com/dv.html |
| *Comments* | Aliza Sherman's Cybergrrls Web site contains a large space for domestic violence resources including statistics, bibliographies, projects, organizations, a handbook, and links to related sites such as training materials for health care providers. |
| *What* | **SASH (Sociologists Against Sexual Harassment)** |
| *How* | Mailing list |
| *Where* | Send message to Phoebe Stambaugh at AZPXS@ASUACAD (BITNET) or AZPXZ@ASUVM.INRE.ASU.EDU (Internet) to subscribe. |
| *Comments* | Moderated discussion on sexual harassment. |
| *What* | **STOPRAPE** |
| *How* | Mailing list |
| *Where* | Send message to LISTSERV@BROWNVM (BITNET) or LISTSERV@BROWNVM.BROWN.EDU (Internet) to subscribe. |
| *Comments* | Discussions on sexual assault activism. |

# 2

# INTERNATIONALIZING THE COMPUTER AGE
## Women's Networks Around the World

In the winter of 1995 I was playing midwife to the creation of an electronic communications *network* for feminist groups in the former Soviet Union and Eastern Europe. From my office in Washington, D.C., I tracked the path of three women *e-mail* trainers who had fanned out across twenty countries, with *modems* and software in tow, to bring *telecommunications* to countries that had long suffered from censorship and cultural isolation. In some towns, women were receiving their first computers, e-mail, telephones, and telephone lines all at once, enabling them to leap over decades of backward technology and head toward the twenty-first century.

During their travels, the trainers (who were Russian, Polish, and American) and I communicated via e-mail. Each of them would spend a week with one women's group per city, teaching basic computer and e-mail skills as well as some advanced techniques—for example, how to use e-mail as an advocacy tool; how to distribute electronic resources to people who lack e-mail access; and how to integrate e-mail into office routines.

As soon as a group signed up with a service provider, chose a *userid,* and installed its modem, the members learned how to send their first e-mail message, which was usually sent to me, thousands of miles away in Washington. I would immediately send a welcome message back to them. In this way, they (and I) would experience e-mail's power to instantly connect people across time and space with relatively little cost.

During one particular weekend (because sometimes a midwife must work on weekends) I received a message and immediately returned one to a newly linked group in Siberia which was in the middle of an all-day training session. When the women saw my message, just a few hours after I had sent it, the entire group cried. The immediacy, the sudden realization of the world's availability, even in the middle of an isolating Siberian winter, had moved them to tears—so the feminist legend is told.

In the international arena, e-mail now replaces fax machines and telephones for the communication needs of civic activists who have access to the technology; as long as the electricity and phone lines are working, it's the most efficient and cost-effective means of informational exchange.

Without e-mail, women from countries such as Kyrgyzstan, Albania, Latvia, and the United States might never talk to one another, might never get to know one another's social change priorities, personal lives, political problems, costs of living, or our wide-ranging and unjustly distributed expenses for using e-mail. (In Russia, e-mail costs at least fifty dollars per month; in

Poland sixty-five dollars per month; in Kyrgyzstan one hundred dollars per month; and in the United States, an average of twenty dollars per month. Add to this comparison that an average monthly salary in Russia or Central Asia is approximately five hundred dollars. So be aware that e-mail is not necessarily inexpensive in some parts of the world, but is still less costly than telephoning calling, or than faxing, which can range from five to thirty dollars per page!)

Working on women's issues internationally, I soon learned that varying technical capacities and financial and cultural differences greatly influence the ways in which people think about and use the Internet. In most parts of the world, people only have e-mail access; they cannot access the Internet or the *World Wide Web.* Consequently, *Listservs* and *conferences* become the main vehicles for dialogue and exchange, along with regular e-mail usage. Within these modes of access lie fruitful connections to people and events throughout the world.

I also learned that people living outside the United States often think about and use electronic communications differently than we do. The kind of media hype that North Americans might associate with the Net—the new frontier in infotainment—carries little or no appeal or relevance in Albania or Ghana, for example, where people rely on e-mail to learn about the world at large, to access real news, to overcome an acculturated sense of isolation. In the United States, e-mail is a luxury; in Romania it's a lifeline.

Women who use electronic communications for international collaborations share mutual concerns and questions, including the following:

- To what extent, and how, might computer networking become an effective tool for cross-cultural collaborations?
- With whom will users speak, in what languages, and about what?
- Who won't use it and why not?
- Will the electronic technology change the roles and relationships of its users?
- Will it help break down complex ethnic and other elitisms that tend to keep information always in the same hands, often in national capitals?
- Will it create links among people inside each country as well as internationally?
- Will it draw women closer together, North and South, East and West?

In 1995, women's on-line activities soared throughout the world as women's nongovernmental organizations (NGOs) prepared for the United Nations Fourth World Conference on Women in Beijing. Almost a year after the historic gathering, the United Nations began to explore establishing global electronic forums to sustain the discussions and activities of women who are working to implement the Beijing Platform for Action in their countries. Several UN departments, including UNIFEM (United Nations Development Fund for Women), DAW (United Nations Division for the Advancement of Women), and INSTRAW (International Research and Training Institute for the Advancement of Women), began consulting with feminist technical advisers who work in Africa, Asia, Europe, and North and South America to develop appropriate communication channels and access for broad-based, global use. For the most part, these experts advised the UN representatives to create the kinds of electronic forums that could be most democratically accessed from anywhere in the world. In other words, it was suggested that *mailing lists* rather than *Web sites* offer greatest global access; their use should be maximized to reach and link women and to enable women to address the United Nations with the kinds of common, global concerns that make up the Beijing Platform for Action. The years ahead should prove very promising for international women's rights advocacy via electronic networking—and for improving the quality of life for women everywhere.

So what better time than the present to explore the increasing tide of global on-line resources? Barbara Ann O'Leary of Virtual Sisterhood and I have collected and organized resources, largely according to region, presenting what we hope reflects women's wide-ranging use of e-mail and the Internet in various parts of the world. The categories in this chapter include:

- International women's organizations and assistance programs—labor, health, population, development
- General international resources—women's electronic networks and services around the world, categorized by region

Note: Resources appearing in this chapter are in English unless otherwise specified.

### ACCESSING THE INTERNET VIA E-MAIL

The Sabre Foundation Gopher contains documents on the sophisticated techniques one can employ to navigate the Internet using only e-mail. The address for the ReadMe file is: `gopher://ftp.std.com/11/nonprofits/Sabre.Foundation.Inc/Reference/Basic.Copyright.Information.`

## INTERNATIONAL WOMEN'S ORGANIZATION AND ASSISTANCE PROGRAMS

| | |
|---|---|
| *What* | **Association for Progressive Communications** |
| *How* | Web |
| *Where* | `http://www.gn.apc.org/gn/` |
| *Comments* | Includes a wide range of information and services from the largest global computer communications and information network dedicated to serving nongovernmental organizations (NGOs) and citizen activists working for social justice, environmental sustainability, human rights, women's empowerment, and other progressive issues. Composed of an international consortium of 21-member networks, APC provides computer communications and information-sharing tools to over forty thousand NGOs, activists, educators, policy-makers, and community leaders in 133 countries. APC member networks share a common mission: to develop and maintain the informational system that allows for geographically dispersed people who are working for social and environmental change to coordinate activities on-line at |

the cheapest possible rate. APC works to reduce the gap between the information-poor and the information-rich. Toward this end, southern and northern members of APC regularly exchange information and technical expertise. In addition, APC members collaborate with over forty partner networks in southern countries, increasing information flow from South to North and between South and South. Many of these partner systems provide the only e-mail access for NGOs in their countries.

|   |   |
|---|---|
| *What* | **APC Women's Networking Support Program** |
| *How* | Web |
| *Where* | http://www.gn.apc.org/gn/women/index.html |
| *Comments* | To redress the gender gap in the use of computer technology that exists in all countries of the world, the Association for Progressive Communications in 1993 launched the Women's Networking Support Program. This initiative works to increase access to and use of networking technologies and information sources for women and women's NGOs, both nationally and internationally. The program also facilitates technical training for women so they can develop the technical skills necessary to install, operate, and develop the system. APC's Women's Networking Support Program provided the Internet connection and Electronic Information Services at the United Nations Fourth World Conference on Women and the NGO Forum on Women. This site provides information about the program as well as about information flow among the North, South, East, and West on gender issues. |
| *Language(s)* | English, with some resources in other languages, including Spanish |

In the past six years, beginning notably with the Earth Summit, there has been a trail of success stories from feminist activists using computer networking to organize for social change. From e-mail to electronic conferencing, "virtual" protests to World Wide Web publishing, these activists have captured the spirit and political potential of connecting women from all over the globe via the (still) public and (relatively) inexpensive communication medium, the Internet. . . . The essence of [computer networking] strategies—e-mail training, travel advice, UN Conference coalition building, NGO Forum event planning—is the linking of local perspectives with global action. Women on-line are sharing experiences with each other, reflecting and developing the strategies for change in international arenas as well as backyard initiatives. The use of the technology is fairly new, so the possibilities for NGOs and social change movements are yet to be discovered. . . . What remains speculative is the range of influence computer networking will have on policymaking and the structure of social groups.

—NINA BETH HUNTEMANN
University of Massachusetts
from "Abstract: The New Girls' Network," May 1995

|   |   |
|---|---|
| *What* | **BEIJING95-L** |
| *How* | Listserv |

| | |
|---|---|
| *Where* | Send message to `listserv@netcom.com` to subscribe. |
| *Comments* | Dedicated to UN Fourth World Conference on Women, with subscribers mostly from the United States, Canada, China, and Australia. |

| | |
|---|---|
| *What* | **Center for Women's Global Leadership (CWGL)** |
| *How* | Gopher |
| *Where* | `gopher://gopher.igc.apc.org:70/11/orgs/cwgl` |
| *Comments* | Based at Rutgers University in New Jersey, CWGL has provided intellectual leadership on issues regarding women's human rights, playing a crucial role at the Beijing conference. CWGL conducts leadership training for women from around the world and makes use of its Gopher space to disseminate related information worldwide. |
| *Tidbit* | Contact CWGL's Gopher Coordinator, Neida Jimenez, via e-mail at `cwgl@igc.apc.org` for more information. |
| *Language(s)* | English, with some resources in Spanish and French |

| | |
|---|---|
| *What* | **FEMISA** |
| *How* | Listserv |
| *Where* | Send message to `LISTSERV@CSF.COLORADO.EDU` to subscribe. |
| *Comments* | Discussions on feminism, gender, women, and  international relations. |

| | |
|---|---|
| *What* | **Gender-CG** |
| *How* | Mailing list |
| *Where* | Send message to `h.feldstein@cgnet.com` to subscribe. |
| *Comments* | Links researchers working on gender and intrahousehold issues in agriculture, natural resource management, food security, and nutrition. |

| | |
|---|---|
| *What* | **Gender Training Electronic Forum** |
| *How* | Mailing list |
| *Where* | E-mail `wsource@igc.apc.org` for subscription information. |
| *Comments* | Network and resource for gender trainers that is co-moderated by regional centers in the United States, South Africa, Uganda, Mexico, Uruguay, Malaysia, Bangladesh, and the Netherlands. |

| | |
|---|---|
| *What* | **GEOGFEM (Geographical Feminism)** |
| *How* | Listserv |
| *Where* | Send message to `LISTSERV@LSV.UKY.EDU` to subscribe. |
| *Comments* | Discussions on feminist issues in geography. |

| | |
|---|---|
| *What* | **Global Net/Global FaxNet** |
| *How* | Mailing list |
| *Where* | Send message to `iwtc@igc.apc.org` to subscribe. |
| *Comments* | Produced by the International Women's Tribune Centre, this one-page bulletin pub- |

lishes follow-up news to the Beijing conference as well as updates on UN meetings and related topics.

| | |
|---|---|
| *What* | **Interaction** |
| *How* | Web; Gopher |
| *Where* | `http://www.interaction.org` for Web site; `gopher://gopher.` `interaction.org:7050` for Gopher |
| *Comments* | Washington, D.C.–based consortium of 150+ nonprofits working worldwide on women-in-development issues, humanitarian aid, and advocacy. A well-developed, informative site, with quality graphics and links to Interaction's mission statement, calendar, newsletters and publications, employment/volunteer opportunities, and related organizations. Special pages on Congressional Action and Media Action. |

| | |
|---|---|
| *What* | **Third World Women** |
| *How* | Listserv |
| *Where* | Send the message `SUBSCRIBE THIRD-WORLD-WOMEN` to `MAJORDOMO@JEFFERSON.` `VILLAGE.VIRGINIA.EDU` to subscribe. |
| *Comments* | Forum on issues related to the representation of third world women, such as identity and personal and professional life. |

| | |
|---|---|
| *What* | **United Nations Development Fund for Women (UNIFEM)** |
| *How* | Web |
| *Where* | `http://un.fem.ingenia.com:80/unifem` |
| *Comments* | Provides direct support to women's projects and to the inclusion of women in mainstream development programs. |

| | |
|---|---|
| *What* | **Virtual Sisterhood** |
| *How* | Web |
| *Where* | `http://www.igc.apc.org/vsister/` |
| *Comments* | Global women's electronic support network, providing information and forums on global feminist activism via electronic communication. |

| | |
|---|---|
| *What* | **WIDNET (Women & Development—Femmes & Developpement)** |
| *How* | Web |
| *Where* | `http://www.synapse.net/~focusint/` |
| *Comments* | Provides statistics on women's issues and a directory of women's development organizations. |
| *Language(s)* | English and French |

| | |
|---|---|
| *What* | **Women-On-line-News** |
| *How* | Mailing list |

| | |
|---|---|
| *Where* | Send message to `women-online-news-request@lists1.best.com` to subscribe. In the body of the message type `subsingle`. |
| *Comments* | International resource list for women using electronic communications featuring a monthly newsletter sponsored by Women On-line and World Wide Women. |
| *Tidbit* | Women On-line will soon have a Web site, too. Check the mailing list for updates. |

| | |
|---|---|
| *What* | **Women's Environment and Development Organization (WEDO)** |
| *How* | Gopher |
| *Where* | `gopher://gopher.igc.apc.org:70/11/orgs/wedo` |
| *Comments* | WEDO supports women's advocacy throughout the world in the areas of development, the environment, population, and gender equity. Its Gopher space takes you to its Women's Action Agenda in five languages, as well as newsletters, updates on advocacy at the United Nations, and on-line action. |
| *Language(s)* | English, with some resources in Spanish and French |

| | |
|---|---|
| *What* | **Women's Info by Gopher** |
| *How* | Gopher |
| *Where* | `liberty.uc.wlu.edu:3002/7?women` |
| *Comments* | Massive list of women's issues and women's studies issues from around the world. |

| | |
|---|---|
| *What* | **WorldWideWomen** |
| *How* | Web |
| *Where* | `http://www.euro.net/5thworld/women/women.html` |
| *Comments* | "Equal but not the same" is this home page's motto, and it contains hotlists for international women's resources. |

## GENERAL INTERNATIONAL RESOURCES

| | |
|---|---|
| *What* | **International Service Agencies Page** |
| *How* | Web |
| *Where* | `http://www.netmarket.com/isa/html/disaster.html` |
| *Comments* | Lists and links to international relief organizations that provide aid in times of war and natural disaster, including CARE and Oxfam. |

| | |
|---|---|
| *What* | **United Nations** |
| *How* | Web; Gopher |
| *Where* | `http://www.un.org/` for Web site; `gopher://gopher.un.org` for Gopher |
| *Comments* | Will link you to the numerous UN departments such as the Fourth World Conference on Women, the Division for the Advancement of Women, and the International Research and Training Institute for the Advancement of Women. |

141

## AFRICA

### General

| | |
|---|---|
| *What* | **Africa On-line: Women** |
| *How* | Web |
| *Where* | `http://www.africaon-line.com/AfricaOnline/women/intro.html` |
| *Comments* | Women's section of Africa On-line; includes chat space, articles, professional networks, profiles of African women in history, gender and development programs, and gender studies. |
| *Tidbit* | Send comments or questions to `women@africaon-line.com`. |
| *What* | **Information Bank on African Development Studies (IBADS)** |
| *How* | Gopher |
| *Where* | `gopher://ftp.worldbank.org:70/00/ibads/RegStudies/wid/wid112` |
| *Comments* | Includes documents on development and women in Africa, finance and enterprise development for women in Africa, and country case studies on women's legal status. |
| *What* | **Women in Law and Development in Africa (WILDAF)** |
| *How* | E-mail |
| *Where* | `WILDAF@mango.zw` |
| *Comments* | Women's rights advocacy network, comprised largely of lawyers and activists throughout Africa. There are offices and contact people in the twenty-three countries where WILDAF operates, with headquarters in Zimbabwe under the directorship of Joanna Foster. |
| *What* | **Women of Africa Resources** |
| *How* | Web |
| *Where* | `http://www.lawrence.edu/~bradleyc/war.html` |
| *Comments* | Bibliographies of African women, syllabi and articles by and for African women. Sources on women in development, international women's rights, female circumcision. Links to related Web sites. |
| *What* | **FEMNET: The African Women's Development and Communication Network** |
| *How* | E-mail |
| *Where* | `Gikori@mukla.gn.apc.org` |
| *Comments* | According to Sarah Macharia of FEMNET, Nairobi, Kenya: "FEMNET is an umbrella organization for African women's NGOs and other NGOs working for the advancement of women in Africa. FEMNET has the distinctive mandate of enhancing networking within its constituency through information dissemination and communication . . . increasingly through electronic mail, whose most attractive advantages over other means of communication include its cost-effectiveness and the outreach to a wider audience." |

**WHAT THE WORLD NEEDS NOW**

The focus [of the Net] is too often on the types of problems which computers can deal with, rather than the differing needs of girls and women around the world. We need to consider that almost half of the people in developing countries are under twenty, compared to less than a third in developed countries. Girls and women make up the majority of the poor and the illiterate almost everywhere. Nations vary a great deal in their resources and needs; currently approximately half of the computer host machines are in the United States. Most telephone systems are state-owned and expensive. Some people are advocating the development of a grid of low-orbiting satellites to link schools and people in the development world (Nicholas Negroponte, *Being Digital,* [New York: Random House, 1996] 220).

But the satellites would not solve all problems and needs. Alisa Gravitz, executive director of Co-op American, has listed the major responses to the question people in many parts of the world are asked: What do you want the world to look like? The list reads: clean, safe, beautiful environment; a clean and adequate supply of water; enough clothing; a balanced diet; basic health care; communication with each other; good education; fuel; simple housing; and spiritual and cultural satisfaction.

We could do well to ask: In what ways can a global Internet assist with these values? We recommend the following strategies:

1. That publicly funded information infrastructure projects be subject to systematic mandated assessment of the degree to which gender equity is reached; be conducted by gender-balanced committees of people involved in research, education, and library communities, consumer and public interest groups, and technology and information industries.

2. That new standards based in equity be developed and applied to ensure the creation, access to, and preservation of networked digital resources for, about, and by women.

3. That network environments be accessible and hospitable to women and girls regardless of race, ethnic background, religion, cultural background, economic status, and sexual orientation.

4. That the principles above be incorporated and upheld by designing training and support program for women and girls; applying and (where necessary) reformulating current laws to guarantee women's rights in the networked environment; fostering civic networks that offer affordable and equitable access; encouraging continued research on the gendered use of electronic networks.

—CHERIS KRAMARAE
Women, InformationTechnology & Scholarship (WITS)

## Mozambique

|          |                                                      |
| -------- | ---------------------------------------------------- |
| *What*   | **Solid Africa**                                     |
| *How*    | Web                                                  |
| *Where*  | http://humanism.org/SolidAfrica/Welcome.html         |
| *Comments* | Programs to support the economic empowerment of women in areas of socioeconomic crisis and hardship with an emphasis on work in Mozambique. Includes calendar/events, articles, links, advisory board, lists of volunteers, and general information on Mozambique. |

## South Africa

| | |
|---|---|
| *What* | **Centre for Gender Studies, University of Natal, South Africa** |
| *How* | Web |
| *Where* | http://www.unp.ac.za/UNPDepartments/politics/gender/gem |
| *Comments* | Provides information about cross-disciplinary gender studies programs in South Africa, links to gender studies around the world, and subscription details for GEN-NET, a listserv hosted by the Centre. |

| | |
|---|---|
| *What* | **GENNET (Gender Issues)** |
| *How* | Mailing list |
| *Where* | Send the message subscribe gennet firstname lastname to maiser@listserv.und.ac.za to subscribe. |
| *Comments* | Facilitates networking between people concerned with issues relating to women and gender primarily (but not exclusively) in Kwa Zulu-Natal, South Africa. |
| *Tidbit* | Further information about GENNET is available at the Web site http://www.unp.ac.za/UNPDepartments/politics/gender/gennet.htm. |

| | |
|---|---|
| *What* | **SANGONeT (South African NGO Secretariat)—Women** |
| *How* | Web |
| *Where* | http://wn.apc.org/women/women.html |
| *Comments* | Networking and information-sharing about the status of women in South Africa, including reports on legislation, the South African NGO Secretariat for Beijing, the Women in Development Network in Angola, and numerous international links. |
| *Tidbit* | E-mail questions and comments to women@wn.apc.org. |

| | |
|---|---|
| *What* | **South African Women in Science and Technology (SA WISE)** |
| *How* | Web |
| *Where* | http://www.sea.uct.ac.za/sawise/index.html |
| *Comments* | Features SA WISE information and bulletin including events calendar, articles, membership materials. |

## ASIA/PACIFIC

### General

| | |
|---|---|
| *What* | **Journal of South Asian Women's Studies** |
| *How* | Web |
| *Where* | http://www.shore.net/~india/jsaws/index.htm |
| *Comments* | Electronic journal for scholars of South Asian women's studies, on theoretical and practical issues in law, civil rights, gender issues, religion, philosophy, politics, and feminism—in other words, everything. Areas of study include India, Nepal, Tibet, |

Afghanistan, Pakistan, Sri Lanka, Bangladesh, Bhutan, Burma, Thailand, Laos, Vietnam, Cambodia, Taiwan, Maldives, Malaysia, Indonesia, Philippines. Includes both published and unpublished articles. A hard copy version of all the contributions is published once a year and distributed upon request.

*Tidbit*    E-mail inquiries to `jsaws@shore.net`.

*What*    **SAWNET (South Asian Women's Net)**

*How*    Mailing list; Web

*Where*    Send the one-word message `subscribe` to `sawnet-request@cs.concordia.ca` to subscribe to the mailing list; go to `http://www.umiacs.umd.edu/users/sawweb/sawnet` for the Web site.

*Comments*    Forum for South Asian women and those interested in issues relevant to South Asian women, such as literacy for women. "South Asia" is taken to include Bangladesh, Bhutan, Burma, India, Nepal, Pakistan, and Sri Lanka. The Web site includes lists of women's organizations, charities, political organizations, and electronic forums; resources on domestic violence, women's health care, funding and career information, literature, and cinema; news updates; and home pages of SAWNET members.

*What*    **Self-Help Women's Association (SEWA)**

*How*    Web

*Where*    `http://titsoc.soc.titech.ac.jp/titsoc/higuchi-lab/icm/sewa-1.html`

*Comments*    Women's trade union, registered in 1972 at Ahmedabad in India. Among its services, it operates a cooperative bank, started in 1974, that helps women become financially independent and start their own economic activity. The site contains facts and figures related to the bank, as well as case studies of SEWA in people-centered financial institutions.

*What*    **Trikone Home Page**

*How*    Web

*Where*    `http://www.rahul.net/trikone/index/html`

*Comments*    Lesbian and gay resource for South Asia; includes listings of events, publications, and groups for Bangladesh, Ghutan, India, Maldives, Nepal, Pakistan, Sri Lanka.

*What*    **The Women's Caravan and Cyber-Harem**

*How*    Mailing list

*Where*    E-mail `fazia@exit109.com` asking for an application to subscribe.

*Comments*    Forum for women interested in South Asia.

*What*    **Women's Issues in Asia**

*How*    Gopher

*Where*    `csf.Colorado.edu/11/ipe/Geographic/Archive/asia/women`

*Comments*    Contains files and links to wide-ranging resources, from the UN Conference in Beijing to the Thai sex trade.

> The challenge here is to keep in mind that our region [Asia] is home to many women with diverse economic and cultural backgrounds. Most of them still have no capability in connecting with other women using this technology. The Internet may be one of the most powerful tools of communicating and accessing information, but it may also be . . . alienating other women who have no equipment and no proper training.
>
> —RHONA BAUTISTA
> Isis International, Manila, Philippines

## India

*What*    **Manushi**

*How*    Web

*Where*    http://www.imsc.ernet.in/~tabish/manushi/

*Comments*    Journal of academic and popular literature on women's work and personal lives. The site contains articles from current and past issues, news updates, subscription details, and links to related sites.

## Japan

*What*    **Women's Energy Network—Japan**

*How*    Web

*Where*    http://rainbow.rmii.com/~jgraham/wen.html

*Comments*    Information for and about women in energy fields, especially nuclear energy, who are concerned about the environmental and political implications of energy use.

*What*    **Women's On-line Media Project**

*How*    Web

*Where*    http://www.suehiro.nakano.tokyo.jp/WOM/

*Comments*    Introduces women to electronic communications and related organizations and activities.

*Language(s)*    Japanese and English

## Singapore

*What*    **Engender—Centre for Environment, Gender, and Development**

*How*    Web

*Where*    http://www.engender.org.sg/

*Comments*    Engender focuses on innovative thinking and strategies on sustainable livelihoods, health, and habitats in regions of Asia affected by rapid developmental changes. The site contains information on GEDNET, a research network focusing on gender, environment, and development; Gaia Crafts, a micro-enterprise program in craft for income, waste recycling, and "therapy"; the Gender and Development Resource Bank, a networking vehicle for the economic empowerment of women and local communities; and a Resource Bank On-line, described as "a place in cyberspace to bridge the gap between the resource-rich and -poor."

*Tidbit*    Questions or comments can be e-mailed to `info@engender.org.sg`.

## Taiwan

*What*    **TW-WOMEN (Taiwanese Women)**

*How*    Listserv

*Where*    Send the message `SUBSCRIBE TW-WOMEN Firstname Lastname` to `MAILSERV@ UTARLG.UTA.EDU` to subscribe.

*Comments*    Discussion on feminist issues regarding Taiwanese women. A central location for those involved in the women's movement in Taiwan.

## Tibet

*What*    **A Tribute to Tibetan Women's Association**

*How*    Web

*Where*    `http://www.grannyg.bc.ca/tibet/tibet.html`

*Comments*    Nongovernmental organization based in Dharamsala, India, with over thirty-seven branches in India and abroad. Its major concerns are violence against women in the home and in public life, reproductive rights, torture and imprisonment of Tibetan women, and gender discrimination in education, health, and employment. The site contains press reports, publications, fundraising projects, and links to Free Tibet, the Dalai Lama, and other Tibetan human rights projects.

## Australia

*What*    **AUSFEM-POLNET (Australian Feminist Politics)**

*How*    Mailing list

*Where*    Send message to `majordomo@postoffice.utas.edu.au` to subscribe; type `subscribe` in the body of the message.

*Comments*    Electronic network for practitioners and scholars who are actively involved in feminist politics.

*What*    **Australian Women's Issues**

*How*    Web

*Where*    `http://www.women2.net.au/`

*Comments*    Complete search engine to Australian gender studies, women's health issues and centers, women in agriculture, women's policy research, fellowships, and publications, filled with colorful graphics.

| | |
|---|---|
| *What* | **Wollongong's World's Women On-line (WWWOn-line)** |
| *How* | Web |
| *Where* | http://www.uow.edu.au/wwwo/ |
| *Comments* | Part of the World's Women On-line series of Web sites that were created in conjunction with the UN Fourth World Conference on Women. Exploring "hypermediality" as a form for exhibition, the site includes the works of artists, writers, and researchers in the performing arts, crafts, literature, sociology, and information technology. |

| | |
|---|---|
| *What* | **Women's Electoral Lobby (WEL), Australia** |
| *How* | Web |
| *Where* | http://www.pcug.org.au/other/wel/ |
| *Comments* | Newsletters, announcements, and other information related to the lobby. |

| | |
|---|---|
| *What* | **Women's Infolink** |
| *How* | Web |
| *Where* | http://www.womens-infolink.qld.gov.au/ |
| *Comments* | Queensland-wide, free information and referral service for women provided by the Queensland state government. |

| | |
|---|---|
| *What* | **WomenzNet** |
| *How* | Web |
| *Where* | http://www.womenz.net.au/ |
| *Comments* | Contains valuable access to activists using computer networks for information-sharing, broadcasting, and collaboration. Women are also encouraged to link to other women's Web sites: health centers, business networks, girls' schools, home education for rural women. |

## EUROPE AND THE FORMER SOVIET UNION

### General

| | |
|---|---|
| *What* | **Euro-Sappho** |
| *How* | Mailing list |
| *Where* | Send message to majordomo@seta.fi with a blank subject line to subscribe; type subscribe euro-sappho firstname lastname in the body of the message. |
| *Comments* | Discussion on topics of interest to European lesbians. Membership is open to all women and is restricted to women. |

| | |
|---|---|
| *Language(s)* | Postings may be in any of the major European languages. |
| *Tidbit* | If you have problems subscribing, write to `EURO-SAPPHO-REQUEST@SETA.FI`. |

| | |
|---|---|
| *What* | **European Network of Women in Decision-Making** |
| *How* | Web |
| *Where* | `http://drum.reference.be/wo-mancracy/` |
| *Comments* | Network of experts working for the European Commission which seeks to increase women's participation in political decision-making. The site contains facts and figures on women's political participation in all the European Union member states, documentation and literature, as well as information on the network. |

| | |
|---|---|
| *What* | **Mixture—Antisexist Alternative—European Mixed Group of Students Against Sexism** |
| *How* | Web |
| *Where* | `http://www-users.informatik.rwth-aachen.de/~florath/Mi` |
| *Comments* | Information, news, articles, and pictures about sexism, racism, and feminism, with refreshingly thoughtful content. |
| *Language(s)* | English, French, German, Spanish, Polish, and Esperanto |

## Austria

| | |
|---|---|
| *What* | **ARIADNE (Oesterreichische Nationalbibliothek)** |
| *How* | Web |
| *Where* | `http://www.onb.ac.at/ariadne.htm` |
| *Comments* | Women-specific information and documentation center within Austria. |
| *Language(s)* | German |

| | |
|---|---|
| *What* | **The Pheminist Cyber Roadshow** |
| *How* | Web |
| *Where* | `http://www.oeh.uni-linz.ac.at:8001/~lisa/#index` |
| *Comments* | Gopher and Web resources, including Surfin' Pheminism. |
| *Language(s)* | German and English |

## Belgium

| | |
|---|---|
| *What* | **A Web of One's Own Home Page** |
| *How* | Web |
| *Where* | `http://www.reference.be/womweb/index.html` |
| *Comments* | Inspired by Virginia Woolf, this site was created for women to share essays, stories, and reviews on women's use of the Internet. |
| *Language(s)* | Dutch, with English summaries |

## Czech Republic

| | |
|---|---|
| *What* | **Gender Studies Centre** |
| *How* | Web |
| *Where* | http://www.ecn.cz/gender/ |
| *Comments* | Forum for the gathering, processing, and spreading of information connected with gender issues. |

## Denmark

| | |
|---|---|
| *What* | **Danish Centre for Information on Women and Gender (KVINFO)** |
| *How* | Web |
| *Where* | http://www.kulturnet.dk/homes/kvinfo/kvinfoe.htm |
| *Comments* | Information on women and gender, including a research library and catalog, excerpts from the Centre's quarterly magazine, *Forum,* and major Nordic and Danish research projects, including a photo archive. |
| *Language(s)* | Danish and English |

## Eastern Europe and the Former Soviet Union

| | |
|---|---|
| *What* | **AWSS-L (Association for Women in Slavic Studies)** |
| *How* | Listserv |
| *Where* | Send the message SUBSCRIBE ASWW-L Firstname Lastname to LIST-SERV@MSU.EDU to subscribe. |
| *Comments* | Moderated list serving professional and academic needs of women in Slavic studies. |

| | |
|---|---|
| *What* | **EE-WOMEN (Eastern European Women)** |
| *How* | Mailing list |
| *Where* | Send message to LISTPROC@CEP.NONPROFIT.NET to subscribe. |
| *Comments* | Unmoderated list on women's issues in the former Soviet Union and Central and Eastern Europe. Most information comes from the United States. |

| | |
|---|---|
| *What* | **GLAS-SISTERS** |
| *How* | Mailing list |
| *Where* | Send message to Irina Doskich at neww@glas.apc.org to subscribe; type Subscribe Glas-Sisters Firstname Lastname and your e-mail address in the body of the message. |
| *Comments* | Network on East-West Women's Russian-language discussion of gender issues in the former Soviet Union, moderated from Moscow. |
| *Language(s)* | Russian |

| | |
|---|---|
| *What* | **Glasnet** |
| *How* | Web |

| | |
|---|---|
| *Where* | http://www.glasnet.ru/ |
| *Comments* | Not-for-profit organization offering e-mail and Internet access accounts in Russia and electronic conferences. |
| *Tidbit* | For more information on how to adapt a western modem to the old Soviet telephone system, contact http://www.glasnet.ru/brochure/modems.html. |

| | |
|---|---|
| *What* | **Network of East-West Women (NEWW)** |
| *How* | Web |
| *Where* | http://www.igc.apc.org/neww (English); http://www.glasnet.ru/neww/neww_r.htm (Russian) |
| *Comments* | Both sites provide information about NEWW's programs, members, feminist as well as Internet developments in the post-Communist region, and free Web space to women's NGOs in "the region." |

| | |
|---|---|
| *What* | **NEWW-RIGHTS** |
| *How* | Mailing list |
| *Where* | Send the message SUBSCRIBE NEWW-RIGHTS to MAJORDOMO@IGC.APC.ORG to subscribe to the English-language version. |
| *Comments* | Well-organized, moderated digest of legal services and resources on women's legal and human rights issues pertinent to the legal reform process in new democracies. |
| *Tidbit* | Echoed in Russian on the Glasnet service provider at GLAS-WOMEN-RIGHTS. To subscribe, contact Irina Doskich via e-mail at neww@glas.apc.org. |

| | |
|---|---|
| *What* | **Russian Feminism** |
| *How* | Web |
| *Where* | http://www.geocities.com/Athens/2533/russfem.html |
| *Comments* | Provides information and links to Russian feminist organizations, literature, art, and updates on Russian women's social position in the post-Communist transition. A very informative location with vivid graphics, created in Australia by a Polish feminist emigrè. |
| *Language(s)* | Russian and English |

| | |
|---|---|
| *What* | **WOMEN-EAST-WEST** |
| *How* | Mailing list |
| *Where* | Send the message SUBSCRIBE WOMEN-EAST-WEST (with a hyphen after WOMEN rather than a period) to MAJORDOMO@IGC.APC.ORG to subscribe. |
| *Comments* | Sponsored by the Network of East-West Women, the list contains announcements and topical discussions from women and women's groups in the former Soviet Union and Central and Eastern Europe; for all interested in women's changing social position in post-Communist societies. More than half of the postings come from women's groups in post-Communist countries. |

## Finland

*What*  **The Christina Institute for Women's Studies (Kristiina-instituutti)**

*How*  Web

*Where*  `http://www.helsinki.fi/~kris_ntk/eindex.html`

*Comments*  Founded in 1991 as a separate institute within the Faculty of Arts at the University of Helsinki, the institute has opened a Web site that presents information on the teaching of women's studies, graduate programs, reference libraries, and contacts.

*Language(s)*  Finnish and English

*What*  **Women's World Wide Web**

*How*  Web

*Where*  `http://www.vicino.fi/WWWW`

*Comments*  Includes an on-line international databased network.

*Language(s)*  Finnish, soon to be available in English

## Former Yugoslavia

*What*  **Electronic Witches**

*How*  Gopher

*Where*  `gopher://gopher.igc.apc.org:70/00/orgs/ew`

*Comments*  E-mail training program for women and women's grassroots groups throughout the former Yugoslavia.

> Citizens of Tuzla [Bosnia] used e-mail to express their rage and grief at the deliberate shelling of the center of the city on the Day of Youth, 1995, which resulted in the deaths of 67 youth and injuries to 128. Women in [other countries] used e-mail to send messages of solidarity to people in Tuzla. While the international media had moved on to the next story (the hostage-taking of UN soldiers), e-mail expressions of solidarity and support continued to flow into Tuzla and countered a general sentiment of their grief having been too quickly forgotten.
> —KATHRYN TURNIPSEED
> *Feminist Collections*, 17: 2 (Winter 1996), 22

## Germany

*What*  **FeMAIdL**

*How*  Web

*Where*  `http://www.muenster.de/femaidl/index.html`

*Comments*  The "girl project" of the WWW (World Wide White) Rose in Muenster, Germany. The site provides links to "antifacism, girlism, leftism, and help for refugees."

*Language(s)*  German, English, French, Turkish, Spanish, and Dutch

| | |
|---|---|
| *What* | **Women Only Mail and News (WOMAN)** |
| *How* | Web |
| *Where* | http://www.woman.de/ (German); http://www.woman.de/index-e.html (English) |
| *Comments* | Information about WOMAN, a women-only BBS for news, networking, Internet research, directories, and links to other women's pages. |
| *Language(s)* | German, with some English |

## Hungary

| | |
|---|---|
| *What* | **GESTH-L (Hungarian Gender Studies)** |
| *How* | Listserv |
| *Where* | GESTH-L |
| *Where* | Send the message SUBSCRIBE GESTH-L Firstname Lastname to LISTSERV@ HUEARN.SZTAKI.HU to subscribe. |
| *Comments* | List for networking and informational exchange for Hungarian activists and researchers on gender issues. |
| *Language(s)* | Hungarian |

## Ireland

| | |
|---|---|
| *What* | **Attic Press** |
| *How* | Web |
| *Where* | http://www.iol.ie/~atticirl/ |
| *Comments* | Publishers of Irish/women's studies, history, and reference books list their works here. Includes a list of Fairytales for Feminists, a Health and Lifestyle series, and Bright Sparks fiction series for teenagers. |
| *Tidbit* | Further information can be e-mailed to atticirl@iol.ie. |

| | |
|---|---|
| *What* | **IRWMST-L (Irish Women's Studies)** |
| *How* | Mailing list |
| *Where* | Send the message SUB IRWMST-L Firstname Lastname to LISTSERV@ IRLEARN.UCD.IE to subscribe. |
| *Comments* | Sponsored by the Irish Higher Education Equality Unit for people involved or interested in women's studies in Ireland. |

## Italy

| | |
|---|---|
| *What* | **DWPress (Women's Press Agency)** |
| *How* | Web |
| *Where* | http://www.mclink.it/n/dwpress/ (Italian); http://www.mclink.it/n/dwpress/index_e.htm (English) |

| | |
|---|---|
| *Comments* | The Rome-based DWPress is issued by the Cooperative Society Quotidiana with "the aim of looking at and informing about the world through women's eyes" on labor, economics, culture, ecofeminism, health, bioethics, virtual reality, theology, peace, law, foreign countries. At the site you can order back issues, subscribe, or visit the Italian version. |
| *Language(s)* | Italian and English |

| | |
|---|---|
| *What* | **Gopher Donne** |
| *How* | Web |
| *Where* | `http://www.idg.fi.cnr.it/www.donna/donna.htm` |
| *Comments* | Devoted to helping Italian women historians locate pertinent bibliographic sources, including the history of suffragism and women's labor force participation. |
| *Language(s)* | Italian and English |

| | |
|---|---|
| *What* | **Le Donne** |
| *How* | Mailing List |
| *Where* | Send the message `subscribe ledonne firstname lastname` to `listserver@CitInv.it`. |
| *Comments* | Italian list on and of women. |
| *Language(s)* | Italian |

## The Netherlands

| | |
|---|---|
| *What* | **House of Renewal (Beit Ha Chidush)** |
| *How* | Web |
| *Where* | `http://huizen.dds.nl/~chidush/` |
| *Comments* | Information about the "first gender-egalitarian synagogue in Holland," including Sabbath services and holiday events. Also contains links to Jewish gay and lesbian resources in Europe, Israel, and the United States. |
| *Language(s)* | Dutch and English |

| | |
|---|---|
| *What* | **WorldWideWomen** |
| *How* | Web |
| *Where* | `http://www.euro.net:80/5thworld/women/` |
| *Comments* | Examines the distinction between male/female and masculine/feminine. |

## Norway

| | |
|---|---|
| *What* | **Nettkledd/AmaZone** |
| *How* | Web |
| *Where* | `http://www.sn.no/~amazone/` |

*Comments*   For the lesbian community in Norway, information about happenings, news alerts, etc.

*Language(s)*   Norwegian

## Sweden

*What*   **Kvinnor Kan Foundation**

*How*   Web

*Where*   http://www.kvinnorkan.se:80/foundation.html

*Comments*   Information about Women's World Fair organized by Kvinnor Kan Foundation.

*Language(s)*   Swedish

*What*   **Q Web Sweden Women's Empowerment Base**

*How*   Web

*Where*   http://www.pi.se/qwebse/qwebhome.htm

*Comments*   Communication network for the exchange of knowledge, experience, and ideas.

*Language(s)*   Swedish and English

## United Kingdom

*What*   **Women's Electronic Village Hall, Manchester**

*How*   Web

*Where*   http://www.u-net.com/set/wevh/wevh1b.html

*Comments*   Information, technology, and telecommunications resource center for women, featuring training courses and equipment reports.

# LATIN AMERICA/CARIBBEAN

## General

*What*   **ALAI (Agencia Latinoamericana de Informacion) Women's Program**

*How*   Web

*Where*   http://www.ecuanex.apc.org/alai/women.html (English);
http://www.ecuanex.apc.org/alai/womespa.html (Spanish);
http://www.ecuanex.apc.org/alai/womefra.html (French)

*Comments*   Ecuador-based regional communications initiative serving women's and feminist movements in Latin America and the Caribbean. The program aims to facilitate channels of expression to women's and feminist movements, help bridge the gap between women's organizations and other social movements, and advocate a gender perspective in communication. The site gathers documentary material on gender and communication issues.

*Language(s)*   Spanish, French, and English

**SNAPSHOT: WOMEN NETWORKING**

On May 28, 1996, International Day of Action for Women's Health, the Mexico City Women's Health Network held a public tribunal in defense of women's reproductive health, where, for the first time in Mexican history, individual women collectively filed suit against the Mexican state's health care apparatus. Charges of involuntary sterilization and grievous medical malpractice resulting in child or maternal death were heard by a jury of experts in human rights and reproductive health, in a packed auditorium and in APC conferences across Latin America. The search for claimants and publicity of the event began in local LaNeta conferences and later through a simple Tribunal Web site. As the individual cases and determinations were heard, the women's e-mail network ModemMujer posted analysis and results in APC conferences and to a mailing list of women activists in non-APC nodes. ModemMujer received responses from all over Latin America reporting further dissemination of the tribunal initiative in other media as well as interest in reproducing this creative and informative style of protest in their countries. As a result of this response, women's health organizations in Mexico learned of on-line counterparts in Latin America. The creation of a Spanish electronic forum to share information and activities on women's reproductive health throughout Mexico and Latin America is in the final planning stages.

—ERIKA SMITH
LaNeta

| | |
|---|---|
| *What* | **Regional NGO Coordination of Latin America and the Caribbean to Beijing '95** |
| *How* | Web |
| *Where* | http://WEB.nando.net/prof/beijing/in.html |
| *Comments* | Contains UN conventions such as CEDAW (Convention on the Elimination of All Forms of Discrimination Against Women) and articles on women's economic rights, reproductive and sexual rights, culture and traditional practices, legal realities, violence. |
| *Language(s)* | Spanish, with some English |

## Brazil

| | |
|---|---|
| *What* | **Brazilian Breastfeeding Page** |
| *How* | Web |
| *Where* | http://bbs.elogica.com.br/aleitamento/ |
| *Comments* | Grupo Origem's Brazilian Breastfeeding Page includes articles on maternal and child nutrition as a basic right; responsive health care systems; breastmilk as a world resource; breastfeeding advocacy; ecology and economy/food production and marketing forces; and numerous topics. |
| *Language(s)* | Portuguese and English |

## Costa Rica

| | |
|---|---|
| *What* | **Our Words, Our Voices: Young Women for Change!** |
| *How* | Web |

| | |
|---|---|
| *Where* | http://terra.ecouncil.ac.cr/confere/idioms.htm |
| *Comments* | Report from the project "Young Women's Portraits Beyond Beijing." |
| *Language(s)* | Spanish, French, and English |

### Mexico

| | |
|---|---|
| *What* | **LaNeta** |
| *How* | Web |
| *Where* | http://www.apc.org.laneta/ |
| *Comments* | An APC sister node, LaNeta, which is Mexican slang for "truth," officially opened in 1993 with the objective of strengthening NGO coordination and communication and offering a transparent and horizontal media in a country with a prohibitive communications monopoly. LaNeta offers special hands-on training for women to improve the gender balance of Net users, develops women's resources and encourages women's groups to join the network. |
| *Tidbit* | For more information, e-mail LaNeta's Women's On-line Networking Promoter, Erika Smith, at erika@laneta.apc.org. |

### Trinidad and Tobago

| | |
|---|---|
| *What* | **Rape Crisis Centre of Trinidad and Tobago** |
| *How* | Web |
| *Where* | http://iisd1.iisd.ca/50comm/commdb/list/c31.htm |
| *Comments* | Features Rape Crisis Centre's education, prevention, and counseling programs. Begun in 1984, these programs are models in the Caribbean for educating the population about violence prevention and reduction. With a staff of seven and a volunteer corps of 140, the Centre reaches 200 students each month through outreach to Trinidad schools. The site provides information about effective advocacy, support services, legislation on violence against women in Trinidad. |

## ADDITIONAL INTERNATIONAL SITES

Joan Korenman has compiled an international subsection of her Women's Studies/Women's Issues WWW Sites Web page. It has links to women-related sites in many countries and many languages, including Finnish, German, Hungarian, Italian, Japanese, Norwegian, and Spanish. Some, though not all, of these links already have been translated into English. The international URL is http://www.umbc.edu/wmst/links_intl.html. The entire listing for Women's Studies/Women's Issues WWW Sites Web page can be found at http://www.umbc.edu.wmst/.

In addition, many listservs of special relevance to women's international issues appear on the Association for Progressive Communications conference list, which can be found at the APC Web site at http://www.gn.apc.org/gn.

Note: I extend a special thank you to Barbara Ann O'Leary, creator of Virtual Sisterhood, who collected many of the resources for this chapter.

# 3

# RAISING CONSCIOUSNESS
## Gender Studies and General Educational Programs and Opportunities
### *Nina Beth Huntemann*

Women's studies scholars and students were among the first to grasp the value of electronic communications, and they still make up one of the most active and prolific on-line communities. Joan Korenman, a researcher at the University of Maryland, has been collecting lists of women's studies and gender-related on-line resources since 1991. She regularly roams the Internet searching for new resources and evaluates their usefulness. She updates her lists, making corrections and additions as needed. This is very time-consuming work, the mark of a dedicated virtual-oso. In a July 1996 *e-mail* interview with Shana Penn she described her transformation into an electronic librarian for women's studies:

> When I started WMST-L, an e-mail list for women's studies teaching, research, and program administration, I found I needed to know about other women- and gender-related lists so that when I told people that their messages lay outside WMST-L's focus, I could make concrete suggestions about where those messages might be sent. The first versions of the WMST-L User's Guide included a section providing that information. As the number of women-related lists became, that section grew too large for the User's Guide, and so I made it available as a file called OTHER LISTS. In time, I also made it available via Gopher and then the World Wide Web, where it is called Gender Related Electronic Forums. It's still available in all three formats. I think one reason it's valued is that it contains up-to-date information. This kind of information changes constantly. I usually make fifteen to twenty additions, changes, and deletions each month, and sometimes more than that. Part of the advantage of putting information on-line is that it can be so easily updated.

This chapter contains a wealth of resources related to education—both general sites that may be of special interest to women, and sites particularly related to women's educational issues and women's studies. The resources are divided into the following categories:

- Indices
- Academic associations and support networks
- Alternative education
- Equity in education
- Funding (grants, fellowships, scholarships, financial aid)

- K–12 education
- Lesbian, gay, and bisexual studies
- Libraries
- Multicultural education, bilingual, and ESL resources
- Publications
- Women's history
- Women's studies

## INDICES

| | |
|---|---|
| *What* | **College and University Home Pages** |
| *How* | Web |
| *Where* | http://www.mit.edu:8001/people/cdemello/univ.html |
| *Comments* | Over 2,500 listings of colleges and universities worldwide, in alphabetical and geographical order. |
| *Tidbit* | This site is mirrored at six other university computers for faster service. If MIT's server is too slow, jump to another site. |

| | |
|---|---|
| *What* | **CollegeNet** |
| *How* | Web |
| *Where* | http://www.collegenet.com/ |
| *Comments* | General information for young adults seeking entrance into college. The site's most useful features are its lists of U.S. colleges. In addition to a comprehensive list of schools (searchable by region, major, enrollment, and tuition), there are separate lists for Ivy League colleges, women's schools, and historically African-American universities. CollegeNet also has a list of community, junior, and technical schools. |

| | |
|---|---|
| *What* | **Community College Web** |
| *How* | Web |
| *Where* | http://www.mcli.dist.maricopa.edu/cc/ |
| *Comments* | Searchable Web links to over 460 community (two-year) colleges located in the United States, Canada, and Europe. |

| | |
|---|---|
| *What* | **Index of American Universities** |
| *How* | Web |
| *Where* | http://www.clas.ufl.edu/CLAS/american-universities.html |
| *Comments* | Giant alphabetical list of U.S. universities that have World Wide Web pages. |

## ACADEMIC ASSOCIATIONS AND SUPPORT NETWORKS

| | |
|---|---|
| *What* | **The American Association of University Women** |
| *How* | Web |

| | |
|---|---|
| *Where* | http://www.aauw.org/ |
| *Comments* | General information about the organization, fellowship and grant opportunities, and suggestions for participating in AAUW activities. Useful resources include several paper abstracts about the gender imbalance in grade school and university education, as well as a fax and e-mail list for mailings about congressional actions that affect the future of women's and girls' education. There is a small cost to subscribe. |
| *What* | **Center for Advanced Feminist Studies (CAFS)** |
| *How* | Web |
| *Where* | http://rhetoric.agoff.umn.edu/~cafs/ |
| *Comments* | Most of the information here is specific to the academic program at the University of Minnesota, such as its visiting scholar program and graduate studies curriculum. |
| *What* | **Feminist University Network** |
| *How* | Web |
| *Where* | http://www.feminist.org/campus/1_campus.html |
| *Comments* | Part of the Feminist Majority Foundation Web site, the Feminist University Network is primarily a database of university faculty and students who have interests in feminist academic topics. The database is searchable and anyone is welcome to add her or his name to the list. Also available at the site are a description of Feminist Majority Foundation internship opportunities and a list of U.S. women's studies programs and centers with postal mail addresses, e-mail addresses, and Web page links. |
| *What* | **FEMPED-L (Feminist Pedagogy List)** |
| *How* | Listserv |
| *Where* | Send message to listserv@uga.cc.uga.edu with no subject line to subscribe; type SUBSCRIBE FEMPED-L Firstname Lastname in the body of the message. |
| *Comments* | "Designed for discussing issues of power and positionality in the classroom and how feminist pedagogy can be used to challenge patriarchal models and methods that silence and intimidate women in educational settings." |
| *What* | **The Gay, Lesbian, and Straight Teachers Network (GLSTN)** |
| *How* | Web |
| *Where* | http://www.glstn.org/freedom/ |
| *Comments* | Hours worth of reading material, this site bursts with content. GLSTN has provided educators with supporting information about: addressing homophobia in K–12 schools; coming-out issues for teachers and students; how students can establish a gay-straight alliance in their school; legal principles governing the employment of gay teachers; conferences for gay-straight teacher alliances; and much more. |
| *What* | **LESAC-NET** |
| *How* | Mailing list |

*Where*   Send message to majordomo@queernet.org with no subject line to subscribe; type SUBSCRIBE LESAC-NET in the body of the message.

*Comments*   "This list is open to self-identified lesbians or bisexual women who are academics (graduate students, professors, or other faculty members) and it serves the fairly limited purpose of enabling women to connect with others who have similar research interests. The list also provides a space . . . to discuss what it means to be a lesbian or bisexual woman in academia—the perils of being out, the problems of sexism and homophobia, the lack of respect for lesbian issues as research material, etc."

*What*   **WRAC-L (Women's Resource and Action Centers)**

*How*   Listserv

*Where*   Send message to listserv@dartmouth.edu with no subject line to subscribe; type SUBSCRIBE WRAC-L Firstname Lastname in the body of the message.

*Comments*   List specifically for discussing issues of significance to women's centers. Staff and affiliates of community-based and academic-affiliated women's centers are encouraged to join. The list's purpose is "to support the outreach, advocacy, and counseling activities of women's centers and to facilitate communication and networking between them."

## ALTERNATIVE EDUCATION

*What*   **Alternative Education**

*How*   Usenet newsgroup

*Where*   alt.education.alternative

*Comments*   Lively discussion about all aspects of alternative education: public versus private, education vouchers, unschooling, etc.

*What*   **The Alternative Higher Education Network**

*How*   Web

*Where*   http://hampshire.edu/html/cs/ahen/ahen.html

*Comments*   Started with four main goals in mind: "to provide a forum for the discussion of what alternative education and education mean, to provide tools for the collaborative assessment of existing programs within the schools, to provide a tool for the creation of new programs, and to help individuals meet their own individual networking needs." This site provides links to alternative colleges across the country.

*What*   **Alternative Education Resource Organization**

*How*   Web

*Where*   http://www.speakeasy.org/~aero/

*Comments*   Tons of links to alternative education information! "AERO helps individuals and groups of people who want to start new community schools, public and private, or who want to change existing schools. It also provides information to people interested in homeschooling their children, or finding private or public alternative schools."

| | |
|---|---|
| *What* | **HOME-ED (Home Education)** |
| *How* | Mailing list |
| *Where* | Send message to `home-ed@world.std.com` with no subject line to subscribe; type `SUBSCRIBE HOME-ED Firstname Lastname` in the body of the message. |
| *Comments* | Very busy list on home schooling, with over 150 messages a day. |
| *Tidbit* | A digest version is available, which is posted daily to the `misc.education.home-school.misc` newsgroup. |

| | |
|---|---|
| *What* | **Home Education's Homeschooling Information and Resource Pages** |
| *How* | Web |
| *Where* | `http://www.home-ed-press.com/` |
| *Comments* | Full of content, Home Ed's site is an invaluable resource for homeschooling parents. Published first in the *Home Ed* magazine, the articles here offer practical advice for testing assessment and evaluation tools, teaching a child with learning disabilities, current research on homeschooled children, unschooling topics, and curriculum ideas for all areas of academics. |

| | |
|---|---|
| *What* | **Homeschooling Information Center Annex** |
| *How* | Web |
| *Where* | `http://pages.prodigy.com/K/I/S/kids/hmsc.htm` |
| *Comments* | Part of a larger site hosted by Prodigy and only fully available to Prodigy members. The public access site, however, is chock-full of resources for homeschooling: lesson plans, upcoming conferences, books for home education, history exercises, foreign language teaching tools and more. |

| | |
|---|---|
| *What* | **Yahoo's Alternative Education Links** |
| *How* | Web |
| *Where* | `http://www.yahoo.com/Education/Alternative/` |
| *Comments* | There's no need to list every alternative education site available on the Web in this chapter, because you can check out Yahoo's comprehensive compilation, with links to individual programs and schools as well as resource clearinghouse Web sites. |

## EQUITY IN EDUCATION

| | |
|---|---|
| *What* | **GENED (Gender and Education)** |
| *How* | Mailing list |
| *Where* | Send message to `majordomo@acpub.duke.edu` with no subject line to subscribe; type `SUBSCRIBE GENED` in the body of the message. |

*Comments*  "This mailing list was designed for K–12 teachers, interested parents, university researchers, and other educators and professionals. Discussion here may address such topics as gender issues for schools; gender equity; gender issues in K–12 curriculum; gender as an element of development and growth; gender and health; gender issues in science, mathematics, and technology education; construction, in school and home, of gender identity and gender roles; and similar topics."

*What*  **EDEQUITY (Equity in Education)**

*How*  Mailing list

*Where*  Send message to `majordomo@confer.edu.org` with no subject line to subscribe; type `SUBSCRIBE EDEQUITY` in the body of the message.

*Comments*  Discussion of multiculturalism and equity in education.

*What*  **Advocate for Women in Science, Engineering, and Mathematics (AWSEM)**

*How*  Web

*Where*  `http://wwide.com/awsem.html`

*Comments*  AWSEM aims to keep girls between the ages twelve and eighteen who are interested in science, math, or engineering, challenged and encouraged to continue studies in the traditional hard sciences, including biology, chemistry, and physics. Based in Oregon, the organization offers mentorship programs, individual tutoring, and study groups.

*What*  **Expect the Best from a Girl. That's What You'll Get.**

*How*  Web

*Where*  `http://www.academic.org/`

*Comments*  In an effort to help girls maintain self-confidence in school, especially in areas of math and science, this Web site offers practical information and advice for parents of elementary and secondary school-age daughters. Also available here: a list of women's colleges and programs for girls, summer camps for girls interested in technology and the sciences, and current statistics about women and the workplace.

*What*  **Pathways to School Improvement**

*How*  Web

*Where*  `http://www.ncrel.org/ncrel/sdrs/pathways.htm`

*Comments*  Maintained by an educational research and development organization called the Regional Educational Laboratories, which is supported by contracts with the U.S. Education Department's Office of Educational Research and Improvement (OERI). Here you will find resources for K–12 school assessment and reform. Educational areas such as math, science, literacy, and technology are separated into "critical issues" categories, each with links to articles and references for securing equal education for minorities, girls, and rural and urban students. Information is geared for parents as well as educators, with real-life examples of equity programs in U.S. elementary and secondary schools.

## FUNDING (GRANTS, FELLOWSHIPS, SCHOLARSHIPS AND FINANCIAL AID)

*What*    **Ada Project at Yale University—Fellowship, Grant, and Award Information**

*How*    Web

*Where*    http://www.cs.yale.edu/HTML/YALE/CS/HyPlans/tap/fellowships.html

*Comments*    The Ada Project Web site honors Ada Lovelace, considered the first computer programmer and colleague of computing pioneer Charles Babbage. This Web page lists organizations with funding programs for women exploring engineering, mathematics, computer science, and other hard science fields.

*What*    **The Cornell University Graduate School Fellowships Notebook**

*How*    Web

*Where*    http://www.cornell.edu/Student/GRFN/

*Comments*    A wonderful and extensive resource for searching fellowship and grant programs for postsecondary study and research.

*What*    **FinAid: The Financial Aid Information Page**

*How*    Web

*Where*    http://www.cs.cmu.edu/afs/cs/user/mkant/Public/FinAid/finaid.html

*Comments*    This huge resource for students has information and links to everything you need to know about funding your education. From loans to scholarships, study abroad to co-ops, FinAid has it all, including a section of financial aid opportunities exclusively for women.

*What*    **The Global Fund for Women**

*How*    Web

*Where*    http://www.igc.apc.org/gfw/

*Comments*    "The Global Fund for Women is the only U.S.-based organization that exclusively supports international women's rights groups." The Fund's three areas of concern are: female human rights, women's access to media and communications technology, and women's economic autonomy. Grants are awarded to non U.S.-based not-for-profit organizations only.

*What*    **GRANTS-L (Grants for Educational Research)**

*How*    Listserv

*Where*    Send message to listproc@.gsu.edu with no subject line to subscribe; type SUBSCRIBE GRANTS-L Firstname Lastname in the body of the message.

*Comments*    "Serves to promote external funding for international education and research. The Listserv is intended to provide a forum for sharing experience, ideas, thoughts, comments, and sources of information on the preparation and administration of contracts and grants."

| | |
|---|---|
| *What* | **Illinois Researcher Information Services (IRIS)** |
| *How* | Web |
| *Where* | http://surya.grainger.uiuc.edu/iris/ |
| *Comments* | Free grant-search service for members of the University of Illinois, Urbana-Champaign, community and a subscription-based service for outside academic institutions. "The IRIS database currently contains approximately 7,000 federal and nonfederal funding opportunities in the sciences, social sciences, arts, and humanities." |

| | |
|---|---|
| *What* | **MOLIS: The Minority On-line Information System** |
| *How* | Web |
| *Where* | http://web.fie.com/web/mol/ |
| *Comments* | "Provides a free source of information about the research and educational capabilities of historically black colleges and universities and Hispanic-serving institutions. MOLIS is also a source of federal education and research opportunities for the minority higher education community." Search the database of historically black colleges by state, school name, or major field of study. Find federal job listings, current events, and minority scholarship and fellowship program information. |

| | |
|---|---|
| *What* | **Research Funding Agencies** |
| *How* | Web |
| *Where* | http://www.cs.virginia.edu/~seas/resdev/sponsors.html |
| *Comments* | Listing of government and private corporation granting agencies for science and technology research projects. |

| | |
|---|---|
| *What* | **Financial Aid Information** |
| *How* | Usenet newsgroup |
| *Where* | soc.college.financial-aid |
| *Comments* | Friendly discussion forum for exchanging financial aid information. Most participants are current students looking for educational funding and sharing financial aid horrors stories and victories. |

| | |
|---|---|
| *What* | **State and Federal Grants** |
| *How* | Web |
| *Where* | http://www.window.texas.gov/window-on-state-gov.html |
| *Comments* | Guide to state and federal government grants only. The index can be searched by topic or keyword. |

| | |
|---|---|
| *What* | **The Student Guide to Financial Aid from the U.S. Department of Education** |
| *How* | Web |
| *Where* | http://www.ed.gov/prog_info/SFA/StudentGuide/ |
| *Comments* | Published every year in print, the *Student Guide* is now available on the Web. All the information a new or continuing student and her/his parents need to know about |

government-sponsored loans. You will find specific information on the types of loans available, how to apply, when to apply, and how loans are repaid.

## K–12 EDUCATION

| | |
|---|---|
| *What* | **EdWeb** |
| *How* | Web |
| *Where* | `http://k12.cnidr.org:90/` |
| *Comments* | Devoted to advancing the use of technology, particularly Internet technology, in K–12 education. Educators will find the HTML crash course useful for learning and planning Web publishing activities for the classroom. EdWeb provides a long list of education-related Listservs/e-mailing lists, with the entire list of K–12 Listserv groups. Sprinklings of information about girls and technology are a part of the text regarding school reform. |

| | |
|---|---|
| *What* | **Teacher's Edition On-line** |
| *How* | Web; Listserv |
| *Where* | `http://www.teachnet.com/` for the Web; send message to `majordomo@teachernet.com` with no subject line to subscribe; type `SUBSCRIBE NEWSLETTER your e-mail address` in the body of the message for the Listserv. |
| *Comments* | A gold mine of resources for K–12 educators! Updated weekly with lesson plan ideas, classroom decor (how to build a classroom pond), time management tips, record-keeping tools, and teacher-to-teacher discussions. If you don't have time to browse the Web site, Teacher's Edition can be sent directly to your e-mail address. |

| | |
|---|---|
| *What* | **Web66: A K–12 World Wide Web Project** |
| *How* | Web |
| *Where* | `http://web66.coled.umn.edu/` |
| *Comments* | University of Minnesota project to link educators and students to Web tools, with over five hundred schools listed. Find practical information on how to link a school district to the Internet (Web66 Network Construction Set) and building a Web site in the classroom (Classroom Internet Server Cookbook). |

## LESBIAN, GAY, AND BISEXUAL STUDIES

| | |
|---|---|
| *What* | **BITHRY-L (Bisexuality)** |
| *How* | Listserv |
| *Where* | Send message to `listserv@brownvm.brown.edu` with no subject line to subscribe; type `SUBSCRIBE BITHRY-L Firstname Lastname` in the body of the message. |
| *Comments* | "For the discussion of bisexuality and gender studies." Incoming e-mail is light. |

| | |
|---|---|
| *What* | **LESBIAN-STUDIES** |
| *How* | Listserv |

| | |
|---|---|
| *Where* | Send message to majordomo@queernet.org with no subject line to subscribe; type INFO LESBIAN-STUDIES in the body of the message. |
| *Comments* | "This list is open to women ONLY, in order to create a safe and independent space . . . to discuss research in the field of lesbian studies. The list is for academic discussions only, relating to lesbian and bi history, literature, cultures, politics, theories, etc., and should not be used for general chat." |

| | |
|---|---|
| *What* | **QSTUDY-L (Queer Studies)** |
| *How* | Listserv |
| *Where* | Send message to listserv@ubvmcc.buffalo.edu with no subject line to subscribe; type SUBSCRIBE QSTUDY-L Firstname Lastname in the body of the message. |
| *Comments* | This list is for academic discussions of queer theory, including lesbian, gay, bisexual, and transsexual/transgender studies. "QSTUDY-L is also intended to promote networking and information sharing between teachers, researchers, librarians, and students—anyone involved or interested in the field of queer studies. Posting announcements about relevant conferences or publications, calls for papers, job opportunities, or anything else relevant to the topic of queer studies is encouraged." |

| | |
|---|---|
| *What* | **University of California at Berkeley Bisexual/Lesbian/Gay/Queer Gopher** |
| *How* | Gopher |
| *Where* | gopher uclink.berkeley.edu/Other U.C. Berkeley Information Servers/Community Topics/Multicultural Bisexual Lesbian Gay Alliance/Lesbian & Gay Studies |
| *Comments* | Information about the academic departments and interdisciplinary programs available at UC-Berkeley in Lesbian & Gay Studies, as well as campus activities, calls for papers, book reviews, and publications. |
| *Tidbit* | Check out the hot links to Lesbian/Gay Studies programs at other universities and the Queer Resources Directory: http://server.berkeley.edu/queer/ucb/ucb.html. |

## LIBRARIES

| | |
|---|---|
| *What* | **Bryn Mawr College** |
| *How* | Telnet |
| *Where* | telnet tripod.brynmawr.edu; log-in name: tripod |
| *Comments* | This Telnet address will connect you to the library catalogs for Bryn Mawr, Haverford, and Swarthmore colleges. |

| | |
|---|---|
| *What* | **Duke University Library Women's Studies Resources** |
| *How* | Web |
| *Where* | http://odyssey.lib.duke.edu/women/ |

*Comments*    Specific to Duke University's collection, this site provides a list of Women's Studies periodicals, microfilm titles, a few bibliographies and research grant opportunities.

*What*    **Index of OPAC (On-line Public Access Catalogs) Libraries World Wide**

*How*    Gopher

*Where*    `gopher libgopher.yale.edu`

*Comments*    Indexed by region and state, this large collection of on-line library catalogs provides links via Telnet or Web directly to the listed libraries.

*What*    **Library of Congress Information System**

*How*    Telnet

*Where*    `telnet locis.loc.gov`

*Comments*    Access to the gigantic Library of Congress collection, which can be searched. FTP services are also available for downloading papers and bibliographies published by the Library of Congress, `ftp ftp.loc.gov`. Once logged in, type `cd /pub` to change to the public access directory, and then type `dir` to see a list of available document directories.

*What*    **The Schlesinger Library on the History of Women in America, Radcliffe College**

*How*    Telnet; Gopher

*Where*    `telnet hollis.harvard.edu` for Telnet; `gopher gopher.harvard.edu/ Harvard Library Resources` for Gopher

*Comments*    The Schlesinger Library holds "personal and family papers and organizational records documenting the history of women in the United States, with some emphasis on New England and Massachusetts."

*What*    **Smith College Library Collection**

*How*    Gopher

*Where*    `gopher marge.smith.edu/Smith College Libraries`

*Comments*    Access to the catalog of holdings of Massachusetts all-women's college libraries: Hillyer (Fine) Arts, Josten Performing Arts, and Young Science Libraries.

*What*    **Texas Women's University Library**

*How*    Telnet

*Where*    `telnet venus.twu.edu`; log-in name: `IRIS`

*Comments*    Catalog of Texas Women's University Library collection.

*What*    **University of North Carolina–Chapel Hill Library System**

*How*    Telnet

*Where*    `telnet librot1.lib.unc.edu`; log-in name: `LIBRARY`

*Comments*    "The University of North Carolina–Chapel Hill has the most extensive holdings of library materials on women's studies in the South. Although resources on women in nearly all areas of the social sciences are collected to some extent, library holdings are particularly strong in history, politics, and socioeconomic conditions and for southern women, African-American women, feminism/women's rights, and labor."

*Tidbit*    Also check out UNC-Greensboro's Library: `telnet steffi.uncg.edu`; log-in name: `jaclin`

*What*    **University of Wisconsin System Women's Studies Librarian's Office**

*How*    Web

*Where*    `http://www.library.wisc.edu/libraries/WomensStudies`

*Comments*    Wonderful collection of women's studies bibliographies, such as the recently added Women in Technology annotated bibliography, plus women's studies journals and papers.

*What*    **WOMCOLLIB (Women in College Libraries)**

*How*    Listserv

*Where*    Send message to `list-request@catt.cochran.edu` to subscribe; type `SUBSCRIBE WOMCOLLIB Firstname Lastname` in the subject line; leave the body of the message completely blank.

*Comments*    Specifically for women working in libraries at women's colleges. Topics of discussion include women's access to information technologies, academic resources available for women's studies, and general talk about working with a women's college.

## MULTICULTURAL EDUCATION, BILINGUAL, AND ESL RESOURCES

*What*    **Black Collegian: A Career and Self-Development Site for Students of Color**

*How*    Web

*Where*    `http://www.black-collegian.com/`

*Comments*    Building on its paper edition, the *Black Collegian* magazine has developed a Web site for a wide variety of campus life topics. Features include readings and bibliographies for black studies, book reviews, interviews, campus news and opinion, a directory of graduate and professional studies programs, and fellowship information.

*Tidbit*    Black Collegian Job Assistant Selection Service is for those about to graduate. It contains job listings, interviewing tips, career reports, and résumé advice.

*What*    **Bilingual and ESL Network (BEN)**

*How*    Web

*Where*    `http://tism.bevc.blacksburg.va.us/BEN.html`

*Comments*    A great starting point for bilingual and English as a second language educational information. Full of links to resources for K–12 and university classrooms.

|          |   |
|----------|---|
| *Tidbit* | BEN also hosts a discussion forum for bilingual and ESL topics. To subscribe send an e-mail message requesting subscription information to nieves@vt.edu. |

| *What* | **CLNet's Chicana Studies Web Pages** |
|--------|----------------------------------------|
| *How* | Web |
| *Where* | http://latino.sscnet.ucla.edu/women/womenHP.html |
| *Comments* | Hosted by the University of California Los Angeles Latino/Latina Studies Department, this Web site offers up tons of academic resources: calls for papers, conferences, Net links to Latina/Chicana research centers, profiles and interviews with Chicana and Latina scholars/activists (recently featured: Rigoberta Menchu Tum), course syllabi, and video and bibliographic reference materials. |
| *Tidbit* | CLNet provides Web space for Chicanas and Latinas to develop personal Web pages, which will be added to CLNet's "Bronze Pages." |

| *What* | **MULTC-ED (Multicultural Education)** |
|--------|----------------------------------------|
| *How* | Listserv |
| *Where* | Send message to listserv@umdd.umd.edu with no subject line to subscribe; type SUBSCRIBE MULTC-ED in the body of the message. |
| *Comments* | "The MULTC-ED moderated discussion list is intended to serve all educators involved in multicultural curriculum, teaching or research in the following areas of interest: grades preschool–12; colleges and universities; other educationally related agencies; parents of children and youth. The scope of multicultural education for this list includes the full range of diversity which includes ability, age, class, ethnicity, gender, national origin, race, religion, and sexual orientation." Discussion topics include theory and practice focused on teaching, curriculum, research, resources, and materials. |

| *What* | **The Multicultural Alliance** |
|--------|--------------------------------|
| *How* | Web |
| *Where* | http://www.branson.org/mca/ |
| *Comments* | "The Multicultural Alliance is an advocate for diversity in schools, helping elementary, secondary, and postsecondary institutions realize the need to work together to ensure the best education for all children." The Alliance sponsors a teacher internship program for junior and senior college students of color. Other Alliance projects: the Ethnic Studies Training Institute, which provides year-long training seminars addressing issues of multicultural classroom instruction, and the Annual Student of Color Forum lecture series and round table discussion for students and parents of color regarding diversity in community education. |

## PUBLICATIONS

| *What* | **Academe This Week** |
|--------|------------------------|
| *How* | Web |

| *Where* | http://chronicle.merit.edu/ |
|---|---|
| *Comments* | A service of *The Chronicle of Higher Education*, this site is updated weekly with top academic news, university events, books for the classroom, job listings, and *The Chronicle of Higher Education* table of contents. To read entire articles from the paper edition you must register and subscribe to *The Chronicle*. |

| *What* | **Women in Higher Education** |
|---|---|
| *How* | Web |
| *Where* | http://www.itis.com/wihe/ |
| *Comments* | Claims to be "the only national monthly publication to support women on campus." This monthly newsletter is partially published on-line, offering a few full articles from each issue as well as subscription information and on-line ordering for the paper copy. |
| *Tidbit* | Check out "Career Connections," a list of job positions recently appearing in Women in Higher Education. |

## WOMEN'S HISTORY

| *What* | **Distinguished Women of Past and Present** |
|---|---|
| *How* | Web |
| *Where* | http://www.netsrq.com/~dbois/ |
| *Comments* | Large collection of biographies of famous women. The site is indexed alphabetically and by area of expertise (science, art, music, education). Where appropriate, biographical material is linked to relevant Web sites. A wonderful research and teaching tool! |

| *What* | **Encyclopedia of Women's History** |
|---|---|
| *How* | Web |
| *Where* | http://www.teleport.com/~megaines/women.html |
| *Comments* | Started by students in grades 3 through 12 and growing every day, this site is fun to browse and a wonderful teaching tool for any grade level. Search the alphabetical listing of women in history for short biographies and links to additional information on the Net. The Web site also has a forum where visitors can add a name to the encyclopedia. |

| *What* | **H-WOMEN (History of Women)** |
|---|---|
| *How* | Listserv |
| *Where* | Send message to listserv@msu.edu with no subject line to subscribe; type SUBSCRIBE H-WOMEN Firstname Lastname in the body of the message. |
| *Comments* | A moderated discussion forum for women's history teachers, librarians, and scholars. |

| *What* | **Isis: Ourstory—Black Women's History** |
|---|---|
| *How* | Web |

| | |
|---|---|
| *Where* | http://www.netdiva.com/ourstory.html |
| *Comments* | "The Ourstory page at Isis is about historically and culturally important women, places, and things." The links are extensive—for example, first African-American woman neurosurgeon Alexa Canady; home page for Carol Moseley Braun, the first African-American woman senator; excerpt of Coretta Scott King reading from her autobiography; black women and work during World War II; *Journal of Women and Minorities in Science and Engineering* page; a bibliography about black women from the Library of Congress. |

| | |
|---|---|
| *What* | **National Women's History Project** |
| *How* | Web |
| *Where* | http://www.nwhp.org/ |
| *Comments* | This beautiful site is a great resource for teachers, parents, community activists, and librarians. It contains practical and thoughtful ideas for integrating women's history into current curricula and workplace activities. Join the Women's History Network, order a catalog of resources for teaching women's history, participate in Women's History Month activities, read a quote or two by famous women, and take an on-line mini quiz to test your women's history IQ. |

| | |
|---|---|
| *What* | **Social Studies School Service: Women's History** |
| *How* | Web |
| *Where* | http://socialstudies.com/mar/women.html |
| *Comments* | Evaluates educational titles from hundreds of publishers to develop catalogs for social studies teachers at all grade levels. The women's history resources highlighted at this site include essays on women in wartime, the workplace, and politics; lists of available books, posters, videos, CD-ROM titles and curricula; and an on-line exercise based on the Declaration of Sentiment at the Seneca Falls Convention. |

| | |
|---|---|
| *What* | **Women of Achievement in Herstory** |
| *How* | Listserv |
| *Where* | Send message to listserv@netcom.com with no subject line to subscribe; type SUBSCRIBE WOAH-Herstory your e-mail address in the body of the message. |
| *Comments* | This list is not for discussion. Members receive via e-mail a daily account of a noteworthy woman from history. The profile is not always of the most well-known women from history, thus bringing to light many other women of achievement not generally recognized. This "woman of the day" list would be a fun addition to a women's studies or history classroom. |
| *Tidbit* | If you have Web access, check out the Women of Achievement in Herstory calendar. For every day of the year there are several listings of women's birthdays: http://worcester.lm.com/women/history/woacal.html. |

| | |
|---|---|
| *What* | **Women's History: A Todd Library Research Guide** |
| *How* | Web |
| *Where* | http://frank.mtsu.edu/~kmiddlet/history/women.html |
| *Comments* | From Middle Tennessee State University (MTSU) come more women's history resources. Some of the lists are linked to on-line resources, but most are citations for papers, books, journals, and bibliographies. On-line links include encyclopedias, bibliographies, and biographical databases. Also find information on MTSU's women's history video collection and organizations for networking with other women historians. |

## WOMEN'S STUDIES

| | |
|---|---|
| *What* | **Feminist Curricular Resources Clearinghouse** |
| *How* | Web |
| *Where* | http://www.law.indiana.edu/fcrc/fcrc.html |
| *Comments* | "The Clearinghouse provides access to a number of resources related to teaching about feminism and law, including syllabi, reading lists, and bibliographies from courses taught in law schools and other departments. All of these materials deal with legal or jurisprudential issues of concern to women." The site is indexed by contributor and subject. |

| | |
|---|---|
| *What* | **Inform Women's Studies Resources at the University of Maryland** |
| *How* | Web; Gopher |
| *Where* | http://www.inform.umd.edu:8080/EdRes/Topic/WomensStudies for Web site; gopher inform.umd.edu/Educational Resources/Academic Resources By Topic/Women's Studies Resources for Gopher |
| *Comments* | This invaluable site lets you click away a few hours reading the entire text of *Jane Eyre* or *Frankenstein*, or peruse feminist film reviews, women's studies employment opportunities, course outlines and syllabi for undergraduate and graduate level women's studies classes, and calls for papers and conferences. All the timely material is kept up-to-date, and visitors are encouraged to use any information for academic purposes as long as the authors receive proper credit. |
| *Tidbit* | Go to the "reference room" for a directory of women's studies programs worldwide or click your way to several women's studies libraries available on-line. |

| | |
|---|---|
| *What* | **WMST-L** |
| *How* | Listserv |
| *Where* | Send message to listserv@umdd.umd.edu with no subject line to subscribe; type SUBSCRIBE WMST-L Firstname Lastname in the body of the message. |
| *Comments* | "WMST-L is an international electronic forum for people involved in Women's Studies as teachers, researchers, librarians, and program administrators. Topics include: current research; teaching strategies; useful texts and films; innovative |

courses; funding sources; building Women's Studies majors, minors, and graduate programs; relations between Women's Studies and other 'minority studies' programs; and other academic issues. WMST-L also publishes announcements about relevant conferences, calls for papers, job opportunities, and publications, and serves as a file repository for syllabi, bibliographies, and other files related to Women's Studies."

*Tidbit*   With over four thousand members, WMST-L is a heavy e-mail list. A daily digest version is available for those who would prefer to receive fewer individual messages.

*What*   **Women's Resources Project: Women's Studies Listings**

*How*   Web

*Where*   http://sunsite.unc.edu/cheryb/women/otherprogs.html

*Comments*   A perfect starting point for harvesting women's studies information on the Net. There are numerous lists to women's studies academic programs, departments, and research institutes, most of which are in the United States. The women's studies library listing includes precise instructions for linking to on-line libraries via Telnet. Also browse other pages at this site for general women's Internet resources.

*What*   **WOMENS-STUDIES**

*How*   Mailing list

*Where*   Send message to mailbase@mailbase.ac.uk with no subject line to subscribe; type JOIN WOMENS-STUDIES Firstname Lastname in the body of the message.

*Comments*   Designed for members of the Women's Studies Network (United Kingdom) Association and for academic staff and researchers in the field of women's studies. The list will provide a forum for the exchange of information and a notice board for conferences, recent publications, etc.

# 4

# WHEN WOMEN COUNT

## Financial, Business, and Career Opportunities

### *Cheryl Lehman*

Stereotypes, always inhibiting and disempowering, are particularly so in commerce, because economic empowerment fosters, enhances, and reproduces social empowerment. The adage that "women just don't have a head for figures" is not only wrong, it is dangerous because it restrains women from seeking and attaining power and empowerment in financial areas. Knowing that numbers are not such a mystery, women have consistently sought to demystify business and to enter all aspects of commerce, investing, negotiation, and trade; they have networked, shared strategies and frustrations, broken glass ceilings, shattered glass walls, and shaken stereotypes.

Women's economic power is not frequently celebrated in the popular press, but the numbers speak for themselves:

• Women-owned businesses in the United States now account for $1.6 trillion in revenues (this is more than the gross domestic product of all but a few countries) and they employ 35 percent more workers in the United States than the Fortune 500 companies.

• Women provide half their households' income in the United States according to a 1995 Louis Harris & Associates Inc. survey.

• Women worldwide contribute billions of dollars worth of production that is excluded from the United Nations Systems of National Accounts, and thus rendered invisible, as accounted by Marilyn Waring in her pathbreaking book *If Women Counted* (1988).

• A study of thirteen industrialized countries released in 1995 by the United Nations Human Development Program found that women's share of work with economic value is 51 percent; the percentage of women's work that is unpaid is 66 percent; the percentage of men's work that is unpaid is 34 percent.

Women's access to certain work is hard won; stereotyping survives in many spheres of life, and the business community has a dismal record of supporting and promoting women's achievements. Consider these facts of organizational life:

• Although females comprise over 50 percent of accounting graduates, less than 5 percent of partners are female.

• Women with equal or better education earn less on average than men, and there are proportionally fewer women in top positions, concluded a study of career professionals of male and female managers in twenty Fortune 500 companies, although the two groups were alike in almost every other way (Gabriel and Martin, Deloitte and Touche 1993 Annual Report, 18).

• In a "twist of the old-boy network, more women business owners and general counsels prefer to give outside assignments to other women," reveals a *New York Times* article (June 23, 1996). Tevia Barnes, associate general counsel and senior vice president of Bank of America, sends this message: "If you have doubt whether we want a diverse team, let us set the record straight. We want men, women, white and of color, a full spectrum."

There is a wealth of support on the Internet for your dreams and goals if you are in business; are seeking advice; want to network, expand your horizons, and access all kinds of industry, corporate, and government data; or just want to learn and nurture your business sensitivities. To help you capture some of these resources, and to facilitate your search, this chapter is divided into two main sections, with subcategories within each.

The first section includes specifically women-friendly resources. Because sisterhood networks have emerged in business and professional spheres, these sites are listed separately from the general, non–female-centered sites. These networks often recognize the problems of women in business and, as with many of the sites listed in this book, they provide support as well as solid advice about how to manage, organize, and proceed as a female in business. These sites not only offer female-specific strategies and networks, but may also link you with the networks listed in the second section. This first section is subdivided into six subcategories:

- All-encompassing sites
- Networking, managing, and financing
- Women-owned businesses
- Women of color business links
- Non–business-dedicated sites (women's supports which include either a "business" or "financing" or "women's business" category)
- Additional women-friendly sites

The second main section includes sites where women can access what has traditionally been the "old boys' network" and use it to their own benefit. Countless networks have developed for accessing the financing, career, and "day-to-day" business concerns of entrepreneurs, bankers, financial analysts, computer experts, managers, and directors. Within this sampling of nonfemale-specific sites are the following subcategories:

- Business and investing
- Career and job opportunities
- How tos—consulting, managing, and legal advice

- Additional links—domestic
- Additional links—international business

## WOMEN FRIENDLY

### All-Encompassing Sites

| | |
|---|---|
| *What* | **Advancing Women** |
| *How* | Web |
| *Where* | http://www.advancingwomen.com/ |
| *Comments* | Everything about this site is exciting: the right-on topics, cool graphics, endless links, perceptive insights, warmth, support, and shared anger. Self-described as "an international networking site for women in the workplace to meet and network with each other, on a global basis, to develop strategies and shape approaches to advance career or personal goals." |

| | |
|---|---|
| *What* | **BizWomen** |
| *How* | Web |
| *Where* | http://bizcomen.com |
| *Comments* | "BizWomen provides the on-line interactive community for successful women in business: to communicate, network, exchange ideas, and provide support for each other via the Internet." A directory links you to women working in the fields of advertising, arts, finance, electronics, health services, legal services, publishing, and others. Women InterNetworking (WIN) is a good place to begin your business networking. |

| | |
|---|---|
| *What* | **Field of Dreams: Women in Business Cyberspace** |
| *How* | Web |
| *Where* | http://www.gridley.org/~imaging/resource.html |
| *Comments* | Practical site with numerous resource links including: Women Incorporated, Minority and Women Business Enterprises, U.S. Department of Labor Women's Bureau, Russian Securities Market News (in English), All Business Network, International Small Business Consortium. |

| | |
|---|---|
| *What* | **NAFE: National Association for Executive Females** |
| *How* | Web |
| *Where* | http://www.nafe.com |
| *Comments* | Founded by Wendy Rue, NAFE has been advancing women's economic independence for the past twenty-five years. NAFE's 200,000-plus members benefit from the organization's networking and career advancement opportunities. Includes access to an Esteem Team program for disadvantaged teenagers and links to the U.S. Securities and Exchange home page, Management Q & A, Bureau of Labor Statistics' information, advice on starting your business, an ethics watch, Managing Smart, excerpts from NAFE's *Executive Female* magazine, and much more. |

## Networking, Managing, and Financing

| | |
|---|---|
| *What* | **Business Women's Network** |
| *How* | Web |
| *Where* | http://www.tpag.com/BWN.html |
| *Comments* | The Business Women's Network (BWN), a division of *Public Affairs, Inc.,* "was designed to encourage communication and networking among the top business-women's organizations in the United States. BWN enables two million business women and corporate America to find information, network, and procure financing." Lists the twenty "top" business and professional women's organizations. Underdeveloped in comparison with other sites, although the organization itself may be a useful resource. |

| | |
|---|---|
| *What* | **Engender Magazine** |
| *How* | Web |
| *Where* | http://www.cadvision.com/ffap/engender/ |
| *Comments* | Offers short articles on managing, tax planning, and community building for women in small business. |

| | |
|---|---|
| *What* | **Feminist Career Center** |
| *How* | Web |
| *Where* | http://www.feminist.org/911/911jobs.html |
| *Comments* | Features progressive jobs and internships, as well as a résumé posting. Includes a listing of career resources and job banks on the Web. They are happy to post job openings, internship opportunities, and résumés. |

| | |
|---|---|
| *What* | **MBA-WOMENS-MANAGEMENT-L** |
| *How* | Listserv |
| *Where* | Send the message subscribe mba-women-management-l Firstname Lastname to LISTPROC@CORNELL.EDU to subscribe. |
| *Comments* | Discussion for MBAs and professionals interested in women's management. |

| | |
|---|---|
| *What* | **Partnership of Women Entrepreneurs** |
| *How* | Web |
| *Where* | http://www.newdirection.com/thepartnership/ |
| *Comments* | This is a national membership service organization "to promote and support women business owners through useful networking vehicles, education/training workshops and personal services." Includes an excellent listing of Web sites devoted to consulting, government, business, and women. |

| | |
|---|---|
| *What* | **Small Business Administration: Office of Women's Business Ownership** |
| *How* | Web |

| | |
|---|---|
| *Where* | http://www.sbaon-line.sba.gov/womeninbusiness/ |
| *Comments* | Numerous statistics on women's contribution to the economy. Site is run by federal government agency, which offers assistance and advice and acts as an intermediary with banks and other lending institutions. Includes links to National Women's Business Council and much more. |
| *What* | **WomenBiz** |
| *How* | Web |
| *Where* | http://www.frsa.com/womenbiz/ |
| *Comments* | Features a discussion with a variety of services and networking possibilities. Biz Tips, Money Matters, and Women Business-Related Resources offer follow-up resources and advice. |
| *What* | **Womenet: The Women Owned Business Network** |
| *How* | Web |
| *Where* | http://womenet.com/ |
| *Comments* | Features a Women's Business Resource site that gives short advice on starting a business and suggests books and reports. A Good Ol' Girls Network section posts news, questions, and suggestions. Contains information on women-owned businesses listed by geographical area and specialty. |
| *What* | **Women's Wire** |
| *How* | Web |
| *Where* | http://www.women.com/ |
| *Comments* | Offers links and articles on careers, health, news, and personal finance. Under Work you can ask the "biz shrink" for advice or get the list of the 100 Best Companies for working mothers. A Women's Wire "Web" includes a section on women's businesses that currently lists over thirty sites: how to develop a home page, a speakers' and consultants' guide, female financial planners, and advertising professionals (plus tropical flowers, CDs, and women's clothes on-line). |
| *What* | **Women's World Banking** |
| *How* | E-mail |
| *Where* | wwb@igc.apc.org |
| *Comments* | Women's World Banking is a global not-for-profit institution established in 1979 that aims to promote the involvement of women in creating business enterprises. Through more than fifty international affiliates it assists millions of women entrepreneurs. It strives to get the policies, practices, and attitudes of governments, banks, and businesses to recognize the importance of women entrepreneurs. It also works to create innovative practices, new relationships, and effective systems to improve women's access to banking services, markets, and information. |

## Women-Owned Businesses

*What* **The Business of Women**

*How* Web

*Where* http://www.web-search.com/women.html

*Comments* Fifty categories, ranging from accounting to automotive to design to insurance to office support to telecommunications. Some categories include helpful organizations while other offerings are thin.

*What* **Links to Women Pages and Sites**

*How* Web

*Where* http://web.idirect.com/~klg/women.html

*Comments* Categories include women in business, and women and computers. The site's business link has over six thousand listings, including accounting, banks, and economic and business resources. Note that the sites are not designed for women only, but are great information sources for your specific needs.

*What* **Pleiades Women's Business Directory**

*How* Web

*Where* http://www.pleiades-net.com/lists/bus.html

*Comments* Organized into subcategories on a variety of subjects, including accounting and finance, legal issues, computers, and insurance.

*What* **WOMEN-LIST**

*How* Listserv

*Where* Send the message SUBSCRIBE WOMEN-LIST to MAJORDOMO@CGIM.COM to subscribe.

*Comments* Business-related support group for women who own businesses or plan to start a business. Includes information on how to manage a business, write a business plan, start-up to apply for loans, market a business, and develop a clientele.

*What* **The Women's White Pages**

*How* Web

*Where* http://www.femail.com

*Comments* White pages directory searchable by name, locale, and keywords to find e-mail addresses, street addresses, and Web sites of women and women-owned businesses both on and off the Internet. Any woman or woman-owned business or organization can add its contact information via the Women's White Pages Web site. The only information required is your first and last names and e-mail address; the rest is optional.

## Women of Color Business Links

| | |
|---|---|
| *What* | **Isis Plus** |
| *How* | Web |
| *Where* | http://www.netdiva.com/isisplus.html |
| *Comments* | Supporting and eloquently displaying arts and culture of women of the African diaspora, this site also offers links to the "Universal Black Pages"; Black Data Processing Associates (BDPA), dedicated to educating and training minority professionals working within the information technology industry, and supportive institutions, such as the National Bar Association (NBA), which seeks "to uphold the honor of the legal profession . . . and protect the civil and political rights of all citizens of the several states of the United States." You can attain info on their career opportunities, events, LawFax, the NBA magazine, and Internet legal resources. |

| | |
|---|---|
| *What* | **Minority Business Entrepreneur (MBE)** |
| *How* | Web |
| *Where* | http://www.mbemag.com/ |
| *Comments* | This is the Web site for the magazine *Minority Business Entrepreneur,* a bimonthly publication for and about minority and women business owners. Recent article topics included high-tech industries, banking, and telecommunications, all in relation to minority business and development. Enter keywords to search for articles of interest. |

## Non–Business-Dedicated Sites

| | |
|---|---|
| *What* | **Angel Swan's World of Women's Resources** |
| *How* | Web |
| *Where* | http://www.netcreations.com/drmatrix/women.html |
| *Comments* | Stunning graphics and two hundred links. |

| | |
|---|---|
| *What* | **The Computer Café** |
| *How* | Web |
| *Where* | http://www.fstlink.com.au/clients/ccafe/women.html |
| *Comments* | The business section of this wonderfully rich site (which also includes health issues, spirituality, sports, and much more) links you with Field of Dreams, BizWomen, Engender, Working@Home, and many other sites mentioned in this resource. |

| | |
|---|---|
| *What* | **FEMINIST.COM** |
| *How* | Web |
| *Where* | http://www.feminist.com/whatn.htm |
| *Comments* | "Place for women to meet, exchange ideas, get information, and empower themselves, offering resources and links and a Women-Owned Business section." |

| | |
|---|---|
| *What* | **Staci's Home Page** |
| *How* | Web |
| *Where* | `http://www.zoom.com/personal/staci/staci1.html` |
| *Comments* | Link onto Women's Networking and Business at `http://www.zoom.com/personal/staci/network.htm` to find listings of over twenty sites, others more specialized, concentrating on locale (Illinois, Israel, the Netherlands), or issues (computers or technology). |

| | |
|---|---|
| *What* | **Voices of Women** |
| *How* | Web |
| *Where* | `http://www.voiceofwomen.com/VOWworld.html` |
| *Comments* | Features spiritual, sensual, and striking graphics and offers much to heal the spirit and soul; also includes a Marketplace of women-owned, women-operated, and women-friendly businesses. |

## Additional Women-Friendly Sites

- Barnard Business and Professional Women: `http://www.intac.com/~kgs/bbpw/`
- Bay Area Business Women's Calender and Directory: `http://www.slip.net/~bizwomen/`
- Cindy's Women's Issues Links: `http://www.vuse.vanderbilt.edu/~suerkeck/`
- Cybergrrl Webstation: `http://www.cybergrrbcom/cg.html`
- ElectraPages, The Women's Organization and Business Locator: `http://electrapages.com`
- FeMiNa: `http://www.femina.com/`
- Feminism and Women's Resources: `http://www.ibd.nrc.ca/~mansfield/feminism.html`
- The Feminist Majority: `http://www.feminist.org/`
- Feminology—Women's Resources on the Net: `http://galaxy.tradewave.com/ed.phanie-Walker/women.pages.html`
- National Association of Women Business Owners: `http://www.ipcc.com/market/wbo/`
- National Conference for Women in Business: `http://www.sbaon-line.sba.gov/womeninbusiness/awed.html`
- National Bar Association On-line: `http://www.melnet.com/melanet/nba`
- NCS Career Magazine: `http://www.careermag.com/`
- Professional and Businesswomen's Conference: `http://www.mim.com/pbwc/home.html`
- Wharton Graduate Women in Business: `http://equity.wharton.upenn.edu/~swan65/gwib.html`
- Women Incorporated: `http://www.bbai.onrmp.net:80/WomenInc`
- The Women Zone: `http://www.livezone.com/womenzone.html`
- Women's Resources: `http://sunsite.unc.edu/cheryb/women/resources.html`

- Women's Web Resources: http://www.rof.net/links/women.html
- Working@Home!: http://www.cyberxpress.com/working@home/news.htm

## THE OLD BOYS' NETWORK

### Business and Investing

| | |
|---|---|
| *What* | **American Stock Exchange** |
| *How* | Web |
| *Where* | http://www.amex.com |
| *Comments* | Pyramid graphics, a listing of all exchange companies, a forum offering "insights from influential business leaders," and market summaries. |

| | |
|---|---|
| *What* | **Douglas Gerlach's Investorama** |
| *How* | Web |
| *Where* | http://www.users.inerport.net/~gerlach/invest.html |
| *Comments* | Links, links, and more links. Brokers, funds, government, quotes—all topic headings linking you to a range of advisers and investment choices. |

| | |
|---|---|
| *What* | **Finance Wat.ch** |
| *How* | Web |
| *Where* | http://finance.wat.ch/ |
| *Comments* | Business and investing site from Switzerland, which is renowned for its timepieces, offering the same exceptional precision. Includes regularly updated hotlists of the newest financial sites; global market predictions; exchange rate, stock market, and derivatives data; and a financial glossary. Don't drop the "dot" in "wat.ch"—the *ch* is the Net's country code for Switzerland! |

| | |
|---|---|
| *What* | **Money** |
| *How* | Web |
| *Where* | http://www.pathfinder.com/money/invest/hoover/ Hoovers_Home.html |
| *Comments* | Profiles on some four hundred of America's best-known companies, updated and comprehensive; an offshoot from *Money* magazine's Personal Finance Center. |

| | |
|---|---|
| *What* | **InterQuote** |
| *How* | Web |
| *Where* | http://www.interquote.com/ |
| *Comments* | This real-time service offers the opportunity to experience stock prices in motion, as stocks rise and fall on your computer screen. |

| | |
|---|---|
| *What* | **Money and Investing Update** |
| *How* | Web |

| | |
|---|---|
| *Where* | `http://update.wsj.com/` |
| *Comments* | Brought to you by the *Wall Street Journal,* and including much of the same financial analysis. But the site (to which you must subscribe) offers assessment in contrast with waiting for the paper version. |

| | |
|---|---|
| *What* | **NETworth** |
| *How* | Web |
| *Where* | `http://networth.galt.com/` |
| *Comments* | Detailed and comprehensive mutual fund information and stock quotes. The Mutual Fund Market Manager includes five thousand mutual fund profiles, and even some prospectuses. To use any of their services, you must fill out the free registration form. |

## Career and Job Opportunities

| | |
|---|---|
| *What* | **The Business Job Finder** |
| *How* | Web |
| *Where* | `http://www.cob.ohio~state.edu/dept/fin/osujobs.htm` |
| *Comments* | Assists recent college graduates in accessing job searches in areas of accounting, finance, and management, and offers links to numerous organizations. |

| | |
|---|---|
| *What* | **Careerweb** |
| *How* | Web |
| *Where* | `http://www.cweb.com/` |
| *Comments* | Job openings, lists of employers, lists of books, career search strategies. |

| | |
|---|---|
| *What* | **Chancellor and Chancellor, Inc.** |
| *How* | Web |
| *Where* | `http://www.chancellor.com:80/` |
| *Comments* | Brokerage company offering placement for computer and technology professionals. Includes resources for contractors and links to related sites. |

| | |
|---|---|
| *What* | **Employment Opportunities and Job Resources** |
| *How* | Web |
| *Where* | `http://www.wpi.edu/~mfriley/jobguide.html` |
| *Comments* | Comprehensive job guide, maintained by Margaret Riley of the Worcester Polytechnic Institute. Includes a smooth introduction offering advice on how to use the Net for job searching, a mini-course on the general use of the Internet, and an extensive job list: recruiter links, professional services, government job listing, high-tech and computer employment, and the arts and humanities. |

| | |
|---|---|
| *What* | **IntelliMatch On-line Career Services** |
| *How* | Web |

| | |
|---|---|
| *Where* | http://www.intellimatch.com/index.html |
| *Comments* | One of the more extensive resume and employer links, where job-seekers complete lengthy applications—twenty-five Web pages worth—to match mostly technical employers. |

| | |
|---|---|
| *What* | **Jobs** |
| *How* | Web |
| *Where* | http://none.coolware.com/jobs/jobs.html |
| *Comments* | Easy-to-use job listing services. Enter your desired career, field, and employment level, and a listing is provided. You can also place your own advertisement for a small fee. |

| | |
|---|---|
| *What* | **The Monster Board** |
| *How* | Web |
| *Where* | http://www.monster.com/ |
| *Comments* | Interactive career site, with current job openings that you can locate through a number of options: geographically, by profession, by industry, by job title. The service is free to the job seeker, although it would benefit from being a bit more focused. |

| | |
|---|---|
| *What* | **World Wide Web Employment Office** |
| *How* | Web |
| *Where* | http://www.harbornet.com/biz/office/annex.html |
| *Comments* | The price is right: $10 a year for posting your resume; $20 per month if you want your own job-wanted notice displayed. Lots of links to other employment sites as well. |

## How Tos—Consulting, Managing, Legal Advice

| | |
|---|---|
| *What* | **The Benchmarking Exchange** |
| *How* | Web |
| *Where* | http://www.benchnet.com |
| *Comments* | Information and communication site for benchmarking, reengineering, process improvement, and quality improvement. |

| | |
|---|---|
| *What* | **Better Business Bureau** |
| *How* | Web |
| *Where* | http://www.econet.apc.org/cbbb |
| *Comments* | Guides you to the local Better Business Bureau for voicing your consumer rights. This on-line site offers advice on preventing abuse, and can zero you in on the latest "scams." |

| | |
|---|---|
| *What* | **The Business Incorporating Guide** |
| *How* | Web |
| *Where* | http://www.corporate.com/ |

| | |
|---|---|
| *Comments* | How to incorporate your business, in every state. Also includes the whys and hows of incorporating, and Internet resources and software for incorporating. |
| *What* | **Business-to-Business Marketing Exchange** |
| *How* | Web |
| *Where* | http://www.btob.wfu.edu/b2b.html |
| *Comments* | Offers a range of articles and advice from the American Marketing Association and international marketing associations, as well as job listings, bulletin boards, and related resources. |
| *What* | **Copyright Clearance Center On-line** |
| *How* | Web |
| *Where* | http://www.openmarket.com/copyright/ |
| *Comments* | Nonprofit organization providing information, services for obtaining legal permission to use copyrighted materials, and catalogs. |
| *What* | **Counsel Connect Web** |
| *How* | Web |
| *Where* | http://www.counsel.com/ |
| *Comments* | Comprehensive site for legal issues, advice, libraries, and seminars. Search the lawyers database, updated daily, for legal help, classifieds, and many links. |
| *What* | **Get Organized** |
| *How* | Web |
| *Where* | http://www.get~organized.com |
| *Comments* | Professional consulting on how to do what we never seem to be able do—organize time, resources, and all that paper. |
| *What* | **HomeOwners Finance Center** |
| *How* | Web |
| *Where* | http://www.internet-is.com/homeowners/in-yahoo.html |
| *Comments* | Everything you ever dreamed of wanting to know about dream houses, and the reality of covenants, interest rates, and mortgages. Get an instant monthly computation of monthly costs with a nifty mortgage calculator. Also includes daily updates on economic factors affecting home loan rates, and many useful tips on buying and refinancing. |
| *What* | **LEXIS-NEXIS Communication Center** |
| *How* | Web |
| *Where* | http://www.lexis~nexis.com/ |
| *Comments* | A well-known on-line legal, news, and business information site for retrieval, storage, and more. |

| | |
|---|---|
| *What* | **Sharrow Marketing Information Center** |
| *How* | Web |
| *Where* | http://www.dnai.com~/sharrow |
| *Comments* | Advertising and marketing resource center, with some very witty "flukes," ideas, and lots of "assorted stuff." |

## Additional Links—Domestic

- The Divorce Page: http://www.primenet.com/~dean/legal.html
- Family Law: http://www.njlawnet.com/famlaw.htm
- Fortune: http://www.pathfinder.com/fortune.htm
- HomeBuyer's Fair: http://www.fractals.com/realestate.html
- Houselinks U.S. Real Estate Guide: http://www.wirelink.com/houselink/index.html
- Internet Real Estate Listings: http://www.amp.com/irel
- The Real Estate Pages: http://www.newmarkets.com/real_estate.hym
- U.S. Patent and Trademark Office: http://www.uspto.gov/web/patinfo/toc.html
- The World Bank Home Page: http://www.worldbank.org/
- World Currency Converter: http://www.dna.lth.se/cgi~bin/kurt/rates

## Additional Links—International Business

- Agora Language Marketplace: http://www.agoralang.com:2410
- Asian Business Daily: http://infomanage.com/~icr/abd/
- Canada Net Pages: http://www.visions.com
- The Econsult Group WWW Page: http://www.egroup.com/home.html
- The International Law Page: http://www.noord.bart.nl/~bethlehem/law.html
- The NAFTA Watch: http://www.aescon.com/naftam/index.htm
- Octagon Technology Group, Inc.: http://www.otginc.com
- Selling Your Products Abroad:
  http://www/lkcilink.com:80/brc/marketing/v2n10.html
- U.S. Council for International Business: http://www.uscib.org/
- Welcome to the European Market: http://www/sme.com/lukas.consulting

# 5

# VIRTUAL HEALING
## Health Resources for Body and Mind

This chapter contains materials of value to women of all ages who understand that health is not only the struggle to overcome illness, but also a state of well-being nurtured by nutrition, exercise, and lifestyle. It's resources will also be of special interest to health care students and professionals.

The chapter provides starting points for finding health care information. Many of the sites listed include a disclaimer about the information provided, thus we follow suit and offer our own: The medical information and advice you find on the Internet is not intended to replace the diagnosis and treatment suggested by a physician, or even a skilled alternative practitioner. Please consult a qualified health practitioner for diagnosis and treatment of your medical concerns. Use the Internet resources to further educate yourself on subjects of concern. In addition, please be forewarned about the commercial sites you may encounter: While it may appear that the owners of the information intend to provide useful health advice, often they are trying to sell you a miracle cure. So watch out for "info-ads"!

This chapter contains reports, organizations, support services, hotline information, and discussions—as always, with a special focus on issues of concern to women. The resources are organized into the following categories:

- African-American women's health
- Aging
- AIDS
- Alternative health care
- Body image/weight issues
- Cancer
- Chemicals/environment
- Cosmetic surgery
- Death and dying
- Disabilities
- Eating disorders
- General health issues

- General women's health issues
- Government and international resources
- Human rights and health
- Insurance rights
- Media related to health issues
- Mental health
- Native American women's health issues
- Nutrition, exercise, and fitness
- Policy issues
- Reproductive and sexual health
- Support groups

The National Technical Information Service, an agency of the Department of Commerce, introduced FedWorld in 1992 to help the public gain access to U.S. government information on-line with one-stop location. FedWorld is a huge government bulletin board, available via Telnet, FTP, and the Web, which enables a connection to other bulletin boards, including the Consumer Information Center's Bulletin Board (CIC BBS). This and other selections will link you to government publications on health issues that can be downloaded from CIC. Several of the on-line publications are listed in this chapter, and you'll find more if you visit FedWorld via one of these tools:

- The FedWorld Telnet site is the original on-line service, with resources from over fifty agencies and one hundred other government information systems, on-line ordering services, and federal job opportunities.
- The FedWorld FTP site provides access to more than 14,000 files of the FedWorld Libraries, including health, business, safety, and the environment.
- The FedWorld Web site enables you to search the on-line services via key word or to link to the Telnet and FTP sites.

## AFRICAN-AMERICAN WOMEN'S HEALTH

| | |
|---|---|
| *What* | **Cancer and African Americans** |
| *How* | Telnet |
| *Where* | `fedworld.gov`; for information on U.S. government publications on cancer, go to `NFCCANCR.TXT`. |
| *Comments* | Colorectal cancer is increasing among African-American men and women. The National Institutes of Health publishes a booklet on how cancer affects you as an African American, called *Get a New Attitude About Cancer*. It includes prevention and treatment information. |

| | |
|---|---|
| *What* | **National Black Women's Health Project** |
| *How* | E-mail |
| *Where* | `nbwhpdc@aol.com` |
| *Comments* | With two offices, a general clearinghouse in Atlanta, and a public policy office in Washington, D.C., the NBWHP provides up-to-date research, organizational directories, and information on medical conditions and health care policies that affect African-American women. NBWHP has not developed on-line services, but staff will field questions received via e-mail. |

## AGING

| | |
|---|---|
| *What* | **National Institute on Aging Page** |
| *How* | Gopher |

| | |
|---|---|
| *Where* | gopher.os.dhhs.gov/1/dhhs/aoa/aoa/agepapers |
| *Comments* | Contains government documents on Sexuality in Later Life; Hearing and Other Problems; Foot Care; and Dental Care. As a subdivision of the Department of Health and Human Services, this site will link you to any other health-related topics. |

## AIDS

| | |
|---|---|
| *What* | **ACT UP** |
| *How* | Mailing list |
| *Where* | Send message to act-up-request@world.std.com to subscribe. |
| *Comments* | ACT UP is an AIDS activist organization with chapters worldwide. This mailing list is a bulletin board with many announcement postings and a discussion forum on topics related to activism and the politics of AIDS and health care. |

| | |
|---|---|
| *What* | **AIDS Discussion Group** |
| *How* | Usenet newsgroup |
| *Where* | misc.health.aids; go to news://misc.health.aids. |
| *Comments* | Unmoderated listing of Q & As on AIDS. People living with AIDS, their lovers, friends, and families frequent the list. |

| | |
|---|---|
| *What* | **AIDS Issues** |
| *How* | Mailing list |
| *Where* | Send message to listserv@rutvm1.rutgers.edu to subscribe; type subscribe AIDS in the body of the message. |
| *Comments* | Extremely useful mailing list, well-moderated and educational in its coverage of the medical, social, and political aspects of AIDS and HIV. Several newsletters are posted here, such as the *AIDS Treatment News* and *CDC Summary* from the U.S. government's Centers for Disease Control. |

| | |
|---|---|
| *What* | **Center for Women's Policy Studies: National Resource Center on Women and AIDS** |
| *How* | E-mail |
| *Where* | hn4066@connectinc.com |
| *Comments* | Based in Washington, D.C., the center will field your questions via e-mail and send their informational packets on Women and AIDS research. |

| | |
|---|---|
| *What* | **Sisterlove Women's AIDS Project** |
| *How* | Web |
| *Where* | http://www.hidwater.com/sisterlove/slhome.html |
| *Comments* | Based in Atlanta, Georgia, Sisterlove Women's AIDS Project is a community-based, not-for-profit organization that focuses on the needs and goals of HIV positive women, specifically addressing the problem of HIV/AIDS as it affects women of color in the industrialized world. The project's programs include the Healthy Love |

Program in HIV/AIDS education, and the Lovehouse, which provides comfortable transitional housing for women who are HIV positive or living with AIDS.

| | |
|---|---|
| *What* | **Women Living with AIDS** |
| *How* | Usenet newsgroup |
| *Where* | `hivnet.women` |
| *Comments* | Discussion group mainly frequented by women who are HIV positive. Information on treatment, diet, support services, insurance, hospices, medical practitioners. |

## ALTERNATIVE HEALTH CARE

| | |
|---|---|
| *What* | **Acupuncture** |
| *How* | Web |
| *Where* | `http://www.acupuncture.com/acupuncture` |
| *Comments* | Probably the most well-known Web page for acupuncture information in the United States, receiving nearly one hundred visits a day, and its popularity is well-deserved. It covers a lot of ground, with information for skeptics, believers, and practitioners on acupuncture, herbology, diagnosis, state laws, and research. So as not to frustrate the layperson, information requiring heavy medical knowledge is suffixed with "Practitioner's Level." Of particular interest to women is the Acupuncture for Women subdirectory of the acupuncture topic. |

| | |
|---|---|
| *What* | **Alternative Health (formerly known as HerbsPlus)** |
| *How* | Web; e-mail |
| *Where* | `http://alt.medmarket.com/members/reiddds/herbplus/herbplus.html` for Web site; `info@alternativehealthemail.com` for e-mail |
| *Comments* | Directory of holistic, alternative, and complementary medicine providers, pharmacies, organic food restaurants, books, modalities, health insurance, fitness, organizations, herbs and vitamins, articles, hotels/spas/camps, and household products. Alternative Health aims "to assist and motivate health-conscious men and women to take responsibility for their health and well-being." |

| | |
|---|---|
| *What* | **Holistic Treatments** |
| *How* | Listserv |
| *Where* | Send message to `listserv@siucvmb.siu.edu` to subscribe; type `sub holistic Firstname Lastname` in the body of the message. |
| *Comments* | This is a discussion list for topics pertaining to holistic treatments. Here you can find people trading herbal remedies, message therapy tips, and revealing the truths behind myths of ancient Chinese medical practices. |

| | |
|---|---|
| *What* | **Homeopathy Home Page** |
| *How* | Web |

| | |
|---|---|
| *Where* | http://www.dungeon.com/~cam/homeo.html |
| *Comments* | Claims to be "a central jumping off point" that "aims to provide links to every related resource available"—and it delivers on its claims. You can find articles, newsgroups, mailing lists, worldwide address for homeopathic centers, publishing houses that specialize in alternative medicine reference books, on-line data bases for public search use, computer software for the homeopathic practitioner, and commercial Web sites for buying alternative medicine materials. |
| *Tidbit* | You could end up clogging your Web browser bookmark file with all the hyperlinks offered here, so get the FTP download-ready Homeopathic Internet Resources List, and sample one homeopathy page per day to keep the doctor away. |

## BODY IMAGE/WEIGHT ISSUES

| | |
|---|---|
| *What* | **Body Image** |
| *How* | Gopher |
| *Where* | gopher.uiuc.edu; go to University of Illinois at Urbana-Champaign Campus Info/Campus Services/Health Services/Health Information/ Health Promotion/Body Image |
| *Comments* | Offers pamphlets on how the ideal body image affects women's physical and emotional health. |

| | |
|---|---|
| *What* | **National Association to Advance Fat Acceptance** |
| *How* | Web |
| *Where* | http://naafa.org/index.html |
| *Comments* | Home page for the not-for-profit human rights organization, founded in 1969, which is "dedicated to improving the quality of life for fat people." Although some of its areas are still under construction, this site has much to offer, including a list of newsgroups for supportive discussion of body image issues, brief descriptions of legal cases regarding employment discrimination based on body weight, and contact information for finding local NAAFA chapters. |

## CANCER

| | |
|---|---|
| *What* | **Breast Cancer Information Clearinghouse (BCIC)** |
| *How* | Web |
| *Where* | http://nysernet.org/breast/Default.html |
| *Comments* | The BCIC is maintained by the New York State Education and Research Network. Some of the information pertains specifically to events and services in New York State; however, there is definitely enough general and national information to warrant a visit by non–New York residents. The BCIC has an index by subject, as well as a list of information agencies and about two dozen 800-number telephone hotline |

support services. Within their self-proclaimed "resources on this server you should-n't miss," the BCIC lists articles from the National Cancer Institute and the American Cancer Society.

*Tidbit*    The most interesting resource we found was a pamphlet entitled "Questions to Ask Your Doctor About Breast Cancer."

*What*    **Breast Cancer**

*How*    Listserv

*Where*    Send message to `listserv@morgan.ucs.mun.ca` with no subject line; type `subscribe breast-cancer` in the body of the message to subscribe or `information breast-cancer` for more information.

*Comments*    Discussion on a range of breast cancer issues.

*Tidbit*    This Listserv discussion is archived at `gopher.nysernet.org`

*What*    **Breast Self-Examination**

*How*    Gopher

*Where*    `gopher.uiuc.edu`; go to University of Illinois at Urbana-Champaign Campus Info/Campus Services/Health Services/Health Information/ Health Promotion/Breast Self Exam

*Comments*    Detailed instructions for monthly self-exams.

---

Some vital statistics:

- Approximately 20 percent of all breast cancers are not detected on mammograms.
- No proven screening test exists for ovarian cancer, which kills approximately 13,000 women each year.
- More than 50 percent of cervical cancer cases occur among African-American women; the resulting mortality rate is three times higher than it is for white women.

---

*What*    **CancerNet**

*How*    Web

*Where*    `http://www.meb.uni-bonn.de/cancernet/cencernet.html` to subscribe; type `help` in the body of the message.

*Comments*    List supplying information and generating discussion on cancer and cancer issues.

*What*    **Cancer Testing**

*How*    Telnet

*Where*    `fedworld.gov`; for information on U.S. government publications on cancer go to `NFCCANC2.TXT`.

*Comments*    The National Institutes of Health publishes a booklet called *Cancer Tests You Should Know About: A Guide for People 65 and Over*, on the different tests to detect cancer.

| | |
|---|---|
| *What* | **Women's Cancer Resource Center** |
| *How* | E-mail |
| *Where* | wcrc@igc.apc.org |
| *Comments* | The WCRC will send their publication and resource lists upon request. |

## CHEMICALS/ENVIRONMENT

| | |
|---|---|
| *What* | **Cancer Prevention Coalition—Chemical Toxins and Health** |
| *How* | E-mail |
| *Where* | cpc@igc.apc.org |
| *Comments* | Based in New York City, the Cancer Prevention Coalition is a monitor clearinghouse on carcinogens. Every three weeks it publishes the *Green Guide for Everyday Life*, where you can find useful statistics and advice on how to prevent chemical poisoning in the home and workplace; content analyses of consumer products; and research data on food and pesticides. Includes statistics such as the following: "Experts estimate the proportion of non-Hodgkin's lymphoma cases among women attributed to their use of hair dyes at 20 percent." |

| | |
|---|---|
| *What* | **CFS-L (Chronic Fatigue Syndrome)** |
| *How* | Listserv |
| *Where* | Send message to listserv@list.nih.gov to subscribe. |
| *Comments* | Discussion on a broad range of CFS-related topics. |

| | |
|---|---|
| *What* | **CITNET-W (Healthy Cities Women's Network)** |
| *How* | Listserv |
| *Where* | Send message to LISTSERV@INDYCMS.IUPUI.EDU to subscribe. |
| *Comments* | The Healthy Cities Women's Network is a discussion on women's health issues and healthy cities issues. |

## COSMETIC SURGERY

| | |
|---|---|
| *What* | **Cosmetic Surgery Precautions** |
| *How* | Telnet |
| *Where* | fedworld.gov; for information on U.S. government publications on health issues related to cosmetic surgery go to NFCCOS.TXT. |
| *Comments* | The Federal Trade Commission publishes "Cosmetic Surgery," on health and safety issues, and guidelines for choosing a qualified surgeon. |

## DEATH AND DYING

| | |
|---|---|
| *What* | **GriefNet** |
| *How* | Gopher |

| | |
|---|---|
| *Where* | gopher.rivendell.org |
| *Comments* | GriefNet is supported by Rivendall Resources, a nonprofit foundation in Ann Arbor, Michigan, directed by clinical psychologist Dr. Cendra Lynn. The Gopher topics here are for both grieving persons and those who work with bereavement issues. GriefNet's Bereaved Person Resource Center is an excellent place to start looking for other Internet sources about loss and recovery. Entries included support services and information on aging, adoption loss, educational tools, hospice information, suicide and homicide, chronic illness, bereaved parents, grieving children and adolescents, and loss from natural and human disasters. |
| *Tidbit* | Check out the site's library, with loads of bibliographical references to books on death and dying. |

## DISABILITIES

| | |
|---|---|
| *What* | **Access Foundation for the Disabled** |
| *How* | E-mail |
| *Where* | danyaon@savvy.com |
| *Comments* | Upon request, the Access Foundation will send you a list of e-mail addresses and Internet sites for support groups for various disabilities. |

| | |
|---|---|
| *What* | **Americans with Disabilities Act of 1990** |
| *How* | Telnet |
| *Where* | fedworld.gov; for information on U.S. government publications on services for the disabled go to NFCAMDIS.TXT. |
| *Comments* | Includes the text of the act in full, plus services by state and local governments. |

| | |
|---|---|
| *What* | **disABILITY Resources on the Internet** |
| *How* | Web |
| *Where* | http://www.eskimo.com/~jlubin/disabled/html |
| *Comments* | Provides excellent links to research and advocacy programs, equipment resources, financial support. |

## EATING DISORDERS

| | |
|---|---|
| *What* | **Eating Disorders** |
| *How* | Gopher |
| *Where* | gopher.berkeley.edu; go to Libraries and Academic Support/Research Databases and Resources by Subject/Women_Gender Studies/Womens Wire Gopher/Women's Health/Eating Disorders |
| *Comments* | Symptoms and warning signs of anorexia and bulimia, with discussions of treatment. |

## GENERAL HEALTH ISSUES

| | |
|---|---|
| *What* | **HealthNet** |
| *How* | Web |
| *Where* | `http://www.hwc.ca/healthnet/` |
| *Comments* | Provides a directory of health care resources to be found on the Internet and instructions on how to locate health care information on-line. |

| | |
|---|---|
| *What* | **Medical Developments** |
| *How* | Web |
| *Where* | `http://cancer.med.upenn.edu:3000/` |
| *Comments* | Recent developments in medicine are published in *MedNews,* by the Health Info-Com Newsletter, which is distributed internationally. |

| | |
|---|---|
| *What* | **Medical Students** |
| *How* | Listserv |
| *Where* | Send message to `listserv@unmvm` to subscribe; type `SUBSCRIBE MEDSTU-L` in the body of the message. |
| *Comments* | Forum for medical students around the world to meet and network. |

| | |
|---|---|
| *What* | **Personal Diagnosis** |
| *How* | FTP |
| *Where* | `oak.oakland.edu`; go to `SimTel/msdos/windows3/winmed_1.zip`, `winmed_2.zip`, and `winmed_3.zip`. |
| *Comments* | Medical diagnostics program that runs under Windows 3.1. Enables you to enter information and search its database to identify possible diseases and illnesses that might match the data. (This is not a substitute for professional medical advice.) |

| | |
|---|---|
| *What* | **Virtual Hospital** |
| *How* | Web |
| *Where* | `http://indy.radiology.uiowa.edu/` |
| *Comments* | This Web site, maintained by the Department of Radiology at the University of Iowa, is by far the Web's best resource for health and medical information. There are hundreds of documents available on-line, with an outstanding search utility to help virtual hospital visitors find what they need. The entire texts of handbooks, such as *The University of Iowa Family Practice Handbook,* are available on-line and can be searched by key words. |

| | |
|---|---|
| *What* | **Virtual Medical Center** |
| *How* | Web |
| *Where* | `http://www-sci.lib.uci.edu/-martindale/Medical.html` |

| | |
|---|---|
| *Comments* | Information about hospitals and medical schools, medical texts, links to other Web and Gopher sites, and multimedia files. Recommended especially for medical students and practitioners. |

## GENERAL WOMEN'S HEALTH ISSUES

| | |
|---|---|
| *What* | **Health-wise** |
| *How* | Web |
| *Where* | http://www.cybergrrl.com/health/index.html |
| *Comments* | Cybergrrl's health site includes articles from the Medical Reporter on Women's Health; fitness advice from the Personal Trainer; SafetyNet Domestic Violence Resources; PrePARE Self Defense for Women; links to other women's health sources. |

| | |
|---|---|
| *What* | **Our Bodies, Our Selves** |
| *How* | Web |
| *Where* | http://www.healthgate.com |
| *Comments* | The latest edition of the book, which was hailed as a revolutionary effort to demystify women's medicine twenty-five years ago, went on-line in June 1996. The Web site contains instant updates on medical information changes and links to other relevant sites. The on-line version is distributed by HealthGate, an on-line health program in Boston that includes free access to MedLine, the on-line arm of the National Library of Medicine. |
| *Tidbit* | This self-help classic is authored by the Boston Women's Health Book Collective, a renowned organization that conducts education, advacacy, and consulting in women's health. The collective's e-mail address is bwhbc@igc.apc.org. |

| | |
|---|---|
| *What* | **WMN-HLTH (Women's Health)** |
| *How* | Listserv |
| *Where* | Send message to listserv@uwawm.u.washington.edu to subscribe. |
| *Comments* | One of the oldest, most popular Listservs on general women's health issues, from the University of Washington. |

| | |
|---|---|
| *What* | **Women's Health** |
| *How* | Gopher |
| *Where* | gopher.berkeley.edu; go to Libraries and Academic Support/Research Databases and Resources by Subject/Women_Gender Studies/Womens Wire Gopher/Women's Health. |
| *Comments* | Extensive information on women's health, including eating disorders and emotional issues, from the University of California at Berkeley. Contact person: Ann Dobson at adobson@uclink.berkeley.edu |

| | |
|---|---|
| *What* | **Women's Health Action and Mobilization (WHAM)** |
| *How* | Web; Listserv |

| | |
|---|---|
| *Where* | `http://www.echonyc.com/~wham/` for Web site; send message `SUBSCRIBE WHAM Firstname Lastname` to `LISTPROC@LISTPROC.NET` to subscribe to the Listserv. |
| *Comments* | WHAM OnLine provides updated news, actions and resources to feminist activists working on reproductive rights and women's health issues. The mailing list officially began on January 22, 1995, the twenty-second anniversary of the *Roe v. Wade* decision that legalized abortion in the United States. |

| | |
|---|---|
| *What* | **Women's Health Files** |
| *How* | Gopher |
| *Where* | `gopher.uiuc.edu` |
| *Comments* | This gopher site, housed at the University of Illinois, Urbana-Champaign, is chock-full of articles about women's health, including self-help for PMS; Pregnancy Information Resources (a bibliography with text on all aspects of pregnancy); the pill; vaginal discharge. |
| *Tidbit* | Gopher your way here and download the information-rich files for your personal library, health practitioner's waiting room, or employee bulletin board. |

| | |
|---|---|
| *What* | **Women's Health Newsletter** |
| *How* | Listserv |
| *Where* | Send message to `shirlee@carson.uwashington.edu` to subscribe; type `listserv@uwavm.uwashington.edu` in the body of the message. |
| *Comments* | From the University of Washington comes this bulletin board–like newsletter on a range of women's health issues—one of the first Listservs of its kind. |

| | |
|---|---|
| *What* | **Women's Health Research and Information** |
| *How* | Web |
| *Where* | `http://inform.umd.edu:86/educational_resources/ academicresources/bytopic/women'sstudies/genderissues/ women'shealth` |
| *Comments* | Academic-oriented Web site particularly valuable to medical practitioners and students specializing in women's health care, disease prevention, and treatment. |

| | |
|---|---|
| *What* | **Women's Homepage** |
| *How* | Web |
| *Where* | `http://www.mit.edu.8001/people/~sorokin/women/index.html` |
| *Comments* | Contains a large collection of Web documents and Gophers, such as the Breast Cancer Information Clearinghouse, a midwifery server, and the Nightingale Gopher, which covers nursing issues. |

## GOVERNMENT AND INTERNATIONAL ORGANIZATIONS

| | |
|---|---|
| *What* | **American Public Health Association Clearinghouse** |
| *How* | E-mail |

*Where*    apha@apha.permanet.org or aphach@igc.apc.org or PHNLink@worldbank.org

*Comments*    The APHAC is an international center for information and materials on the health and nutrition of women and children. This clearinghouse works with field-based organizations in Africa, Asia, and Latin America to produce and disseminate materials, and promotes networking among organizations and practitioners working in these countries. Articles from its main publication, *Mothers and Children,* are available through the World Bank's PHNFlash archive, an electronic bulletin to which you can subscribe by sending a message to the World Bank address listed above.

*What*    **Centers for Disease Control**

*How*    Web

*Where*    http://www.cdc.gov

*Comments*    Government-sponsored Web site with press releases, newsletters, publications, funding opportunities, and scientific data supplied by the National Center for Health Statistics, which offers a download-ready copy of the electronic data products (mostly databases) available.

*Tidbit*    When planning an overseas trip, check the CDC's travel information. Here you will find all you need to know about vaccination requirements, current disease epidemics listed by country, and specific health recommendations for travelers.

*What*    **The First Lady: Health Care Speeches by Hillary Rodham Clinton**

*How*    Web

*Where*    http://www.whitehouse.gov/White_House.EOP/First_Lady/html/health-care-index.html

*Comments*    WYSIWYG (what you see is what you get) at the First Lady's Web page. The entire texts of her health care reform speeches delivered during her husband's presidency are available on-line to browse, read, and download.

*What*    **International Women's Health Coalition**

*How*    E-mail

*Where*    iwhc@igc.apc.org

*Comments*    IWHC is a private nonprofit organization supporting quality reproductive health care for women in third world countries. Works with health care workers, policymakers, and women's groups. Offers professional and technical assistance to third world health organizations. Provides financial support and offers educational materials. See also Global Feminism and World Peace.

*What*    **National Institutes of Health**

*How*    Gopher

*Where*    gopher.nih.gov

*Comments*    Provides an abundance of health and clinical information. You can also use it to access CancerNet information, a government-run bulletin board that is accessible from the Internet and offers up-to-date data in English and Spanish on cancer research, breakthroughs, prevention, hotlines, support groups. Use this Gopher to explore AIDS and HIV research, drug information, support services for AIDS patients and their families at the National Library of Medicine (NLM).

In 1989, a government investigation revealed that research into women's health had long lagged behind research into men's health. For example, only 14 percent of the National Institutes of Health's budget was being expended on women's health issues. In 1993, in an attempt to redress the imbalance, Dr. Bernadine Healy, the NIH's first woman director, introduced the Women's Health Initiative. The initiative was designed to establish the most extensive statistical profile of women's health ever conducted, and thereby meet head-on the scientific neglect of women's health. In 1992, the U.S. government appropriated $132 million for breast cancer research to the National Cancer Institute, a gain of almost 50 percent over 1991 spending.

*What*    **The Substance Abuse and Mental Health Services Administration**
*How*    Web
*Where*    http://www/samhsa.gov
*Comments*    Government-run public service with programs on substance abuse prevention and treatment. Most of the information available is government documents, with statistical material, national initiatives, and news and public affairs.
*Tidbit*    The list of Internet resources leads to various aspects of public health, including links to the Department of Health and Human Services (http://phs.os. dhhs.gov/phs/phs.html) and the Public Health Service (http://www. os.dhhs.gov).

*What*    **World Health Organization**
*How*    Web
*Where*    http://www.who.ch/
*Comments*    WHO's Web site is a typical international organization site. The table of topics include WHO press releases, newsletters, and publications. If you need to do research on the latest world health statistics, WHO does provide download-ready files of the Global Health Indicators project (662K file for PCs only), but most of WHO's databases are not yet available on-line. WHO's Web site does give you the proper contact information for requesting statistics via letter, fax, or phone. The page is well-updated, with plenty of tables, charts, and country-by-country assessments of particular health issues.

## HUMAN RIGHTS AND HEALTH

| | |
|---|---|
| *What* | **Health and Human Rights Journal** |
| *How* | E-mail |
| *Where* | franl@hsphsun2.harvard.edu |
| *Comments* | According to the journal, "The promotion and protection of health and the promotion/protection of human rights are now being understood to be inextricably linked . . . [and take] health far beyond medical services and a biomedical framework." The editors of the journal, published by the Harvard School of Public Health, will send you a promotional brochure and subscription form in response to your request. |

## INSURANCE RIGHTS

| | |
|---|---|
| *What* | **Employee Health Insurance Coverage** |
| *How* | Telnet |
| *Where* | fedworld.gov; for information on U.S. government publications on health coverage go to COBRA.TXT. |
| *Comments* | A Department of Labor publication, *Health Benefits Under the Consolidated Omnibus Budget Reconciliation Act* (COBRA), explains your rights under this law, which protects your right to extend your employee health insurance after you leave a job. |

## MEDIA RELATED TO HEALTH ISSUES

| | |
|---|---|
| *What* | **Academic Press Journals** |
| *How* | Gopher |
| *Where* | ukoln.bath.ac.uk:7070/11/Link/Tree/Publishing/AcademicPress/APJournals |
| *Comments* | This Gopher site takes you to numerous journals, including medical journals, published by a British company. Recommended for health care practitioners. |

| | |
|---|---|
| *What* | **Health Media** |
| *How* | E-mail |
| *Where* | newsdesk@igc.apc.org |
| *Comments* | Send message for listings of news reports and digests on women's health issues drawn from international news sources such as the Health News Service and Inter Press Service, along with current information on AIDS and U.S. health care reform. |

## MENTAL HEALTH

| | |
|---|---|
| *What* | **John M. Grohol's Mental Health Page** |
| *How* | Web |

| | |
|---|---|
| *Where* | `http://csbh.mhv.net/~grohol` |
| *Comments* | Tremendous stock of resources. Grohol's contribution comprises a weekly IRC session for anonymous discussion of mental health issues. His credentials as a mental health care provider are not apparent, but his effort to construct a useful list of Internet information on topics from alcoholism to Alzheimer's, sexual abuse survivors to cancer recovery support groups, is impressive. |
| *Tidbit* | Check out the vast e-mailing lists and newsgroups available on a huge variety of mental health topics. |

| | |
|---|---|
| *What* | **Psychology Issues** |
| *How* | Gopher |
| *Where* | `panda 1.upttawa.ca`; go to `MENTAL HEALTH` Software; The `PSYCGRAD` `Project`; or `PROJETS DE RECHERCHE`. |
| *Comments* | Psychology-related software, including couples counseling, IQ tests, programs to quit smoking, tests for attention deficit disorder. |

| | |
|---|---|
| *What* | **Sidran Foundation** |
| *How* | Web |
| *Where* | `http://www.access.digex.net/~sidran` |
| *Comments* | The Sidran Foundation is a not-for-profit advocacy, educational, and research organization focusing on psychiatric disabilities related to survivors of catastrophic trauma. Resources include a bookshelf of listings on child sexual abuse, dissociate disorders, and tips for survivors of trauma. Most of the information here is aimed at counselors and mental health practitioners. |

## NATIVE AMERICAN WOMEN'S HEALTH ISSUES

| | |
|---|---|
| *What* | **Native American Women's Health Education Resource Center** |
| *How* | E-mail; Gopher |
| *Where* | `nativewomen@igc.apc.org` for e-mail; `gopher.igc.apc.org.70/11/orgs/` `nawherc` for Gopher |
| *Comments* | Grassroots, community-based organization that provides education and empowerment skills to women and children and self-help skills to the Native American community. Projects include AIDS education, diabetes education, domestic violence programs and a shelter, an adult learning center, child development, a reproductive rights coalition, and education programs in several other health areas. |

## NUTRITION, FITNESS, AND EXERCISE

| | |
|---|---|
| *What* | **Aerobics** |
| *How* | FTP |
| *Where* | `oak.oakland.edu`; go to `SimTel/mdos/database/aerobix.zip` |

| | |
|---|---|
| *Comments* | This program enables you to enter your condition and workout program and provides entry options for jogging, aerobics, stair-climbing. Calculates calories burned. |
| *What* | **Breastfeeding** |
| *How* | Telnet |
| *Where* | `fedworld.gov`; for information on government publications on infant nutrition, go to `NFCBABY.TXT` |
| *Comments* | Advice on breastfeeding and nutrition for babies in their first months. |
| *What* | **Fitness** |
| *How* | Gopher |
| *Where* | `gopher.uiuc.edu`; go to `University of Illinois at Urbana-Champaign Campus Info/Campus Services/Health Services/Health Information/ Fitness` |
| *Comments* | Includes exercise guidelines, advice on how to treat injuries. |
| *What* | **International Food Information Council Foundation (IFICF)** |
| *How* | Web |
| *Where* | `http://ificinfo.health.org.org/` |
| *Comments* | Excellent source of consumer, educator, and health practitioner information about nutrition and food safety. Each type of information is clearly categorized for the consumer, parent, or medical professional. The IFICF newsletter, *Food Insight,* is on-line with articles such as "What You Should Know About Aspartame"; "A Guide About Pesticides and Children"; "Food Allergy Dos and Don'ts;" and "MSG Myths and Facts." |
| *Tidbit* | Educators should check out the elementary and secondary school curricula for teaching children food safety and consumer-savvy nutrition habits. |
| *What* | **Nutrition** |
| *How* | Gopher |
| *Where* | `gopher.uiuc.edu`; go to `University of Illinois at Urbana-Champaign Campus Info/Campus Services/Health Services/Health Information/ Nutrition` |
| *Comments* | Information on weight loss and gain, cholesterol intake, vegetarianism, and recommended healthy diets. |
| *What* | **Vegetarianism** |
| *How* | Gopher |
| *Where* | `quartz.rutgers.edu`; go to `Food, Recipes, Nutrition, Vegetarian-FAQ` |
| *Comments* | Everything you need to know about vegetarianism, including nutrition, recipes, and an international compilation of vegetarian-friendly restaurants and organizations. |

## POLICY ISSUES

| | |
|---|---|
| *What* | **President's Report on Health Care** |
| *How* | Telnet |
| *Where* | `fedworld.gov`; for information on U.S. government publications on health issues go to `HREPORT.EXE` |
| *Comments* | Review of the president's report on the current status of health care in the United States. |

| | |
|---|---|
| *What* | **The Politics of Medicine** |
| *How* | Usenet newsgroup |
| *Where* | `talk.politics.medicine` |
| *Comments* | In this very active newsgroup, participants discuss how the government and the media influence medical practice. One recent discussion addressed the French abortion pill, RU486. |

## REPRODUCTIVE AND SEXUAL HEALTH

| | |
|---|---|
| *What* | **Atlanta Reproductive Health Clinic** |
| *How* | Web |
| *Where* | `http://www.mindspring.com/~mperloe/index.html` |
| *Comments* | Presents range of subjects, including fertility, PMS, contraception, adoption, cervical and breast cancer, and many others. A useful site for women and their partners. |

| | |
|---|---|
| *What* | **The Blowfish Sexuality Information Center** |
| *How* | Web |
| *Where* | `http://www.best.com/blowfish/blowsic.html` |
| *Comments* | Information about sexual health and sexual politics. Includes a catalog of safe sex supplies. |

| | |
|---|---|
| *What* | **Contraception: The Pill** |
| *How* | Gopher |
| *Where* | `gopher.uiuc.edu`; go to `University of Illinois at Urbana-Champaign campus info/Campus Services/Health Services/Health Information/ Women's Health/The Pill` |
| *Comments* | Information on the use of oral contraceptives, including possible side effects, Q & As. |

| | |
|---|---|
| *What* | **MENOPAUS (Menopause)** |
| *How* | Listserv |
| *Where* | Send message to `listserv@psuhmc.hmc.psu.edu` to subscribe. |
| *Comments* | Discussion on menopause and remedies. |

| | |
|---|---|
| *What* | **Planned Parenthood on Sexual Health** |
| *How* | Web |
| *Where* | http://www.ncf.carleton.ca/freeport/social.services/ppo/info/menu |
| *Comments* | Planned Parenthood of Ottawa answers questions about contraception, STDs, infertility, and parenting. |

| | |
|---|---|
| *What* | **The Safer Sex Page** |
| *How* | Web |
| *Where* | http://www.cmpharm.ucsf.edu/~tryoer/safesex.html |
| *Comments* | Hip and information-rich source for various aspects of sexual health. The Safer Sex page aims to please all, including parents looking for tips on how to talk to kids about sex; twenty-somethings wanting accurate information on STDs and HIV/AIDS on college campuses; straight, bisexual, and gay couples who have questions about practicing safe sex; and anybody who has a burning question for the Safer Sex Forum. Download Safer Sex informational brochures and a picture-based pamphlet describing how to insert the Reality female condom. |
| *Tidbits* | The Safer Sex Forum found on this Web page is an IRC group for anonymous (if preferred) participation in a topic-based discussion about sexual health issues. Topics are decided prior to a chat meeting (see the Web site for topic voting and meeting times), and the discussions are archived at the Safer Sex page. |

| | |
|---|---|
| *What* | **Sex During Pregnancy** |
| *How* | Gopher |
| *Where* | gopher.uiuc.edu; go to University of Illinois at Urbana-Champaign Campus Info/Campus Services/Health Services/Health Information/ Women's Health/Sex During Pregnancy. |
| *Comments* | A discussion of safe sex practices during pregnancy. |

| | |
|---|---|
| *What* | **Sexually Transmitted Diseases** |
| *How* | Gopher |
| *Where* | riceinfo.rice.edu; go to Health and Safety at Rice/Health Info/ Sexually Transmitted Diseases. |
| *Comments* | Information on contraction, prevention, and treatments for chlamydia, genital warts, and other STDs, and on the use of condoms. |

| | |
|---|---|
| *What* | **Toxic Shock Syndrome** |
| *How* | Gopher |
| *Where* | gopher.uiuc.edu; go to University of Illinois at Urbana-Champaign Campus Info/Campus Services/Health Services/Health Information/Women's Health/Toxic Shock Syndrome |

| | |
|---|---|
| *Comments* | Information on the causes of TSS, symptoms and prevention, and the disease's relationship to tampon use. |
| *What* | **WITSENDO (Endometriosis)** |
| *How* | Listserv |
| *Where* | Send an message to `listserv@dartcms1.bitnet` or `listserv@dartcms1.dartmouth.edu` to subscribe. |
| *Comments* | Open to anyone who is interested in the subject, though mainly used by those who suffer from endometriosis. |

## SUPPORT GROUPS

The following list of support and discussion groups is only a sampling of the hundreds of health-related Usenet newsgroups, `alt.support` groups, that meet on-line. Participants usually include people who suffer from the designated health problem as well as their lovers, families, and friends.

- Abuse: `alt.abuse.recovery`
- Alcohol and drug recovery: `alt.recovery.na`
- Arthritis: `alt.support.arthritis`
- Asthma: `alt.support.asthma`
- Breastfeeding: `alt.support.breastfeeding`
- Cancer: `alt.support.cancer`
- Childhood-onset diabetes: `alt.support.diabetes.kids`
- Death and dying: `alt.support.grief`
- Depression: `alt.support.depression`
- Eating disorders: `alt.support.eating-disord`
- Epilepsy: `alt.support.epilepsy`
- Infertility: `alt.infertility`
- Menopause: `alt.support.menopause`
- Multiple sclerosis: `alt.support.mult-sclerosis`
- Obesity: `alt.support.obesity`
- Sleep disorders: `alt.support.sleep-disorder`

# 6

# MY SISTAH'S SPACE
## Resources for Women of African Descent
### *Debra K. Floyd*

When I began using the Internet six years ago, nothing was developed for use by the African-descent community; there were no African conferences. I said, "Oh, here's my niche." At the Institute for Global Communications (IGC) where I was working, I developed African-American Networking. I designed informational brochures to go out with IGC's promo materials. I didn't want African-descent people to have to work hard to find what we had to offer. I wanted people to see what we had to offer them right away.

Since those early days in the computer-generated information business, my personal mission has been to bring as many people of African descent as possible into the digital information age. I designed this chapter as a guide to the on-line resources available to women of African descent; my aim is to make available the information necessary to help African-descent women survive and flourish in the technological world.

In doing the research for this chapter, I discovered that too few sites on any of the on-line services speak exclusively to the needs of African-descent women. Even when I discovered women-only areas on-line, I could still feel the effect of difference between white women and black women. There was something missing; I couldn't hang. Sistahs need a homespot, too. It became apparent that we must be self-creators of our on-line presence: through classes that teach us how to use the coding language called HTML, used for designing Web sites, or by creating mailing lists centered around topics of interest to you and other on-line sistahs.

One way to get started is to ask either friends or sistahs you have met through business or social activities if they have an e-mail address. As you check out their interests, take note of the issues they find important and see how their interests match your own. Then see if you can exchange e-mail with each other about your shared interests, and invite others to join your discussions. By taking these small steps, you can develop an e-mail discussion group, create your own electronic network, and help to strengthen African-descent women's on-line presence.

Here are a few helpful tips for Web page exposure and networking with other sistahs on-line:

1. Be sure to place your Web site on a frequently used Internet Service Provider (ISP).
2. Register with Internet search engines, like Yahoo and Infoseek.
3. Put your URL (Web page address) as well as your e-mail address on your business cards and stationery.

4. Encourage and support other sistahs to obtain e-mail accounts and create Web pages of their own.

5. Develop partnerships with sistahs with similar interests.

6. Be confident in your creative abilities and remember: I support you in taking on this venture of self-expression on the Internet, whether this expression comes in the form of creating your own Web page, starting an e-mail mailing list, or contributing statistical information to on-line database searches!

This chapter can be an inspiration to you as you pursue your own endeavors. Compiled from on-line sources including the Web, Gophers, FTP locations, and various mailing lists, this chapter includes resource listings on a wide array of topics: Since the technology of on-line services continues to change and develop, with new on-line informational areas being created daily, some of your favorite locations may have been left out of this chapter unintentionally. But this is only the beginning of this kind of documentation, and I certainly hope that during your on-line surfing, you'll find My Sistah's Place useful and enjoyable.

Materials found in this chapter are listed under the following headings:

- The Arts
- Education
- Family
- General sites

- Lesbian issues
- Networks
- Politics, advocacy, gender/race
- Spirituality

Note: I don't like to say "African American" because it's limiting. There are African Canadians, African Caribbeans, Africans from the motherland, and so on. That's why I began using the word *diaspora* to describe our reality; I began playing around with how to convey "African descent," which is what I usually say. I prefer to use "African descent" to encompass and include more people.

## THE ARTS

| | |
|---|---|
| *What* | **African-American Artists** |
| *How* | Web |
| *Where* | http://www.arton-line.com/aol/afam.html |
| *Comments* | Contains a mixture of women and men visual artists. Just scroll down the page and you will come to sistahs such as Verna Hart and Lavarne Ross. |

| | |
|---|---|
| *What* | **The African American Home Page Distributor of Fine Art** |
| *How* | Web |
| *Where* | http://www.thenerve.com/aahp/annlee/annlee.htm |
| *Comments* | Home to a sistah who distributes fine-art work. |

| | |
|---|---|
| *What* | **Black Stars Past and Present** |
| *How* | Web |
| *Where* | http://www.igc.apc.org/africanam/resources/stars.html |
| *Comments* | African-American directory which draws together some very fine women artists in one location—and the list is growing. |

| | |
|---|---|
| *What* | **Daughters of the Dust** |
| *How* | Web |
| *Where* | http://www.pacificnet.net/geechee/Daughter1.html |
| *Comments* | From the Web site: "Welcome to the Daughters of the Dust home page. This page is a tribute to the spirit of women of color exemplified in the dramatic feature film *Daughters of the Dust,* written and directed by Julie Dash." There really are no words to describe the beauty found on this site—a must on your bookmark list. (The movie is also well worth renting!) |

| | |
|---|---|
| *What* | **IBBU-OKUN** |
| *How* | Web |
| *Where* | http://sunsite.oit.unc.edu/mao/musicians/ibbu_okun.html |
| *Comments* | IBBU-OKUN, an all female Afro-Cuban folkloric group from Cuba, made its U.S. debut in March 1995. The group was formed in Havana in 1993 and performs a repertoire of Afro-Cuban music and dance traditions: Palo, Yuca, Arara Iloosa, and the various styles of Rumba (Yambu, Guaguanco, and Columbia). |

| | |
|---|---|
| *What* | **Isis: Performing Arts** |
| *How* | Web |
| *Where* | http://www.netdiva.com/perform.html |
| *Comments* | The great actress Hattie McDaniel once said, "This is not the way I am, but they don't want me the way I am. So I put my handkerchief on and I am the best mammy that they've ever seen, and when I came home I take that handkerchief off." This quote opens the Isis Performing Arts site which includes many sistahs in the performing arts and is a section of the Isis Plus home page. Isis Plus was created by NetDiva Communications. |

| | |
|---|---|
| *What* | **Lady Day Images** |
| *How* | FTP |
| *Where* | ftp://ftp.njit.edu/pub/images/ |
| *Comments* | Here you can find pictures of the great Billie Holiday. To find the images, go to ftp://ftp.njit.edu/pub/images/ladyday.xbm and ftp://ftp.njit.edu/pub/images/ladyday.gif. |

| | |
|---|---|
| *What* | **Zora Neale Hurston** |
| *How* | Web |

| | |
|---|---|
| *Where* | http://www-hsc.usc.edu/%7Egallaher/hurston/hurston.html |
| *Comments* | A site to honor our sistah, writer Zora Neale Hurston, author of *Their Eyes Were Watching God* and an important figure in our literary language. |

## EDUCATION

| | |
|---|---|
| *What* | **African American Studies** |
| *How* | Gopher |
| *Where* | gopher://lib-gopher.lib.indiana.edu:3050/11m/gpraaamc.rpt |
| *Comments* | Contains information on people of African descent from A to Z, including many women. |

| | |
|---|---|
| *What* | **African-American Women's Identity/A Bibliography** |
| *How* | Gopher |
| *Where* | gopher://gopher.kenyon.edu:70/00GOPHER_ROOT%3a% 5b000000.depts.acad.wmns.biblio%5dblkwomen |
| *Comments* | "The majority of the items included in the bibliography deal with either gender identity or racial identity, very few deal with gender and race as they relate to black women specifically. However, we feel that it is necessary to include all of these articles/chapters in our writing and research. This bibliography is not offered as the sole bibliography on black women's identity. Instead it is being offered as a starting point for researchers interested in issues relative to African-American female identity." |

| | |
|---|---|
| *What* | **Bennett College** |
| *How* | Web |
| *Where* | http://www.bennett.edu |
| *Comments* | Bennett College in Greensboro, North Carolina, is an academic institution serving African-descent women. Its site describes its academic program, campus life, and special activities. It also links to other sites, including the African University and a directory of historically black colleges and universities. |
| *Tidbit* | For more information, send e-mail to bcinfo@bennett1.bennett.edu |

| | |
|---|---|
| *What* | **Historically Black Colleges and Universities** |
| *How* | Web |
| *Where* | http://www.smart.net/~pope/hbcu/hbculist.htm |
| *Comments* | Lists the black colleges and universities that are in the United States |

| | |
|---|---|
| *What* | **National Council of Negro Women** |
| *How* | Web |
| *Where* | http://www.ncnw.com |
| *Comments* | Informational listing for this organization. Housed within the National Academy of Sciences home page. |

| | |
|---|---|
| *What* | **Sororities** |
| *How* | Web |
| *Where* | http://www.gatech.edu/bgsa/blackpages/frats.html |
| *Comments* | Includes a list of all the sites for the "Soror" sistahs out there. |

| | |
|---|---|
| *What* | **Spelman College** |
| *How* | Web |
| *Where* | http://www.auc.edu/ |
| *Comments* | Spelman College, an outstanding historically black college for women, is recognized for excellence in liberal arts education. This predominately residential college is a member of the Atlanta University Center (AUC). This site contains registration and class schedule information, housing tips, and a student e-mail directory. |

## FAMILY

| | |
|---|---|
| *What* | **Maligned Wedding Guide** |
| *How* | Web |
| *Where* | http://www.melanet.com/wedding/ |
| *Comments* | Offers sistahs detailed information about traditional African wedding ceremonies. Find out about the history of African weddings or learn how to pick African cloth, how to finance the ceremony, and how to organize such weddings. |

| | |
|---|---|
| *What* | **Watoto World** |
| *How* | Web |
| *Where* | http://www.melanet.com/watoto/parents.html |
| *Comments* | One of the many insightful sites from Maligned—this one on parenting. It gives you the National Black Parents Code and the Black Family Pledge written by Dr. Maya Angelou. Unfortunately, single parenting issues are missing. |

## GENERAL SITES

| | |
|---|---|
| *What* | **AFROAM-L** |
| *How* | Listserv; Web |
| *Where* | Send message to listserv@harvarda.harvard.edu to subscribe; type SUBSCRIBE AFROAM-L Firstname Lastname in the body of the message for Listserv; http://qualcomm.com/people/gnah/AFROAM-L.html for Web site. |
| *Comments* | General informational mailing list and site on topics of interest to African Americans. |

| | |
|---|---|
| *What* | **African-American Discussion** |
| *How* | Usenet newsgroup |

| | |
|---|---|
| *Where* | soc.culture.afam |
| *Comments* | Unmoderated discussion on topics related to African-American interests. |

| | |
|---|---|
| *What* | **African-American Women Online** |
| *How* | Web |
| *Where* | http:/www.uoknor.edu/jmc/home/gmccauley/black.html |
| *Comments* | This fine site is created by Gina McCauley who claims to be a newbie in web work. Yea, sistah Gina. The beginning of her mission statement says, "I would like this page to focus on Black women and issues that concern and intrigue them." |

| | |
|---|---|
| *What* | **Harambee** |
| *How* | Web |
| *Where* | http://www.voicenet.com/~lynsilk/blkwomen.htm |
| *Comments* | This site is filled with resourcful Sistah selections. |

## Additional General Sites

- African Human Rights Resource Center:
  http://www.umn.edu/humanrts/africa/index.html
- Black Information Network: http://www.bin.com/
- Redemption: http://www~personal.engin.umich.edu/~louielou/Redemption
- Universal Black Pages: http://www.gatech.edu/bgsa/blackpages.html
- Vibe magazine: http://www.vibe.com

## LESBIAN ISSUES

| | |
|---|---|
| *What* | **The Black Stripe** |
| *How* | Web |
| *Where* | http://www.qrd.org/qrd/www/culture/black/blackstripe.html |
| *Comments* | Quoting from the site: "Welcome to the Rainbow's Black Stripe. This Web site represents the cooperative effort of Queers: lesbians, gay men, bisexuals, and transgendered people of African descent. It was inspired by discussions on GLBPOC and SistahNet. As gays and lesbians of African descent, we claim and are claimed by two communities—the black community and the gay community. Neither community fully accepts, appreciates, or understands us." |

| | |
|---|---|
| *What* | **National Black Gay and Lesbian Leadership Forum** |
| *How* | Web |
| *Where* | http://abacus.oxy.edu/qrd/www/orgs/nbgllf/ |
| *Comments* | Site is home for the National Black Gay and Lesbian Leadership Forum. Housed are its national newsletter, press releases, and information concerning the national conference. |

| | |
|---|---|
| *What* | **SistahNet** |
| *How* | Listserv |
| *Where* | Send e-mail message to majordomo@igc.org to subscribe; type subject bio in the subject line and subscribe SistahNet as the first line of the message. Include a brief bio of yourself. |
| *Comments* | A list of and for African-American lesbians, bi, and transgendered women. |

## NETWORKS

| | |
|---|---|
| *What* | **African-American Networking** |
| *How* | Web; Gopher |
| *Where* | http:www.africanam.org |
| *Comments* | This Megellan Internet Award–winning site, African-American Networking and the African-American Directory, was designed to give the African diaspora community networking access on the Web. It receives an estimated 3,200 hits per week. The sections found here are: Hot Topics (burning issues of the day, week, month); Resources (other African diaspora-based Web locations); Education; Lavender Light (Spirituality); the Diaspora NewzCenter (housing the African-American NewService and Real Newz . . . Newz Reel); Black Hilites; Dates; Let's Talk About It (an interactive area moderated by Nailah Jenkins of Real Newz . . . Newz Reel). |

| | |
|---|---|
| *What* | **AfroNet** |
| *How* | Web |
| *Where* | http://www.afronet.com/ |
| *Comments* | Contains sections pertaining to Business Discussion (topics change frequently); the 411 (Politics, Culture, News of the week, the Box, and the Black Directory); Junior Pose; the Waiting to Exhale area; Total African-American Product Store (the latest on-line catalog featuring high-quality African and African-American inspired products). |

| | |
|---|---|
| *What* | **Maligned** |
| *How* | Web |
| *Where* | http://www.melanet.com |
| *Comments* | Family-owned site containing useful African-American Resources, including an On-line Marketplace, the Ida Wells Media Center, and the Year Round Kwanza Bazaar. |

| | |
|---|---|
| *What* | **NetNoir** |
| *How* | Web |
| *Where* | http://www.netnoir.com/index.html |
| *Comments* | Part of America Online, this site is open to all people of African descent. NetNoir also has a site on the Internet separate from America Online. |

| | |
|---|---|
| *What* | **Web Diva** |
| *How* | Web |
| *Where* | `http://www.afrinet.net/~hallh/` |
| *Comments* | African diaspora–based Web site with Gopher links. Well-developed, with lots of informational resources. |

---

**RACISM ON-LINE**

**Shana Penn:** Have you dealt with racism on-line?

**Debra Floyd:** Oh yeah. You know how the word "black" is used to connote bad things: you're the "black" sheep, "black" Monday, etc. Once I was in a conference and someone on-line talked about a blacklist, or something like that. I wrote a message asking "Why use that term, why not use another term?" And somebody went to an alias computer and read me up one side and down the other: "What do you people want to become? What's wrong with using the word 'black'? What are you gonna be called this year? You don't know what you wanna be." Here, let me find it on my computer. It's dated December 1994:

> So here we have—caught in the act—another politically correct liberal asshole trying to ram proper wording down people's throat.
>
> So what do you want? Why don't you sit down with a dictionary and start identifying and listing all words that have "black" in it. Then start a campaign trying to have them changed.
>
> I guess white folks should have the name "Whitewater" changed (maybe to "blackwater") because of the negative connotations attached to the term?
>
> Besides, why are you so worked up about the word "black"? I thought this had long been replaced by "African-American." Not to mention "Moorish-American." Or—of course—the currently fashionable "people of color" (until you'll start feeling that particular term doesn't quite do you justice either, and start looking for another one. Something that's bound to happen soon . . . )
>
> —XYZ

I wasn't even thinking in that frame of mind. When I read the person's response, I couldn't believe it. My colleagues were very supportive. They got on-line and wrote: "You got your nerve; you couldn't be up-front about it—you had to go to an alias . . . "

---

## POLITICS, ADVOCACY, GENDER/RACE

| | |
|---|---|
| *What* | **African-American Women's Issues** |
| *How* | Gopher |
| *Where* | `gopher://lib-gopher.lib.indiana.edu:3050/` |
| *Comments* | Scroll down to the African-American section and scroll through the list until you come to the various listing on African-American women's issues. |

| | |
|---|---|
| *What* | **BlackSysterNetwork** |
| *How* | Listserv |

| | |
|---|---|
| *Where* | Send message to BKSYSNET-REQUEST@AVNET.CO.UK to subscribe; type subscribe in the body of the message. |
| *Comments* | Discussions on issues about African-descent women the world over. |

| | |
|---|---|
| *What* | **GIRLFRIEND** |
| *How* | Listserv |
| *Where* | Send message to LETT@HAVEN.IOS.COM to subscribe; type subscribe in the body of the message, and also include a brief biographical profile. |
| *Comments* | "Girlfriends can be black women by birth or by choice of any political orientation and sexual preference." A wide range of topics is discussed, from politics to spirituality, work, children, men, sexuality, current events. |

| | |
|---|---|
| *What* | **Isis Plus—Listing of Organizations, Institutions, and Events** |
| *How* | Web |
| *Where* | http://www.netdiva.com/oie.html |
| *Comments* | NetDiva's extensive list includes the Universal Black Pages events calendar, the Fifth Annual Women of Color Film Festival, National Black Women's Health Project Domestic Violence Campaign, National Council of Negro Women, Afrikan Cultural Arts Network, and more. |
| *Tidbit* | The list is hyperlinked to the Isis Plus Web page, http://www.netdiva.com/isisplus.html, which features the art and culture of African-descent women. |

| | |
|---|---|
| *What* | **My Sistah's Room** |
| *How* | Web |
| *Where* | http://www.ourspace.com |
| *Comments* | Designed to give sistahs their own "room" on the Web. Feel free to browse around and comment on what you find there. |
| *Tidbit* | To contact Debra, e-mail: OurSpace@ourspace.com |

## SPIRITUALITY

| | |
|---|---|
| *What* | **Christian African-American Women** |
| *How* | Web |
| *Where* | http://www.zondervan.com/history5.htm |
| *Comments* | *Women to Women* . . . perspectives of fourteen African-American Christian Women. Editors Dr. Nobella Carter and Matthew Parker have compiled an encyclopedia of Christian living for the African-American woman, as publicized on this Web page. |

| | |
|---|---|
| *What* | **Harlem Week of Prayer** |
| *How* | Web |

| | |
|---|---|
| *Where* | http://www.hsph.harvard.edu/Organizations/hai/hai_ini/conferen/ministry.html#Pernessa C. Seele |
| *Comments* | Harlem Week of Prayer for Healing of AIDS, founded by Pernessa C. Seele. Harvard AIDS Institute, Harvard Divinity School, and Harvard AIDS Ministries co-published a report on the spiritual challenge of AIDS in 1994, with contributions by, among others, Sonya Hunt Gray, Reverend Kim Crawford Harvie, and Reverend Renee McCoy. |

| | |
|---|---|
| *What* | **Inspirations: Spiritual Writings for the Mind, Body, and Soul** |
| *How* | Web |
| *Where* | http://www.africanam.org/lavendar/lambright |
| *Comments* | Contains the inspirational writings of Sunshine Michelle Lambright. Check out this site for inspiring commentary from this Bay Area sistah. |

| | |
|---|---|
| *What* | **Luisah Teish** |
| *How* | Web |
| *Where* | http://www.harpercollins.com/afroamer/spirita.htm and http://www.newdimensions.org/95VOLUME/november.htm |
| *Comments* | Two areas on the internationally acclaimed storyteller, actress, teacher of African spirituality, and Yoruba priestess, Luisah Teish. |

| | |
|---|---|
| *What* | **Mary Reynolds** |
| *How* | Web |
| *Where* | http://www.netnoir.com/spotlight/women/maryreynolds.html |
| *Comments* | Mary Reynolds's *The Endurance of Prayer* is a memoir of her life recorded in the 1930s, when she was one hundred years old. |

| | |
|---|---|
| *What* | **Muslim Women** |
| *How* | Web |
| *Where* | http://www.mpac.org/mwl/transcript.html |
| *Comments* | Challenges and opportunities facing American Muslim women. |

| | |
|---|---|
| *What* | **Oya's Daughters** |
| *How* | Web |
| *Where* | http://www.azstarnet.com/~cdm/oya1.html |
| *Comments* | Maintained by Cynthia M. Dagnal-Myron, this site speaks to people of African and Native American heritage. This is not a women-only space, yet there are elements here that sistahs can appreciate. |

| | |
|---|---|
| *What* | **Women's Spirituality** |
| *How* | Web |
| *Where* | http://www.beacon.org/Beacon/wadeg.html |
| *Comments* | Home page for *My Soul Is a Witness,* a book about African-American women's spirituality by Gloria Wade Gayles. |

# 7

# THE MULTICULTURAL WEB
## Resources for Women of Color

On-line resources for women of color commonly have their origins in academia, evolving out of university-based cultural studies programs such as Asian-American studies, Chicano/Latino studies, Native American studies, and so forth, much as general on-line resources for women grew out of women's studies and other academic programs.

Today you can access research and bibliographies on topics concerning women of color in university libraries and research collections, from MIT to UCLA. You can also join discussion groups on cultural diversity; on gender, class, and race; and on the double jeopardy of being a woman and ethnic or racial minority. And you can explore arts and literature on-line as created by or about women of color. The offerings are relatively small in number but, for the most part, intelligently and creatively organized and expressive of the specific culture and social concerns being presented.

The resource listings in this chapter begin with two general categories followed by categories keyed to specific cultural heritages:

- General gender and race/ethnicity/class—related sites
- General race/ethnicity/class—related sites
- Asian American
- Latina
- Native American
- Other related organizations

Note that while many of the sites in this chapter are of relevance to African-American women, sites specifically about/for women of African descent are listed in part 2, chapter 6.

> Being a woman of color or of a nonwhite ethnicity is not just about defining ourselves as part of a group that experiences racism. It is about having a common history with other women of color, about celebrating different cultures, art, languages, religions, holidays. It's about defining what each woman sees as important in her own life, about learning to reclaim an identity that society does not automatically value.
> —from "Community and Identity: Women of Color"
> *The Barnard/Columbia Women's Handbook,* `gopher:// gopher.cc.columbia.edu:71/00/publications/women/wh3`

## GENERAL GENDER AND RACE/ETHNICITY/CLASS-RELATED SITES

| | |
|---|---|
| *What* | **Diversity Page** |
| *How* | Web |
| *Where* | http://latino.sscnet.ucla.edu/diversity1.html |
| *Comments* | The ultimate jumping-off point to excellent Web and Gopher resources for Asian Americans, Latinas, Native Americans, and people of African descent, including special links to women's issues. Begin your explorations here. |

| | |
|---|---|
| *What* | **FEMINIST (Women, Racism, Ethnic Diversity, and Librarianship)** |
| *How* | Listserv |
| *Where* | Send e-mail message to LISTSERV@MITVMA.MIT.EDU to subscribe. |
| *Comments* | Owned by the Feminist Task Force of the American Library Association, this list discusses issues including racism and ethnic diversity in librarianship. |

| | |
|---|---|
| *What* | **Gender, Ethnicity, and Class** |
| *How* | Web |
| *Where* | http://www.aber.ac.uk/~dgc/gender.html |
| *Comments* | Contains indices on Class, Ethnicity, Gender, Representation, and Social and Personal Identity. Also includes articles, publications, and institutions addressing these categories. Located at the Media and Communication Studies site. |

| | |
|---|---|
| *What* | **Technomama** |
| *How* | E-mail |
| *Where* | technomama@igc.apc.org |
| *Comments* | Information from this California-based group, which provides computer training and technical support for women of color. |

| | |
|---|---|
| *What* | **Women and Minorities in Science and Engineering** |
| *How* | Web |
| *Where* | http://www.ai.mit.edu/people/ellens/Gender/wom_and_ min.html |
| *Comments* | Provides links to publications and articles, professional organizations, and profiles of scientists. |

| | |
|---|---|
| *What* | **Women of Color** |
| *How* | Web |
| *Where* | http://www.gu.edu.au/gwis/aiwrap/AIWRAP.colour.html |
| *Comments* | Contains Web resources such as the Urban Black Women's Cultural Salon and Gopher resources such as the Women's Handbook, Aboriginal Women, and others. |

| | |
|---|---|
| *What* | **Women of Color Handbook** |
| *How* | Gopher |

| | |
|---|---|
| *Where* | gopher://gopher.cc.columbia.edu:71/00/publications/women/wh38 |
| *Comments* | Contains excerpts from the *Barnard/Columbia Women's Handbook on Women of Color: Community and Identity.* |

| | |
|---|---|
| *What* | **Women of Color Resource Center** |
| *How* | Gopher |
| *Where* | gopher://gopher.igc.apc.org:70:1/org/wcrc |
| *Comments* | Site will take you to the Resource Center's general information materials and newsletters. |

## GENERAL RACE/CLASS/ETHNICITY/CLASS-RELATED SITES

| | |
|---|---|
| *What* | **ERaM (Ethnicity, Racism, and the Media)** |
| *How* | Mailing list |
| *Where* | Send message to majordomo@bradford.ac.uk with no subject line to subscribe; type SUBSCRIBE ERAM-LIST in the body of the message. |
| *Comments* | General discussion regarding race and ethnicity issues in the media. |

| | |
|---|---|
| *What* | **Inner-City Software: "Brains in the Hood"** |
| *How* | Web |
| *Where* | http://www.innercity.com/ |
| *Comments* | Inner-City Software, an innovative software development company based in Dorchester, Massachusetts, is dedicated to "bringing Blacks, Hispanics, and Native Americans into the Information Age. Our primary strategy for pulling this off is to develop as much ethnically oriented computer software as we can . . . the most realistic way to get people of color interested in and using computers and information technology. . . . [We] see technology as an enabling tool to work against the problems of poverty, low self-esteem and lack of self-determination." |
| *Tidbit* | Inner-City Access Project is a group of businesses and individuals in the Boston area who create Web sites for Boston's inner-city neighborhoods of Roxbury, Dorchester, and Mattapan, and provide Boston's communities of color with information about their neighborhoods and the world. Features neighborhood businesses, community organizations, events, announcements, and ads. |

| | |
|---|---|
| *What* | **Interracial Voice** |
| *How* | Web |
| *Where* | http://www.webcom.com/intvoice/ |
| *Comments* | Published every other month, *Interracial Voice* is an "information-oriented, networking news journal serving the mixed-race/interracial community in cyberspace." Recent articles (written by women and men) focused on affirmative action and immigration law reform. Also included are book reviews, editorials, and relevant newswire stories. |

## ASIAN AMERICAN

| | |
|---|---|
| *What* | **Asian American Resources** |
| *How* | Web |
| *Where* | http://www.mit.edu:8001/afs/athena.mit.edu/user/i/r/irie/ www/aar.html |
| *Comments* | Begun in 1994, this well-stocked Web site links you to e-zines, cultural events, educational resources, business opportunities, political and social trends, calls for action, and more, all of which serve the interests of Asian Americans. There are numerous links to related organizations such as the Asian-American Graduate and Professional Organization, the National Asian-American Telecommunication Association, the Asian-American Legal Defense and Education Fund, the Anti-Asian Violence Page, the Asian-American Census Statistics, and the Asian-American Studies Center at the University of California. |

| | |
|---|---|
| *What* | **Asian Community On-line Network (ACON)** |
| *How* | Web |
| *Where* | http://www.igc.apc.org/acon/ |
| *Comments* | ACON, a community resource for Asian Pacific American community-based organizations, aims to provide on-line information and technical assistance to groups learning to use the Internet. Member organizations include the Vietnamese Community Health Promotion Project; Asian Immigrant Women Advocates, Asian Neighborhood Design, Filipino American Women's Network, and the National Asian Pacific American Women's Forum. |

## LATINA

| | |
|---|---|
| *What* | **Chicana Latina Studies at UCLA** |
| *How* | Web |
| *Where* | http://latino.sscnet.ucla.edu/women.links.html |
| *Comments* | Provides access to information on Chicanas and Latinas, including profiles, interviews, links to related sites, announcements, calendars of events, directories of educational and professional organizations, anthologies, bibliographies, syllabi, archives, general women's studies networks around the world, and information on Latina lesbians and bisexuals. |

| | |
|---|---|
| *What* | **Chicano/LatinoNet (CLNET)** |
| *How* | Web |
| *Where* | http://latino.sscnet.ucla.edu |
| *Comments* | Originally conceived as a location for educational research, CLNET has become a multipurpose Web site, providing information on women, employment opportunities, legal and social services, housing, the environment, and the arts. Educational materials remain its foundation, with information on research collections, archives, |

and libraries. CLNET also links to the on-line catalogs of major collections that house Latino resources and publications. Some of the Gopher, Web, and newsgroup sites include the Azteca Web Page, EgoWeb, Hispanic/ Latino Telarana, LatInfo, Summit of the Americas, Virtual Barrio, Chicano/Latino Studies Videos, and Latino Newsgroups.

| | |
|---|---|
| *What* | **LatinoLink** |
| *How* | Web |
| *Where* | http://www.latinolink.com/ |
| *Comments* | With articles available in English and Spanish, *LatinoLink* is a monthly magazine for the Latino/Latina community. Contents include news (from wire services like AP), business, commentary, lifestyles, job listings, personals, and a reader forum. Coming soon: *LatinaLink!* |

| | |
|---|---|
| *What* | **MUJER-L** |
| *How* | Listserv |
| *Where* | Send message to LISTPROC@LMRINET.GSE.UCSB.ECU to subscribe. |
| *Comments* | Discussion on Chicana and Latina issues, begun by the creators of CLNET's Chicana Studies Home Page at UCLA. |
| *Tidbit* | The list owners hope to develop this into an international list. |

## NATIVE AMERICAN

| | |
|---|---|
| *What* | **Center for World Indigenous Studies Information** |
| *How* | Web |
| *Where* | http://www.halcyon.com/FWDP/cwisinfo.html |
| *Comments* | The Center for World Indigenous Studies is a nonprofit research and education organization that manages archives on tribal governments and related research and inter-tribal groups' initiatives to regain sovereignty and sustain tribal cultures. The archives contain documents recording tribal and intertribal decisions and issues with which indigenous people contend. The Web site contains records such as United Nations papers, testimonies, resolutions, and treaties from indigenous peoples in North and South America, Africa, Asia, Europe, Melanesia, and the Pacific. |

| | |
|---|---|
| *What* | **Electronic Pathways, Native American Internet Information** |
| *How* | Web |
| *Where* | http://hanksville.phast.umass.edu/defs/independent/Elecpath/elecpath.html |
| *Comments* | Creator Karen Strom simulates a Native American infrastructure on this Web site, with information on councils, related organizations, and more. |

| | |
|---|---|
| *What* | **Native American Internet Sites** |
| *How* | Web |
| *Where* | http://latino.sscnet.ucla.edu/Native.links.html |

| | |
|---|---|
| *Comments* | This Web page links you to Listservs, Gophers, newsgroups, and Web sites such as Native American Net Server, National Indian Policy Center, American Indian College Fund, NativeNet, Indian Health Service, Pueblo Cultural Center, Index of Native American Resources on the Internet, Indigenous People's Literature. |
| *What* | **Native American Women's Health and Resource Center** |
| *How* | Gopher |
| *Where* | `gopher://gopher.igc.apc.org:70/11/orgs/nawhrc` |
| *Comments* | Based in South Dakota, this not-for-profit information clearinghouse offers its materials on-line, including publication lists, newsletters, resources relating to culture and language, youth, and of course, health. |

## OTHER RELATED ORGANIZATIONS

Organizations with valuable information and perspectives on gender and race/ethnicity/class-related issues can be contacted via the following e-mail addresses.

- Asian Immigrant Women Advocates: `aiwa@igc.apc.org`
- Canadian Advisory Council on the Status of Women: `cacsw@web.apc.org`
- Casa de Colores: `casadcolores@igc.apc.org`
- Equal Means: `equalmeans@igc.apc.org`
- Mujer a Mujer (Canada): `perg@web.apc.org`
- National Organization of Immigrant and Visible Minority Women of Canada: `noivmwc@web.apc.org`
- Native American Women's Health Education Resource Center: `nativewoman@igc.apc.org`
- Native Women's Resource Center: `nwrc@web.apc.org`
- Women and Environmental Education Development: `weed@web.apc.org`
- Women and Rural Economic Development: `wredstr@web.apc.org`

---

Debra Floyd of the Institute for Global Communications in Washington, D.C., recommends these related resources for underserved populations:

- Community Technology Centers' Network (CTCNet), headquartered in Newton, Massachusetts, aims to create a community technology movement throughout the United States. For information, contact: CTCNet, Education Development Center, Inc., 55 Chapel Street, Newton, MA 02158-1060; Tel: 617/969-7100 x2727; e-mail: `ctcnet@edc.org`

- Urban Internet Project (UIP) helps public housing residents tap the Internet. Made up of a coalition of federal agencies, not-for-profit groups, and charities, UIP solicits donations to place computers in the recreation and community rooms of Washington, D.C., public housing complexes. UIP also offers computer and Internet trainings for residents. For more information, contact John Rosenthall by telephone at 703-922-7653.

# 8

# OUT ON-LINE

## Lesbian Lives on the Internet

*Amy Goodloe*

For many lesbians today, the Internet has played a key role in the coming out process, either by providing access to resources that answer commonly asked questions or by offering "virtual communities" in which women can feel free to explore and discover their identities. The Internet also plays an important role in promoting lesbian rights and visibility, providing activists with the ability to exchange information quickly and broadly, and offering the mainstream population a glimpse into "real" lesbian lives that they might otherwise never see.

But the Internet is just a tool. And it is the work of hundreds of lesbians, devoted to providing information and resources to lesbians around the world, that has made the Internet such a *powerful* tool for promoting lesbian visibility. This chapter focuses on the work of these women, highlighting a wide variety of on-line resources that covers everything from news, information, and history to personal life stories to venues for "real time" interactions between lesbians.

Resources appear in the following categories:

- Activism and advocacy
- Arts and entertainment
- General queer sites
- Health and sexuality
- Lesbian hot-lists and collections
- On-line meeting places
- Products and services
- Publications and literary links

## ACTIVISM AND ADVOCACY

| | |
|---|---|
| *What* | **Foundation Group 7152: Dutch Organization for Lesbian and Bisexual Women** |
| *How* | Web |
| *Where* | `http://www.cybercomm.nl/~lonys` |
| *Comments* | "Foundation Group 7152 is a Dutch organization for lesbian and bisexual women. Its goal is to support these women during the awakening of their feelings toward women and accepting them. Moreover it offers possibilities for meeting each other. Every woman, young or old, married or not, can become a contributor of Group 7152. The privacy of the contributors is optimally protected." |
| *What* | **International Lesbian Information Service** |
| *How* | Web |

| | |
|---|---|
| *Where* | http://www.helsinki.fi/~kris_ntk/ilis.html |
| *Comments* | The ILIS is an international network of lesbians working toward lesbian rights. "The five basic ILIS demands are: We have the unconditional right to control our own bodies; we have a right to education that is not sexist or heterosexist and which includes positive information about lesbian lifestyles; we need the right to self-organization; all governments must repeal legislation which criminalizes us or discriminates against us. Therefore, all governments must pass human rights legislation to protect individuals against discrimination based on color, class, creed, sex, and sexual preference." |

**Shana Penn:** What kinds of on-line information would be valuable for lesbians?

**Amy Goodloe:** I'd especially like to get more lesbian studies information on the Net, to make this information available to academics everywhere, and I'm encouraging those teaching such courses to get their students to submit work for publication on Lesbian.org. It'd be great to offer space to publish the works of women who aren't quite ready to be published in academic journals, but whose research would be of great interest to many readers.

| | |
|---|---|
| *What* | **Lesbian Avengers New York City Chapter** |
| *How* | Web |
| *Where* | http://www.cc.columbia.edu/~vk20/lesbian/avenger.html |
| *Comments* | "The Lesbian Avengers is a direct action group focused on issues vital to lesbian survival and visibility. . . . Direct action means turning our ideas into concrete action. Lesbian Avenger actions have ranged from invading a hate-mongering radio station and taking over the airwaves to demand an end to their racist and homophobic attacks, to sending lesbophobic politicians turkeys on Thanksgiving. We have also developed the Lesbian Avenger Civil Rights Organizing Project (LA CROP), which has organized against homophobic legislation in Maine and Idaho, and the FREE NY project which is fighting for lesbian and gay civil rights right here in New York State." |

| | |
|---|---|
| *What* | **Lesbian Avengers San Francisco Chapter** |
| *How* | Web |
| *Where* | http://www.lesbian.org/sfavengers/ |
| *Comments* | "The Lesbian Avengers of San Francisco is a direct action group of lesbian, bisexual, and transgendered women focused on issues vital to our survival and visibility." |

| | |
|---|---|
| *What* | **Lesbian Caucus of the Hellenic Homosexual Society** |
| *How* | Web |
| *Where* | http://www.cyberzine.org/html/GLAIDS/Color/greeklesbians.html |
| *Comments* | "The Hellenic Homosexual Community (EOK) has formed a Lesbian Caucus with the aim to address lesbian issues and help lesbians solve problems related to being |

a lesbian in modern Greece. We are women relatively experienced in the gay movement and other arenas of social activism but we have a lot to confront."

| | |
|---|---|
| *What* | **Lesbian.org** |
| *How* | Web |
| *Where* | http://www.lesbian.org/ |
| *Comments* | Lesbian.org is a Web site dedicated to promoting lesbian visibility on the Internet by offering free Web space to lesbian not-for-profit and activist groups, publishing a wide range of lesbian news, resources, and information, and sponsoring five lesbian mailing lists. |

| | |
|---|---|
| *What* | **National Lesbian Political Action Committee** |
| *How* | Web |
| *Where* | http://www.lesbian.org/nlpac/ |
| *Comments* | The mission of the NLPAC is to "provide a continuous forum for women to work with women on lesbian issues on a political level; help lesbians identify and strengthen their priorities; make lesbian issues visible at the national level; unite and energize lesbian activists; educate our national leaders; inspire new leadership; influence the political process and make a difference." |

| | |
|---|---|
| *What* | **NOW-Lesbian Rights** |
| *How* | Web |
| *Where* | http://now.org/now/issues/lgbi/lgbi.html |
| *Comments* | "NOW is committed to fighting discrimination based on sexual orientation in all areas, including employment, housing, public accommodations, child custody, and military and immigration policy. NOW asserts the right of lesbians and gays to live their lives with dignity and security." The site contains information about NOW's policies, history, and recent actions, and you can search the whole site by the key word "lesbian" to learn more about other ways that NOW works toward lesbian rights. |

## ARTS AND ENTERTAINMENT

| | |
|---|---|
| *What* | **Derivative Duo** |
| *How* | Web |
| *Where* | http://www.nwlink.com/~rainier/duo.htm |
| *Comments* | "The Derivative Duo wreaks havoc on the classical music scene. Their outrageous opera parodies illuminate the pressing social issues of our day: PMS, gays in the military, cat psychology. Once you've heard the Derivative Duo, opera will not be the same. Listen to their original songs on the Internet using Real Audio. (A modem connection of 28.8 or better is essential to fully enjoy this site.)" |

| | |
|---|---|
| *What* | **Dyke Street** |
| *How* | Web |
| *Where* | http://www.demon.co.uk/world/ukgay/ukg000f.html |
| *Comments* | Dyke Street is an interactive soap opera on the Web. Readers are encouraged to suggest new characters or plot twists, and they can tune in each month for a new episode. Previous episodes are archived on the site for the benefit of newcomers, making it easy to get up to speed with what's happening on Dyke Street. |

| | |
|---|---|
| *What* | **Dyke TV** |
| *How* | Web |
| *Where* | http://www.dyketv.org |
| *Comments* | "Dyke TV is a half-hour weekly television program produced by lesbians, for lesbians. We mix news, political commentary, the arts, health, sports, and much more to present lesbian lives—in all our variety—with intelligence and humor." The site contains information on when and where Dyke TV airs, as well as contact information for volunteers. And the opening page features a really nifty animated graphic: a lavender TV with changing images on the screen. |

| | |
|---|---|
| *What* | **Ladyslipper Records** |
| *How* | Web |
| *Where* | http://www.ladyslipper.org |
| *Comments* | "Ladyslipper is a nonprofit organization whose primary purpose is to heighten public awareness of the achievements of women artists and musicians, and to expand the scope and availability of recordings by women." From the site you can order music, request a free catalog, or learn more about featured women artists. |

| | |
|---|---|
| *What* | **Lesbian and Bisexual Actresses** |
| *How* | Web |
| *Where* | http://www.blarg.com/~dhua/films/women/actresses1.html |
| *Comments* | Interesting list of actresses who are known to be or thought to be lesbian or bisexual. |

| | |
|---|---|
| *What* | **Lesbian-centered European Films** |
| *How* | Web |
| *Where* | http://www.helsinki.fi/~kris_ntk/film.html |
| *Comments* | Long list of European films with a sapphic slant. |

| | |
|---|---|
| *What* | **Sweet Music: Sisters on Stage** |
| *How* | Web |
| *Where* | http://www.qworld.org/DykesWorld/sweetmusic.html |
| *Comments* | Contains information on and links to Web sites about lesbian musicians around the world, lovingly compiled by Indina Bueche. According to Bueche, this is "no outing |

list," as all the musicians she features are publicly open as women-loving women. The list is delightfully long and diverse, and international in scope.

## GENERAL QUEER SITES

*What*       **Community United Against Violence (CUAV)**

*How*        Web

*Where*      http://www.xq.com/cuav/

*Comments*   CUAV is a fifteen-year-old nonprofit agency which addresses and prevents hate violence directed at lesbians, gay men, bisexuals, and transgender persons. CUAV also provides services to gay men who are battered by their partners. CUAV offers crisis intervention, short-term counseling, advocacy with the criminal justice system, support groups, and a twenty-four-hour CrisisLine. In addition to documenting and publicizing anti-lesbian/gay violence, CUAV offers speakers for schools and community groups and safety monitoring for community events. We routinely distribute safety information, and provide whistles and self-defense classes as preventative measures."

*What*       **Digital Queers (DQ)**

*How*        Web

*Where*      http://www.dq.org/dq/

*Comments*   Digital Queers is a not-for-profit organization dedicated to promoting the use of computer technology among queer activist groups.

*What*       **Gay and Lesbian Alliance Against Defamation (GLAAD)**

*How*        Web

*Where*      http://www.glaad.org/

*Comments*   The Web site for the Gay and Lesbian Alliance Against Defamation bills itself as "your on-line resource for promoting fair, accurate, and inclusive representation of individuals and events as a means of challenging discrimination based on sexual orientation or identity."

*What*       **The Human Rights Campaign**

*How*        Web

*Where*      http://www.hrcusa.org

*Comments*   "The Human Rights Campaign (HRC), the nation's largest lesbian and gay political organization, works to end discrimination, secure equal rights, and protect the health and safety of all Americans. With a national staff, and volunteers and members throughout the country, HRC lobbies the federal government on gay, lesbian, and AIDS issues; educates the general public; participates in election campaigns; organizes volunteers; and provides expertise and training at the state and local level." This site is nicely designed and chock-full of political news and information for anyone interested in lesbian and gay rights.

| | |
|---|---|
| *What* | **The National Lesbian and Gay Health Association** |
| *How* | Web |
| *Where* | http://www.serve.com/nlgha/index.htm |
| *Comments* | "The National Lesbian and Gay Health Association is the only national lesbian and gay organization in the nation's capitol dedicated solely to our communities' health and health care. . . . With the formation of the National Lesbian and Gay Health Association (NLGHA), the lesbian and gay community now has a single, comprehensive resource for physical and mental health–related issues, advocacy, education, technical assistance, and research, as well as a powerful voice for educating public health officials and leaders on the importance of lesbian and gay health." |

| | |
|---|---|
| *What* | **The National Gay and Lesbian Task Force (NGLTF)** |
| *How* | Web |
| *Where* | http://www.ngltf.org/ |
| *Comments* | "The National Gay and Lesbian Task Force (NGLTF) is a leading progressive civil rights organization that has supported grassroots organizing and advocacy since 1973. Since its inception, NGLTF has been at the forefront of every major initiative for lesbian, gay, bisexual, and transgender rights. In all its efforts, NGLTF helps to strengthen the gay and lesbian movement at the state and local level while connecting these activities to a national vision of change." |

| | |
|---|---|
| *What* | **PlanetOut** |
| *How* | Web |
| *Where* | http://www.planetout.com |
| *Comments* | Easily one of the coolest sites on the Web, PlanetOut features news and information on queer culture, politics, fashion, relationships, and more, in the style of a high quality, glossy, full-color magazine. Highlights include searchable databases on a variety of topics and interactive chat rooms and message boards. Beautifully designed and breathtakingly comprehensive, this is one of the best queers resources on the Net—and they don't leave the "lesbian" out of lesbian and gay either! |

## HEALTH AND SEXUALITY

| | |
|---|---|
| *What* | **Dykes, Disabilities & Stuff** |
| *How* | Web |
| *Where* | http://tps.stdorg.wisc.edu/MGLRC/Groups/DykesDisabilitiesStuff. html |
| *Comments* | "This quarterly newsletter is unique as the only publication in the country (and, to the best of our knowledge, in the world) that is expressly devoted to the health and disability concerns of lesbians. It is also unique in the range of accessible media available: standard print, large print, audio cassette, braille, DOS diskette, and modem transfer. *Dykes, Disabilities & Stuff* (*DD&S*) is a grassroots publication. We promise |

news, reviews, verse, controversy, essays, and art—all with the disabled lesbian's perspective!"

*What*          **Eve's Garden: An Erotic Boutique for Women**

*How*           Web

*Where*         http://www.evesgarden.com/

*Comments*      The unusual and very tasteful graphics on this site are a treat for Web-weary eyes, and the information is sure to please as well. In addition to a fully illustrated catalog of erotic toys, the site also features important information about sexual health and exploring one's sexuality with erotic toys.

*What*          **Getting Hot: Lesbians and Sex**

*How*           Web

*Where*         http://www.qworld.org/DykesWorld/Getting_hot.html

*Comments*      Marvelous hot-list of links to lesbian erotica and information about lesbian sex and sexuality.

*What*          **Helping Our Women (HOW)**

*How*           Web

*Where*         http://www.provincetown.com/village/organizations/how/how.html

*Comments*      "We are a nonprofit and support organization of women concerned about the increasing number of women who are facing major illnesses without adequate care. HOW was formed in the fall of 1992 to educate, empower, and support women with chronic and life-challenging illnesses. Our goal is to promote the health and well-being of all women."

*What*          **Lesbian Health Resources**

*How*           Web

*Where*         http://www-personal.umich.edu/~druid/les.html

*Comments*      Information and contacts for lesbian health resources around the country.

*What*          **The Lesbian Safer Sex Page**

*How*           Web

*Where*         http://www.cmpharm.ucsf.edu/~troyer/safesex/lesbianss.html

*Comments*      Excellent resources and information about lesbian sexuality, including a printable stand-up display with safer sex information!

## LESBIAN HOT-LISTS AND COLLECTIONS

*What*          **Amazon.org**

*How*           Web

*Where*         http://www.amazon.org

| | |
|---|---|
| *Comments* | Collection of links of interest to lesbians and bi women, with a special emphasis on northern California resources. Most of the links here are not specifically lesbian oriented, but are mostly queer- and/or woman-friendly. |
| *What* | **Caryl's Lesbian Links** |
| *How* | Web |
| *Where* | http://www.sirius.com/~caryls/ |
| *Comments* | Caryl Shaw guides you through her favorite lesbian Web sites, providing helpful annotations and a ranking system based on quality of design and content. |
| *What* | **A Dyke's World** |
| *How* | Web |
| *Where* | http://www.qworld.org/DykesWorld/index2.htm |
| *Comments* | This site is actually composed of lots of parts, and they're all great! The site is the work of Indina Beuche in Germany, and it's a nice blend of great information, interesting stories, hard-to-find lesbian links, and really fantastic graphics, design, and layout. Some of what you'll find on A Dyke's World: Sweet Music—Sisters on Stage, an annotated list of links to lesbians in the music industry; an annotated guide to some of our worst enemies, so you can know what they're up to and be prepared to fight them; lots of great Web design resources; and of course a great lesbian hot-list. |
| *What* | **June L. Mazer Lesbian Collection** |
| *How* | Web |
| *Where* | http://www.lesbian.org/mazer/ |
| *Comments* | "Dedicated exclusively to preserving lesbian history and to guaranteeing that those who come after us will not have to believe that they 'walk alone.' The Collection is committed to gathering and preserving materials by and about lesbians of all classes, ethnicities, races, and experiences. Included are personal letters and scrapbooks, lesbian artwork, manuscripts, books, records, newspapers, magazines, photographs, videotapes, flyers, papers of lesbian organizations, private papers, and even clothing, such as softball uniforms from the 1940s and 1950s." |
| *What* | **The Lesbian History Project** |
| *How* | Web |
| *Where* | http://www-lib.usc.edu/~retter/main.html |
| *Comments* | The mission of this site is "to support efforts to gather, record, publicize, and preserve work on lesbian history in any geographic area or time period, with an emphasis on lesbians of color in general and southern California in particular." |
| *What* | **Searchable Lesbian Links** |
| *How* | Web |
| *Where* | http://www.lesbian.org/lesbian/ |
| *Comments* | Joint effort between WWWomen (http://www.wwwomen.com) and Lesbian.org |

(http://www.lesbian.org). Provides the most comprehensive index of lesbian-specific links on the Web today. The index is updated on a regular basis and is fully searchable by key word.

| | |
|---|---|
| *What* | **Swade Lesbian Tribal Voice: Glimpses of Our History** |
| *How* | Web |
| *Where* | http://www.mindspring.com/~swade/les_hist.htm |
| *Comments* | As the name implies, this site provides readers a glimpse into lesbian history in the form of a timeline, starting with poet Sappho in the 580s B.C. and ranging across the continents and through time until the present. |

| | |
|---|---|
| *What* | **Yoohoo! Lesbians!** |
| *How* | Web |
| *Where* | http://www.sappho.com/yoohoo/ |
| *Comments* | Annotated and beautifully designed guide to lesbian and gay Web sites, in a hierarchical directory format similar to Yahoo's. |

## ON-LINE MEETING PLACES

| | |
|---|---|
| *What* | **D.Y.K.E.** |
| *How* | Web |
| *Where* | http://dspace.dial.pipex.com/town/square/ad454/ |
| *Comments* | D.Y.K.E. is an unusual site, with heavy emphasis on the lesbian bar scene, both virtual and real. You can learn more about the fine art of cruising in the "Cruise Me Now" café, or leave a message on the virtual wall of the Ladies Lounge. The site also features links to the Oscar Wilde Society, Fan's Private Salon, and the D.Y.K.E. News. |

**SP:** What are the most popular on-line forums for lesbians?

**AG:** Lesbian mailing lists. At last count I believe there were some forty-six e-mail lists for lesbians, and although I don't have exact numbers, I feel sure there aren't the same number of discussion lists for gay men. These are discussion lists (not news or announcements lists), so that is significant, and they're all pretty high volume.

| | |
|---|---|
| *What* | **GrrlTalk** |
| *How* | IRC |
| *Where* | http://www.geocities.com/WestHollywood/1123/grrl.html |
| *Comments* | Billed as "a guide to lesbian IRC," the GrrlTalk Web site features comprehensive information about how to use Internet Relay Chat and how to find lesbian IRC channels. |

| | |
|---|---|
| *What* | **Guide to Lesbian Mailing Lists** |
| *How* | Web |

| | |
|---|---|
| *Where* | `http://www.helsinki.fi/~kris_ntk/lezlist/lezl.html` |
| *Comments* | Mailing lists are the most popular way to have interactive communication on the Internet, and not surprisingly, the best way to meet and have conversations with other lesbians. This site contains the most comprehensive information on lesbian mailing lists to date, including a description of each list's purpose and instructions for what's happening on Dyke Street! |
| *What* | **Lesbian-Themed Newsgroups** |
| *How* | Usenet newsgroups |
| *Where* | `alt.lesbian.feminist.poetry`; `alt.shoe.lesbian`; `soc.support.youth.gay-lesbian-bi`; and `soc.women.lesbian-and-bi` |
| *Comments* | Of the thousands of newsgroups, only a handful address lesbian themes. These four groups are primarily for lesbians and bisexual women, with special interests as the names imply. |
| *Tidbit* | A broader range of queer and or women's issues are discussed in the following newsgroups: `soc.motss`; `soc.feminism`; `soc.women`. |
| *What* | **Pleiades, Qworld, and Women Online Worldwide (WOWomen)** |
| *How* | Web |
| *Where* | `http://www.pleiades-net.com`; `http://www.qworld.org`; and `http://www.wowwomen.com` |
| *Comments* | On each of these sites you can find Web-based message boards on topics directly or indirectly relating to lesbians and lesbian issues. QWorld and WOWomen also feature regular, hosted "live chat" sessions on lesbian topics; check the sites for a calendar and more information. |

## PRODUCTS AND SERVICES

| | |
|---|---|
| *What* | **Alternative Creations** |
| *How* | Web |
| *Where* | `http://www.alternative-creations.com/` |
| *Comments* | "Alternative Creations is a lesbian-owned and operated business that produces and promotes art for and by women. Our primary goal is to be an asset to our community by designing products that are not only fun but are also needed in our society." |
| *What* | **Artemis On-line Mall** |
| *How* | Web |
| *Where* | `http://www.Webgal.com/artemis` |
| *Comments* | Functions as a gallery of lesbian-owned businesses that are currently on the Web. Here you can browse through the different on-line offerings of a wide variety of companies, selling products and services that range from consulting to travel to clothing and jewelry. |

| | |
|---|---|
| *What* | **Olivia Travel** |
| *How* | Web |
| *Where* | http://www.oliviatravel.com |
| *Comments* | Olivia Travel offers cruises and travel packages for women only, to destinations around the world. "Olivia is committed to creating adventures as priceless as the women who take them. Hard to imagine? Not for the more than 12,000 women who have traveled with us in the past six years. And their experience will be yours: a world class vacation in the company of women, with all the freedom you need to be who you are!" Check out the site for details on upcoming cruises and vacation packages. |

| | |
|---|---|
| *What* | **We'Moon Lesbian Calendar** |
| *How* | Web |
| *Where* | http://www.teleport.com/~wemoon/ |
| *Comments* | "We'moon is not just a calendar, it's a way of life: an astrological moon calendar, ecofeminist appointment book, daily guide to natural rhythm, and lunar perspective through the thirteen moons of the year. It also provides access to an international Web of fabulous, creative womyn, with art and writing from womyn around the world; womyn-loving, Goddess-inspired themes; and an active network of womyn sharing work and ideas across the planet." |

## PUBLICATIONS AND LITERARY LINKS

| | |
|---|---|
| *What* | **Escape Magazine** |
| *How* | Web |
| *Where* | http://web.idirect.com/~mistress/escape.htm |
| *Comments* | "Escape magazine is a full off-line publication geared specifically toward lesbian and bisexual women. With the help of a wonderful volunteer staff, our ideas and creativity are only the start of what we hope will become the place women turn to when they want to get away. Although we work far away [from each other], we communicate by computer, therefore bringing our talents and ideas closer." |

| | |
|---|---|
| *What* | **For Lesbians: The Art and Poetry of Women** |
| *How* | Web |
| *Where* | http://www.goodnet.com/~stacey/staceys_other.html |
| *Comments* | Stacey Coleman keeps up this page of useful links to information about lesbian poetry and art. From this page you can also reach her list of links for lesbian writers of poetry and fiction. |

| | |
|---|---|
| *What* | **HotHead Paisan: Homicidal Lesbian Terrorist** |
| *How* | Web |
| *Where* | http://www.marystreet.com/HH/ |
| *Comments* | In the parallel universe of comic books, Hothead Paisan lives out the revenge fantasies |

of thousands of women who've been assaulted and abused by men. Her adventures are a tad too violent for some, and refreshingly cathartic for others. Hothead isn't for everyone, so before you buy a print copy, check out the Web site for more info.

| | |
|---|---|
| *What* | **The Isle of Lesbos: Lesbian Images in Art** |
| *How* | Web |
| *Where* | http://www.sappho.com/lart/ |
| *Comments* | Painstakingly compiled by Alix North, this collection of lesbian images in art spans four centuries and three continents, and features both thumbnail and full-size versions of each image. |

| | |
|---|---|
| *What* | **The Isle of Lesbos: Lesbian Poetry** |
| *How* | Web |
| *Where* | http://www.sappho.com/poetry/ |
| *Comments* | Like the Lesbian Images in Art site, this site is truly a labor of love—a collection of poetry by women with lesbian themes from the Renaissance to the present, carefully researched and annotated. Alix North provides extensive resources for further study and has written original commentaries on all of the poets featured here. The graphics on the site are also tastefully done and quick to load. |

| | |
|---|---|
| *What* | **The Lesbian-Writers Page** |
| *How* | Web |
| *Where* | http://www.lesbian.org/lesbian-writers/ |
| *Comments* | Resources and information about lesbian books, writers, and publications. Also includes information on the lesbian-writers mailing list. |

| | |
|---|---|
| *What* | **Matrices** |
| *How* | Web |
| *Where* | http://www.lesbian.org/matrices/ |
| *Comments* | "*Matrices: A Lesbian and Lesbian Feminist Research and Network Newsletter,* is a nonprofit endeavor to increase communication and networking among those interested in lesbian scholarship." The site provides subscription information as well as copies of back issues. |

| | |
|---|---|
| *What* | **Sapphic Ink** |
| *How* | Web |
| *Where* | http://www.lesbian.org/sapphic-ink/ |
| *Comments* | Sapphic Ink is a lesbian literary journal on the Web, published quarterly and featuring the work of lesbian writers from around the world. |

| | |
|---|---|
| *What* | **Visibilities** |
| *How* | Web |

| | |
|---|---|
| *Where* | http://www.qworld.org/Visi/visib_home.html |
| *Comments* | Visibilities is an on-line magazine for lesbians, featuring stories, regular columns, cartoons, poetry, and on-line discussion forums on a variety of topics. |
| *What* | **The Writing Pad** |
| *How* | Web |
| *Where* | http://www.goodnet.com/~stacey/writing_pad.html |
| *Comments* | Showcases lesbian writers every month or so, including interviews with an author and excerpts from her work. |

# 9

# WHAT WE TALK ABOUT WHEN WE TALK ABOUT ON-LINE LOVE AND SEX

## Resources for Relationships

Sex changes everything. It certainly did so on the Internet. When people discovered that libido-driven pleasures can be created or reached with the click of a mouse, usage suddenly skyrocketed, making sex and love one of the most popular subject areas in cyberspace. Erotic explorations on Web sites, on mailing lists, in newsgroups, and in chat rooms seem to be changing the way we desire and engage in amorous encounters, as much as computers have changed the way we think, work, and converse with one another. Sherry Turkle, a professor of the sociology of science at MIT, notes that "computer screens are the new location for our fantasies, both erotic and intellectual" (Samantha Miller, "NetWorth," PEOPLE Online Web site).

Women users have much to say about their experiments with on-line love and sex. For example, in an essay in the anthology *Wired Women,* Ellen Ullman describes her electronic love affair: "I fell in love by e-mail. It was as intense as any other falling in love—no, more so. For this love happened in my substitute body, the one on-line, a body that stays up later, is more playful, more inclined to games of innuendo—all the stuff of romantic love."

The anonymity is titillating; the meeting of minds and shared fantasies excites; the absence of the body, and thus the lack of judgment of physical appearance, is liberating. A friend who goes by the userid Trixie42 says:

> When you have cybersex, you can really enter another person's mind. It's a true meeting of minds, and I love that. Whereas with real sex, the bodies are always mediating between the minds. But in cybersex, nothing interferes. Plus, if your mind wanders, no one notices because they're not there physically. Or if you don't like something the other person says, you can just walk away and they'll never know.

New questions arise: Is cybersex a safe-sex solution in the computer age? Or is it an illusion—all talk, no action? Carla Sinclair, author of *Net Chick* asks: "If a married person indulges on-line, is adultery being committed?" Trixie42 ponders: "Do you *have* cybersex or do you *do* cybersex? I think you *do* it," she says. "It's so different from having sex with your body." Perhaps the computer screen is the new mediator between the minds. One races home to turn on the PC and retrieve the next *billet-doux* or set of erotic instructions. Communication technology enables users to indulge in turn-of-the-last-century romantics with a next-century immediacy. Ellen Ullman describes the thrill of chasing her object of desire through cyberspace:

What followed were months of e-mail that rode back and forth between us with increasing speed. Once a day, twice a day, hourly. It got so I had to set a clock to force myself to work uninterruptedly for an hour then—ring!—my reward was to check my mail. We described our lives, interests, favorite writers, past projects and, finally, past lovers. Once we got to lovers, the deed was done. It was inevitable that we would have to go out, *see* each other. Yet we delayed. We wanted to stay where we were: in the overwhelming sensation of words, machine, imagination.

New experiences are to be had on-line, along with old ones, such as joining singles groups or browsing through bridal directories and sex toy catalogs. There's no paucity of venues for exploring sex and love on-line, no matter your sexual orientation or preference. For example, you can find familiar spokespersons and media, such as Susie Bright, Dr. Ruth, *Yellow Silk,* and personal ads. The nonexploitative, erotica Web sites are as colorful, exciting, playful, animated, and interactive as Web sites should be—and are among the best, from the standpoint of design and engagement.

The creative possibilities do not exclude the existence of new paths to age-old vulnerabilities and dangers for women. As most of us know by now, violent, sex-as-power venues occupy plenty of space on the Internet. For the most part, you still have to go to them; they don't come to you. However, wherever you go on-line, you have to be prepared to protect yourself. The medium that you are exploring is deceptive: you are alone in front of your computer screen, but you can be found. When roaming cyberspace for erotic encounters, it is easy to forget that you are vulnerable, as you would be at a local singles bar. First cases are erupting: a Columbia University student was allegedly sexually assaulted by a man she met on-line; a woman was stalked on-line by a harasser she met in a chat room. Always take precautions. The Internet may know no boundaries; your life, however, depends on having them.

This chapter provides you with resources on love and sex for every sexual orientation and many sexual tastes, and includes safe sex tips, personal ads, and even romantic getaways.

| | |
|---|---|
| *What* | **Blowfish** |
| *How* | Web |
| *Where* | http://www.blowfish.com/catalog.html |
| *Comments* | Warehouse of videos, safe sex supplies, erotic arts and crafts, edibles, 'zines. |
| *Tidbit* | While you're visiting, check out the Blowfish Sexuality Information Center. |
| *What* | **Cafe Queer** |
| *How* | Web |
| *Where* | http://www.interport.net:80/~sorel/cafe-queer.html |
| *Comments* | Leathermom Supervises the "cafe", and Sexy Matilda is a regular. There's plenty of room for hanging out and meeting "OUTspoken dykes, faggots, disco queens, queer boys, muffdivers, purple-socked womyn, A-list society fags, transgendered ppl, and differently sexualled folks of all kinds." |

| | |
|---|---|
| *What* | **COUPLES-L** |
| *How* | Listserv |
| *Where* | Send message to `LISTPROC@CORNELL.EDU` to subscribe. |
| *Comments* | Moderated list on "significant relationships." Topics include love, romance, sex, patterns, and dynamics. More serious and instructive than some of the Usenet newsgroups listed here. |

| | |
|---|---|
| *What* | **Cyber Queer Lounge** |
| *How* | Web |
| *Where* | `http://cyberzine.org/html/GLAIDS/glaidshomepage.html` |
| *Comments* | This site contains alphabetized links to recreational, cultural, and political forums and resources, from Queer Studies and AIDS alerts to private play rooms, coming out sites, peep shows, and a museum of famous queers, to name a few. "Love sees no gender." |

| | |
|---|---|
| *What* | **Cyber-Romance 101** |
| *How* | Web |
| *Where* | `http://web2.airmail.net/walraven/romance.htm` |
| *Comments* | Links to articles and advice columns about on-line romance, addressing questions such as: "Are on-line romances healthy?" "How to prepare for the first F2F (face-to-face) date," "Lust in Space," and "The Scarlet Letter." |

| | |
|---|---|
| *What* | **Erotica** |
| *How* | Web |
| *Where* | `http://www.erotica-toys.com/` |
| *Comments* | Catalog of sex-oriented products. |

| | |
|---|---|
| *What* | **Free to be . . .** |
| *How* | Usenet newsgroup |
| *Where* | `soc.support.youth.gay-lesbian-bi` |
| *Comments* | Supportive discussions on sexual orientation, coming out, and so on. |

| | |
|---|---|
| *What* | **Libido** |
| *How* | Web |
| *Where* | `http://www.indra.com/libido` |
| *Comments* | The Chicago-based magazine on erotica is now on-line. |

| | |
|---|---|
| *What* | **The Love Port** |
| *How* | Web |
| *Where* | `http://www.amore.com` |
| *Comments* | Meet Natasha the sex goddess, visit her video library and toy box, and tell her your secret desires. |

| | |
|---|---|
| *What* | **Masturbation** |
| *How* | Usenet newsgroup |
| *Where* | `alt.sex.masturbation` |
| *Comments* | It's never too late to learn some new techniques. |

| | |
|---|---|
| *What* | **Personal Ads for Bisexuals** |
| *How* | Usenet newsgroup |
| *Where* | `alt.motss.bisexual` |
| *Comments* | Space to browse for personal ads. |

| | |
|---|---|
| *What* | **Polygamy** |
| *How* | Usenet Newsgroup |
| *Where* | alt.polyamory |
| *Comments* | Talk about polygamy, and multiple sex partners. |

| | |
|---|---|
| *What* | **Romantic Adventures** |
| *How* | Web |
| *Where* | `http://www.sos.net.romance/romantic.tips.html` |
| *Comments* | Global sampling of romantic spots. |

| | |
|---|---|
| *What* | **Romantic Getaways** |
| *How* | Web |
| *Where* | `http://www.users.interport.net/~dolphin/netwomen.html` |
| *Comments* | Colorful, abundantly illustrated and informative Web site, which takes you on site tours of seductive vacation spots in places like Hawaii and the Caribbean. Includes a Destination Finder and Travel Forum with Q and As. Helpful and inspiring. |

| | |
|---|---|
| *What* | **S&M** |
| *How* | Usenet newsgroup |
| *Where* | `alt.bondage` |
| *Comments* | Discussion on sadomasochism, bondage, and domination; nothing innocent here. |

| | |
|---|---|
| *What* | **Safe Sex** |
| *How* | Usenet newsgroup |
| *Where* | `alt.sex.safe` |
| *Comments* | Discussion forum for many types of safe sex, from sex with condoms to masturbation to cybersex. |

| | |
|---|---|
| *What* | **Sex** |
| *How* | Usenet newsgroup |
| *Where* | `alt.sex` |

*Comments*   Runs the gamut, from memorable and forgetable pick-up lines to graphic details of sexual encounters. For hard-core, second-chakra types.

*What*   **Single Search National/International**

*How*   Web

*Where*   http://nsns.com/single-search/

*Comments*   Commercial dating network, which offers its services in the United States and around the world.

*What*   **True Romance**

*How*   Usenet newsgroup

*Where*   alt.romance

*Comments*   All matters of the heart are talked about here—heart throbs, heartache, sonnets, love songs.

*What*   **The World of Romance**

*How*   Web

*Where*   http://www.sos.net/romance/romance.html

*Comments*   Links to romantic getaways around the world.

*What*   **Yellow Silk**

*How*   Web

*Where*   http://www.enews.com:80/magazines/yellow_silk/

*Comments*   California-based erotica magazine, now on-line. The illustrations and photos are on the Web site but the literature is to be found only on the Gopher site.

# 10

# FAMILY MATTERS

## Resources for Parents and Children

*Liza Weiman Hanks*

The questions start the minute your child is born and they don't ever let up. Being a parent means a lifetime of encountering new experiences while simultaneously having to make critical decisions—after all, you're the grown-up in the room. The only consolation is that every parent experiences the same befuddling, amusing, and occasionally terrifying process; we're all reinventing the same wheel. Parents are a tremendous resource for each other and this chapter offers you the Internet sites that best offer support and information. Best of all, you can go on-line and ask questions or do research twenty-four hours a day without worrying about waking up those lucky enough to be getting their rest.

I've tried to select sites here that take real advantage of the Internet and offer interactivity, so that you can communicate directly with other parents, as well as comprehensive content, so that you feel like you're doing more than reading the back of a box or watching an advertisement. I've tried to avoid sites that simply offer items for sale, since buying things for children is easily done and is one of the least interesting parts of parenthood.

I've found that the Internet works best if you think of it as a combination of a great library and your favorite café (or maybe your pediatrician's waiting room). It is a terrific place for finding information that is not widely available, such as detailed medical information on rare children's diseases, or for making contact with others when too many days alone with your four-year-old leave you feeling isolated. I've also tried to offer a mixture of commercial Web sites, where professional editors have the time to present well-organized, edited texts, and passionate amateur sites, where well-meaning and well-informed people bring you the best of whatever it is that they want to present. Because the Internet is constantly growing and changing, most of these sites also contain updated lists of other related resources so that you'll always be able to find the newest parenting sites.

You'll find sites here that offer parenting information on just about any topic imaginable, including specialized listings on becoming parents, children's health, mothering, single parenting, stepparenting, grandparenting, and gay parenting. In some cases, a resource suits more than one category, so check all that apply to you! While most of the listings are for the World Wide Web, there are also newsgroups listed for most topics, with group discussions that are often quite active and opinionated. Finally, resources are included for those concerned about the safety of their children on the Internet, providing you with positive information that you can use to counter those who would like to ban children's use altogether, as well as tips and guidelines to help keep their use safe. These sites also provide links to companies who are marketing Net-watching software, which is designed to allow parental control of children's computer use.

Resources in this chapter are divided into the following categories:

- Becoming a parent: pregnancy, infertility, birth, and adoption
- Gay parenting
- General
- Grandparenting
- Health
- Mothering
- Net safety and Net censorship
- Single parenting
- Stepparenting

## BECOMING A PARENT: PREGNANCY, INFERTILITY, BIRTH, AND ADOPTION

| | |
|---|---|
| *What* | **The Adoption Connection Project** |
| *How* | Web |
| *Where* | http://www.sover.net/~adopt/ |
| *Comments* | The Adoption Connection Project was created by a group of women dedicated to bringing together birth mothers, adopted daughters, adoptive mothers, foster mothers, and stepmothers. |

| | |
|---|---|
| *What* | **Adoption Online Connection** |
| *How* | Web |
| *Where* | http://www.clark.net/pub/crc/open.html |
| *Comments* | Resource for connecting birthparents and prospective adoptive parents. Families can post names, photograph, and letter of introduction. Personal replies can be e-mailed directly to prospective parents. |

| | |
|---|---|
| *What* | **Childbirth** |
| *How* | Web |
| *Where* | http://www.childbirth.org |
| *Comments* | Provides extensive information on all matters related to birth and interesting links to other pregnancy resources. |
| *Tidbit* | My favorite line is to an interactive pregnancy calendar that builds you a developmental record of the developing fetus: www.olen.com/baby. |

| | |
|---|---|
| *What* | **Doulas of North America** |
| *How* | Web |
| *Where* | http://www.dona.com/index.html |
| *Comments* | Here's an example of high-technology being used for old-fashioned comfort. Use this site to find yourself a doula (a trained labor assistant) to assist at your birth or learn how to become one. |

| | |
|---|---|
| *What* | **Fetal Alcohol Syndrome** |
| *How* | Telnet |
| *Where* | `fedworld.gov`; for information on U.S. government publications on fetal alcohol syndrome go to `FETALALC.TXT`. |
| *Comments* | Contains an essay by the National Council on Alcoholism. Includes information on alcoholism research and treatment. |

| | |
|---|---|
| *What* | **Infertility and Health** |
| *How* | Usenet newsgroup |
| *Where* | `alt.infertility & misc.health.infertility` |
| *Comments* | Discussions on infertility issues. |

| | |
|---|---|
| *What* | **Midwifery** |
| *How* | Usenet newsgroup |
| *Where* | `sci.med.midwifery` |
| *Comments* | Discussions on midwifery. |

| | |
|---|---|
| *What* | **Online Birth Center** |
| *How* | Web |
| *Where* | `http://www.efn.org/~djz/birth/birthindex.html` |
| *Comments* | Provides all sorts of information for parents and expectant parents, including a midwifery page for practicing and aspiring midwives. Start here to track down more specialized organizations, mailing lists, newsgroups, and women's resources concerning birthing and related issues. |

| | |
|---|---|
| *What* | **Parenting Resources** |
| *How* | Web |
| *Where* | `http://www.adopting.org/sitparnt.html` |
| *Comments* | Here is virtually everything you might want to know about how to adopt a child. The site provides access to a community of support for adoptive parents and children. |

| | |
|---|---|
| *What* | **Pregnancy** |
| *How* | Usenet newsgroup |
| *Where* | `misc.kids.pregnancy` |
| *Comments* | Discussions on pregnancy. |

| | |
|---|---|
| *What* | **Resolve** |
| *How* | Web |
| *Where* | `http://www.resolve.org` |
| *Comments* | This is the home page for the national not-for-profit group that assists people in resolving their infertility by providing information, support, and advocacy. |

## GAY PARENTING

| | |
|---|---|
| *What* | **FamilyQ** |
| *How* | Web |
| *Where* | http://www.athens.net/~familyq/ |
| *Comments* | Offers resources for the queer family, including legal information and resources, as well as links and articles on adoption, surrogate motherhood, and foster parenting. |

| | |
|---|---|
| *What* | **The Lesbian Mom's Web Page** |
| *How* | Web; e-mail |
| *Where* | http://www.lesbian.org/moms/ |
| *Comments* | "This Web site was designed to help those women out there, specifically lesbians, who want to have babies through nontraditional means. A disclaimer feels rather obligatory at this point, so here it goes: If you need a doctor, get one; if you need legal advice, see a lawyer; if you are looking for the wisdom and life experiences of other lesbian moms . . . read on." |
| *Tidbit* | The Web site also contains instructions for subscribing to the lesbian moms' mailing list. |

| | |
|---|---|
| *What* | **The Lesbian Mother's Support Society** |
| *How* | Web |
| *Where* | http://www.lesbian.org/lesbian-moms/ |
| *Comments* | "Lesbian Mothers Support Society or LMSS, a nonprofit group, strives to provide peer support for lesbian parents (biological and nonbiological) and their children, as well as those lesbians considering parenthood. Through social functions such as potlucks and children's activities, lesbian families are able to share experiences and support each other in a positive environment. We also attempt to provide legal/medical/psychosocial referrals as needed." |

| | |
|---|---|
| *What* | **MOMS** |
| *How* | Listserv |
| *Where* | Send the message Subscribe Moms Firstname Lastname your e-mail address to MAJORDOMO@QICLAB.SCN.RAIN.COM to subscribe. |
| *Comments* | For lesbian mothers, co-mothers, and women, especially lesbians, who want to be mothers. |
| *Tidbit* | Contact the listowner directly at: moms-owner@qiclab.scn.rain.com |

| | |
|---|---|
| *What* | **Parents, Families, and Friends of Lesbians and Gays (PFLAG)** |
| *How* | Web |
| *Where* | http://www.critpath.org/pflag-talk |
| *Comments* | Web site for the organization PFLAG offers on-line help, FAQs, and information on upcoming conferences and advocacy issues. |

## GENERAL

| | |
|---|---|
| *What* | **Annie's Bookstop** |
| *How* | Web |
| *Where* | http://www.owt.com/anniesbk |
| *Comments* | Though Web shopping isn't always my cup of tea, I have to give this site points for passion. It is clear that they love children's books, make thoughtful recommendations, and even offer book/puppet packages that would make anyone smile. |

---

**CYBERSEXISM/CYBER EMPOWERMENT FOR GIRLS**

Which would you rather buy for your daughter? McKenzie and Co. is a CD-ROM game for 10-15 year-old girls that features cheerleaders and aspiring actresses chasing males and developing choices as to how to act to snag a boy. Let's Talk About Me is an interactive resource for girls to meet other girls from around the world through e-mail, learn about their developing bodies, look in on successful women, and get fitness, sports, and nutrition information. If you want to tell Her Interactive, the makers of McKenzie, to send their cheerleaders to the locker room, call 800-561-0908. Order Let's Talk from Girl Games, 221 East 9th Street Suite 302, Austin, TX 78701 http://www.sccsi.com/girlgames.

—from Feminist FaxNet, May 31, 1996

---

| | |
|---|---|
| *What* | **BabyBag Online** |
| *How* | Web |
| *Where* | http://www.babybag.com |
| *Comments* | In addition to general-purpose parenting information, this site offers good health and safety information on topics like sun safety and pesticides. It also offers business and job opportunities and a recipe exchange. |

| | |
|---|---|
| *What* | **Children's Literature** |
| *How* | Usenet newsgroup |
| *Where* | rec.arts.books.children |
| *Comments* | Discussions on finding and enjoying children's literature. |

| | |
|---|---|
| *What* | **Children's Software Reviews** |
| *How* | Web |
| *Where* | http://qv3pluto.leidenuniv.nl/steve/reviews/welcome.htm |
| *Comments* | Repository for volunteer reviews of children's software produced by users of a newsgroup on the topic. What's great about it is its honesty—these are unvarnished opinions by real consumers: "The children never got to play with this program; I sent it back." |
| *Tidbit* | Visit the Usenet newsgroup at misc.kids.computer. |

| | |
|---|---|
| *What* | **Family Surfboard** |
| *How* | Web |
| *Where* | http://www.familysurf.com |
| *Comments* | What makes this site stand out is that it is activity oriented—you'll find useful information here on how to make the Internet useful, engaging, and educational for yourself and your kids. In addition to offering a list of good Web sites, as well as demos of popular kids' software, each Web site recommendation comes with ideas for using the site as a springboard for further discussion, thoughts and actions. And the authors (Ruth and Steve Bennett) ought to have good ideas: They've published *365 TV-Free Activities You Can Do with Your Child* and *Kick the TV Habit: A Simple Program for Changing Your Family's Television Viewing and Video Game Habit.* |

| | |
|---|---|
| *What* | **KidsSource OnLine** |
| *How* | Web |
| *Where* | http://www.kidsource.com |
| *Comments* | This general parenting site offers particularly good information on safety issues, with a full library of toy recall announcements from the United States Product Safety Commission. It also has interesting, slightly offbeat parenting tips, such as "tips that all baseball coaches should know." |

| | |
|---|---|
| *What* | **Parenting Solution** |
| *How* | Usenet newsgroup |
| *Where* | alt.support.parenting.solutions |
| *Comments* | Discussions on general parenting concerns. |

| | |
|---|---|
| *What* | **Parents at Home** |
| *How* | Web |
| *Where* | http://iquest.com/~jsm/moms/ |
| *Comments* | This is a site for parents, both moms and dads, who choose to stay home and raise their children full time. It has information on parenting, books, money issues, a place to link up with an e-mail pen pal, and a good list of organizations for stay-at-home parents. |

| | |
|---|---|
| *What* | **ParentsPlace** |
| *How* | Web |
| *Where* | http://www.parentsplace.com |
| *Comments* | This parenting resource site offers well-designed and well-used bulletin boards, live chat opportunities, and an on-line mall, but best of all it has extensive reading rooms full of articles, book excerpts, and hard-to-find on-line newsletters and links to other useful Web sites on a wide variety of parenting issues. Its bulletin boards are well organized and interesting. For research on all of the topics covered in this chapter, start here. |

| | |
|---|---|
| *What* | **ParentSoup** |
| *How* | Web |
| *Where* | `http://www.parentsoup.com` |
| *Comments* | This Web site offers bulletin boards; live chat opportunities on varied parenting topics; a general store with interesting baby products; and fourteen topic areas, organized like a magazine for information on such things as sports, travel, and money. It is lively, well designed, and another good place to start your Web explorations, especially if you're looking for bulletin boards on parenting topics. |

## GRANDPARENTING

| | |
|---|---|
| *What* | **Caring Grandparents of America** |
| *How* | Web |
| *Where* | `http://www.uconnect.com/cga` |
| *Comments* | Allows access to articles from *The Grandparents Times* newsletter and offers discussion groups as well. |

| | |
|---|---|
| *What* | **Grandparent E-Mail Pen Pals** |
| *How* | Web |
| *Where* | `http://iquest.com/~jsm/moms/grand.html` |
| *Comments* | List of grandparents who are interested in conversing with other grandparents or children and younger parents. |

| | |
|---|---|
| *What* | **Grandparenting** |
| *How* | Web |
| *Where* | `http://seniors-site.com/retiremt/grandpar.html` |
| *Comments* | Offers articles about grandparenting, books and newsletters, and bulletins on topics such as grandparents' rights in custody cases. |

| | |
|---|---|
| *What* | **Grandparents Board** |
| *How* | Web |
| *Where* | `http://www.parentsoup.com/cgi-bin/genobject/dgr000` |
| *Comments* | Bulletin board offering conversation about grandparenting and dialog among grandparents. |

| | |
|---|---|
| *What* | **Grandparents Bulletin Board** |
| *How* | Web |
| *Where* | `http://www.parentsplace.com/dialog/get/grandparents.html` |
| *Comments* | In addition to providing a place for grandparents to get together and discuss their grandchildren, this site offers a weekly support group for grandparents, which meets on Tuesdays and Saturdays. |

## HEALTH

| | |
|---|---|
| *What* | **Internet Resources for Special Children** |
| *How* | Web |
| *Where* | http://w3.one.net/~julio_c/ |
| *Comments* | This is the place to start researching information on children with special needs. It has a comprehensive directory of Web sites for everything from Attention Deficit Disorder to Visual Impairment, organized both alphabetically and topically. |

| | |
|---|---|
| *What* | **KidsHealth** |
| *How* | Web |
| *Where* | http://kidshealth.org/ai/cht/spring.1995/cht1.html |
| *Comments* | A comprehensive health information site published by the Nemours Foundation Center for Biomedical Communications. The information (which covers nutrition, behavior, development, immunizations, and childhood diseases) is detailed, easy to find, and useful. It also offers information designed for children on bodies and feelings. |

| | |
|---|---|
| *What* | **Parents Helping Parents** |
| *How* | Web |
| *Where* | http://www.portal.com/~cbntmkr/php.html |
| *Comments* | Searchable human services resource directory with a focus on the needs of children. It includes condition and disability files as well as shareware. It also offers a long list of specialized Web sites, such as the Down Syndrome Listserv, National Parent Information Network, and Parent to Parent (a project that puts parents of children with disabilities in touch with one another). |

| | |
|---|---|
| *What* | **Rare Genetic Diseases in Children** |
| *How* | Web |
| *Where* | http://mcrcr4.med.nyu.edu/~murphp01/homenew.htm |
| *Comments* | In addition to providing an excellent directory of disability resources on the Web, this site offers a directory of resources concerning such nitty-gritty details as health insurance, SSI, Medicaid, and government grants. It also provides a worldwide messaging center for people who want to trade information with others struggling with similar diseases. |

## MOTHERING

| | |
|---|---|
| *What* | **Mothers' Groups** |
| *How* | Usenet newsgroup |
| *Where* | alt.mothers |
| *Comments* | Discussion group for mothers about childrearing, fathers, managing careers, and managing grandparents. |

| | |
|---|---|
| *What* | **Between Moms** |
| *How* | Web |
| *Where* | http://www.cadvision.com/moms |
| *Comments* | Designed to be a network for mothers of infants and preschool-aged children, this site offers mom-tested ideas and issues of the *Between Moms* newsletter. |

| | |
|---|---|
| *What* | **BIG-MOMS** |
| *How* | Listserv |
| *Where* | Send the message SUBSCRIBE your e-mail address to BIG_MOMS_LIST-REQUEST@BUTLER.HPL.HP.COM to subscribe. |
| *Comments* | A discussion for "large moms (be they tall or obese or both) and large women who want to be moms" on social issues, fertility, parenting, and so forth. |

| | |
|---|---|
| *What* | **Feminist Mothers at Home** |
| *How* | Listserv |
| *Where* | Contact Ann Allen at amallen@millcomm.com |
| *Comments* | "For thinking women who choose to stay at home with their children and do something more than watch Regis and Kathie Lee." |

| | |
|---|---|
| *What* | **A Space Made for Moms** |
| *How* | Web |
| *Where* | http://almond.srv.cs.cmu.edu/afs/cs.cmu.edu/user/jeanc/mom/space.html |
| *Comments* | Offers links for women's reproductive policy issues as well as general women's interest issues, and includes helpful personal stories on balancing careers and kids. |

| | |
|---|---|
| *What* | **Work at Home Moms** |
| *How* | Web |
| *Where* | http://www.maricle.com/wahm |
| *Comments* | On-line magazine for mothers who work at home. |

## NET SAFETY AND NET CENSORSHIP

| | |
|---|---|
| *What* | **Fridge Art KidSafe** |
| *How* | Web |
| *Where* | http://www.go-interface.com/fridgeartz/kidsafe.html |
| *Comments* | Includes helpful tips for kids, parents, and teachers on keeping the Internet safe, plus a list of sites to get demos of popular Net-watching software such as CyberPatrol, NetNanny, SurfWatch, and CYBERsitter. |

| | |
|---|---|
| *What* | **Interesting Places for Parents** |
| *How* | Web |

| | |
|---|---|
| *Where* | http://www.crc.ricoh.com/people/steve/parents.html |
| *Comments* | In addition to offering a lot of interesting links to educational resources for kids on the Internet, this site has a strong commitment to combatting Net censorship and providing access to Web sites that provide information about safety on the Web. |
| *What* | **Larry's KidPage** |
| *How* | Web |
| *Where* | http://www.larrysworld.com/kids.html |
| *Comments* | This is the kid's section of Larrysworld, a site written by Larry J. Magid, a syndicated columnist whose work appears in the *Los Angeles Times, Washington Post, San Jose Mercury News,* and many other publications. He wrote *Child Safety on the Information Highway* (available at this Web site), a pamphlet that educates parents on the nature of on-line systems, outlines its risks to children, and discusses ways that parents can reduce these risks. This site also provides links to great sites for kids, parents, and teachers, and a listing of companies that make parental control software which includes links to the companies' Web sites, where demo software is usually available. |

## SINGLE PARENTING

| | |
|---|---|
| *What* | **Single Parents' Support Group** |
| *How* | Usenet newsgroup |
| *Where* | alt.support.single-parents |
| *Comments* | A good place to turn for advice and support if you are: a single mom or dad; divorced; widowed; unmarried; or gay. |
| *What* | **At Home Dads** |
| *How* | Web |
| *Where* | http://www.parentsplace.com/readroom/athomedad/index.html |
| *Comments* | This is the on-line version of a quarterly newsletter promoting the home-based father, both single and not single. Especially helpful is the At-Home Dads Network, a national list of at-home dads published quarterly to inspire playgroups. |
| *What* | **Single Parents Reading Room** |
| *How* | Web |
| *Where* | http://www.parentsplace.com/readroom/single.html |
| *Comments* | Includes especially good bulletin boards for single and soon-to-be single parents, newsletters, and links to other resources for single parents. |
| *What* | **Single Dad's Index** |
| *How* | Web |
| *Where* | http://www.vix.com/pub/men/single-dad.html |

| | |
|---|---|
| *Comments* | Policy-oriented site with an index to child support issues, paternity, visitation and access, custody, missing kids, divorce, alimony, and fatherhood tips and advice. |
| *What* | **Sole Mothers International** |
| *How* | Web |
| *Where* | `http://home.navisoft.com/solemom` |
| *Comments* | Web site for the group Sole Mothers International has good articles and self-help resources. Its Operation Net Support provides help and resources on how to get help enforcing child support obligations. |

## STEPPARENTING

| | |
|---|---|
| *What* | **Stepfamilies Bulletin Board** |
| *How* | Web |
| *Where* | `http://www.parentsoup.com/cgi-bin/bboard/message/4/5` |
| *Comments* | Turn here to discuss the problems and pleasures of being a stepparent. |
| *What* | **Stepfamilies Bulletin Board** |
| *How* | Web |
| *Where* | `http://www.parentsplace.com/dialog/get/stepfamily.html` |
| *Comments* | Another good place to discuss tough issues such as fighting with stepchildren, integrating new babies, dealing with child support, and struggling with teenagers. |
| *What* | **Step-parents' Support Group** |
| *How* | Usenet newsgroup |
| *Where* | `alt.support.step-parent` |
| *Comments* | Great place to find companionship and advice on difficult issues such as introducing children to your new partner, blending families, or how to deal with angry stepchildren. |

# 11

# ALL THE NEWS THAT'S FIT TO UPLOAD

## On-line Media

### *Nina Beth Huntemann*

The print and broadcast media with which you're familiar, whether it's mainstream, alternative, or feminist, from *The New York Times* to CNN and PBS, to National Public Radio and *On The Issues*, are likely to be found on the Internet. Along with easy access to the hard news, several locations provide excellent updates on Internet-related topics, such as the ongoing legal arguments over regulation on the Net. There's also a wealth of international resources, such as OMRI (Open Media Research Institute), formerly Radio Free Europe.

In addition, the Internet is a medium in itself, and individuals and organizations have used it creatively (and sometimes uncreatively) to disseminate news alerts, current events and analyses, creative writing, animation, artwork, and so forth. Electronic magazines, called e-zines, abound, as do newsletters and bulletin boards. You can find the news on the Internet, and you can also make it.

This new medium has already demonstrated its unique power to circulate real news to people: the unedited, hard-core facts behind a mainstream presentation—and sometimes, the information that whole populations desperately need to have and may not be able to otherwise access, as a result of political crises such as government censorship or civil war. During the August 1991 coup in the Soviet Union, when tanks were rolling into Moscow and the Parliament building was under siege, one of the only means for sending news in and out of the Russian capital was via e-mail. The Communist party had closed down the regular media, and foreign correspondants based in the country were forced to depend solely on e-mail. Without e-mail, people inside and outside the country wouldn't have known what was really happening. "Technology limits the tyrant," a friend of mine underscored when recalling the historic uprising.

When civil war erupted in Yugoslavia in 1991, the Zamir Network (*zamir* means "for peace" in Serbo-Croat) was quickly created to link Croatia, Serbia, Slovenia, and Bosnia via a host computer in Germany. Transcending spiraling ethnic and national conflicts, peace groups mobilized across borders with the help of e-mail. It was a radical solution for overcoming the dislocation and isolation wrought by war.

In this chapter, you'll find a thoughtful and interesting selection of resources, divided into the following:

- Indices
- Books, publishers, and distributors
- Broadcast media
- Communications

- E-zines
- Film and video
- Magazines
- Media literacy and education
- Newspapers, newsletters, and news wire services

## INDICES

| | |
|---|---|
| *What* | **InfoSearch Broadcasting Links** |
| *How* | Web |
| *Where* | http://www.searcher.com/links.html |
| *Comments* | Huge list of U.S. radio- and television-related Net links, such as Nickelodeon, National Public Radio, CSPAN, major networks (ABC, NBC, CBS, FOX), and local affiliates. |

| | |
|---|---|
| *What* | **Mega Media-Links** |
| *How* | Web |
| *Where* | http://www.rtvf.nwu.edu/links/ |
| *Comments* | Gigantic source for anything on the Net related to television, radio, film, video, and new media. This site is definitely one for your Web browser bookmark. Find Net information on newsgroups, Listservs, BBSs, Web pages, and e-mail addresses. Categories include: TV shows and stars; news and reviews; media history and education; databases and organizations; festivals and conferences; and new media technology. |

| | |
|---|---|
| *What* | **Parrot Media Network** |
| *How* | Web |
| *Where* | http://www.parrotmedia.com/ |
| *Comments* | Directory of U.S. television stations ranked by Nielsen markets, locations, and station affiliation. Find detailed information about station program managers, directors, postal mail addresses, e-mail, and telephone and fax numbers. Coming soon: radio, cable, and newspaper directories. |

## BOOKS

| | |
|---|---|
| *What* | **BOOKFIENDS** |
| *How* | Listserv |
| *Where* | Send message to Felice Newman at Cleis Press at cleis@english.hss.cmu.edu to subscribe; type Firstname Lastname e-mail address in the body of the message. |
| *Comments* | List for feminist, lesbian, and other alternative editors, publishers, booksellers, and distributors. |

| | |
|---|---|
| *What* | **Celebration of Women Writers** |
| *How* | Web |
| *Where* | http://www.cs.cmu.edu/Web/People/mmbt/women/writers.html/ |
| *Comments* | Great links to the writings of women. |

| | |
|---|---|
| *What* | **Directory of Feminist Bookstores** |
| *How* | Web |
| *Where* | http://www.igc.apc.org/women/bookstores/booknets.html |
| *Comments* | Index of feminist bookstores in the United States and Canada arranged by province and state, then area code. This site also has links to a European and worldwide feminist bookstore index, a Canada/USA gay and lesbian bookstore index, and a European and worldwide gay and lesbian bookstore index. |
| *What* | **FEMEDIT** |
| *How* | Mailing list |
| *Where* | Send message to listproc@wheatonma.edu with no subject line to subscribe; type SUBSCRIBE FEMEDIT Firstname Lastname in the body of the message. |
| *Comments* | List dedicated to the discussion of all aspects of feminist publishing. "Anyone with an interest in feminist publishing is welcome to subscribe." |
| *What* | **Feminist Research Center** |
| *How* | Web |
| *Where* | http://www.feminist.org/research/1_public.html |
| *Comments* | Created by the Feminist Majority Foundation, the Feminist Research Center on-line provides listings of feminist fiction and nonfiction. |
| *Tidbit* | New section, called Feminist Arts, Entertainment, and Literature, lists artists, performers, and writers and other art-related sites on the Web as well as concerts, readings, and other events from the FMF's expanded Feminist Calendar. The site is located at: http://www.feminist.org/news/1_calndr.html |
| *What* | **Spinsters Ink** |
| *How* | Web |
| *Where* | http://www.lesbian.org/spinsters-ink/index.html |
| *Comments* | Feminist publishing house specializing in "novels and nonfiction works that deal with significant issues in women's lives from a feminist perspective." Spinsters Ink's catalog is on-line, with beautiful book cover graphics and chapter excerpts. |
| *What* | **Women's Books On-line: A Cooperative Book Review** |
| *How* | Web |
| *Where* | http://www.cybergrrl.com/review/ |
| *Comments* | Books written and reviewed by women. Three reviewers offer insights and recommendations for feminist fiction. Also featured is a searchable index of feminist booksellers. |
| *What* | **Women's National Book Association (WNBA)** |
| *How* | Web |
| *Where* | http://www.bentoni.com/wnba/ |

*Comments*    Organization supporting women in publishing. Back issues of the monthly newsletter *Signature* are featured, as well as membership information and Washington, D.C.–area WNBA activities.

## BROADCAST MEDIA—RADIO AND TELEVISION

*What*    **Alternative and Recreational Television**

*How*     Usenet newsgroup

*Where*    `alt.tv.*` or `rec.arts.tv`

*Comments*    Over seventy newsgroups discuss television shows, exchanging information about stars, griping about plot development, and bickering over which show is better, "90210" or "Melrose Place." For fun (and flaming) check out everything from `alt.tv.roseanne` and `alt.tv.seinfeld` to `alt.tv.x-files` and `alt.tv.talkshows.daytime`. See the newsgroup `rec.arts.tv` for a more general discussion of television programming.

*What*    **Iconoclast Productions**

*How*     Web

*Where*    `http://www.best.com:80/~iconocla/`

*Comments*    Cable television production company based in San Francisco. Focusing on progressive multicultural programming, Iconoclast is an African-American and women-owned company. For those in the Bay Area, Iconoclast offers television production training, particularly for differently abled persons.

*What*    **ShopTalk**

*How*     Mailing list

*Where*    Send message to `listserv@vm3090.ege.edu.tr` with no subject line to subscribe; type `SUBSCRIBE SHOPTALK Firstname Lastname` in the body of the message.

*Comments*    Mailing list not designed for discussion. Members receive an industry newsletter distributed by a media consulting firm in California. "The focus of ShopTalk is mostly on television news, but it often adds notes on radio, information technologies, and humor."

*What*    **TV-L**

*How*     Mailing list

*Where*    Send message to `listserv@vm3090.ege.edu.tr` with no subject line to subscribe; type `SUBSCRIBE TV-L Firstname Lastname` in the body of the message.

*Comments*    Mailing list that runs a general discussion about television programming. This list is often busy, depending on the current topic. For example, discussion about television soap operas draws much attention. However, the list has a nice feature that allows you to block out certain discussion topics.

| | |
|---|---|
| *What* | **WINGS (Women's International News Gathering Service)** |
| *How* | Web |
| *Where* | http://www.hypercity.com/hyp/wings.html |
| *Comments* | Independent radio production company, creating programs about women's actions and views on current events. The site provides information on ordering back cassette tapes of WINGS productions, a list of radio stations worldwide broadcasting WINGS shows, and RealAudio samples of WINGS programs for instant listening with the RealAudio Player. |
| *Tidbit* | Visit the RealAudio Web Site at http://www.realaudio.com for more information on downloading the RealAudio Player. |

## COMMUNICATION

| | |
|---|---|
| *What* | **Women On-line Worldwide** |
| *How* | Web |
| *Where* | http://www.wowwomen.com:80/ |
| *Comments* | Interactive forum on the Web that has free nightly hosted chats, message boards, a zine, a shareware library, and more. Covers a wide range of women's issues—education, on-line writings, work and money, women and the Internet. |

**Q:** Now as electronic communications becomes increasingly popular in the United States, how should feminists be thinking about its use?

**A:** Feminists should be planning and taking action on how to secure access to electronic communications technology for all women. We must strive to influence public policy and commercial interests, always emphasizing the need for public access channels to the Internet. Already computer communications technology is being bought up by the entertainment, software, and telecommunications industries. Their concern is profit, monopoly, lowest common denominator content for the widest audience. Just look at cable and broadcast television for the future of the Internet, unless we act now to retain bandwidth for diverse points of view.

—NINA BETH HUNTEMANN
University of Massachusetts, Amherst

| | |
|---|---|
| *What* | **MECCA** |
| *How* | Web |
| *Where* | http://www.systers.org/mecca |
| *Comments* | Communication and information system for "Systers." |

## E-'ZINES

| | |
|---|---|
| *What* | **Elight** |
| *How* | Web |

| | |
|---|---|
| *Where* | http://www.youth.org/elight/ |
| *Comments* | E-zine for the Web created by and for gay youth and young adults in cyberspace. Light on graphics, heavy on fun; this electronic rag provides Web space for gay youth to express themselves. *Elight* features poetry, fiction, nonfiction, and coming-out forums, and welcomes unsolicited submissions. |

| | |
|---|---|
| *What* | **Queer Jewish Women WebZine** |
| *How* | Web |
| *Where* | http://www.zoom.com/personal/staci/staci1.htm |
| *Comments* | Monthly webzine for lesbian and bisexual Jewish women focusing on the past, present, and future of queer Jewish women's identity. The editors welcome submissions of articles, herstory, interviews, stories, poems, photos, and artwork about what it means to be a queer Jewish woman. Send questions via e-mail to Staci Schoenfeld at staci@zoom.com. |

| | |
|---|---|
| *What* | **Women's Web Magazine** |
| *How* | Web |
| *Where* | http://www.womenswebmagazine.com |
| *Comments* | On-line magazine aiming to "reach that ever-increasing number of women who call cyberspace home. Besides being one of the few women's magazines on the Net, it uses the interactive capabilities of the medium to its fullest potential. Readers can interact with one another, respond to articles, and even shape the editorial content of the magazine. Its motto is 'building a community of women on-line.'" Sophisticated design and easy navigation. |

## FILM AND VIDEO

| | |
|---|---|
| *What* | **Black Film Center/Archive (BFCA)** |
| *How* | Web |
| *Where* | http://www.indiana.edu/~bfca/index.html |
| *Comments* | Indiana University BFCA houses over seven hundred film and video titles related to and/or written by African-Americans. You can view an almost complete catalog of the collection at the site, but the film and videos are not for public distribution. Those interested in viewing a title are encouraged to contact the BFCA and arrange a viewing time. Information about and a table of contents of the BFCA newsletter, Black Camera, are also available here. |

| | |
|---|---|
| *What* | **CINEMA-L** |
| *How* | Mailing list |
| *Where* | Send message to listserv@auvm.american.edu with no subject line to subscribe; type SUBSCRIBE CINEMA-L Firstname Lastname in the body of the message. |
| *Comments* | Created as a forum for general chat about movies. This extremely busy e-mailing list will fill up your mailbox in no time. Discussions focus primarily on popular films, |

what participants liked or didn't like about a movie, rumors about upcoming Hollywood productions, etc.

| | |
|---|---|
| *What* | **Frameline On-line** |
| *How* | Web |
| *Where* | http://www.frameline.org/ |
| *Comments* | Excellent Web resource with over 160 titles of lesbian and gay films available for purchase or rental. Frameline's entire catalog is on-line and indexed by title, director, and genre. Most film and video descriptions have a short plot synopsis, viewing time and price. In addition, Frameline—a nonprofit organization supporting the exhibition, production, distribution, and funding of lesbian and gay films—features information on Frameline programs and activities, such as the annual San Francisco International Lesbian and Gay Film Festival. |

| | |
|---|---|
| *What* | **Girls on Film: Chicks, Flicks, and Politicks** |
| *How* | Web |
| *Where* | http://www.itp.tsoa.nyu.edu/~gof/ |
| *Comments* | Movie reviews brought to you by four women film buffs, Academy Awards commentary, a reader forum, and "Notes from the Aisle" all make this Web site a must for both the passive and fanatic film goer. Recent features included "On the '96 Campaign Trail" and a discussion of Hollywood's obsession with rape scenes. |

| | |
|---|---|
| *What* | **Inform Women's Studies: Film Reviews** |
| *How* | Web |
| *Where* | http://www.inform.umd.edu:8080/EdRes/Topic/WomensStudies/FilmReviews |
| *Comments* | Hosted by the University of Maryland's Women's Studies Department, this Web site has a huge collection feminist film reviews. Browsing through the archive of recent box office hits and timeless faves is made easy with a text-only alphabetical listing of film titles. |

| | |
|---|---|
| *What* | **National Black Programming Consortium (NBPC)** |
| *How* | Web |
| *Where* | http://www.supptec.com/business/nbpc/ |
| *Comments* | Not-for-profit media arts organization supporting the improvement of African-American programming on public television. This Web site lists video titles available for rent from NBPC, membership information, and funding opportunities for independent film and video productions. |

| | |
|---|---|
| *What* | **Video Production** |
| *How* | Usenet newsgroup |
| *Where* | rec.video.production |

| | |
|---|---|
| *Comments* | Thoughtful discussion about equipment, costs and headaches of video production. Some video production experience required for useful feedback. |
| *What* | **Women in Cinema: A Reference Guide** |
| *How* | Web |
| *Where* | `http://poe.acc.virginia.edu/~pm9k/libsci/womFilm.html` |
| *Comments* | Chock-full of film references. Find a list of annotated bibliographies and anthologies of women in film, and links to feminist film review Web sites. Great resource for researching women in film or creating a syllabus for a history of film class. |
| *What* | **Women in Film & Video of Maryland, Inc.** |
| *How* | Web |
| *Where* | `http://mail.bcpl.lib.md.us/~ddavison/wifv.html` |
| *Comments* | Maryland chapter of the not-for-profit group Women in Film & Video. Membership information, local chapter listings, WFV workshop schedule, and the monthly chapter newsletter, *The Projector,* can be found at this site. |

## MAGAZINES

| | |
|---|---|
| *What* | **Essence Magazine On-line** |
| *How* | Web |
| *Where* | `http://www.essence.com/home.cgi` |
| *Comments* | Offers a variation from the magazine including Susan Taylor's "In the Spirit" and information about the World of Essence Empowerment Seminars. |
| *What* | **HUES: Hear Us Emerging Sisters** |
| *How* | Web |
| *Where* | `http://www.hues.net/` |
| *Comments* | Offers readers anything but powder-puff fluff. No makeup ads here—just the straight (and not so straight) dope. Includes well-written satire like "Dinner Roll Barbie, and Other Dolls I'd Like to See." Published on paper twice a year, the Web edition of *HUES* features a handful of complete articles, plus some Web-only material. |
| *What* | **LGNY: Lesbian and Gay New York** |
| *How* | Web |
| *Where* | `http://www.fly.net/~lgny/` |
| *Comments* | Electronic version of the hard copy *LGNY* magazine focusing on New York City lesbian and gay politics, news and entertainment. Be sure to bookmark *LGNY*'s extensive index of NYC Queer organizations. It's got everything from ACT UP and All the Queens' Women (a lesbian rap group in Queens, N.Y.), to the Women's Action Coalition and We Wah Bar-Chee Ampee (Native American lesbian and gay organization). The site also features a a listing of N.Y.C. gay bars and night clubs, including an events calendar of week-to-week entertainment, for those traveling to the Big Apple. |

| | |
|---|---|
| *What* | **Lilith** |
| *How* | Web |
| *Where* | http://cybergrrls.com/info/lilith/index.htm |
| *Comments* | Independent Jewish women's magazine, named for the predecessor of Eve who, according to the legend, insisted on equality with Adam. Published quarterly in New York. Its editors invite articles, fiction, memoirs, poetry, and original artwork. |
| *Tidbit* | Lilith on-line sends and receives information on Jewish women's activities and issues on the Internet. E-mail the editors at lilithmag@aol.com. |
| *What* | **On the Issues: The Progressive Woman's Quarterly** |
| *How* | Web |
| *Where* | http://www.igc.apc.org/onissues/ |
| *Comments* | The complete texts for a few feature articles per issue are available as well as Web-only stories. Check out live coverage from the September 1995 United Nations Fourth World Conference on Women, and bookmark the *On the Issues* women-related Net links. Subscribe to the paper edition on-line, or review a free copy sent via postal mail. |
| *What* | **Redbook** |
| *How* | Web |
| *Where* | http://homearts.com/rb/toc/00rbhpc1.htm |
| *Comments* | Visually pleasing, the Net version of *Redbook* serves up full articles from the current issue. Each article is sectioned into readable pieces, with lots of clean graphics. Hosted by a division of the Hearst Corporation, Redbook shares on-line space with *Good Housekeeping, Country Living,* and *Popular Mechanics.* |
| *What* | **Utne Reader** |
| *How* | Usenet newsgroup |
| *Where* | utne.buzz |
| *Comments* | Read-only comments on the *Utne Reader*, books, salons and on-line services. |
| *What* | **Women's Web (WomWeb)** |
| *How* | Web |
| *Where* | http://www.womweb.com/ |
| *Comments* | A joint collaboration between *Ms., Working Mother,* and *Working Woman,* Women's Web offers content from all three printed magazines, plus articles particular to on-line technology. Each magazine has the same subject headings: Departments, Talk (reader forum), and Biz (subscription information). Recently featured on Women's Web: tips on finding quality child care, and legal rights for women in the workplace. |
| *Tidbit* | Women's Web has unnecessarily large graphics and an image map on the home page. Turn off your graphics viewer for faster downloading. |

## MEDIA LITERACY AND EDUCATION

| | |
|---|---|
| *What* | **Center for Media Literacy** |
| *How* | Web |
| *Where* | http://websites.earthlink.net/~cml/ |
| *Comments* | Produces and distributes media literacy resources for schools and community education programs. A catalog includes an impressive list of books, videos, primary and secondary school curriculum, and links to other media literacy Net sites. |

| | |
|---|---|
| *What* | **Fairness and Accuracy in Reporting (FAIR)** |
| *How* | Web |
| *Where* | http://www.igc.apc.org/fair/ |
| *Comments* | National media-watch group publishing a bimonthly newsletter, *Extra!*, a half-hour syndicated radio broadcast, "CounterSpin," and several other nationally distributed critiques of the media industry. This Web site offers partial articles from *Extra!* and transcripts of "CounterSpin"; papers on the insensitive coverage of women, labor, minorities, and other public interest groups; and a brief list of contact information for major media corporations. |
| *Tidbit* | Check out the Women's Desk portion of FAIR's *Extra!* magazine. All articles are related to the portrayal of women in the media and its impact on society. Go to: http://www.fair.org/fair/womensdesk.html. |

| | |
|---|---|
| *What* | **KIDMEDIA** |
| *How* | Mailing list |
| *Where* | Send message to kidmedia-request@airwaves.com to subscribe; type SUBSCRIBE in the subject line and leave the body blank. |
| *Comments* | "Dedicated to the furthering of communications between people interested in, or involved in, the creation, production, distribution and/or consumption of media whose primary target audience is children." Recent topics of discussion included children's public and commercial television programs and their impact; producing children's media; how so-called "adult" or mainstream media affect kids; and how media does (or does not) affect children, and what is being done in that arena. |

| | |
|---|---|
| *What* | **Media Education Foundation** |
| *How* | Web |
| *Where* | http://www.igc.apc.org/mef/ |
| *Comments* | A not-for-profit organization devoted to producing educational materials that highlight the role of the media in the lives of Americans. The foundation produces media literacy videos, such as *Slim Hopes: Advertising and the Obsession with Thinness; Dreamworlds II: Desire/Sex/Power in Rock Video;* and *Pack of Lies: The Advertising of Tobacco.* The site also features a video catalog, as well as a list of media literacy Net links and statistics regarding violence and images of women in the media. |

| | |
|---|---|
| *What* | **Media-L** |
| *How* | Listserv |
| *Where* | Send message to `listserv@nmsu.edu` with no subject line to subscribe; type `SUBSCRIBE MEDIA-L Firstname Lastname, Your Position, Your Organization` in the body of the message. |
| *Comments* | Open to teachers, administrators, media professionals, researchers, and others with an active involvement in projects or issues related to media literacy. The major focus of the list is to provide a forum for the exchange of ideas and information related to a broad scope of media literacy subjects, activities, research, and teaching. Media-L is sponsored by KRWG-TV, the New Mexico State University Department of Journalism and Mass Communications, and the Southern New Mexico Media Literacy Coalition. |

| | |
|---|---|
| *What* | **Media Literacy On-line Project** |
| *How* | Web |
| *Where* | `http://interact.uoregon.edu/MediaLit/HomePage` |
| *Comments* | Based at the University of Oregon, this site is a clearinghouse for resources, Net links, and general information about media literacy. Add this site to your bookmark file as a jumping off point to bibliographies, organizations, article databases, school curricula, and educator guides and lists for media awareness. |

## NEWSPAPER, NEWSLETTERS, AND NEWS WIRE SERVICES

| | |
|---|---|
| *What* | **Catt's Claws: A Frequently Appearing Feminist Newsletter** |
| *How* | Mailing list |
| *Where* | Send message to `listserv@netcom.com` with no subject line to subscribe; type `SUBSCRIBE CATTS-CLAWS Firstname Lastname` in the body of the message. |
| *Comments* | Delivered directly to your e-mail inbox, this mixed bag of important feminist news is a must-read. Articles range from what's new in breast cancer research to sassy media criticism. Editor Irene Stuber keeps a watchful eye with a swift keyboard on the religious right, exposing contradictions in right rhetoric and antiwomen legislative endeavors. |
| *Tidbit* | Current and back issues also available on the World Wide Web at `http://worcester.lm.com/women/is/cattsclaws.html`. |

| | |
|---|---|
| *What* | **Clarinet** |
| *How* | Usenet newsgroup |
| *Where* | `clari.news.*` |
| *Comments* | Electronic news wire service. Most of the headlines are from existing news wire services, such as the Associated Press and Reuters. All news items are broken down by topic, such as `clari.news.women`, `clari.news.childrn+family`, `clari.news.blacks`, `clari.news.gays`, and `clari.news.issues.reproduction`. |

| | |
|---|---|
| *Tidbit* | You cannot post to Clarinet newsgroups and there are strict guidelines as to how you can reproduce Clarinet articles. |
| *What* | **Feminist News** |
| *How* | Web |
| *Where* | http://www.feminist.org/news/news.html |
| *Comments* | Feminist Majority Foundation news service gathers headlines from *The New York Times*, Associated Press, *Washington Post*, and other top U.S. newspapers and news services to create an impressive database of feminist news items. The headlines are updated daily and archived back to August 1995. |
| *Tidbit* | Bookmark the media links page which includes an extensive listing of major U.S. media providers. |
| *What* | **National NOW Times** |
| *How* | Web |
| *Where* | http://now.org/now/nnt/nntindex.html |
| *Comments* | Published every other month on paper and electronically. Contents include updates on NOW activities, editorials about current legislative events, and ongoing NOW campaigns with information on how to participate. Full articles are available with links to related information and past issues. |
| *What* | **New York Times on the Web** |
| *How* | Web |
| *Where* | http://www.nytimes.com/ |
| *Comments* | Updated daily with crisp photos and complete articles, the Web version of *The New York Times* may one day edge out the paper copy. Full articles are displayed with links to related current stories and even back issue articles. One can browse through the current *New York Times* issue by key word without charge and, for a fee per article, search issues back to June 1980. |
| *Tidbit* | Interested readers must register to access *The New York Times* on the Web (name and e-mail address required). If you don't want to be placed on a mailing list, be sure to uncheck the box asking permission to use your e-mail information. |
| *What* | **Political Woman Hotline** |
| *How* | Mailing list |
| *Where* | Send to polwoman@aol.com; type Interested in the subject line to subscribe. |
| *Comments* | Electronic newsletter of Women Leaders On-line http://worcester.lm.com/women/women.html. The site supports women running for public office and battles the political right. The newsletter features savvy analysis of the political process, news on the campaign trail, and biting critiques of media coverage. Back issues are available on the Web at http://worcester.lm.com/women/pw/hotlineinfo.html. |

| | |
|---|---|
| *What* | **Voices of Women (VOW)** |
| *How* | Web |
| *Where* | `http://www.voiceofwomen.com/` |
| *Comments* | On-line version of printed newsletter includes additional articles and artwork celebrating women's creative lives. VOW accepts submission of nonfiction, essays, poetry, and art. |
| *Tidbit* | Check out the VOW list of women-owned businesses. Search or submit your own. |

What will the newspaper of the future look like? Esther Dyson, hailed by the *New York Times* as the most powerful woman in "Net-erati," replies: "If you're looking twenty to thirty years from now, they will probably be printed out on local printers by whomever wants one. People will still want their news, but a lot of the traditional newspaper will disappear. With electronic distribution, there's no real reason for recipes and foreign coverage to be stuck together in one big wad of paper. Instead, the newspaper of the future will be customized to a consumer's needs. Stock prices and classifieds will probably drop off first—and this should happen in a very few years. After that, the data-intensive items will go—like local movie listings. These are sections that are so much more valuable when they can be electronically searched, filtered, and graphed.

It's really stupid to print out thousands of apartment listings for thousands of people. Just put them on line and let people select what they want by neighborhood and price range. As for investments, I want all the stock prices covered and filtered. I want to be able to call up all the securities that went up ten percent in the last two months."

—ESTHER DYSON
EDventures and Electronic Frontiers Foundation
(from "The Cyber-Maxims of Esther Dyson," interview with Claudia Dreifus,
*The New York Times Magazine,* 7 July 1996, 16–17)

| | |
|---|---|
| *What* | **Women's Feature Service** |
| *How* | Mailing list |
| *Where* | Send message to `wfs@igc.apc.org` asking for more information and subscription costs. |
| *Comments* | International news of interest to women including women's issues and women-related topics. All articles are written by women. Paid subscription includes six articles e-mailed in a weekly digest. Summaries of each week's articles are also available on the Association for Progressive Communications Conference at `wfs.english`. |

# 12

# CYBER R & R
## Travel and Recreation
### *Melissa Leigh Stone*

Electronic communications is an important source for work, education, activism, and much more! It also has a lighter side: The Internet can be a rich resource—and even a stimulating companion—for the purely enjoyable things in life. Whether you are an intrepid traveler, a gourmand, an athlete, or a couch potato who likes to relax with a good book or video, there's something for you in cyberspace.

Through your computer, you can access a wealth of resources on travel and recreational activities, some of them designed especially for women. In addition, your computer itself can be a source of recreation and a useful co-pilot on your journeys.

If you are looking for useful information, personal adventure, or an inexpensive, efficient way to retrieve your messages when on the road, you may want to consider packing a laptop computer with modem. Many airports and hotels in the United States provide public pay telephones that have standard modular (RJ-11) phone jacks like the one you normally use in your home or office to plug in the cord from your modem. Keep in mind that, especially in airports, these telephone locations are usually short of workspace and a comfortable place to sit, so it may be more convenient to unpack your computer when you get to a destination where you will be lodging.

If you decide to travel with your computer, know what you need to bring. First, all laptop computers automatically adapt to power sources of 110V and 60Hz (U.S.), or 220V and 50Hz (Europe, Asia, etc.) without a transformer, but for non–U.S. destinations, you will need an adapter plug for the power cord to your computer so that it will fit the local electricity sockets wherever you are. Second, it is always a good idea to carry the list of local dial-ups for Internet access numbers in your computer case with your computer. Your Internet Service Provider can supply you with its list of numbers, or can give you a list of other local hosts through which you can Telnet to your usual host network. Third, you will need to physically connect your computer modem to the local telephone system. This connection is easy if there is a standard modular telephone jack (RJ-11), which almost all U.S. telephones use.

However, many countries use nonstandard telephone plugs that you will not be able to use to connect your modem. The good news is that you can make almost any telephone in the world modem-friendly with a screwdriver and one essential tool, which you can make at home. I call this tool a "phone gizmo," and have made at least a hundred of them at my kitchen table. For instructions on how to construct this device, contact me at mstone@igc.apc.org.

This chapter is divided into two parts. The first provides practical sources of information for domestic and international traveling. The second offers descriptions of recreational activities that may be of interest while traveling, during weekends at home, or while experiencing a cyber-vacation in front of the computer.

Every day, more and more vacation destinations and purveyors of recreational activities are creating Web sites of their own. So in addition to these listings, we suggest that you initiate a quick search of your own so that you can quickly locate information that best suits your needs.

The listings are categorized as follows:

- Domestic and international travel
- Recreation and cyber-vacations
  - Books
  - Food, cooking, and restaurants
  - Hobbies
  - Music and dance
  - New Age interests
  - Pets
  - Self-defense
  - Sports

## DOMESTIC AND INTERNATIONAL TRAVEL

| | |
|---|---|
| *What* | **Ecotourism** |
| *How* | Usenet newsgroup |
| *Where* | green.travel |
| *Comments* | Information and discussion about environmentally and socially responsible travel and ecotourism, from the Amazon to Burma to Siberia to Nevada. A great place to plan your next vacation. |

| | |
|---|---|
| *What* | **Lowest Airfares** |
| *How* | Usenet newsgroup |
| *Where* | rec.travel.air |
| *Comments* | Resource for finding the lowest prices on international airfares, travel protection, and travel groups. |

| | |
|---|---|
| *What* | **Maiden Voyages Travel Guide** |
| *How* | Web |
| *Where* | http://maiden-voyages.com |
| *Comments* | Quarterly magazine and Web site featuring information on women's travel around the world. |

| | |
|---|---|
| *What* | **Region, Country, and World Guides** |
| *How* | Web |
| *Where* | http://gnn.com/gnn/wic/wics/trav.new.html |
| *Comments* | Geographic and subject guides of adventure travel, food and wine, lodging, guide-books and tips, magazines and news, maps and weather, reference and currency, |

transportation, travel agent resources, travel and health, travel narratives, and work/study abroad.

| | |
|---|---|
| *What* | **Travel Agents, Tickets, and Lodging** |
| *How* | Web |
| *Where* | http://www.travelassist.com/ |
| *Comments* | Listings of bed and breakfasts, inns and small hotels across the United States, a monthly travel magazine, and travel agents for different regions, and discount airfares. Also provides detailed indices of on-line travel services. Includes a section for travelers with "alternative lifestyles." |

## TIPS FOR WOMEN TRAVELERS

Being a stranger in a new place is an adventurous challenge, but the following advance preparations can help to ensure that you will be able to relax and enjoy yourself during your time away from home, whether you are traveling within the United States or abroad:

• Take a self-defense course, preferably one taught by women, that covers strategies for staying safe, how to detect the warning signs of potential attack, and physical self-defense techniques designed for adult women. (See the listings on self-defense for women in this chapter.)

• Assemble one or two packets of important information, and stash them in different pieces of luggage. In each packet include a photocopy of the following: your passport, relevant visas, credit cards, lists of traveler's checks with their amounts and serial numbers, telephone numbers of local U.S. embassies or consulates in the cities you plan to visit, relevant medical insurance information, contact person(s) in case of an emergency, local emergency numbers (other countries have equivalents to 911), and reference information for like-minded feminist women from local women's groups.

• Purchase traveler's medical insurance, including emergency medical evacuation if you are traveling to an area where adequate medical care is not available. Verify that your homeowner's or renter's insurance policy covers lost or stolen luggage. Purchase tickets and rent cars with credit cards that offer complimentary travel protection services.

| | |
|---|---|
| *What* | **Travel Commentary** |
| *How* | Usenet newsgroup |
| *Where* | gen.travel |
| *Comments* | Commentary by travelers on unique and interesting global travel adventures, such as Cuban International Youth Festivals. Also includes job vacancies for travel guides, helpful tips about hotels, travel services, discount airline tickets, and the latest listings of computer BBS dial-up numbers. |

| | |
|---|---|
| *What* | **Travel in . . .** |
| *How* | Usenet newsgroups |

| | |
|---|---|
| *Where* | `rec.travel.afr; rec.travel.asi; rec.travel.eur; rec.travel.lat;`<br>`rec.travel.usa` |
| *Comments* | Places to connect with people with extensive knowledge about travel in Africa; Asia, Europe, Latin America and the Caribbean, and the United States and Canada, respectively. |

## RECREATION AND CYBER-VACATIONS

### Books

| | |
|---|---|
| *What* | **BOOKWOMAN** |
| *How* | Mailing list |
| *Where* | Send message to `majordomo@vector.casti.com` with no subject line to subscribe; type `SUBSCRIBE BOOKWOMAN Firstname Lastname e-mail address` in the body of the message. |
| *Comments* | Women-only list devoted to discussing writing by women. |

| | |
|---|---|
| *What* | **FEM-BIBLIO** |
| *How* | Mailing list |
| *Where* | Send message to `listserv@listserv.aol.com` with no subject line to subscribe; type `SUBSCRIBE FEM-BIBLIO Firstname Lastname` in the body of the message. |
| *Comments* | On-line reading group created for the discussion of books relating to women and spirituality. One book is chosen in a round. A reading schedule, usually separated by a chapter or section per week, organizes the discussion. Participants are asked to stay strictly on topic. This is not a list for general discussion of women's literature. |

| | |
|---|---|
| *What* | **Mystery Lovers Readings** |
| *How* | Usenet newsgroup |
| *Where* | `rec.arts.myste` |
| *Comments* | Reviews, discussion, and references to mystery and crime books, plays, films, and author readings and appearances. |

| | |
|---|---|
| *What* | **RRA-L (Romance Readers Anonymous)** |
| *How* | Mailing list |
| *Where* | Send e-mail message to `listserv@kentvm.kent.edu` with no subject line to subscribe; type `SUBSCRIBE Firstname Lastname RRA-L` in the body of the message. |

### Food, Cooking, and Restaurants

| | |
|---|---|
| *What* | **Chocolate** |
| *How* | Usenet newsgroup |

| | |
|---|---|
| *Where* | rec.food.choco |
| *Comments* | Discussion of chocolate in its many forms. |

| | |
|---|---|
| *What* | **Cooking Tips and Recipes** |
| *How* | Usenet newsgroup |
| *Where* | rec.food.cooki |
| *Comments* | Discussion group for cooking enthusiasts. Archives include new and innovative foods and food preparation suggestions, as well as cookbook recommendations and recipes. |

| | |
|---|---|
| *What* | **Healthy Vegetarian Meals** |
| *How* | Usenet newsgroup |
| *Where* | rec.food.veg.c |
| *Comments* | Vegetarian recipes of all types, with cooking and nutrition suggestions. |

| | |
|---|---|
| *What* | **Lowfat and Fat-free Cuisine** |
| *How* | Usenet newsgroup |
| *Where* | alt.food.fat-f |
| *Comments* | Tips on lowfat and no-fat diets, food, and cooking. |

| | |
|---|---|
| *What* | **New York City Food** |
| *How* | Usenet newsgroup |
| *Where* | nyc.food |
| *Comments* | Tips for making the best of your dining experience in New York City and its surrounding area. |

| | |
|---|---|
| *What* | **Preservation** |
| *How* | Usenet newsgroup |
| *Where* | rec.food.prese |
| *Comments* | Tips and techniques on preserving foodstuffs, herbs, and medicinals. |

| | |
|---|---|
| *What* | **San Francisco Food** |
| *How* | Usenet newsgroup |
| *Where* | ba.food |
| *Comments* | San Francisco Bay Area restaurants, eating places, and recommendations. |

## Hobbies

| | |
|---|---|
| *What* | **Gardening** |
| *How* | Usenet newsgroup |
| *Where* | rec.gardens |
| *Comments* | Tips for green thumbs on what to plant, how to spruce up a yard, how much to water your garden, mulch it, or how to save it from blight, flying pests, or raccoons. |

| | |
|---|---|
| *Tidbit* | Visit the GardenNet home page on the Web at `http://trine.com/GardenNet/InternetGuide/` for detailed gardening tips by topic. |

| | |
|---|---|
| *What* | **Humor** |
| *How* | Usenet newsgroup |
| *Where* | `rec.humor` |
| *Comments* | Funny jokes, stories, anecdotes posted daily. |

| | |
|---|---|
| *What* | **Juggling Information Service** |
| *How* | Web |
| *Where* | `http://www.juggling.org/` |
| *Comments* | Includes news, home pages, festivals, meetings, shopping, organizations, and commentary. |

| | |
|---|---|
| *What* | **Photography** |
| *How* | Usenet newsgroup |
| *Where* | `rec.photo.mode` |
| *Comments* | Good tips for amateurs about cameras, lenses, lighting, etc. |
| *Tidbit* | View a photo of Mt. Kilimanjaro, the highest mountain in Africa, at `http://www.bgsu.edu/~hern/kil.jpeg`. For a photo exhibit of the Temple Mount in Jerusalem, go to `http://www.tiac.net/users/ccstar/temple/`. |

| | |
|---|---|
| *What* | **Woman Motorist** |
| *How* | Web |
| *Where* | `http://www.womanmotorist.com` |
| *Comments* | Free e-zine on automotives, cars, and motorsports for women. Topics include car and automobile maintenance, reviews, racing, safety, and travel. |

| | |
|---|---|
| *What* | **World Wide Quilting Page** |
| *How* | Web |
| *Where* | `http://ttsw.com/mainquiltingpage.html` |
| *Comments* | All kinds of information on quilting. Find out who won the "worst quilt in the world" award (for a total of $2,400) and see the classifieds, bulletin board, and trading post. |

## Music and Dance

| | |
|---|---|
| *What* | **Bluenote Music** |
| *How* | Usenet newsgroup |
| *Where* | `rec.music.bluenote` |
| *Comments* | Information on recordings, artists, and live shows for jazz and blues enthusiasts. |

| | |
|---|---|
| *What* | **Classical Music** |
| *How* | Usenet newsgroup |

| | |
|---|---|
| *Where* | rec.music.classical |
| *Comments* | Serious discussions about classical music and its makers. |

| | |
|---|---|
| *What* | **Folk Festivals** |
| *How* | Usenet newsgroup |
| *Where* | rec.music.folk |
| *Comments* | Features song lyrics, scheduled folksinger appearances, and weekend dance seminars. |

| | |
|---|---|
| *What* | **Funky Music** |
| *How* | Usenet newsgroup |
| *Where* | rec.music.funky |
| *Comments* | Includes concert information, newly released compact discs, lyrics, and artist mailing list information. |

| | |
|---|---|
| *What* | **Guitars and Music** |
| *How* | Usenet newsgroup |
| *Where* | rec.music.classical.guitar |
| *Comments* | Buy or sell guitars, learn where to find guitar music on the Internet, and find schedules of fabulous guitar players performing in your area.   Includes information on Flamenco. |

| | |
|---|---|
| *What* | **Indigo Girls** |
| *How* | Mailing list |
| *Where* | Send message to indigo-girls-request@cgrg.ohio-state.edu to subscribe. |
| *Comments* | Updates on Indigo Girls' tour information, concert reviews, discussion of music and lyrics. |

| | |
|---|---|
| *What* | **International Dances** |
| *How* | Usenet newsgroup |
| *Where* | rec.folk-dancing |
| *Comments* | Includes event information and details on international, contra, square, Cajun, barn dancing, and so on. |

| | |
|---|---|
| *What* | **Kate Bush** |
| *How* | Usenet newsgroup |
| *Where* | rec.music.gaffa |
| *Comments* | Fan club discussion of music, concert dates, and personal life. |

| | |
|---|---|
| *What* | **Madonna** |
| *How* | Mailing list |
| *Where* | Send message to madonna-request@athena.mit.edu to subscribe. |
| *Comments* | Information on and discussions about the star. |

| | |
|---|---|
| *What* | **New Age, Irish, and American Indian Music** |
| *How* | Usenet newsgroup |
| *Where* | `rec.music.newage` |
| *Comments* | Recommendations for recordings of various kinds of music and artists. |

| | |
|---|---|
| *What* | **Percussion** |
| *How* | Usenet newsgroup |
| *Where* | `rec.music.makers.percussion` |
| *Comments* | Discussion and tips on drums, percussion, technique, and drummers wanted for bands. |

| | |
|---|---|
| *What* | **Sinead O'Connor** |
| *How* | Mailing list |
| *Where* | Send message to `jump-in-the-river-request@presto.ig.com` to subscribe. |
| *Comments* | Information and discussion about Sinead's music, recordings, lyrics, and tours. |

| | |
|---|---|
| *What* | **Synthesizers** |
| *How* | Usenet newsgroup |
| *Where* | `rec.music.makers.synth` |
| *Comments* | Information on equipment specifications and trouble-shooting, including detailed exchanges on synthesizer and computer components and music. |

## New Age Interests

| | |
|---|---|
| *What* | **Amazons International** |
| *How* | Listserv |
| *Where* | Send message to `thomas@smaug.uio.no` to subscribe. |
| *Comments* | Monthly newsletter for and about women breaking free of gender roles and traditional ideas of femininity. For an archive of back issues, FTP `ftp.css.itd.umich.edu` in `/poli/Amazons.Intl/`. |

| | |
|---|---|
| *What* | **Astrology** |
| *How* | Web |
| *Where* | `http://www.idirect.com/astrology` |
| *Comments* | Instructions for calculating your astrological chart. You will need your date of birth, time of birth in Greenwich-mean time, and the latitude and longitude of the place you were born. |

| | |
|---|---|
| *What* | **Healing Arts** |
| *How* | Web |
| *Where* | `http://search.yahoo.com/bin/search?p=yoga` |

*Comments*    Up-to-date listings of places to practice various disciplines of yoga, meditation, and other healing arts.

*What*    **New Age Spirituality Index**

*How*    Web

*Where*    http://www.spiritweb.org/

*Comments*    Includes descriptions of channeling, lightwork, UFO, light-tech, healing, reincarnation, meditation, out-of-body-experiences, yoga, veda, theosophy, mysteries, and astrology.

*What*    **PSYCHE: An Interdisciplinary Journal of Research on Consciousness**

*How*    Listserv

*Where*    Send message to listserv@nki.bitnet to subscribe; type SUBSCRIBE PSY-CHE-L in the body of the message.

*Comments*    Quarterly publication which explores consciousness and its relationship to the brain from a variety of scientific, psychological, and philosophical perspectives.

*What*    **Salem Tarot Page**

*How*    Web

*Where*    http://www1.usa1.com/~arachne/

*Comments*    Introduction to Tarot, witchcraft, and the Salem witch trials, including e-mail and phone psychic consultations by "Salem witches" who practice healing arts, divination, psychic awareness, midwifery, the medicinal and magical use of herbs, and rituals honoring the Goddess and nature that resemble Celtic and pagan celebrations. Includes a brief history of witch trials, during which over twenty residents of Salem (mainly unmarried women with self-sustaining economic resources) were persecuted and executed by Puritans in 1692.

*What*    **Yoga**

*How*    Web

*Where*    http://search.yahoo.com/bin/search?p=yoga

*Comments*    Up-to-date listings of places to practice various disciplines of yoga, meditation, and other healing arts.

## Pets

*What*    **All About Dogs**

*How*    Usenet newsgroup

*Where*    rec.pets.dogs

*Comments*    Information and discussion on dogs and dog care.

*Tidbit*    Also see the newsgroups rec.pets.dogs.rescue about placing and adopting; rec.pets.dogs.health about health problems; and rec.pets.dogs.behavior about behavioral problems such as housetraining and chewing.

| | |
|---|---|
| *What* | **Birds** |
| *How* | Usenet newsgroup |
| *Where* | `rec.pets.birds` |
| *Comments* | Information for breeders and owners. Macaws, parrots, parakeets, and other birds are discussed. |

| | |
|---|---|
| *What* | **Cat Humor** |
| *How* | Web |
| *Where* | `http://geog.utoronto.ca/reynolds/pethumor/catrules.html` |
| *Comments* | Kitty humor. |

| | |
|---|---|
| *What* | **Domestic Cats** |
| *How* | Usenet newsgroup |
| *Where* | `rec.pets.cats` |
| *Comments* | Includes cats for adoption, health problems and solutions, and general cat correspondence with Internet users. |

| | |
|---|---|
| *What* | **Electronic Zoo** |
| *How* | Web |
| *Where* | `http://netvet.wustl.edu/` |
| *Comments* | Resources on animals from around the world and their unique characteristics and behaviors. |

## Self-Defense

| | |
|---|---|
| *What* | **Assault Prevention Information Network Index** |
| *How* | Web |
| *Where* | `http://galaxy.einet.net/galaxy/Community/Safety/Assault-Prevention/apin/APINindex.html` |
| *Comments* | Excellent resource including lists of Rape Crisis Centers, self-defense instructors, self-protection guidelines, real-life self-defense stories, weapons and protective devices, women in martial arts, violence in society, recommended readings, and reader comments. |

| | |
|---|---|
| *What* | **Martial Arts** |
| *How* | Usenet newsgroup |
| *Where* | `rec.martial-arts` |
| *Comments* | Information on styles, techniques, tournaments, and related topics about aikido, karate, kung fu, tae kwon do, and other martial arts. |
| *Tidbit* | For *Aikido Today* magazine's global dojo directory, go to `http://www.aiki.com/` |

| | |
|---|---|
| *What* | **Self-Defense Courses** |
| *How* | Web |
| *Where* | http://www.ugcs.caltech.edu/~rachel/bamm/html |
| *Comments* | Courses concentrate on full-power, full-contact, physical self-defense techniques for women. These techniques utilize the strongest parts of a woman's body to provide her with strategic advantage against vulnerable target areas of single attackers, multiple attackers, and weapons. Web site includes a list of global locations where courses are regularly offered. |

| | |
|---|---|
| *What* | **Women's Martial Arts Organizations** |
| *How* | Web |
| *Where* | http://galaxy.einet.net/galaxy/Community/Safety/Assault-Prevention/apin/NWMAF.html |
| *Comments* | Information on and listings of women's martial arts organizations. |

## Sports

| | |
|---|---|
| *What* | **Gender Equity** |
| *How* | Web |
| *Where* | http://www.arcade.uiowa.edu/proj/ge/resources.html |
| *Comments* | Information on achieving gender equity and basic information about Title IX for colleges, universities, high schools, and coaches. Includes resources for creating gender-neutral sports programs. |

| | |
|---|---|
| *What* | **Sports Discussion Groups** |
| *How* | Usenet newsgroup |
| *Where* | rec.sport.golf; rec.sport.olympics; rec.sport.tennis; rec.running; rec.scuba; rec.sport.soccer; rec.sport.softball; rec.sport.swimming; rec.sport.triathlon; rec.sport.volleyball; rec.sport.waterski; rec.windsurfing |

| | |
|---|---|
| *What* | **Women's Mountain Bike and Tea Society (WOMBATS)** |
| *How* | Web |
| *Where* | http://www.wombats.org/ |
| *Comments* | Information for women mountain-biking enthusiasts. |
| *Tidbit* | Visit http:\\www-cs-students.stanford.edu/~rsf/mtn-bike.html for detailed trail and race information for rides around the United States, Canada, the Caribbean, Latin America, Europe, Asia, Africa, Australia, and New Zealand. |

| | |
|---|---|
| *What* | **Women's Sports** |
| *How* | Web |
| *Where* | http://fiat.gslis.utexas.edu/~lewisa/womsprt.html |

*Comments*  Index, by sport, of aero sports, baseball, softball, basketball, bicycling, climbing, field sports, golf, gymnastics, metal sports, motor sports, netball, pugilists, racquet sports, track and field, skating, skiing, sports festivals (including the Olympic, Goodwill, and Gay Games), volleyball, water sports, and more.

*What*  **Women's Sports Foundation Information Center**

*How*  Web

*Where*  `http://www.lifetimetv.com/WoSport/index.htm`

*Comments*  Information about enhancing sports and fitness experience for girls and women. The site includes over 150 documents featuring biographies of female athletes, grant opportunities, and other resources.

# 13

# TECHNOPHOBE NO MORE
## Technical Support by and for Women

Where is the best place to learn about women's involvement in electronic communications? On the Internet, of course! This chapter lists sites that offer general information on women and technology, on-line support groups for women in technology professions, and technical support by and for women in the United States.

Through the sites listed in this chapter, you'll discover the various ways women are learning from one another on-line, through computer networks, on-line technical resources, and user groups for technology info-sharing.

All over the Net, women are networking; they are teaching, learning from, and empowering one another. Join in!

| | |
|---|---|
| *What* | **Computer Professionals for Social Responsibility (CPSR)** |
| *How* | Web |
| *Where* | `http://www.cpsr.org/home` |
| *Comments* | Self-described as a public interest alliance of computer scientists and others interested in the impact of computer technology on society. As technical experts, CPSR members provide the public and policy makers with realistic assessments of the power, promise and limitations of computer technology. As concerned citizens, they direct public attention to critical choices concerning the applications of computing and how those choices affect society. |

| | |
|---|---|
| *What* | **GRANITE (Gender and Information Technologies)** |
| *How* | Mailing list |
| *Where* | Send message to `LISTSERV@NIC.SURFNET.NL` or `LISTSERV@HEARN.BITNET` to subscribe. |
| *Comments* | Forum to stimulate research on gender and new information technologies, and discussions on theories and research from a feminist perspective. |

| | |
|---|---|
| *What* | **International Directory of Women Web Designers** |
| *How* | Web |
| *Where* | `http://www.primenet.com/~shauna/women.html` |
| *Comments* | International directory of Web design and related Internet sites by and for women. |

| | |
|---|---|
| *What* | **INTERNET-WOMEN-HELP** |
| *How* | Mailing list |

| | |
|---|---|
| *Where* | Send the message SUBSINGLE to INTERNET-WOMEN-HELP-REQUEST@LISTS1.BEST.COM to subscribe. |
| *Comments* | Women-only list for asking questions and receiving help on a wide variety of Internet-related functions and issues. |

| | |
|---|---|
| *What* | **LIBWAT-L (Library Women and Technology)** |
| *How* | Mailing List |
| *Where* | Send the message SUBLIBWAT-L Firstname Lastname with the subject line blank to LISTSERV@UBVM.CC.BUFFALO.EDU to subscribe. |
| *Comments* | Discussion list for "people with a serious interest in the effect of new technologies on gender roles in the library." |

Women need good technical instruction to cut through the jargon and mystery of telecommunications, same as with computer training. They need to feel like "This is within my reach." Women want to know: "What good is it going to do me? How does it link to my life?" Seeing a demonstration helps. Every women's conference should have an Internet workshop or demo.

—KAREN WICKRE
Planet.Out, San Francisco

| | |
|---|---|
| *What* | **MAC-WOMEN** |
| *How* | Mailing list |
| *Where* | Send the one-word message SUBSINGLE or SUBSCRIBE to MAC-WOMEN-REQUEST@LISTS1.BEST.COM to subscribe. |
| *Comments* | Macintosh help forum for women Mac experts to share their knowledge and network. |

| | |
|---|---|
| *What* | **MAIDEN-L** |
| *How* | Mailing list |
| *Where* | Send the message SUBSCRIBE MAIDEN-L to MAJORDOMO@WOMEN.CA to subscribe. |
| *Comments* | Discussion group for women who are new to the Internet and are seeking support and user tips. |

| | |
|---|---|
| *What* | **Once and Future Action Network (OFAN)** |
| *How* | Web |
| *Where* | http://www.igc.apc.org/womensnet/beijing/ngo/ofan.html |
| *Comments* | OFAN is an "open-ended, growing network of nongovernmental organizations working in the area of gender, science, and technology" to create a "more holistic, people-centered and environmentally sustainable approach to science and technology" and to highlight women's contributions to innovations in these fields. |
| *Tidbit* | OFAN is based in Kingston, Jamaica, and can also be contacted via e-mail at ofan@igc.apc.org. |

| | |
|---|---|
| *What* | **Spiderwoman** |
| *How* | Mailing list |
| *Where* | Send message to Majordomo@lists.primenet.com to subscribe; type subscribe spiderwoman in the body of the message. |
| *Comments* | A support group for women Web developers and consultants. |

I spend about forty hours a week actually logged in, but more time than that at the computer. I work in a home office using a PowerMac 7100 that's connected to all sorts of nifty things, like a CD ROM drive, a scanner, a laser printer, and a color ink jet printer. Your basic home office setup! Ergonomic, too. Best of all, I get to be with my kids all day long (two dogs—Wimsey and Milton).

—AMY GOODLOE
Lesbian.org

| | |
|---|---|
| *What* | **TAP/The Ada Project** |
| *How* | Web |
| *Where* | http://www.cs.yale.edu/HTML/YALE/CS/HyPlans/tap/tap.html |
| *Comments* | Offers education and employment resources, counseling services, program information, statistics on women in computer science, indices and bibliographies, discussion groups, related news. TAP is a volunteer effort. |

| | |
|---|---|
| *What* | **Technomama** |
| *How* | E-mail |
| *Where* | technomama@igc.apc.org |
| *Comments* | California-based group providing computer training and technical support for women of color. |

| | |
|---|---|
| *What* | **UHURA** |
| *How* | Listserv |
| *Where* | Contact Liona Sanderson at fionas@rmplc.co.uk to subscribe. |
| *Comments* | Discussion list for women researching aspects of the Net who want to discuss why women use electronic communications and how it influences women. |

| | |
|---|---|
| *What* | **WATER (Women's Access to Electronic Resources)** |
| *How* | E-mail |
| *Where* | water@igc.apc.org |
| *Comments* | Created by the Foundation for a Compassionate Society in Austin, Texas, WATER aims to provide a safe, comfortable space for women to learn electronic communication skills and their application for furthering advocacy work. |

| | |
|---|---|
| *What* | **Webgrrls** |
| *How* | Web |
| *Where* | http://www.webgrrls.com |
| *Comments* | Webgrrls is a real-world, in-person networking group for women interested in new media. Forty-six chapters currently operate in North America, and there are also chapters in the Philippines, Australia, Japan, New Zealand, the West Indies, the United Kingdom, and the Netherlands. Webgrrls provides job and business leads, as well as news on the latest technologies. Groups and classes aim to mentor, intern, and train women users. |

| | |
|---|---|
| *What* | **WEB-WOMEN-TECH** |
| *How* | Listserv |
| *Where* | Send the message subscribe to WEB-WOMEN-TECH-REQUEST@NIESTU.COM to subscribe. |
| *Comments* | For women working on the technical side of Web site management. |

| | |
|---|---|
| *What* | **Women and Computer Science** |
| *How* | Web |
| *Where* | http://www.ai.mit.edu/people/ellens/gender.html |
| *Comments* | This site contains a healthy collection of articles on women in computer science and links to related interesting sites. The Web page shows a classic 1950s photo of university-aged women holding dinosaur computer parts. |

I did a training at American University. A sistah said, "Oh my god, there's a black woman coming to do a training for all these white people." I was so proud. I feel very responsible to sistahs who want to learn the business. I'll go down to the office on a Sunday to do a training. What do sistahs need? Do I help them get prepared on-line to be up with the technology, to skim the surface, or to be able to go out and get the jobs? Do you know how much that adds to you if you know the technology for any kind of job? I always ask students: Where are you going and how are you going to develop it?

—DEBRA K. FLOYD
African American Networking, Institute for Global Communications

| | |
|---|---|
| *What* | **Women, Information Technology, and Scholarship (WITS)** |
| *How* | Web |
| *Where* | http://www.art.uiuc.edu/wits |
| *Comments* | WITS is a group of women, teachers, and graduate students in many academic fields, now in its seventh year of meetings, workshops, publications, and activism. "The women of WITS believe that women and girls should have integral roles in the conception, design, content, use, implementation, economics, and legal |

policies of electronic communication networks on a local, national, and international level. To help implement these gender equity policies, WITS members participate in both self-education and outreach."

*Tidbit*    For more information, send e-mail message to Cheris Kramarae at `cheris@ uiuc.edu`.

---

### EXORCISING THE TECHNOPHOBE WITHIN

Women, Information Technology, and Scholarship (WITS) holds workshops on new technologies for the classroom, experiments with asynchronous network software, plays with graphic design programs, and, in general, keeps up to date on technology developments. Using small group techniques, we have held collaborative workshops in which we imagine the ideal information technology for our lives. We have discussed sexual harassment on the Internet, issues of censorship, copyright, changes in commercial publishing, methods of scientific computer visualization, and environmental concerns. We have organized reading groups to discuss the social aspects of communication technologies in feminist speculative fiction. We have even had a combination potluck-and-computer demolition, to demystify computer innards. (We used old computers which were going to be junked.) We have invited speakers to talk about their experiences linking women's organizations, ways to make networks more woman-friendly, and social change applications.

We have encouraged individuals and groups to fund activities that may result in policy implementation (for example, establishing summer computer classes or camps for girls and funding public service announcements about gender equity on the Internet). We have taught girls in neighborhoods and local schools how to use computers and networks, spoken to local women's organizations about networks and shown them how to get access. WITS members have become "computer moms" to other women trying to learn computer skills. Individual members have become WITS representatives on campus and community technology policy committees. They have attended and reported on the regular computer workshops offered by the university, and then have offered the workshop organizers suggestions on how to make the sessions more useful. (Women attending the campus workshops found that the short sessions were often almost useless unless each participant had access to continuing help from one person in a system much like our "computer moms" network.) We published a book about our WITS work, so that others would be able to start WITS groups on others campuses. We have a WITS home page, with some of this information.

—CHERIS KRAMARAE
Women, Information Technology, and Scholarship (WITS)

---

*What*        **Women in Technology**
*How*         Web
*Where*       `http://gseweb.harvard.edu/TIEWEB/STUDENTS/STUDENTGROUPS/WIT /wit.html`
*Comments*    Directory for use by women who want to mentor or advance their careers in technology fields.

| | |
|---|---|
| *What* | **Women in Technology International (WITI)** |
| *How* | Web |
| *Where* | http://www.witi.com |
| *Comments* | WITI, a nonexclusionary association of women and men from diverse backgrounds worldwide, has strived since its founding in 1989 to increase the number of women hired and promoted to management and executive-level positions, help women become technology literate, and encourage young women to choose careers in technology and science. The WITI Campus, as the web site is called, offers expert advice, updates on technology developments, on-line articles, a newsletter, calendar, live chats, and numerous links to related resources. |
| *Tidbit* | June is "Women in Science and Technology" Month, officially launched in 1996 by Women in Technology International (WITI). In 1996, activities included "Take Your Children on the Internet Week." |

| | |
|---|---|
| *What* | **WOMEN-L** |
| *How* | Listserv |
| *Where* | Send the message SUBSCRIBE WOMEN-L to MAJORDOMO@HELIX.NET to subscribe. |
| *Comments* | Discussions on women with emphases on the Internet, Net culture, and new technologies. |

# Author and Contributor Biographies

## ABOUT THE AUTHOR

SHANA PENN is a writer and director of media relations at the United States Holocaust Memorial Museum in Washington, D.C. Previously, as the executive director of an international women's rights organization called the Network of East-West Women, she was the driving force behind the creation of an electronic communications network linking hundreds of grassroots women's groups in over twenty countries in the former Soviet Union and Central and Eastern Europe.

Penn is presently completing a book about women's role in pro-democracy movements and the 1989 revolutions in Central Europe. Her work appears in the anthology *The Beacon Book of Essays by Contemporary American Women* and in periodicals including the *Journal of Women's History*, the *Women's Review of Books* and *Tikkun*.

## ABOUT THE CONTRIBUTORS

DEBRA K. FLOYD directs the East Coast Office of the Institute for Global Communications (IGC) in Washington, D.C., and coordinates African American Networking at IGC. In these capacities, Floyd created the African American Directory/World Wide Web and the Diaspora NewzCenter/WWW; designed and executed demo-trainings for new and existing clients; regularly speaks on panels and conducts workshops on basic Internet skills and on Internet access to the "Telecomm Haves and Have Nots"; and frequently consults with a broad range of clients on the use of the Internet and the Web. Floyd is deeply committed to bringing people of African descent on-line and to teaching about computer technology for readiness in future job offerings. Prior to her work in computer telecommunications, Floyd was a professional dancer in the Oakland/San Francisco Bay Area and a dance and women's studies instructor with her own dance company and movement counseling practice. (Shana Penn was one of her former dance students and starry-eyed fans.) She holds a bachelor's degree in physical education and a master's degree in theology.

AMY GOODLOE, who is based in the Bay Area, has been designing Web pages for women's issues and women-owned businesses since March of 1995, when she went into business under the name Women Online. In addition to maintaining Web sites and training women how to use on-line technology, Goodloe runs ten women-only Internet mailing lists and edits three on-line publications for women: *Sapphic Ink*, a lesbian literary journal on the Web, *Women Online News*, a monthly newsletter for women on-line, and *net.dyke*, the magazine of lesbian culture on-line. She is also author of *A Woman's Guide to Online Publishing*, published on-line in 1996.

LIZA WEIMAN HANKS has been working with computers since Ronald Reagan won the 1980 presidential election, because she figured that the Left should have access to the same technology that the Right had used to mobilize grassroots support. Since then she has been the executive director of an organization that taught computer skills and offered computer access to not-for-profit groups, worked as a first grade teacher, written and edited articles for *MacWorld Magazine,* and gotten a law degree from Stanford Law School. A longtime resident of Seattle currently en-route to Sacramento, she recently welcomed the arrival of her daughter, whose changing table is right next to the printer and who thinks the mouse is an input device in the most literal sense.

NINA BETH HUNTEMANN is a graduate student at the University of Massachusetts, Amherst, where she has earned a master's degree and is pursuing a doctoral degree in communication. Her areas of interest include telecommunications policy, new media technologies, gender studies, feminist political theory, and science fiction fandom. Completed in the fall of 1996, Huntemann's master's thesis, *Creating Safe Space in Cyberspace: Electronic Communications Technology and Feminist Social Change*, analyzed the potential contribution of Internet technologies to the women's rights movement. Huntemann says of her experience with electronic communications: "The first computer I ever used was a Texas Instruments-99A, back in 1981; I was ten. My Dad hooked the TI-99A up to an old black-and-white television set in our basement, where my sister Renee and I would play arcade-style games (Pac-Man, Frogger) until 3 A.M. Then we got a Commodore 64 with a color screen and light pen! More games, primitive computer graphics, and a little elementary school word processing, but I quickly became disinterested. After four years at Penn State and one semester at UMass my electronic typewriter finally broke down, and I rediscovered computers. Soon thereafter I found the Internet. I sometimes think that in two years I have seen every corner of the Web. It's neat, it's cool, but it's only the beginning. There is so much potential, and thus so much work to do. Despite all the gadgetry, though, some days I would rather sit in front of the flickering black-and-white set playing Car Wars with Renee until dawn."

CHERYL LEHMAN, professor of accounting at Hofstra University in Hempstead, New York, is the general editor of *Advances in Public Interest Accounting* and associate editor of *Critical Perspectives in Accounting*. Her publications appear in *Accounting; Organizations and Society; Accounting, Auditing and Accountability*, and many other periodicals. Lehman's research and professional work include accounting's role in a global economy, financial accounting disclosure, public policy and regulation, managerial accounting techniques, business ethics, and gender issues. As a visiting scholar, Lehman has lectured in Australia and has presented her research at numerous international conferences in Canada, Cuba, England, Hungary, New Zealand, Peru, Scotland, Spain, and elsewhere. Over the past five years she has participated in numerous seminars and training programs to managers, executives, financial analysts, and business persons in the former Soviet Union.

SONIA JAFFE ROBBINS is a co-founder of the Network of East-West Women and a writer and editor living in New York City. For three years she served as information research coordinator for NEWW's electronic bulletin boards and co-moderated several of NEWW's international board meetings on-line. She teaches journalism at New York University, drawing on more than twenty years' experience editing, copyediting, and writing. Her articles and book reviews have appeared in the *Women's Review of Books, Village Voice, Columbia Journalism Review*, and *Women and Language News*, among other publications. She has been a feminist activist for more than twenty-five years, and is a member of the abortion rights zap group No More Nice Girls. She helped organize the union at the *Village Voice* and is a member of the National Writers Union, where she is a co-plaintiff in the NWU's lawsuit concerning writers' electronic rights. She is currently writing her first novel.

MELISSA LEIGH STONE is communications director and senior program officer at the Center for Communications, Health and the Environment in Washington, D.C. She is also secretary of the Network of East-West Women's board of directors, advisor to NEWW's On-Line Project, and coordinator of NEWW's Women's Self-Defense Project. In addition, she is a women's self-defense instructor and holds a black belt in Tae Kwon Do at the D.C. Self-Defense Karate Association. As the former executive director of Kompass Resources International, Stone founded and published two on-line publications: the monthly *Environmental Cooperation Bulletin*, which concentrates on major environmental projects in the former Soviet Union and Central and Eastern Europe, and the quarterly *NIS Health Promotion Bulletin*, which focuses on wellness and disease prevention based on healthy lifestyle choices. She has also consulted with the World Bank, North Atlantic Treaty Organization, U.S. Department of State, U.S. Agency for International Development, National Science Foundation, and others on the development of Internet and other international technology infrastructures and on multimedia solutions to improve the quality of life in post-Communist nations through information access and public interest projects, particularly in the fields of environment, health, and education.

VICTORIA VRANA, as director of NEWW On-Line, facilitates two of NEWW's Listservs and created its Web page. Vrana has trained hundreds of women in the use of computers and electronic communications technology in Albania, Bulgaria, China, Germany, Russia, Hungary, Kyrgyzstan, Romania, and the U.S. She has also conducted trainings at U.S. institutions such as Columbia University's Center for Religion, Human Rights and Religious Freedom and Georgetown University Law School's African Women Lawyers Fellowship Program. In August 1995 Vrana conducted computer trainings on the United Nations Development Programme's "Beijing Express," which brought two hundred women from the former Soviet Union and Central and Eastern Europe to the UN Fourth World Conference on Women in Beijing, and managed the satellite communications on the train. Vrana also participated in the 24 Hours in Cyberspace project (on the Web at http://www.cyber24.com/htm/4_186.html), which published photos of her trainings of the first women in Albania to use e-mail.

## Research and Editorial Assistants

DONNA AXEL recently survived the New Jersey bar exam and is recovering in Spain before she embarks on a law career as a human rights attorney.

CARLEY HYDUSIK is a master's degree candidate in international relations at Yale University. In 1995, as a Fulbright scholar, she conducted research in the Czech Republic while based in Prague. She is fluent in Russian and German and is learning the Czech language. In the summer of 1996, she interned at the Network of East-West Women in Washington, D.C.

KATHY KOHUT is an experienced "Net techie" who enjoys exploring and learning about all aspects of the Internet, especially the wonders of e-mail. She is a senior at the University of the Pacific in Stockton, California, where her major field of study is international studies with a Russian emphasis and her minor is viola performance. In the summer of 1996, she interned at the Network of East-West Women. Aside from surfing the Web, she enjoys traveling, foreign languages, and spending time with Misha.

DOROTA MAJEWSKA, a program assistant for the Network of East-West Women, is completing her master's degree in foreign and domestic policy, history, and economics at the CERES (Center for Eurasian, Russian, and East European Studies) program of the School of Foreign Service at Georgetown University in Washington, D.C.

BARBARA ANN O'LEARY is founder and director of Virtual Sisterhood, a global women's electronic support network dedicated to increasing women's access to and effective use of electronic communications. During her three years with Women's Environment & Development Organization (WEDO), she contributed to the global women's movement by working with women from around the world to ensure that women's information was being disseminated electronically through e-mail, electronic conferences, and the WEDO Gopher, which she designed and implemented. O'Leary also created an integrated relational database system to track WEDO's 17,000+ contacts worldwide. With the New York Public Interest Research Group (NYPIRG), she organized Brooklyn College students to effect change on environment, education, and other social justice issues. O'Leary, who lives in New Jersey, brings ten years of theatrical stage management organizing experience to her feminist activist work.

GALINA VENEDIKTOVA is a professional programmer and an activist in democratic and women's movements in Russia. As a program coordinator for NEWW On-Line, she provides e-mail trainings and technical assistance to women's non-governmental organizations in the former Soviet Union and the United States.

# Recommended Readings

Braun, Eric. *The Internet Directory.* New York: Fawcett Columbine, 1994.

Broadhurst, Judith A. *The Woman's Guide to Online Services.* New York: McGraw-Hill, 1995.

Carlson, Matt. *Childproof Internet: A Parent's Guide to Safe and Secure Online Access.* New York: MIS Press, 1996.

Cherny, Lynn and Elizabeth Reba Wise, eds. *Wired Women: Gender and New Realities in Cyberspace.* Seattle: Seal Press, 1996.

Clark, David. *Student's Guide to the Internet.* 2nd. ed. Indianapolis: Que Corporation, 1996.

Coffee, Kevin and Ross Scott Rubin. *World Wide Web Starter Kit.* Indianapolis: Hayden Books, 1995.

Davis, Frederic E., ed. *CyberSource.* Emeryville, CA: Ziff-Davis Press, 1995.

Dawson, Jeff. *Gay & Lesbian Online.* Berkeley: Peachpit Press, 1996.

Dern, Daniel P. *The Internet Guide for New Users.* New York: McGraw-Hill, 1994.

Epler, Anita, et al., eds. *Computer and Online Training and Resource Directory.* Dallas: NGLTF Policy Institute, 1994.

Electronic Frontier Foundation. *The Big Dummy's Guide to the Internet.* Washington, D.C.: Electronic Frontier Foundation, 1993.

Gagnon, Eric, ed. *What's On the Web.* Fairfax, VA: Internet Media Corp., 1996.

Gunn, Angela, et al. *Web Guide: Exploring the Weird, the Wild, and the Wonderful on the World Wide Web.* Indianapolis: Macmillan Publishing/SAMS, 1995.

Herring, Susan. "Gender and Democracy in Computer-mediated Communication." *Electronic Journal of Communication* 3:2. Available from `comserve@rpitsvm.bitnet`.

Kramer, Jana, and Cheris Kramarae. "Gendered Ethics on the Internet." In J. Makau and R. Arnett, eds. *Communications Ethics in an Age of Diversity.* Urbana, IL: University of Illinois Press, in press.

Krebs, Nina Boyd. *Changing Women, Changing Work.* Aspen, CO: MacMurray & Beck Communications, 1993.

Krol, Ed. *The Whole Internet User's Guide and Catalog.* 2d ed. Sebastopol, CA: O'Reilly & Associates, 1994.

Leshko, Isa. "Reflections on Gender in Cyberspace." *Sojourner: The Women's Forum.* 20:8 (April 1995). 20–21.

Levine, John R. and Carol Baroudi. *The Internet for Dummies.* San Mateo, CA: IDG Books Worldwide, 1993.

Maloni, Kelly, Nathaniel Wice, and Ben Greenman. *Net Chat: Your Guide to the Debates, Parties and Pick-up Places on the Electronic Highway.* New York: Michael Wolff & Company/Random House Electronic Publishing, 1994.

New Riders Publishing. *The Internet Yellow Pages*. Indianapolis: New Riders Publishing, 1996 (updated biannually).

———. *The World Wide Web Yellow Pages*. Indianapolis: New Riders Publishing, 1996 (updated biannually).

Newson, Stephen L. [CK] *The World Wide Web for Busy People*. Berkeley: Osborne McGraw-Hill, 1996.

Polly, Jean Armour. *The Internet Kids Yellow Pages*. Berkeley: Osborne McGraw-Hill, 1996.

Senjen, Rye and Jane Guthrey. *The Internet for Women*. N. Melbourne, Australia: Spinifex, 1996.

"Sex and Violence in Cyberspace." *Edupage*. 12 February 1995. Available via Gopher at `educom.edu`.

Sinclair, Carla. *Net Chick: A Smart-Girl Guide to the Wired World*. New York: Henry Holt and Company, 1996.

Taylor, H. Jeanie, Cheris Kramarae, and Maureen Ebben, eds. *Women, Information Technology, and Scholarship*. Urbana, IL: Center for Advanced Study, University of Illinois, 1993.

Vincent, Patrick. *Free Stuff From the Internet*. Scottsdale, AZ: Coriolis Group Books, 1994.

Waltz, Mitzi and Steve Schultz. *The Internet International Directory 1997*. Emeryville, CA: Lycos Press, 1996.

Winter, Debra and Chuck Huff. "Adapting the Internet: Comments from a Women-only Electronic Forum." Available from the authors at `dlwinter@uxa.cso.uluc.edu` or `huff@siolaf.edu`.

Women, Information Technology, and Scholarship (WITS). *Gender Equity in Global Communication Networks: A Global Alert*. 1995. Pamphlet available from WITS, Graduate School of Library and Information Science, University of Illinois at Urbana-Champaign, 112 LIS, Champaign, IL 61820.

# Glossary of Terms

In this glossary you will find definitions for all of the terms that appear in the text of the book enclosed in asterisks, *like this.* Boldfaced words found in the text of glossary entries are also defined under their own entries in the glossary. Because terminology can be one of the most mysterious and intimidating facets of electronic communications, especially for new users, this glossary also contains a selection of other terms you may come across in your Internet explorations.

**Agent.** *See* **Knowbot.**

**Application.** A specific type of task or function performed by the computer, such as word processing or spreadsheets; also the software that performs these tasks.

**Anonymous FTP.** A form of **FTP** (file transfer protocol) which enables you to connect to a site, search directories, and **download** files or programs without an assigned **userid.** Instead, the **login** is always "anonymous" and the password is your **e-mail** address. Anonymous FTP can be accessed via the Internet, e-mail, or the **World Wide Web.**

**Archie.** A **search tool** used to find files in **anonymous FTP** sites. Archie is a software program; it is also a system of servers, or computers that contain files. As of 1997 there were over thirty thousand Archie servers in the world.

**Archieplex.** A **World Wide Web interface** to Archie, which is an easy way to interact with the tool.

**Archiving.** A method of storing many files into one file, which is useful for making backup copies of files or for moving a number of files to another system.

**ASCII.** American Standard Code for Information Interchange, a file format that uses only standard text characters as data.

**Attachments.** Files that are attached to an **e-mail** transmission.

**Backbone.** A major **line** or set of connections in a **network.**

**Bandwidth.** The amount of data an on-line connection can transmit, measured in **bits**-per-second.

**Baud rate.** The number of **bits**-per-second a modem can transmit through a phone line.

**BBS.** *See* **Bulletin board system.**

**Binary.** A file with data outside of **ASCII**, which includes text files with formatting, graphics files, **compressed** files, and **archived** files.

**Bit.** Binary digit, the smallest unit of computerized data, represented by a 0 or 1.

**BITNET.** A **network** for educational sites, now decreasing in usage.

**Bookmark.** A tool used to save a **World Wide Web** address in a special file so that you can swiftly access it later.

**Bounced mail**. Sent **e-mail** that reappears in your mailbox, usually because the recipient's address was inaccurate.

**Bozo filter**. A tool for screening out **flaming** or otherwise unpleasant users.

**Bps**. Bits-per-second, the unit for measuring the rate of on-line data transmission.

**Browser**. Software which provides tools (such as **search tools**) to explore Internet resources.

**Bulletin board system**. An on-line system usually made up of local or regional networks. It contains discussion groups, **e-mail**, and occasionally games or libraries and allows various people to participate without being simultaneously connected.

**Byte**. A group of **bits** which represent a single character. There are always eight bits in a byte.

**Channel**. A **virtual** space where users of **Internet Relay Chat** communicate in **real-time**. Anyone can open up a channel with a few IRC commands, and the person who opens a channel becomes the channel operator. Thousands of channels are open at any given time on the Internet.

**Chat room**. A forum for informal discussion on the Internet, usually provided by commercial **Internet service providers** like America Online.

**Client**. A software program that enables its user to access data from a **server** on another computer. Clients and servers need each other to function.

**Command-driven**. A program or tool that is operated by typing in keyboard characters, rather than selecting pre-existing menu items or icons.

**Command-line interface**. **Text-based** software in which commands must be communicated by typing in keyboard characters, rather than by pointing and clicking with a mouse as with **GUI**.

**COM ports**. Communications ports, plug-in sockets found in the back of the computer for hooking up modems, printers, or scanners.

**Compression**. A means of reducing the size of a large file in order to store and/or transfer it, as with **FTP** files. A compression program is software that performs this task.

**Conference**. An electronic discussion or bulletin board, which technically functions like a **Usenet newsgroup** but can only be accessed by users of the **Internet service provider** on which the conference resides.

**Connect time**. The period during which a user is **logged-on** to an **Internet service provider** or other on-line service, a **bulletin board system**, or a **host computer**.

**Content provider**. A person or institution developing and/or **uploading** content to the **World Wide Web** or **FTP** or **Gopher** sites.

**Cyber**. Prefix used to signify a word's connection to the digital or Internet world.

**Cyberspace**. The intangible on-line world in which Internet information "lives" and "travels."

**Default**. Settings or commands that are programmed into your software, under which your computer will operate unless you actively change them.

**Dial-up**. To access the Internet via **modem**.

**Domains**. Terms in an electronic address, appearing to the right of the @ sign, which signify the location and official address of a **host computer** on the Internet. The domain for America Online is aol.com, while the domain for the Institute for Global Communications is igc.apc.org.

**Download**. To retrieve information from another computer to your own.

**Electronic mail**. *See* **E-mail**.

**E-mail**. A communication tool for sending and retrieving messages from one computer to another over telephone lines. E-mail can be used to communicate with one other user or with several users simultaneously.

**E-zine**. A small, independently owned electronic publication.

**Emoticons**. Typographical symbols used on-line to contribute emotion, useful in providing otherwise obtuse text with more accurate expression. An example is a smiley :-)

**Encryption**. A means of encoding messages by using algorithms, thus making the message unreadable by anyone who does not know the code.

**Ethernet**. A system for networking computers within a **LAN** (local area network), which provides the **network** with greater capacity and is widely compatible.

**Eudora**. One of the most popular **e-mail** programs.

**FAQ**. A file on the Internet containing frequently asked questions, with answers provided. These prevent redundant inquiries and are especially helpful for new users.

**File extension**. A three-letter code, which follows the file name and a dot, used to identify the file format, such as text-only, graphic, video, or audio.

**File Transfer Protocol**. *See* **FTP**.

**Filter.** Software used in tandem with a **browser**, which blocks sexually explicit material. One example is SurfWatch.

**Finger**. A tool (and command) for finding people at other Internet sites. Certain sites block finger access.

**Flame**. To attack or rudely criticize someone else on-line. This kind of attack is most prevalent on **Usenet newsgroups** and some unmoderated **mailing lists**.

**Flame war**. An on-line fight, usually abusive and hurtful. Most often occurs on **Usenet newsgroups** or unmoderated **mailing lists** when a comment produces a nasty retort, which in turn provokes many subscribers to respond in kind.

**Freeware**. Software made available on the Internet for public use, at no charge, by the author of the software.

**FTP**. File Transfer Protocol, a standardized, text-based means of retrieving files and programs from data archives on **remote computers**. Known as the library of the Internet.

**Gateway address**. The address of a service that translates between different **protocols**.

**GIF**. A type of graphics file, usually a photo or an illustration.

**Gopher**. A menu-based search-and-retrieve tool for conducting research on the Internet. Gopher sites are hierarchically organized menus, through which users navigate to access databases, text files, and other resources—an action which is described as "burrowing." Gopher is accessible via a Gopher **client**, the **World Wide Web**, or **Telnet**.

**Graphics-based**. Files or software that use graphics as well as text. Graphics-based software is the type that allows you to point and click a mouse rather than type in text commands. Graphics-based files are most often found on the **World Wide Web**.

**GUI**. Graphical user interface, **graphics-based** software with icons or pictures to click on which automates complicated commands the user need not learn, as opposed to **command-line interface**. Windows is an example of GUI software.

**Hacker**. A person who devises original tricks to solve computer problems.

**Hit**. The unit for measuring usage of a **Web site**. Whenever someone visits a Web site it registers as a hit.

**Home page**. The first screen of a **Web site**, and/or the screen to which a user will return upon hitting the "home" button.

**Host computer**. The computer to which you connect to access the Internet, usually a big, powerful computer owned by your **ISP**.

**Hotlist**. A list of **hyperlinks** to favorite **Web sites**.

**HTML**. Hypertext Markup Language, the coding language in which **hypertext** documents are created for the **World Wide Web**.

**HTTP**. Hypertext Transfer Protocol, the **protocol** which enables users to move **hypertext** files within the Internet.

**Hypertext**. A kind of programmed file which allows for user interaction; clicking on a word in a hypertext document calls up another site or file related to that word.

**Hyperlink**. A **Web site** that is accessible from another Web site; also that which makes it possible to move between sites.

**Hypermedia**. Similar to **hypertext**, except that it applies not only to text but to audio and visuals.

**Image map**. A set of pictures used as a map or table of contents for a **Web site**.

**Interactive**. Any two-way system of electronic communication, in which a user not only observes but interacts, especially systems which allow exchanges with other human users, such as **mailing lists**, **Usenet newsgroups**, and **conferences**.

**Interface**. The way the Internet appears on your computer screen; ranges from **text-based** to fully **graphics-based**.

**internet (small i)**. A general term for the connection of two or more **networks.**

**Internet Relay Chat**. An on-line space where many people can simultaneously discuss varying topics. Users establish **channels** for different topics, and everything sent to a given channel is seen by everyone else using that channel.

**Internet service provider**. A company or organization that offers its Internet connection to computer users in exchange for a fee. An ISP may serve a user base that is local, regional, national, or international.

**Intranet**. A private **network** system which functions like a mini-Internet but is only accessible to a certain group, such as employees of a company.

**IRC**. *See* **Internet Relay Chat**.

**ISDN**. Integrated services digital network. Network which uses ordinary telephone lines instead of analog signals to connect to the Internet.

**ISP**. *See* **Internet service provider**.

**Java**. A programming language which enables the user to **download** from the Internet without concern for **viruses** or other causes of harm. Java makes tricks like calculators or animation possible on **Web pages**.

**JPEG**. A graphics file format much like **GIF**.

**Jump**. A move between **Web sites** using a **hyperlink**.

**Kbps**. **Kilobytes** per second, a unit of measurement usually used to indicate the speed of transmissions over a **modem**.

**KILL file**. A file contained on many **newsreader** programs, which helps users deal with **flaming**. It automatically removes all articles with a specific subject line or part of a subject, articles from a specific user or site, cross-posted articles, or follow-ups to other articles.

**Kilobyte**. A thousand **bytes** (to be precise, 1024).

**Knowbot**. A mechanism that automates a series of commands, causing several **paths** to be searched simultaneously. These search programs are often called "spiders" or "worms."

**LAN**. Local area network, a computer **network** for a limited area.

**Listproc**. List processors, which perform the tasks and processes necessary for managing a **mailing list**. **Listserv** and **Majordomo** are also types of list processors.

**Listserv**. A **BITNET** program that manages **mailing lists**, subscribes and unsubscribes users, and distributes messages that are **posted** to the list. Also a term used to describe mailing lists that are maintained by Listserv, which usually have addresses ending with − l.

**Local dial-up**. A service which allows your modem to connect to the Internet via a local telephone number, saving you money on long-distance charges.

**Login**. User **e-mail** "name." The means of identifying yourself to your on-line service.

**Log-in**. Connecting to an **e-mail** account.

**Log-off**. Exiting from an **e-mail** account.

**Lurking**. Reading messages on-line (such as in a **chat room**) without contributing to discussion.

**Macro**. A small software program built into your communications software that automates the **dialing-up** and **logging-in** routine by executing a series of commands whenever you click on an icon or choose an item from the menu.

**Mailing list**. A tool for discussion among people with a shared interest, who subscribe to a list and then receive all messages **posted** to the list and have the opportunity to post messages themselves.

**Majordomo**. A program that manages **mailing lists**, similar to **Listserv**.

**Megabyte**. One million **bytes**, or one thousand **kilobytes**.

**MIME**. Multipurpose Internet mail extensions, a tool for adding non-text files such as graphics, spreadsheets, etc. to Internet mail messages.

**Modem**. Modulator/demodulator, a device that enables a computer to communicate and exchange information with other modem-equipped computers via telephone lines. Modems are either internal, installed inside your computer, or external, attached to your computer's modem **port**. To use a modem, you must connect it to a telephone jack.

**Moderator**. The person who monitors all **postings** to a **mailing list** or **Usenet newsgroup** and, in some cases, facilitates on-line discussion.

**MOO**. **Mud**, object oriented, a **text-based cyber**-"place" for multiple users to conduct role plays.

**MUD**. Multi-user dimension or dungeon, a place in which multiple users create and simulate worlds. The creations remain and may continue to be used by others even after the creator has left the MUD.

**Multimedia**. Involving several different media, such as video, audio, graphic images, and text.

**Netiquette**. Communication etiquette for the on-line world.

**Netizen**. A person who uses the Internet, especially one who respects the on-line community and the responsibilities which accompany Internet usage.

**Netscape Navigator**. A popular **browser** used on the **World Wide Web**.

**Network**. Any set of two or more interconnected computers. Two or more connected networks make up an **internet**.

**Newbie**. A newcomer to the Internet.

**Newsgroup**. *See* **Usenet newsgroup**.

**Newsreader**. A program that enables you to read and respond to messages in a **Usenet newsgroup**.

**NIC**. Networked information center, which coordinates a set of networks and ensures that names and network numbers are consistent from one network to another.

**Nick collision kill**. What happens when you enter a **channel** in **Internet Relay Chat** where someone using the same nickname is also present. You are both "killed," or kicked off your IRC **servers** as soon as the duplicate nicknames are detected, and you must reconnect and re-enter the channel.

**Node**. Any single computer as part of a network.

**Off-line**. Not connected to your **network** or any other computer, and not using your **modem**. To save money, you can read your **e-mail**, print out messages, and write responses while you are off-line.

**On-line service**. A for-profit company which provides users with **e-mail** addresses, on-line activities, and often Internet access.

**Packet switching**. Procedure for moving data within the Internet which increases user capacity of connecting lines by dividing the information to be moved into pieces and reassembling it upon arrival, allowing many data pieces to share the same lines. Each piece contains the addresses of its origin and destination.

**Page**. Each individual subject file shown on a **Web site**. You move between pages by clicking on highlighted words.

**Parameters**. A function that tells your computer and **modem** exactly how to transfer information.

**Path**. The route by which a message travels from one computer to another. The header of an **e-mail** message provides you with information about the path a message has traveled to reach your mailbox.

**POP**. 1. Point of presence, a location (such as a city) to which a **network** can be connected, enabling the use of local phone lines for users in that area. **2. Post office protocol**, a **protocol** which enables the user's **e-mail** software to retrieve mail from a mail **server**.

**Port**. Site where information passes into or out of a computer. Examples are printer and **modem** ports.

**Port number**. The number that comes immediately after a **host computer**'s name; it enables different services to run on a single computer.

**Posting**. A message sent to a **Usenet newsgroup**, **conference**, or **bulletin board**, also sometimes known as an article; also the act of sending the message.

**PPP**. Point-to-point protocol, a **protocol** which connects computers and telephone lines directly through a **modem** using **TCP/IC connections**, without an intermediary **Internet service provider**.

**Protocol**. A language or set of standards that enables different **network** products to work together to do things such as transfer files.

**Real time**. Time calculated as in reality; pertains to on-line interaction in which users participate simultaneously, without a time lag.

**Remote computer**. A computer other than your own, containing files which your computer can access via **Telnet** or **FTP**; also called a **server**.

**Router**. Computer or software which manages the passage of information between **networks** by examining destination addresses and deciding which **path** is most appropriate for that packet of information.

**Scrambling**. *See* **Encryption**.

**Script**. A series of commands and keystrokes you can record which, like a **macro**, automates and simplifies routine tasks like **dialing-up** and **logging-in**.

**Search engine**. A software tool for searching indexes of information on the Internet, using key words which you input. Some examples are Magellan, Excite, Lycos, and Infoseek.

**Search tools**. Software programs used to find information on-line. For example, **Veronica** is a search tool for **Gopher**, **Archie** is a search tool for **FTP**, and **alta Vista** is a search tool for the **World Wide Web**.

**Server**. Software, or the computer containing the software, which performs a duty for **client** software on other computers.

**Shareware**. Software sent out by companies as market testers. Initial use is free, but unregistered, unpaid use after a thirty-day trial is usually illegal.

**Shell account**. An entry-level Internet access account, which does not link your computer directly to the Internet. Instead, you dial in to an Internet-connect host computer operated by an **Internet service provider**.

**SLIP**. Serial line Internet protocol, a **protocol** which performs the same function as **PPP**, but is less common and losing popularity.

**SMDS**. Switched multimegabit data service, a standard for high-speed data transfer.

**Spam**. To clutter **Usenet newsgroups** or **mailing lists** by posting unwanted messages, mail, or advertisements to large numbers of users.

**Spam detector**. A device that monitors **Usenet newsgroups**, looks for messages which are **posted** repeatedly to many different newsgroups, and deletes them.

**Surf**. To jump from site to site on the Internet, often with speed and/or for the purpose of skimming large amounts of information.

**Sysop**. Systems operator, the person responsible for maintenance and operation of a computer system.

**TCP/IP**. Transmission control protocol/Internet protocol, a connection which enables direct access to the Internet, bypassing a commercial network.

**Telecommunications**. The science, technology, and industry of communication by electronic transmission.

**Telnet**. Program and command which enable a user to connect to a different **host computer** in order to **log-on** to the Internet through that computer.

**Terminal**. A device which enables the user to send commands to a computer at another location.

**Terminal server**. **Server** which connects multiple **modems** to a **LAN** or **host computer**, passing connections to the correct **node**.

**Text-based**. Files or software that handle only text data, with no special formatting data, no graphics, no audio or video. Text-only files are stored on computers using **ASCII**.

**Thread**. A line of conversation in a **conference** or **mailing list**.

**TOS**. Terms of service.

**Trolling**. Deliberately **posting** inflammatory messages to provoke others and gain attention.

**UART**. Computer chip inside the computer or **modem**; must be up-to-date for high-speed **modems**.

**UNIX**. Multi-user computer operating system with **TCP/IP** built in, often the system used for Internet **servers**.

**Upload**. Send information from your computer to one or more other computers.

**URL** (**uniform resource locator**). Standard address form, beginning with `http.//`, for Internet resources on the **World Wide Web**.

**Usenet newsgroups**. System of over ten thousand newsgroups worldwide, not all of them part of the Internet. A newsgroup is a non-**real time**, on-line forum in which users discuss topics of mutual interest by reading posted messages from others and **posting** their own messages to the group.

**Userid**. A name that you choose or your **Internet service provider** chooses for you, which enables you to **log-on** to your ISP's **host computer** and connect to the Internet. Also called a username, it is part of your **e-mail** address, appearing to the left of the @ sign.

**UUCP**. Unit to unit copy program, a program which transfers files containing **e-mail** between computers.

**UUencoding**. A common formatting standard for encoding files that are attached to **e-mail** messages.

**Veronica**. Very Easy Rodent Oriented Net-wide Index to Computerized Archives, a perpetually updated database of items on **Gopher servers**, which functions as a **search tool** for Gopher. Veronica can be accessed and searched from many Gopher menus.

**Virtual**. Simulated, almost real; a term sometimes used to describe the functions and experiences available through electronic communications.

**Virus**. Computer program which is "communicable" through disks and destroys stored data. Can be fought using an anti-virus program.

**WAIS**. Wide area information servers, software which enables users to index massive amounts of information for later use across networks such as the Internet; enables searches and subsequent refined searches.

**WAN**. Wide area network, any **network** or **internet** which spans an area larger than a building or campus.

**Web browser**. *See* **Browser**.

**Web site**. **Cyber** location on the **World Wide Web**.

**Wired**. Connected in some fashion to the Internet.

**World Wide Web**. A **hypertext**-based system, often including graphics, for exploring Internet resources.

**Zine**. *See* **E-zine**.

**Zipfile**. A **compressed** file.

# Index

All page numbers appearing in italic type indicate locations of Internet resource listings.